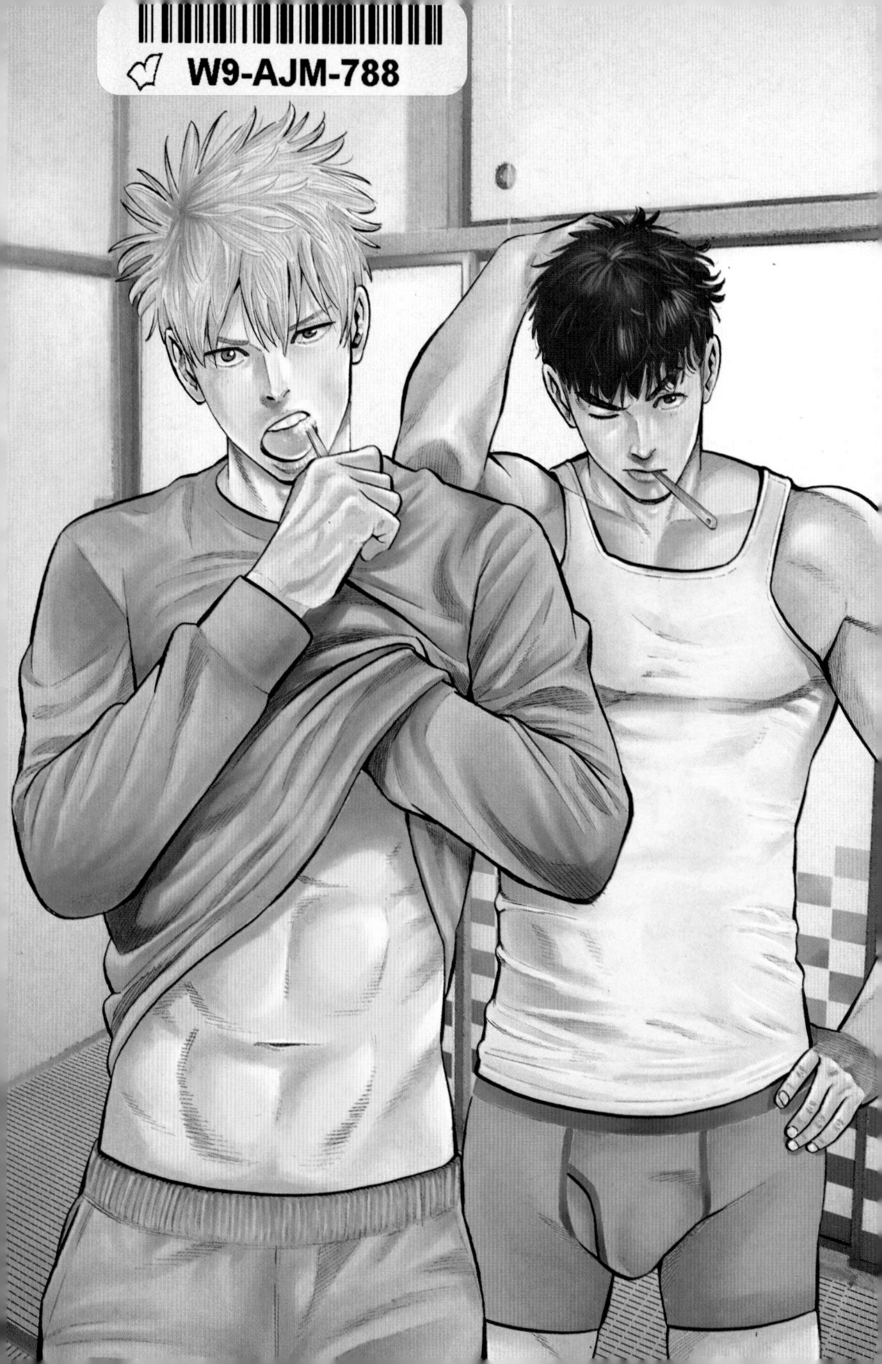

Bad Boys, Happy Home

Story by **SHOOWA** Art by **Hiromasa Okujima**   volume **2**

CONTENTS

SUBLIME
SuBLime Manga Edition

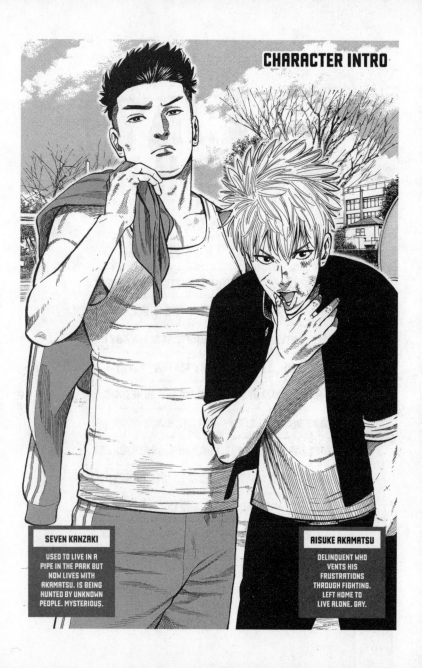

CHARACTER INTRO

SEVEN KANZAKI

USED TO LIVE IN A
PIPE IN THE PARK BUT
NOW LIVES WITH
AKAMATSU. IS BEING
HUNTED BY UNKNOWN
PEOPLE. MYSTERIOUS.

RISUKE AKAMATSU

DELINQUENT WHO
VENTS HIS
FRUSTRATIONS
THROUGH FIGHTING.
LEFT HOME TO
LIVE ALONE. GAY.

BAD BOYS HAPPY HOME

STORY THUS FAR

HIGH SCHOOL DELINQUENT AKAMATSU GOES TO THE

PARK EACH DAY TO PICK A FIGHT WITH A MYSTERIOUS GUY

NAMED SEVEN. AFTER LEARNING THAT SEVEN HAS NO

HOME TO GO TO, AKAMATSU INVITES HIM TO STAY WITH

HIM. THE TWO BEGIN A STRANGE AND SOMETIMES

AWKWARD LIFE TOGETHER. ONE DAY, SEVEN DISCOVERS

THAT AKAMATSU IS GAY, WHICH WAS HIS REASON FOR

LEAVING HOME. SEVEN SUGGESTS HE TALK THINGS OVER

WITH HIS FAMILY, SO HE DOES AND ENDS UP CLEARING

THE AIR WITH HIS DAD. BUT EVEN SO, AKAMATSU DECIDES

TO CONTINUE LIVING WITH SEVEN. NOT LONG AFTER

THAT, SEVEN COMES CLOSE TO KISSING HIM!

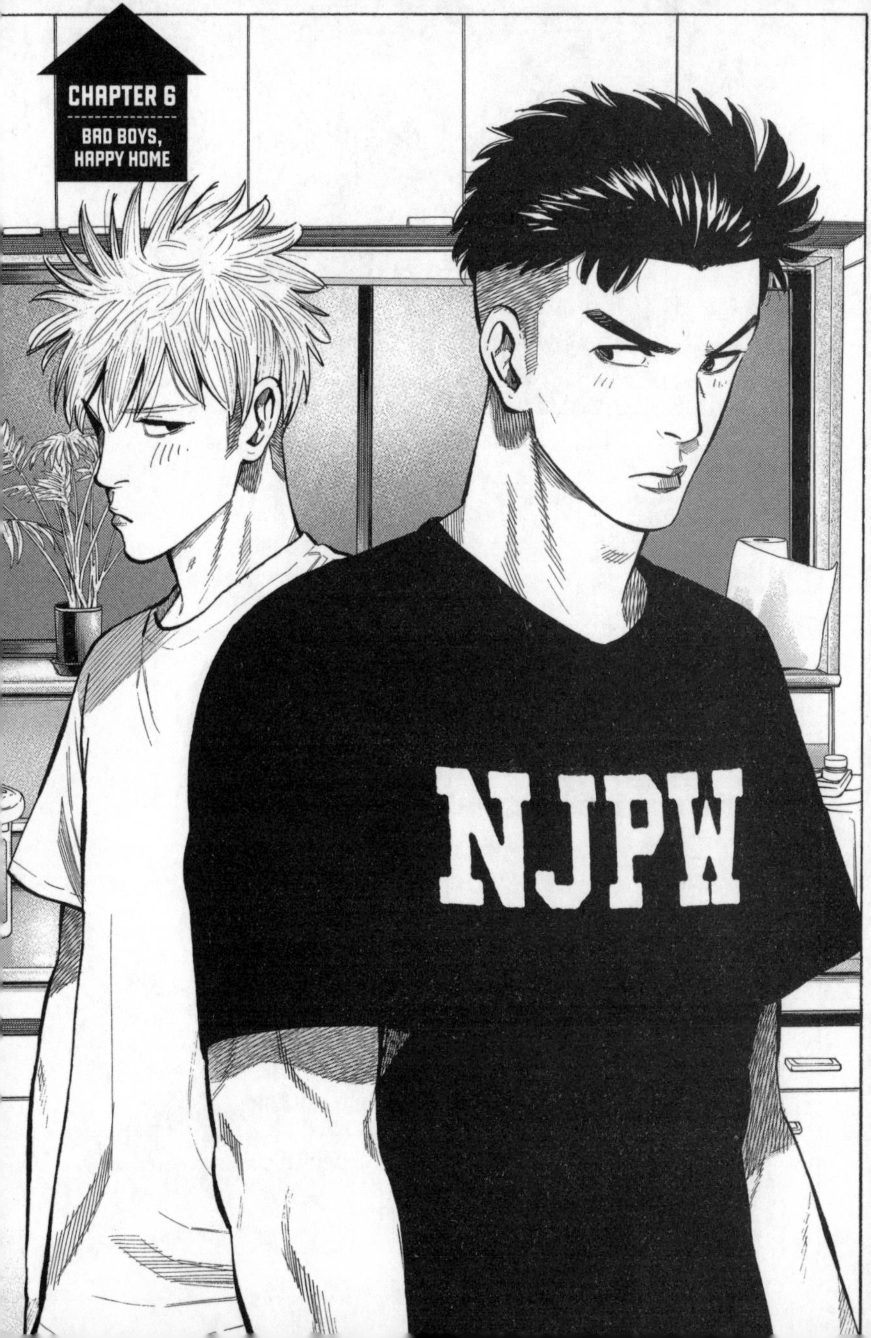
CHAPTER 6
BAD BOYS, HAPPY HOME
NJPW

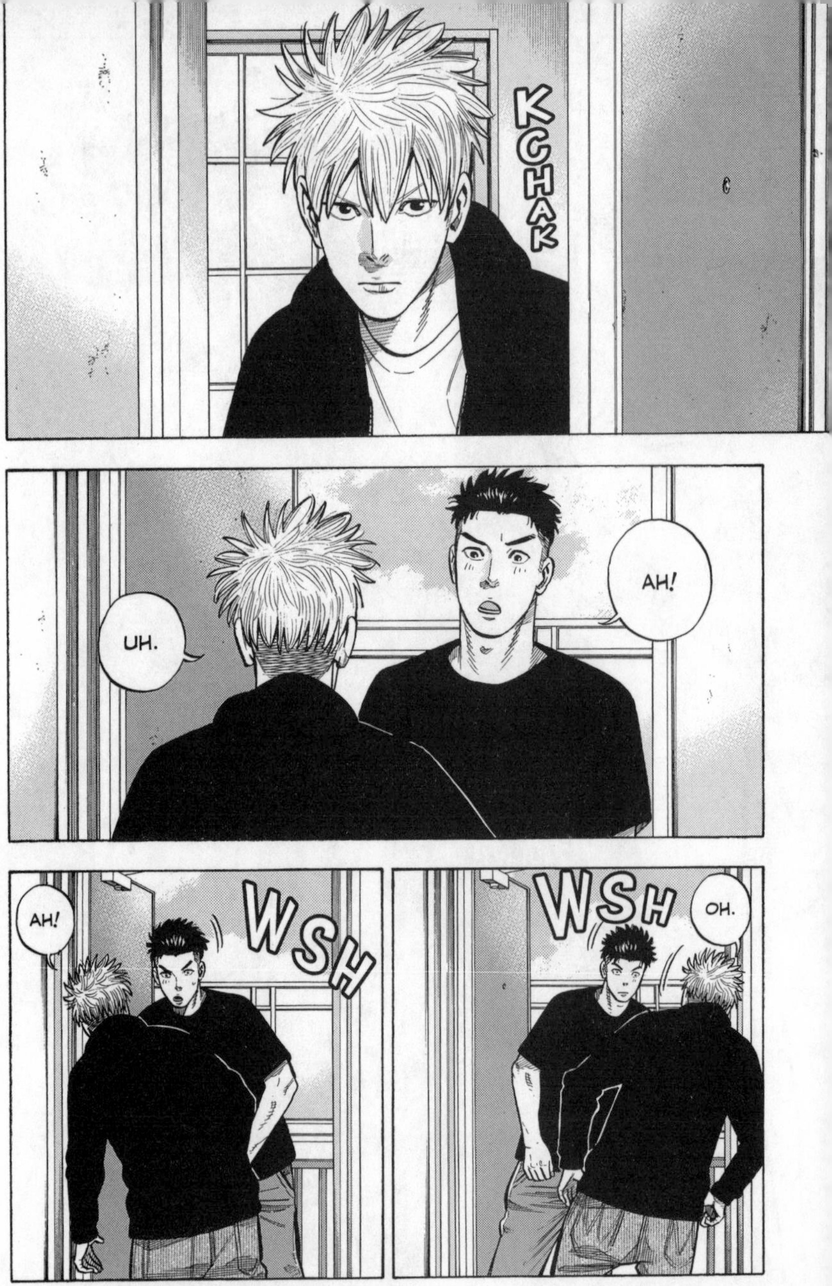
KCHAK
AH!
UH.
OH.
WSH
WSH
AH!

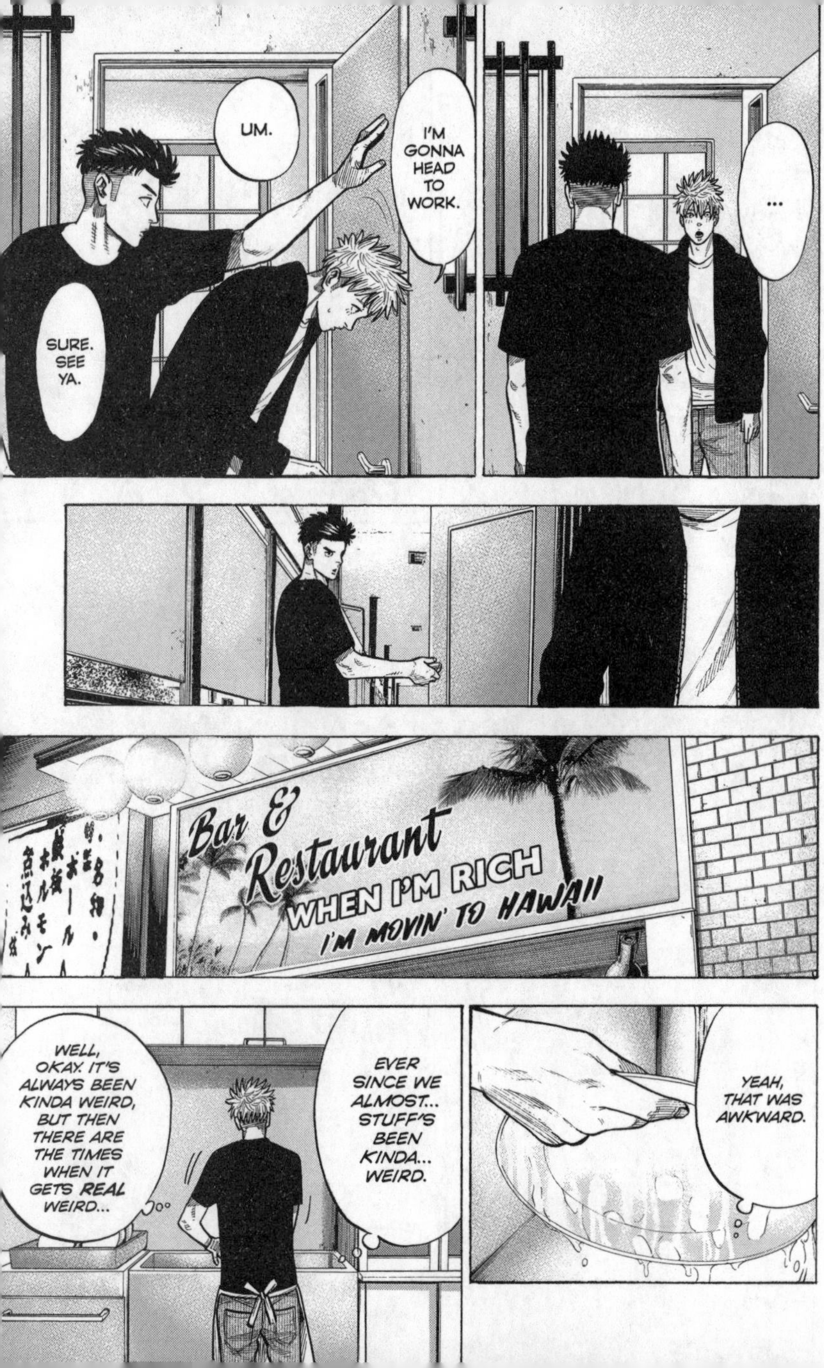
...
I'M GONNA HEAD TO WORK.
UM.
SURE. SEE YA.
Bar & Restaurant
WHEN I'M RICH
I'M MOVIN' TO HAWAII
YEAH, THAT WAS AWKWARD.
EVER SINCE WE ALMOST... STUFF'S BEEN KINDA... WEIRD.
WELL, OKAY. IT'S ALWAYS BEEN KINDA WEIRD, BUT THEN THERE ARE THE TIMES WHEN IT GETS *REAL* WEIRD...

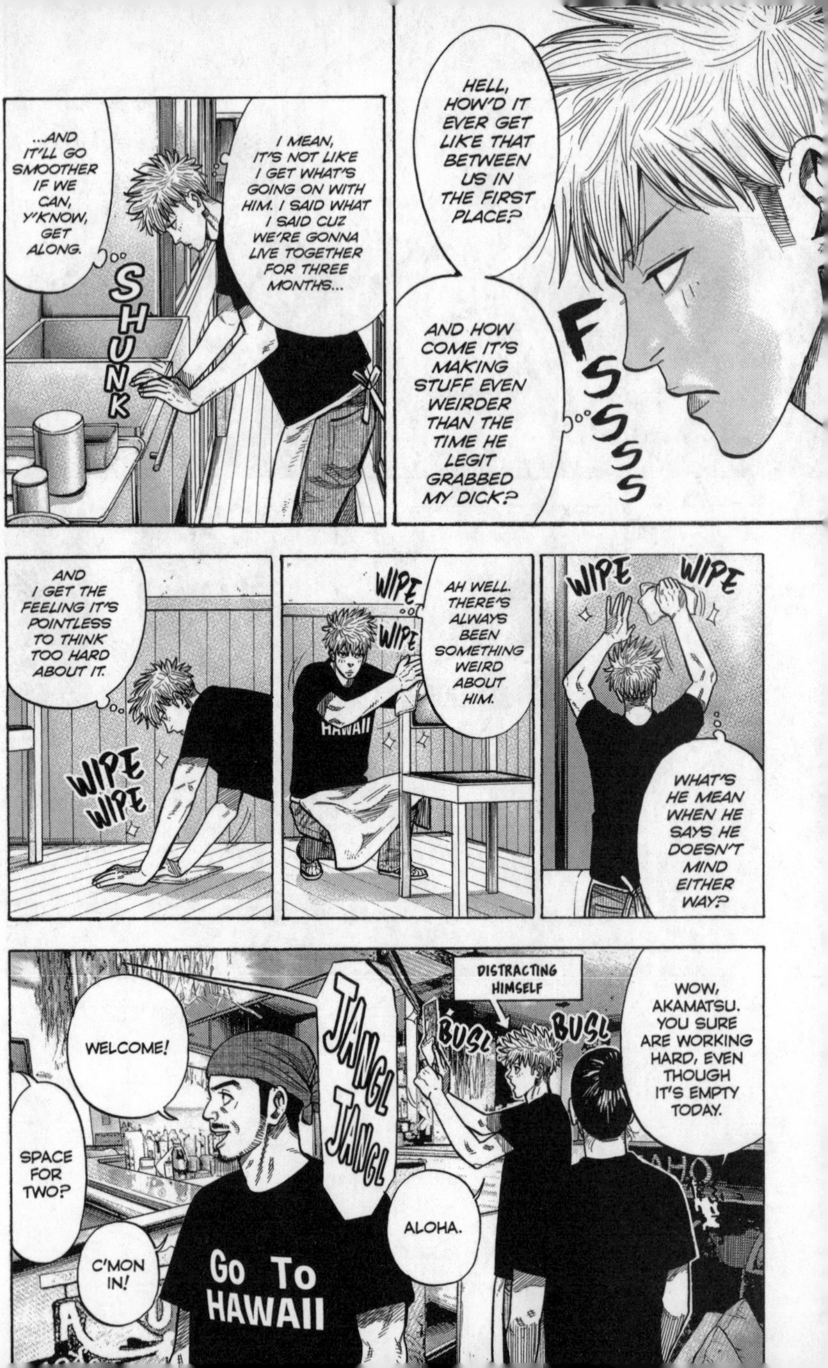
HELL, HOW'D IT EVER GET LIKE THAT BETWEEN US IN THE FIRST PLACE?
AND HOW COME IT'S MAKING STUFF EVEN WEIRDER THAN THE TIME HE LEGIT GRABBED MY DICK?
FSSSS
I MEAN, IT'S NOT LIKE I GET WHAT'S GOING ON WITH HIM. I SAID WHAT I SAID CUZ WE'RE GONNA LIVE TOGETHER FOR THREE MONTHS...
...AND IT'LL GO SMOOTHER IF WE CAN, Y'KNOW, GET ALONG.
SHUNK
WIPE WIPE
WHAT'S HE MEAN WHEN HE SAYS HE DOESN'T MIND EITHER WAY?
WIPE WIPE
AH WELL. THERE'S ALWAYS BEEN SOMETHING WEIRD ABOUT HIM.
HAWAII
AND I GET THE FEELING IT'S POINTLESS TO THINK TOO HARD ABOUT IT.
WIPE WIPE
WOW, AKAMATSU. YOU SURE ARE WORKING HARD, EVEN THOUGH IT'S EMPTY TODAY.
DISTRACTING HIMSELF
BUSL BUSL
JANGL JANGL
ALOHA.
WELCOME!
SPACE FOR TWO?
C'MON IN!
Go To HAWAII

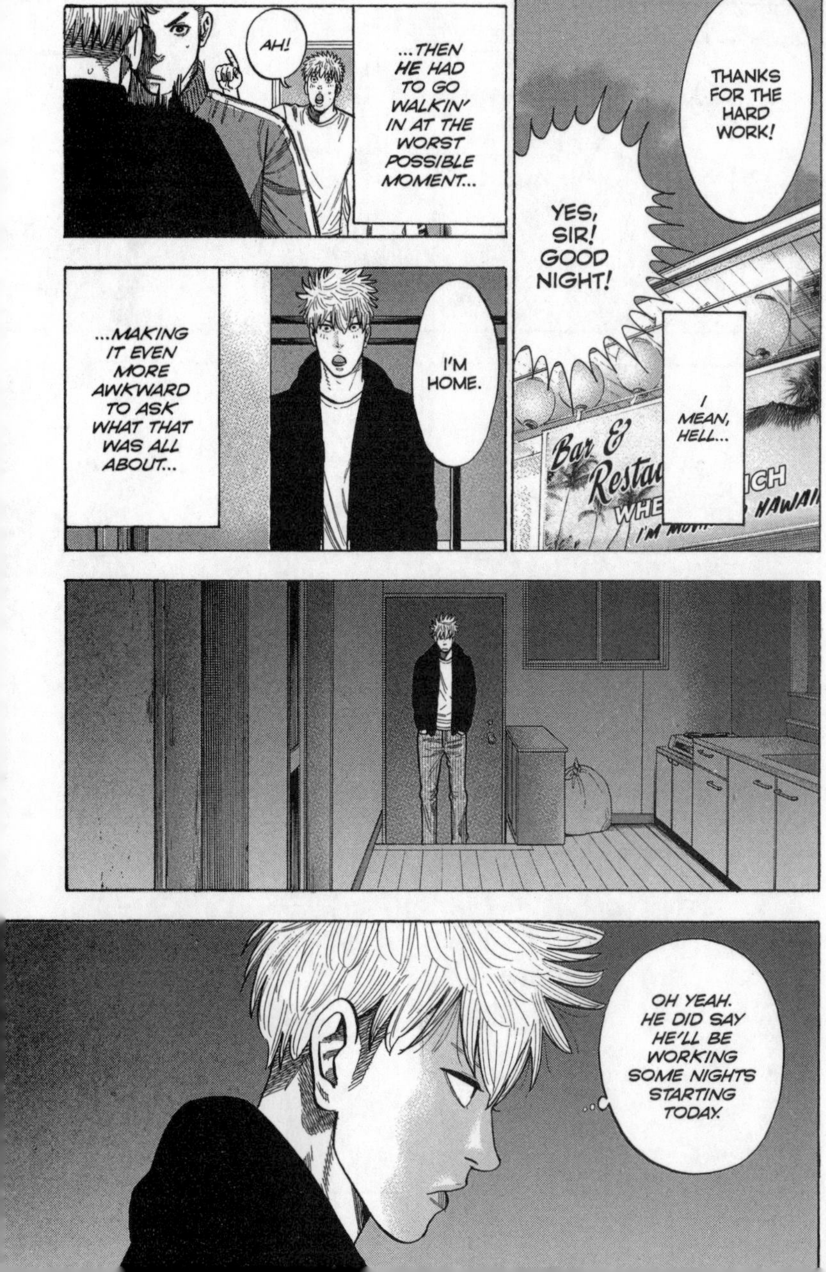
THANKS FOR THE HARD WORK!
YES, SIR! GOOD NIGHT!
I MEAN, HELL...
...THEN HE HAD TO GO WALKIN' IN AT THE WORST POSSIBLE MOMENT...
AH!
I'M HOME.
...MAKING IT EVEN MORE AWKWARD TO ASK WHAT THAT WAS ALL ABOUT...
OH YEAH. HE DID SAY HE'LL BE WORKING SOME NIGHTS STARTING TODAY.

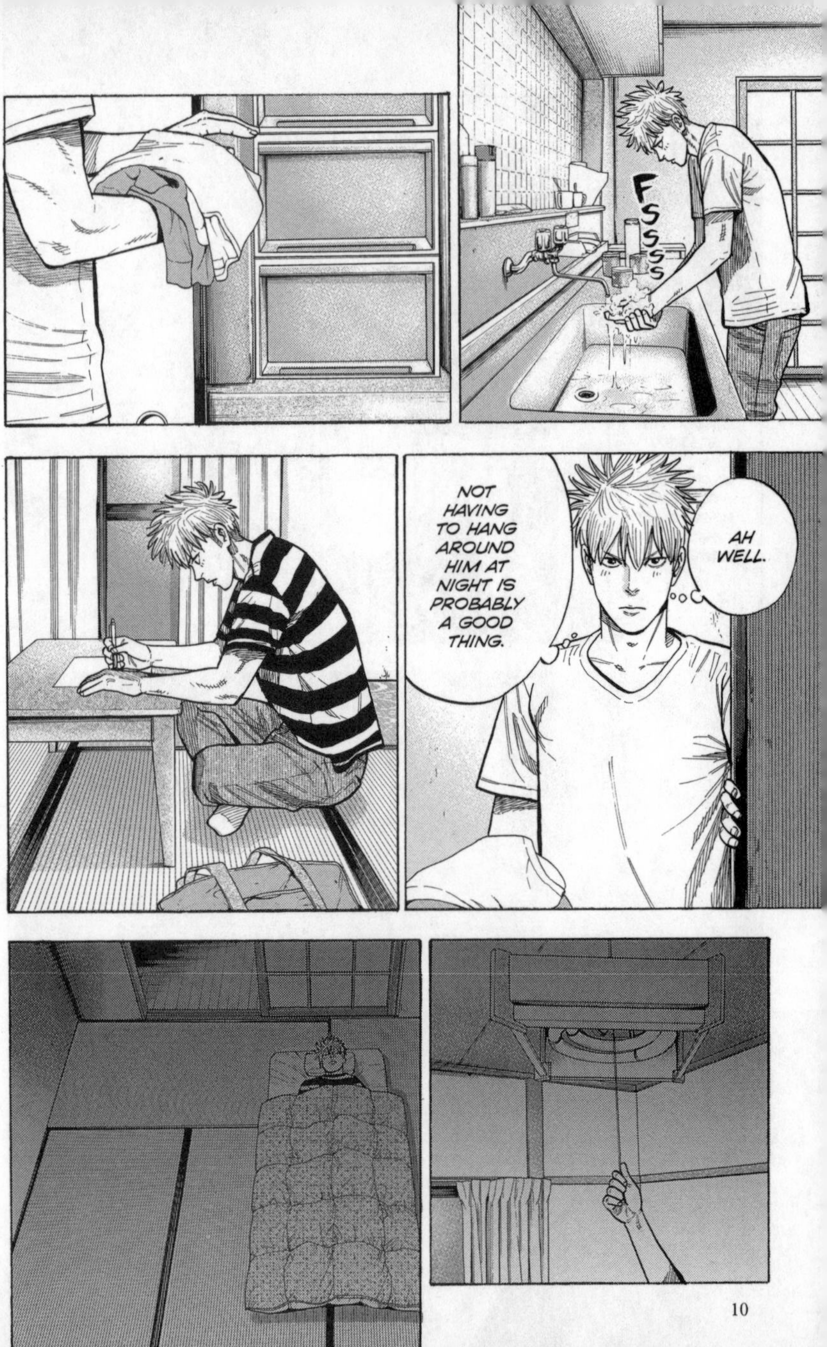
FSSSS
AH WELL.
NOT HAVING TO HANG AROUND HIM AT NIGHT IS PROBABLY A GOOD THING.

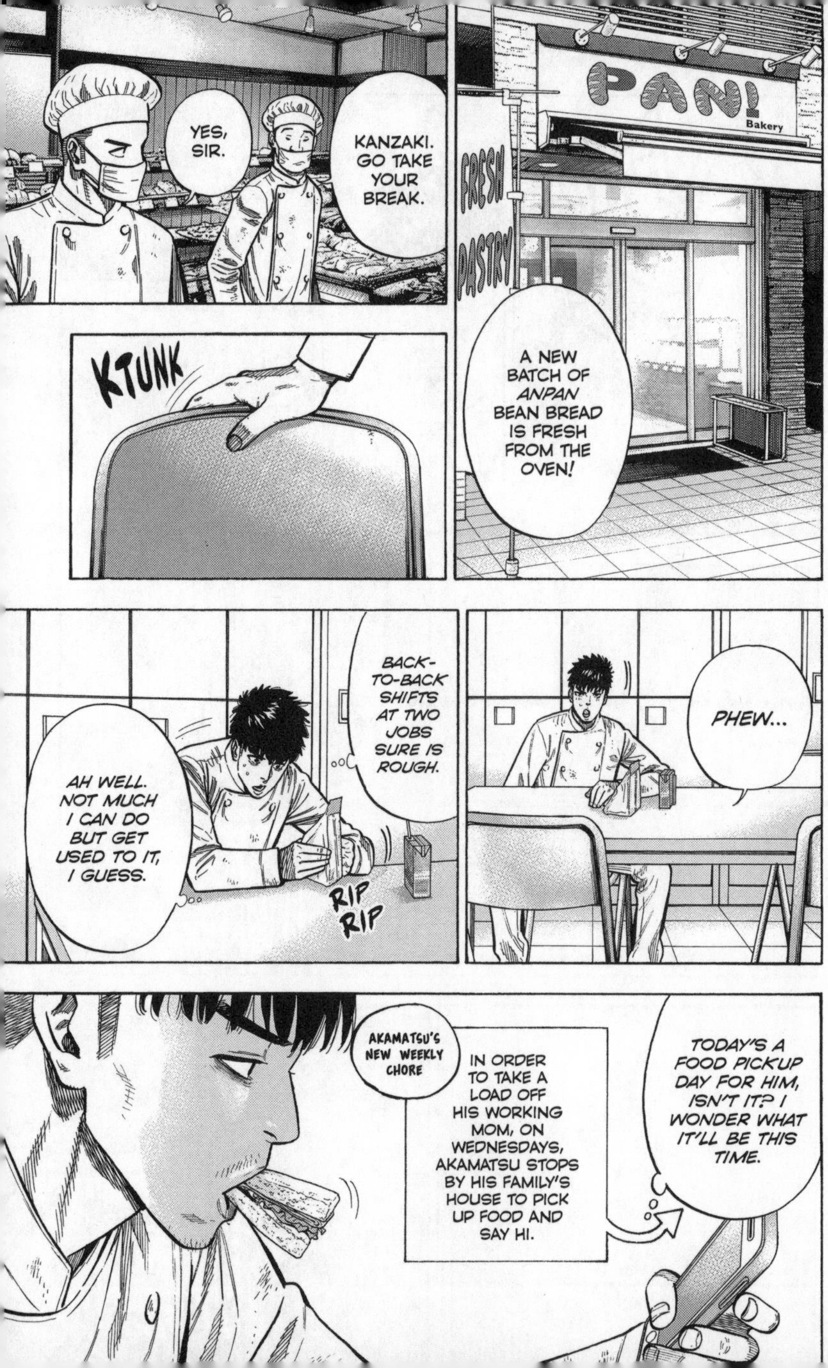
PAN! Bakery
FRESH PASTRY
A NEW BATCH OF *ANPAN* BEAN BREAD IS FRESH FROM THE OVEN!
KANZAKI. GO TAKE YOUR BREAK.
YES, SIR.
KTUNK
PHEW...
BACK-TO-BACK SHIFTS AT TWO JOBS SURE IS ROUGH.
AH WELL. NOT MUCH I CAN DO BUT GET USED TO IT, I GUESS.
RIP RIP
TODAY'S A FOOD PICKUP DAY FOR HIM, ISN'T IT? I WONDER WHAT IT'LL BE THIS TIME.
IN ORDER TO TAKE A LOAD OFF HIS WORKING MOM, ON WEDNESDAYS, AKAMATSU STOPS BY HIS FAMILY'S HOUSE TO PICK UP FOOD AND SAY HI.
AKAMATSU'S NEW WEEKLY CHORE

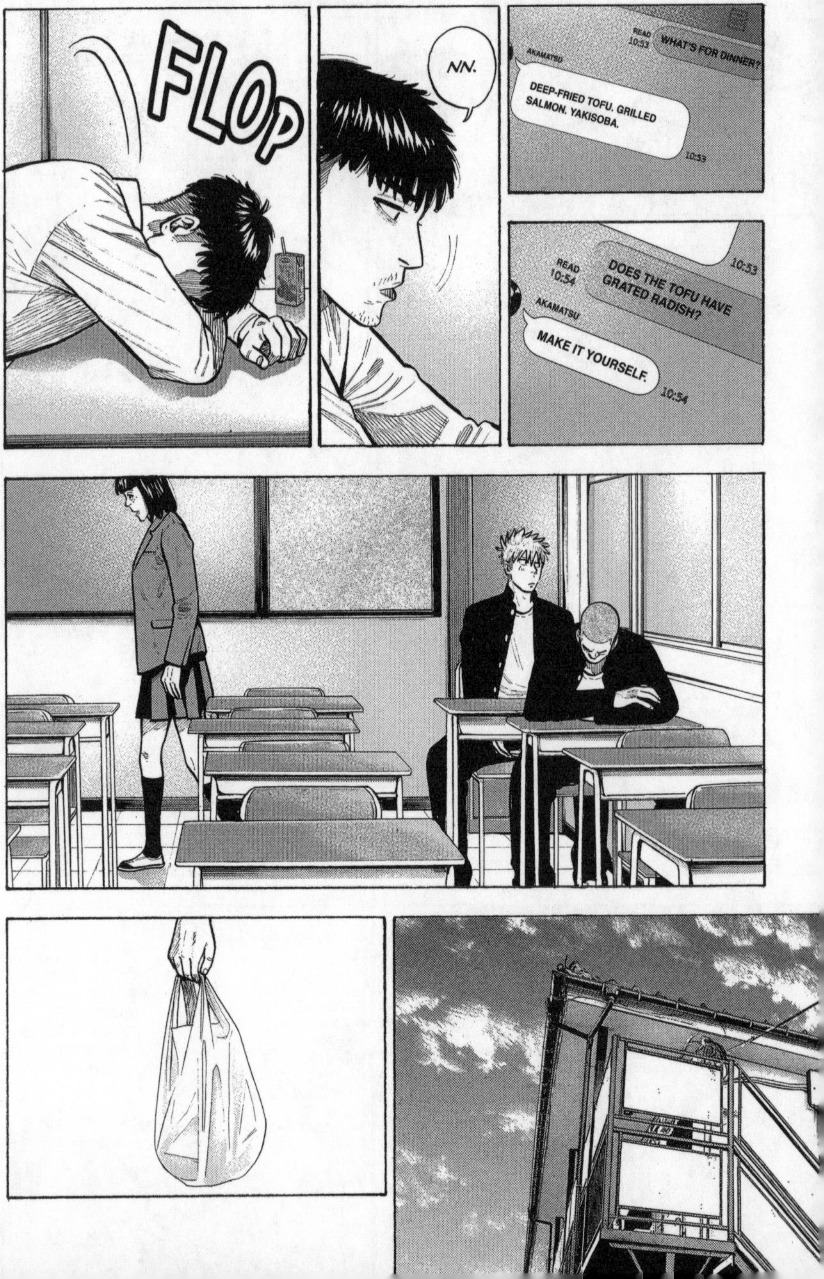
READ
10:53
WHAT'S FOR DINNER?
AKAMATSU
DEEP-FRIED TOFU. GRILLED SALMON. YAKISOBA.
10:53
10:53
READ
10:54
DOES THE TOFU HAVE GRATED RADISH?
AKAMATSU
MAKE IT YOURSELF.
10:54
NN.
FLOP

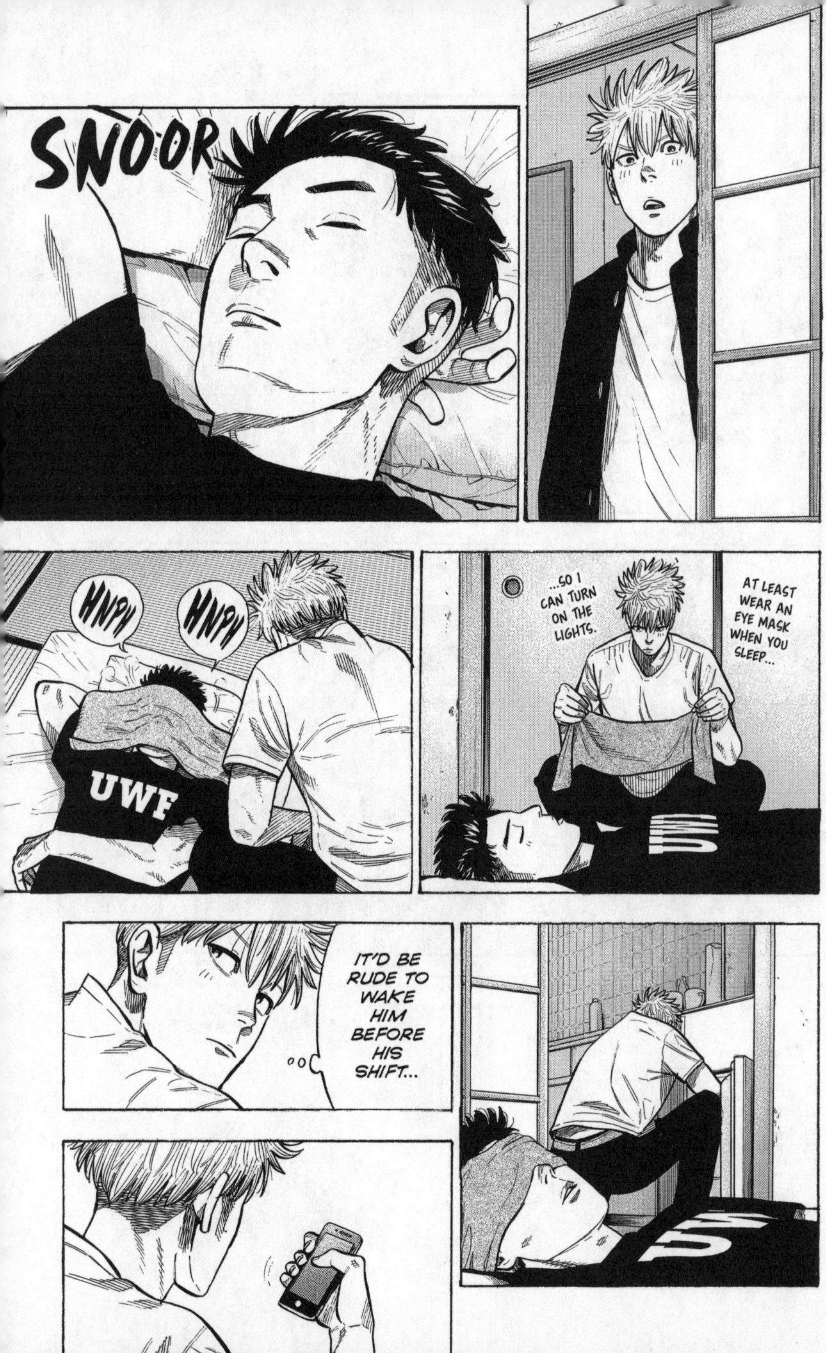
SNOOR
AT LEAST WEAR AN EYE MASK WHEN YOU SLEEP...
...SO I CAN TURN ON THE LIGHTS.
HNGH
HNGH
UWF
IT'D BE RUDE TO WAKE HIM BEFORE HIS SHIFT...

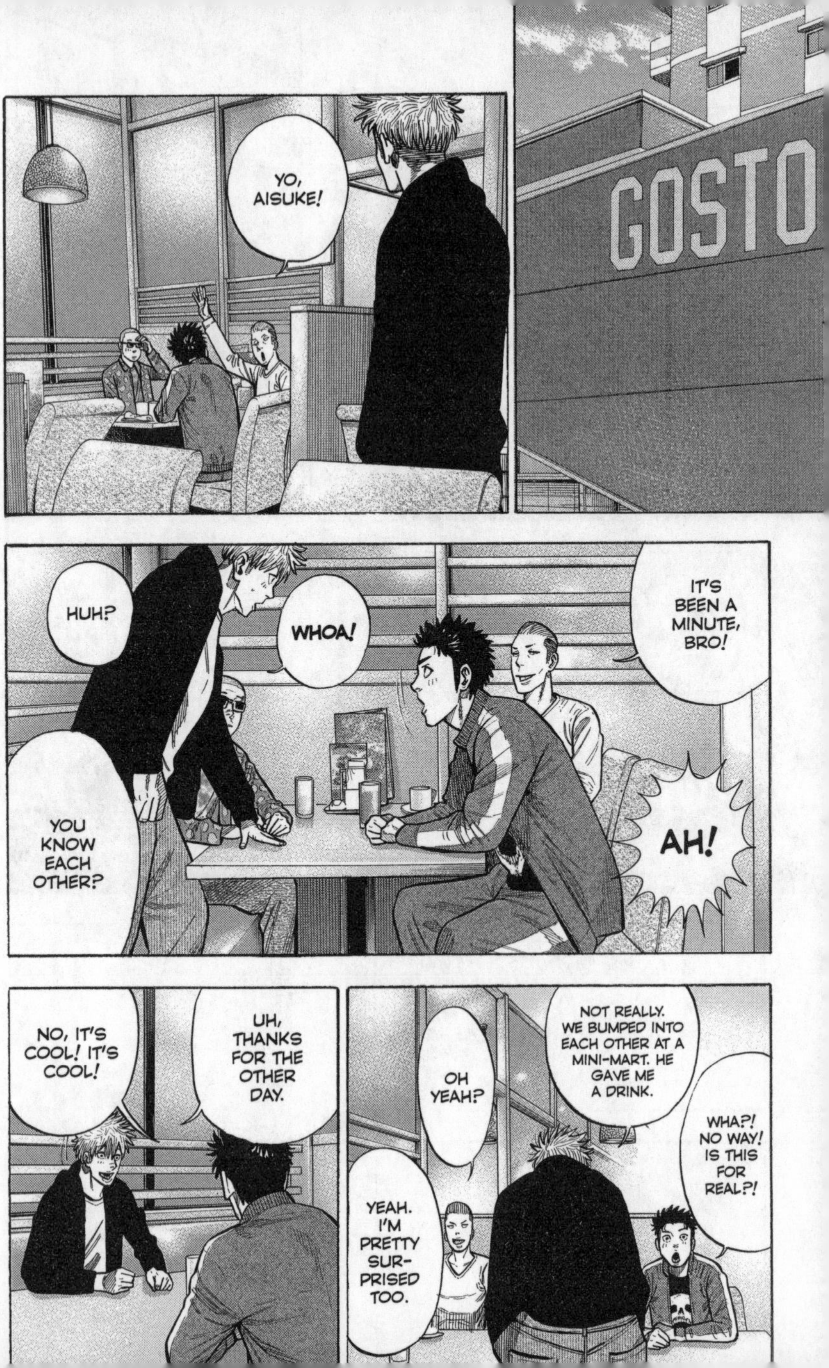
GOSTO
YO, AISUKE!
IT'S BEEN A MINUTE, BRO!
AH!
WHOA!
HUH?
YOU KNOW EACH OTHER?
NOT REALLY. WE BUMPED INTO EACH OTHER AT A MINI-MART. HE GAVE ME A DRINK.
WHA?! NO WAY! IS THIS FOR REAL?!
OH YEAH?
YEAH. I'M PRETTY SUR-PRISED TOO.
UH, THANKS FOR THE OTHER DAY.
NO, IT'S COOL! IT'S COOL!

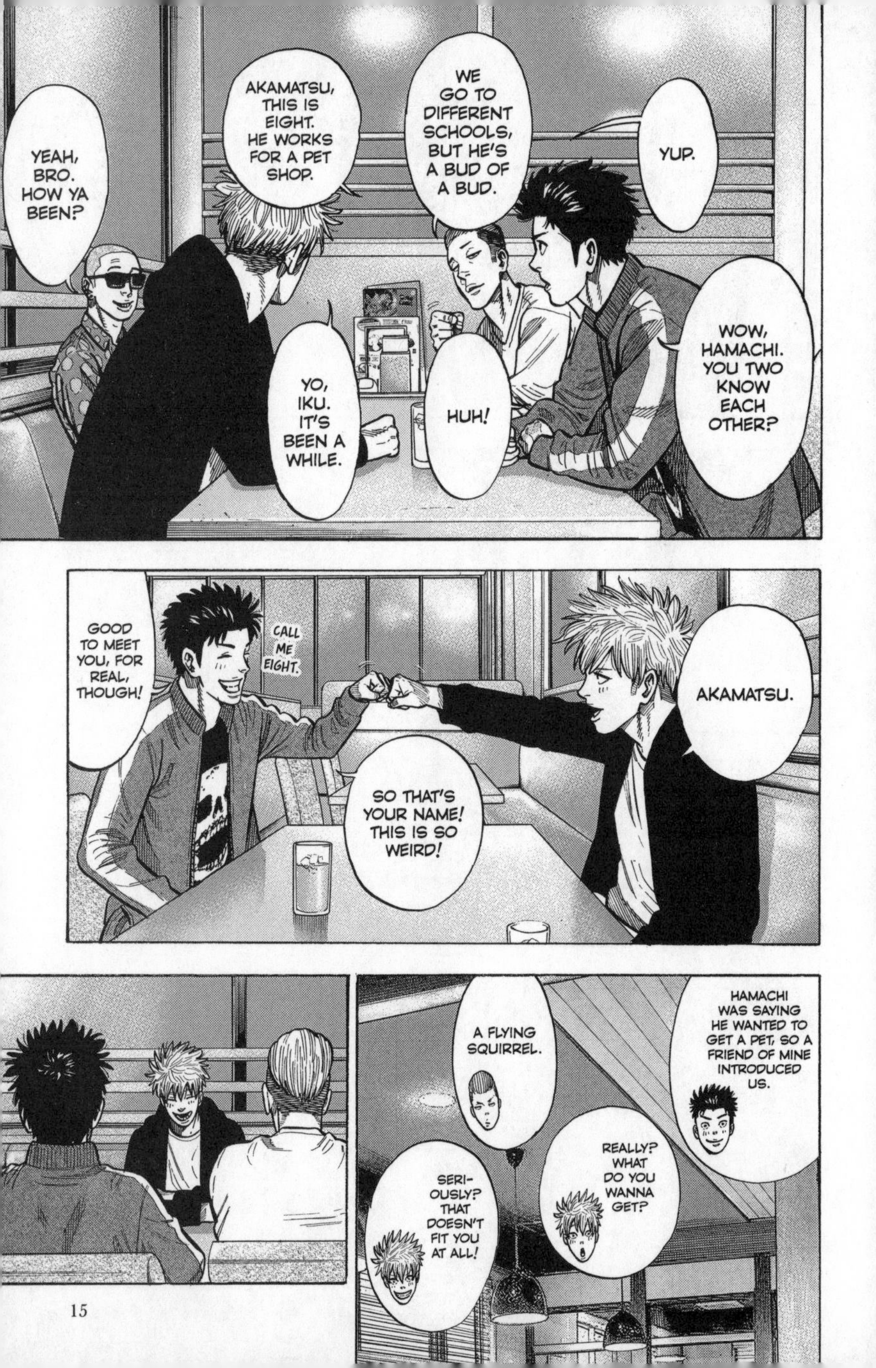
WOW, HAMACHI. YOU TWO KNOW EACH OTHER?
YUP.
WE GO TO DIFFERENT SCHOOLS, BUT HE'S A BUD OF A BUD.
HUH!
AKAMATSU, THIS IS EIGHT. HE WORKS FOR A PET SHOP.
YO, IKU. IT'S BEEN A WHILE.
YEAH, BRO. HOW YA BEEN?
AKAMATSU.
SO THAT'S YOUR NAME! THIS IS SO WEIRD!
CALL ME EIGHT.
GOOD TO MEET YOU, FOR REAL, THOUGH!
HAMACHI WAS SAYING HE WANTED TO GET A PET, SO A FRIEND OF MINE INTRODUCED US.
REALLY? WHAT DO YOU WANNA GET?
A FLYING SQUIRREL.
SERI-OUSLY? THAT DOESN'T FIT YOU AT ALL!

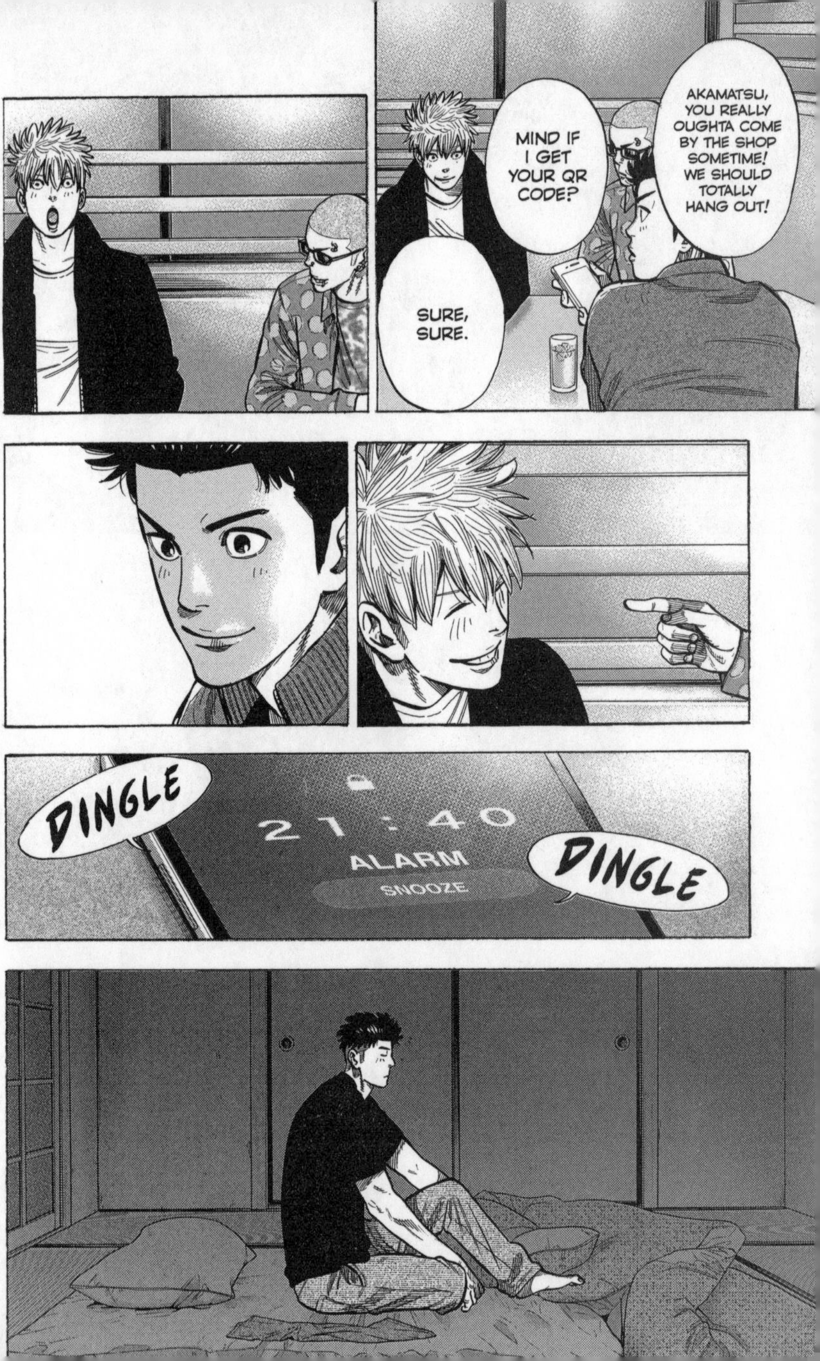
AKAMATSU, YOU REALLY OUGHTA COME BY THE SHOP SOMETIME! WE SHOULD TOTALLY HANG OUT!
MIND IF I GET YOUR QR CODE?
SURE, SURE.
DINGLE
21:40
ALARM
SNOOZE
DINGLE

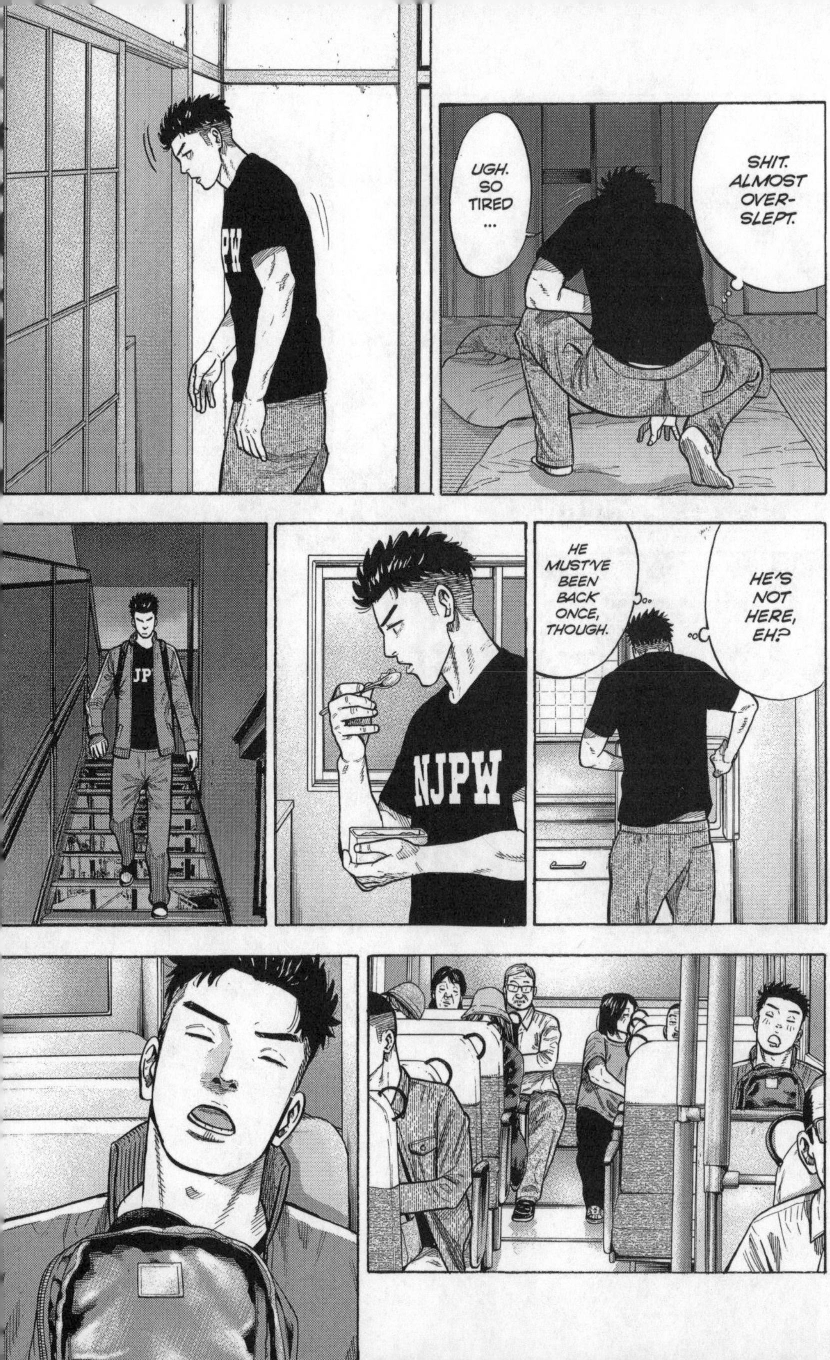
SHIT. ALMOST OVER-SLEPT.
UGH. SO TIRED ...
HE'S NOT HERE, EH?
HE MUST'VE BEEN BACK ONCE, THOUGH.
NJPW

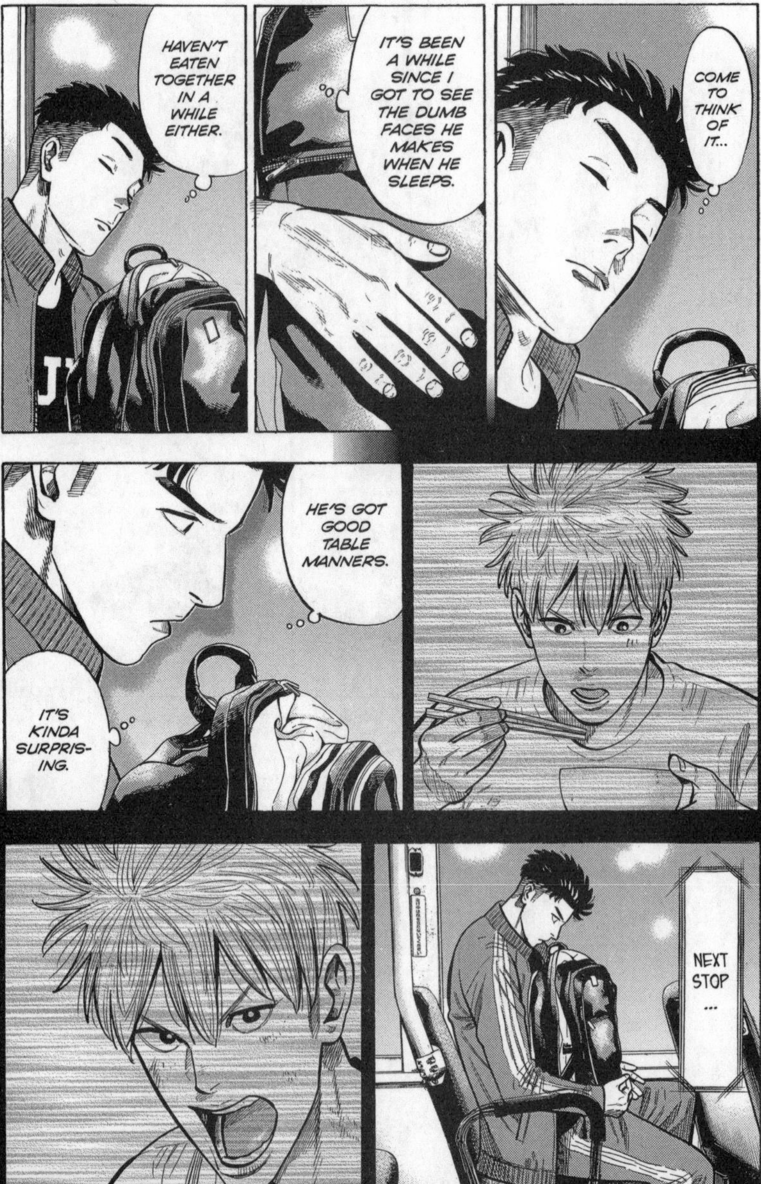
COME TO THINK OF IT...
IT'S BEEN A WHILE SINCE I GOT TO SEE THE DUMB FACES HE MAKES WHEN HE SLEEPS.
HAVEN'T EATEN TOGETHER IN A WHILE EITHER.
HE'S GOT GOOD TABLE MANNERS.
IT'S KINDA SURPRIS-ING.
NEXT STOP ...

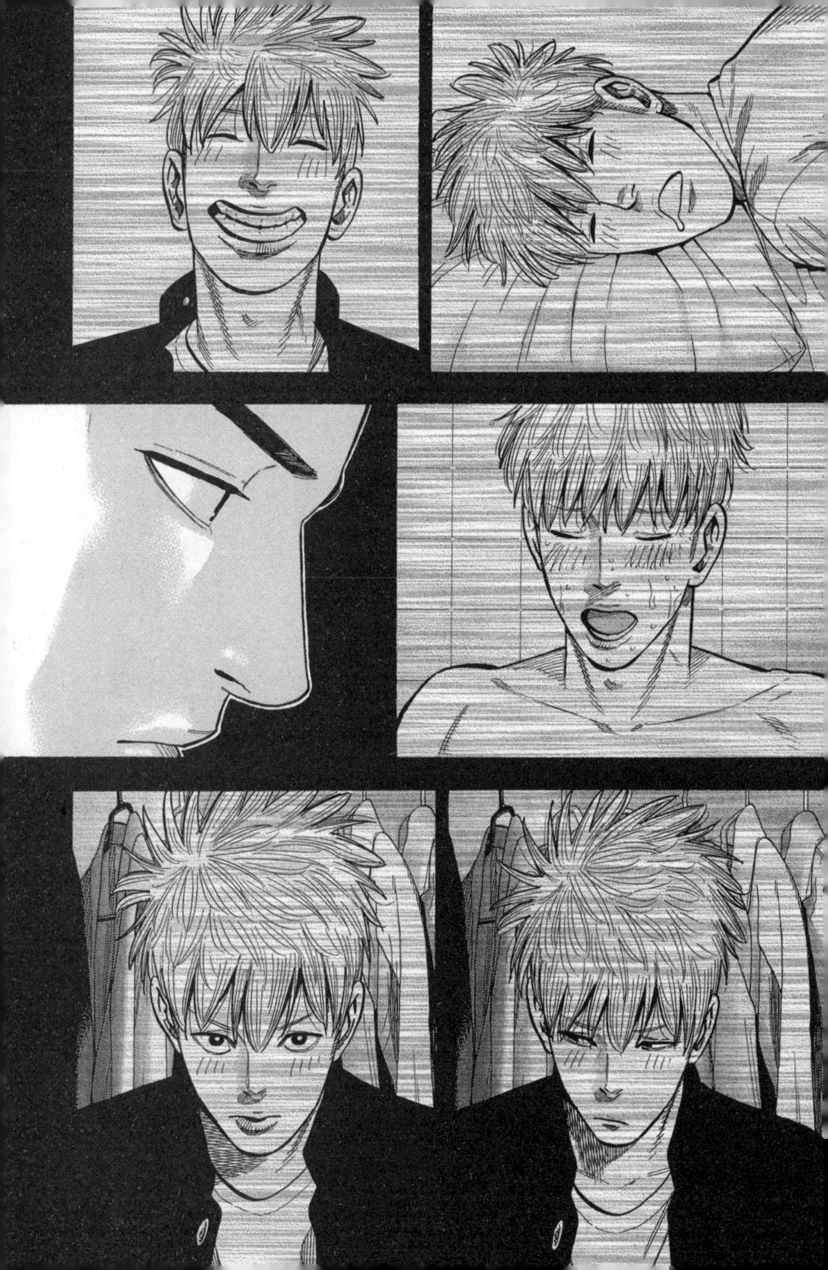

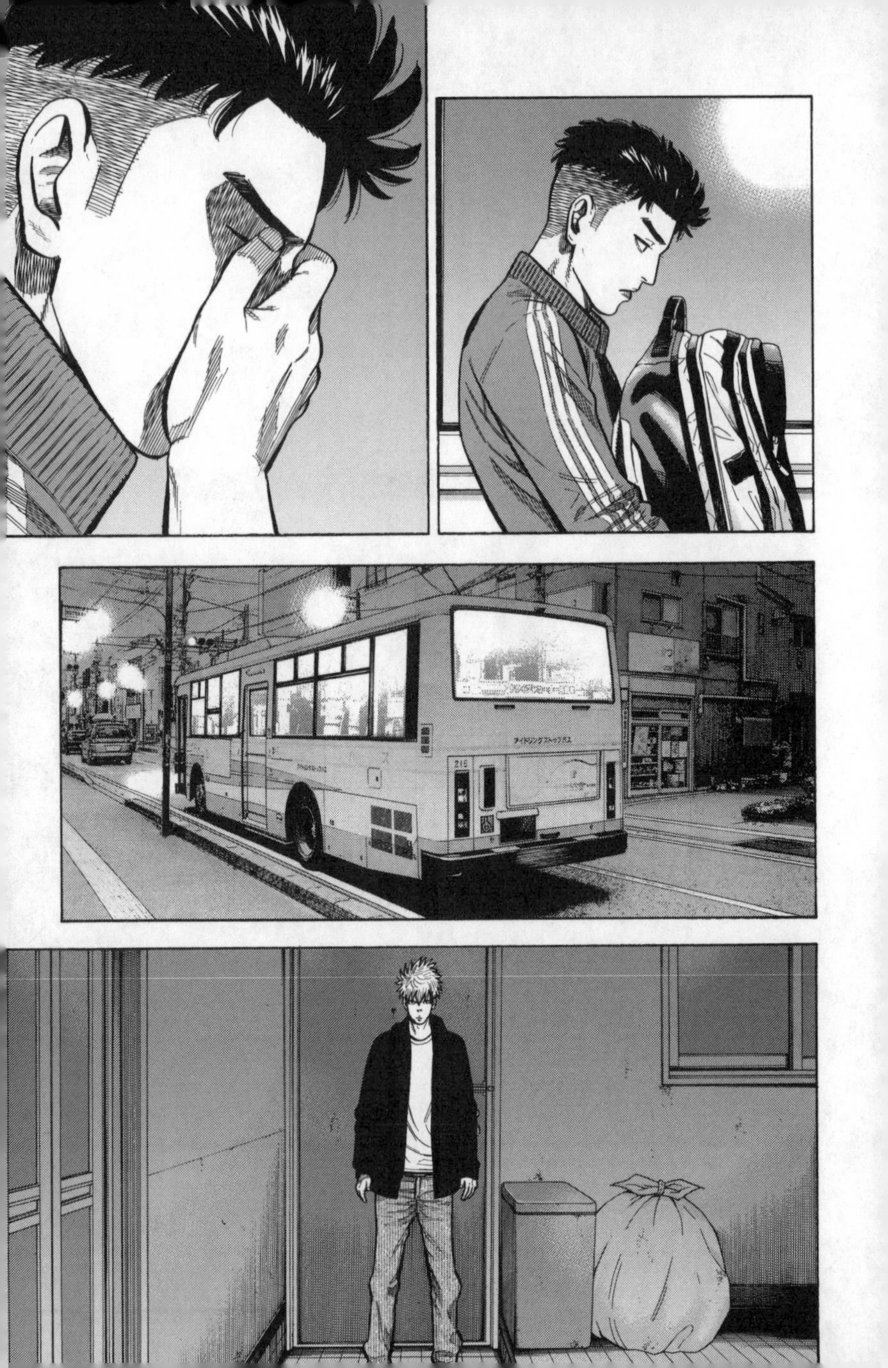
アイドリングストップバス
215

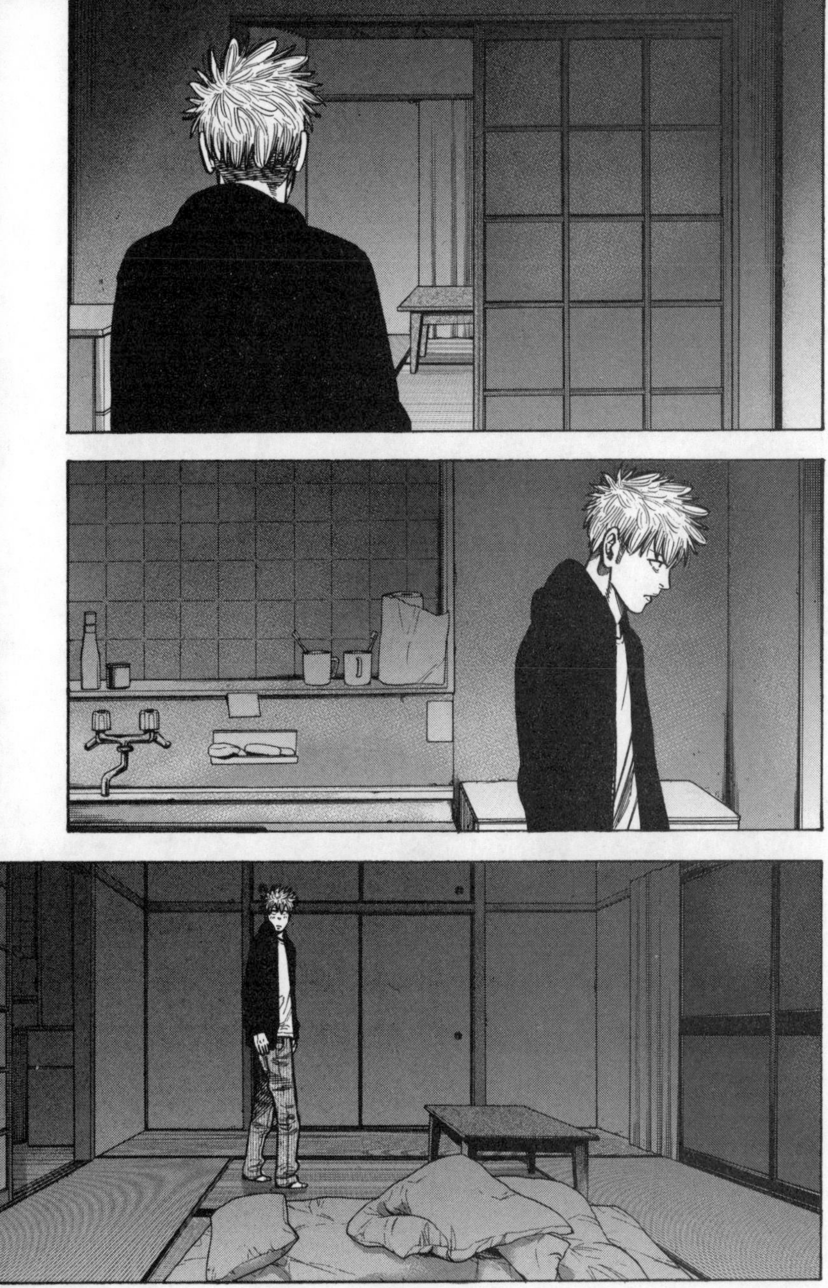

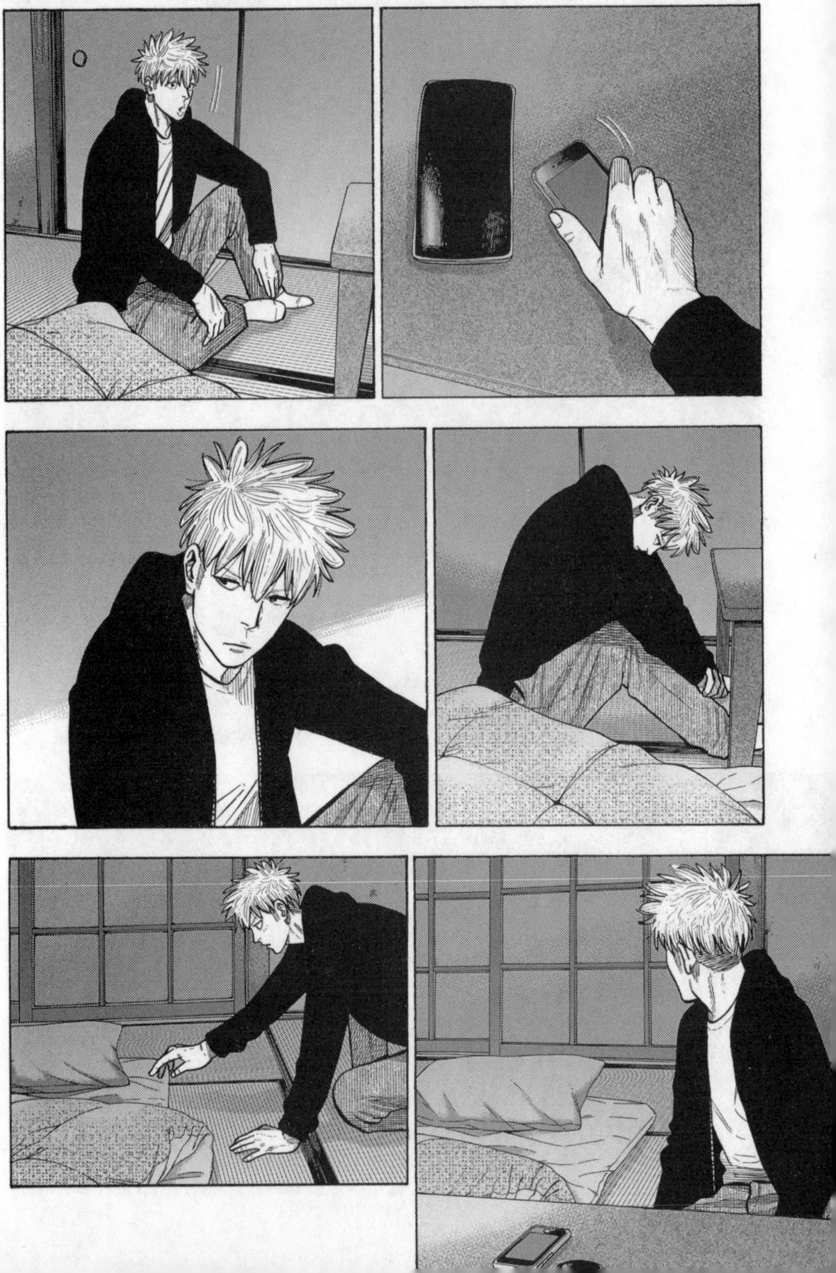

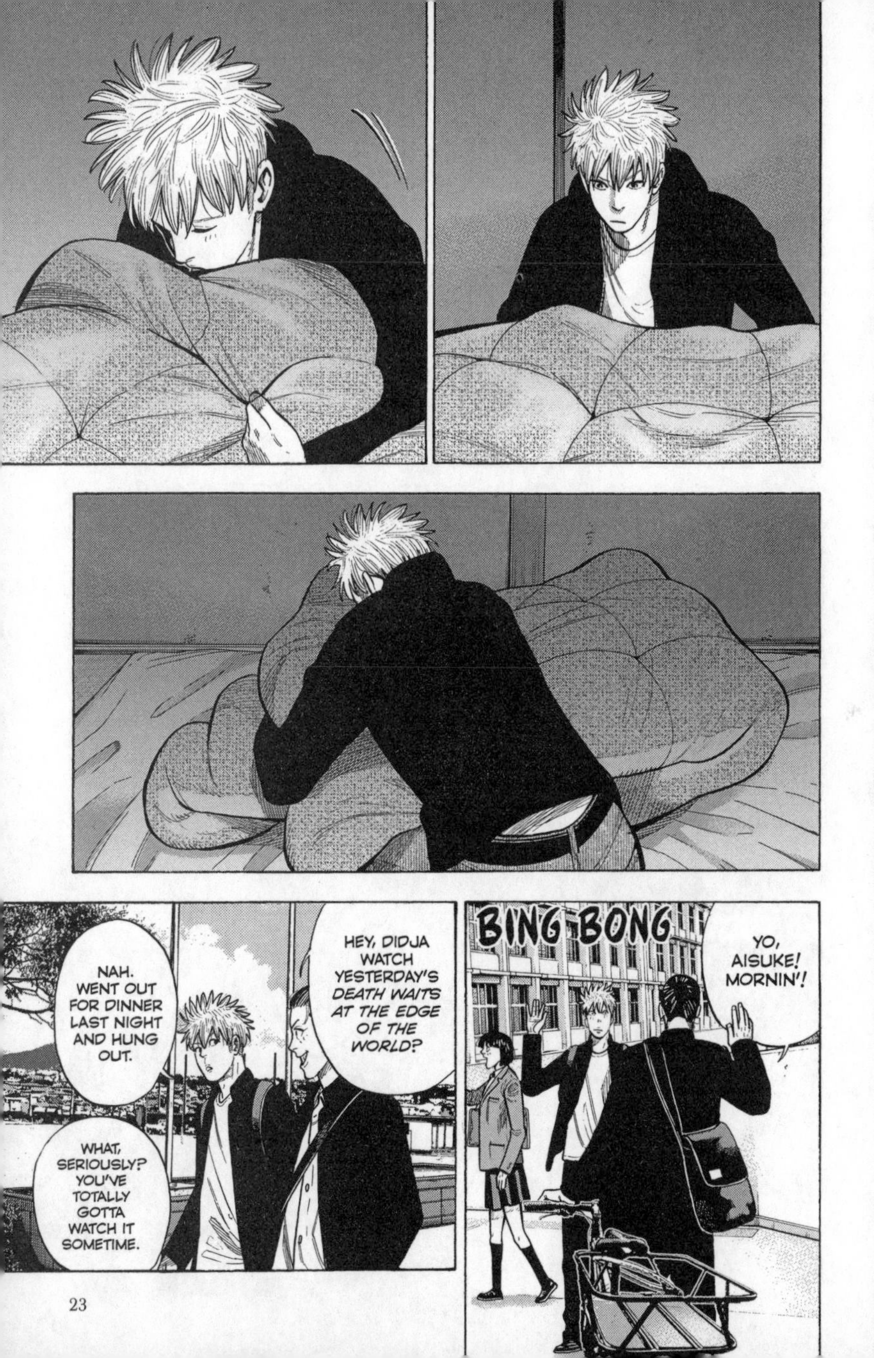
BING BONG
YO, AISUKE! MORNIN'!
HEY, DIDJA WATCH YESTERDAY'S *DEATH WAITS AT THE EDGE OF THE WORLD*?
NAH. WENT OUT FOR DINNER LAST NIGHT AND HUNG OUT.
WHAT, SERIOUSLY? YOU'VE TOTALLY GOTTA WATCH IT SOMETIME.

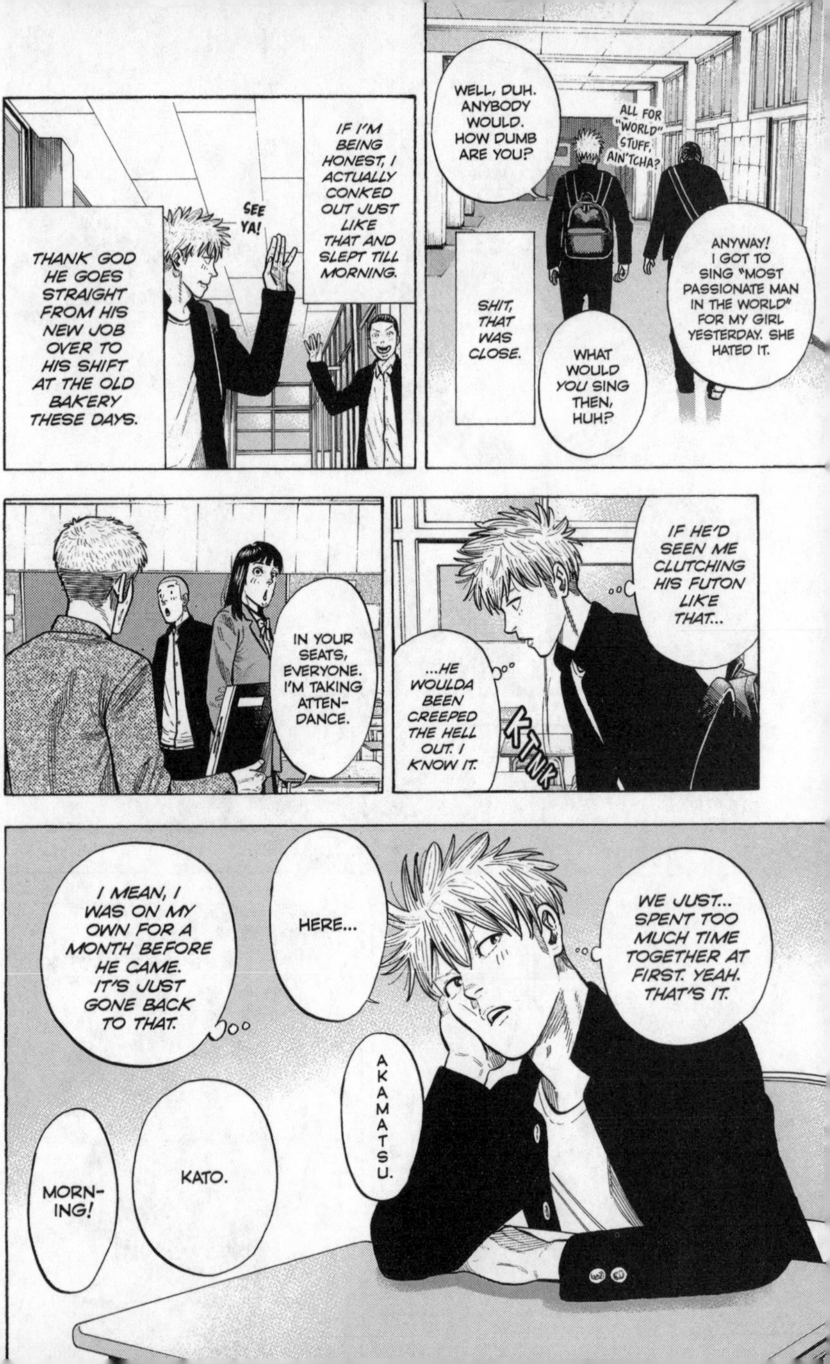
ANYWAY! I GOT TO SING "MOST PASSIONATE MAN IN THE WORLD" FOR MY GIRL YESTERDAY. SHE HATED IT.
WHAT WOULD YOU SING THEN, HUH?
ALL FOR "WORLD" STUFF, AIN'TCHA?
WELL, DUH. ANYBODY WOULD. HOW DUMB ARE YOU?
SHIT, THAT WAS CLOSE.
IF I'M BEING HONEST, I ACTUALLY CONKED OUT JUST LIKE THAT AND SLEPT TILL MORNING.
SEE YA!
THANK GOD HE GOES STRAIGHT FROM HIS NEW JOB OVER TO HIS SHIFT AT THE OLD BAKERY THESE DAYS.
IF HE'D SEEN ME CLUTCHING HIS FUTON LIKE THAT...
...HE WOULDA BEEN CREEPED THE HELL OUT. I KNOW IT.
KTINK
IN YOUR SEATS, EVERYONE. I'M TAKING ATTEN-DANCE.
WE JUST... SPENT TOO MUCH TIME TOGETHER AT FIRST. YEAH. THAT'S IT.
HERE...
I MEAN, I WAS ON MY OWN FOR A MONTH BEFORE HE CAME. IT'S JUST GONE BACK TO THAT.
AKAMATSU.
KATO.
MORN-ING!

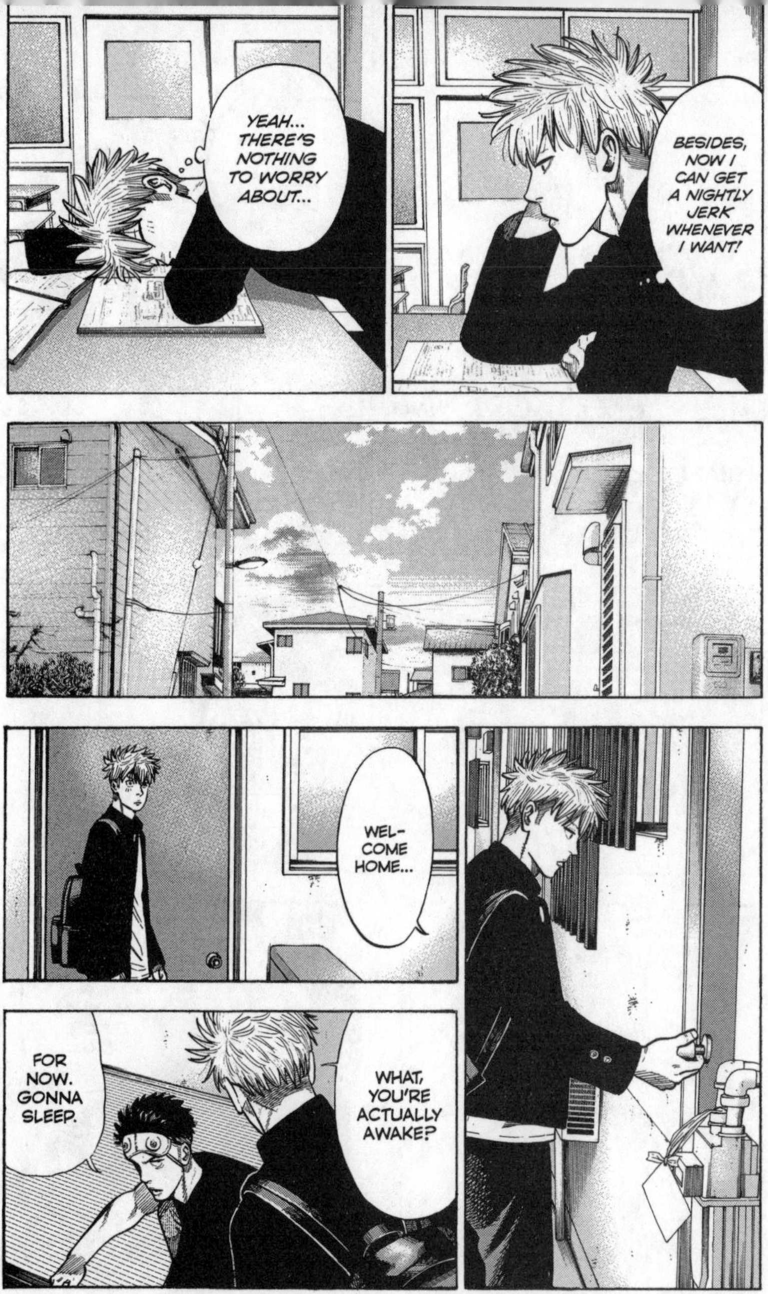
BESIDES, NOW I CAN GET A NIGHTLY JERK WHENEVER I WANT!
YEAH... THERE'S NOTHING TO WORRY ABOUT...
WEL-COME HOME...
WHAT, YOU'RE ACTUALLY AWAKE?
FOR NOW. GONNA SLEEP.

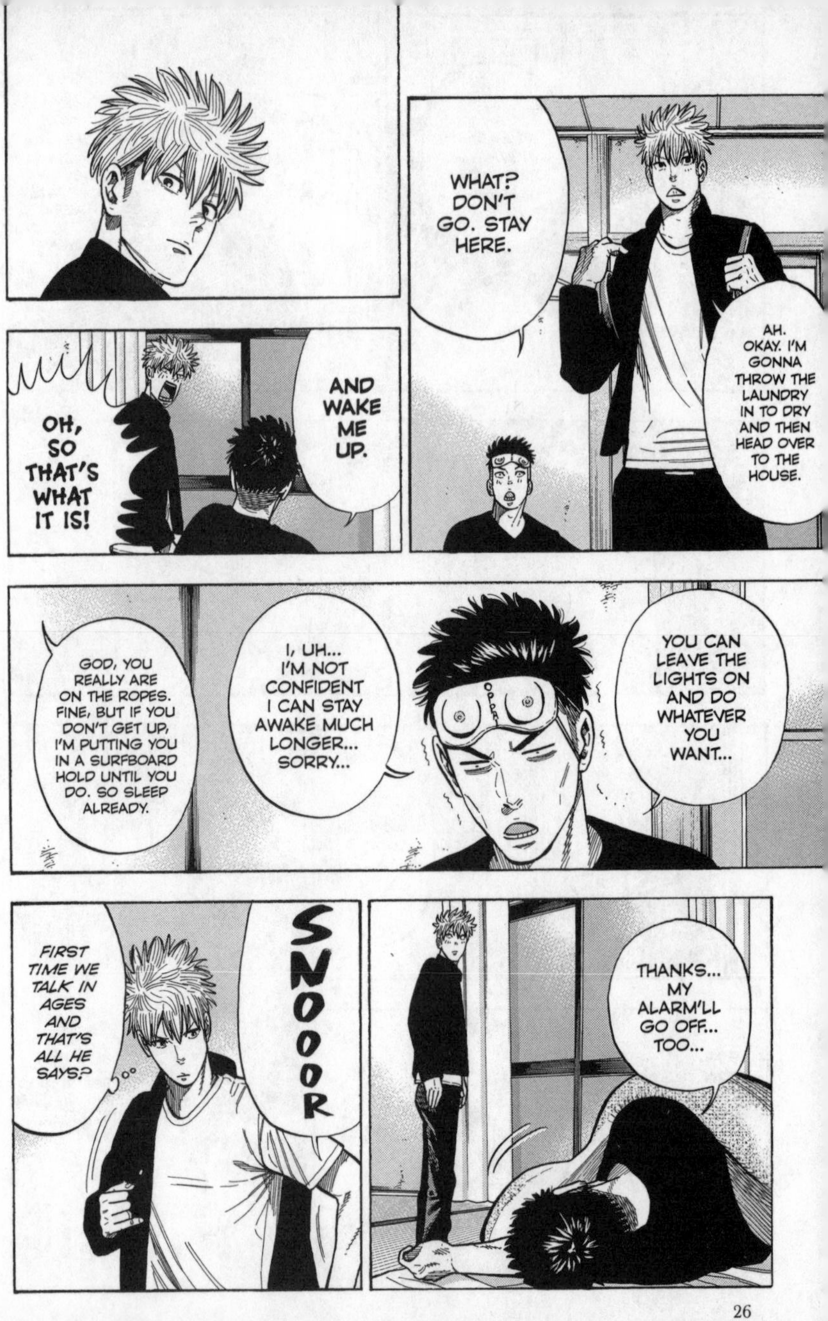
AH. OKAY. I'M GONNA THROW THE LAUNDRY IN TO DRY AND THEN HEAD OVER TO THE HOUSE.
WHAT? DON'T GO. STAY HERE.
AND WAKE ME UP.
OH, SO THAT'S WHAT IT IS!
YOU CAN LEAVE THE LIGHTS ON AND DO WHATEVER YOU WANT...
I, UH... I'M NOT CONFIDENT I CAN STAY AWAKE MUCH LONGER... SORRY...
GOD, YOU REALLY ARE ON THE ROPES. FINE, BUT IF YOU DON'T GET UP, I'M PUTTING YOU IN A SURFBOARD HOLD UNTIL YOU DO. SO SLEEP ALREADY.
THANKS... MY ALARM'LL GO OFF... TOO...
SNOOOR
FIRST TIME WE TALK IN AGES AND THAT'S ALL HE SAYS?

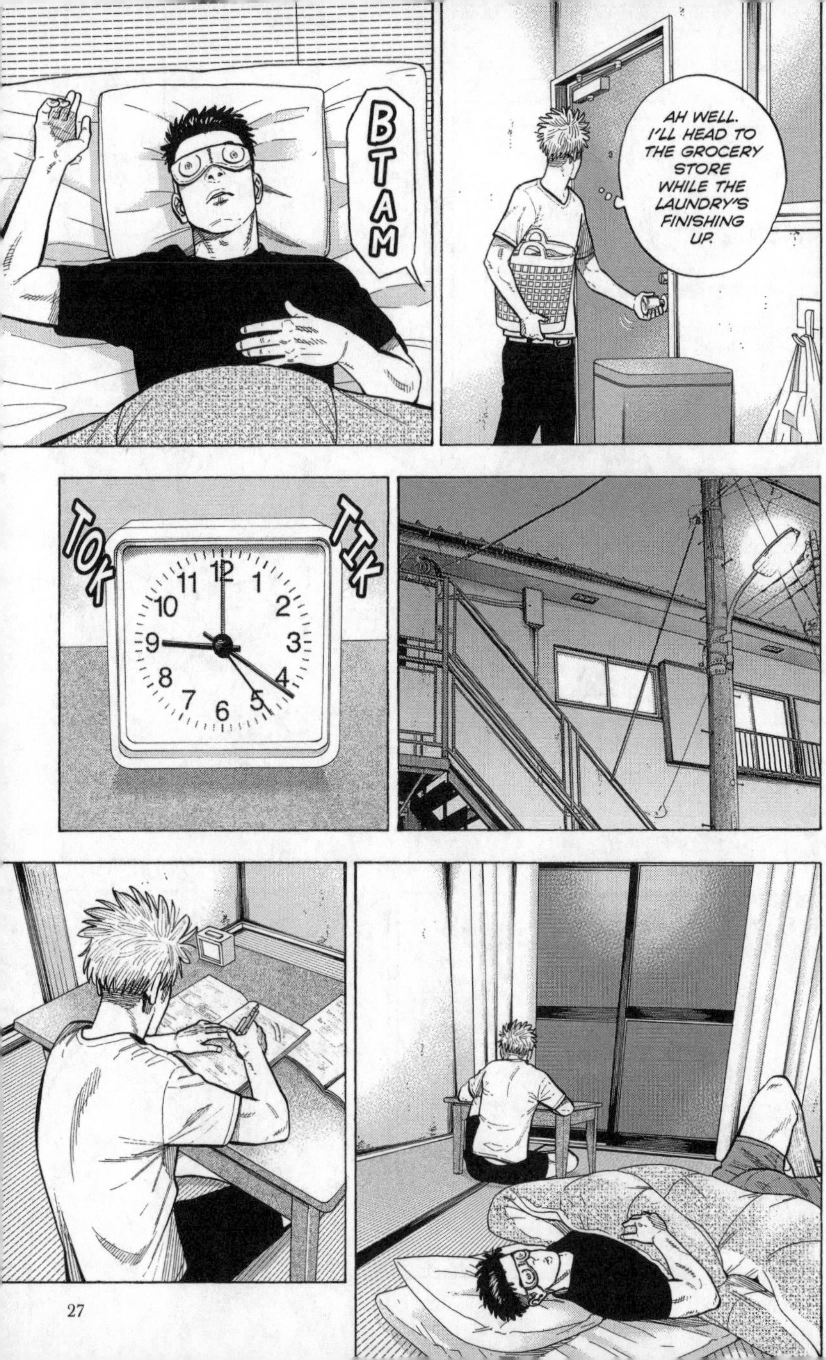
AH WELL. I'LL HEAD TO THE GROCERY STORE WHILE THE LAUNDRY'S FINISHING UP.
BTAM
TIK
TOK

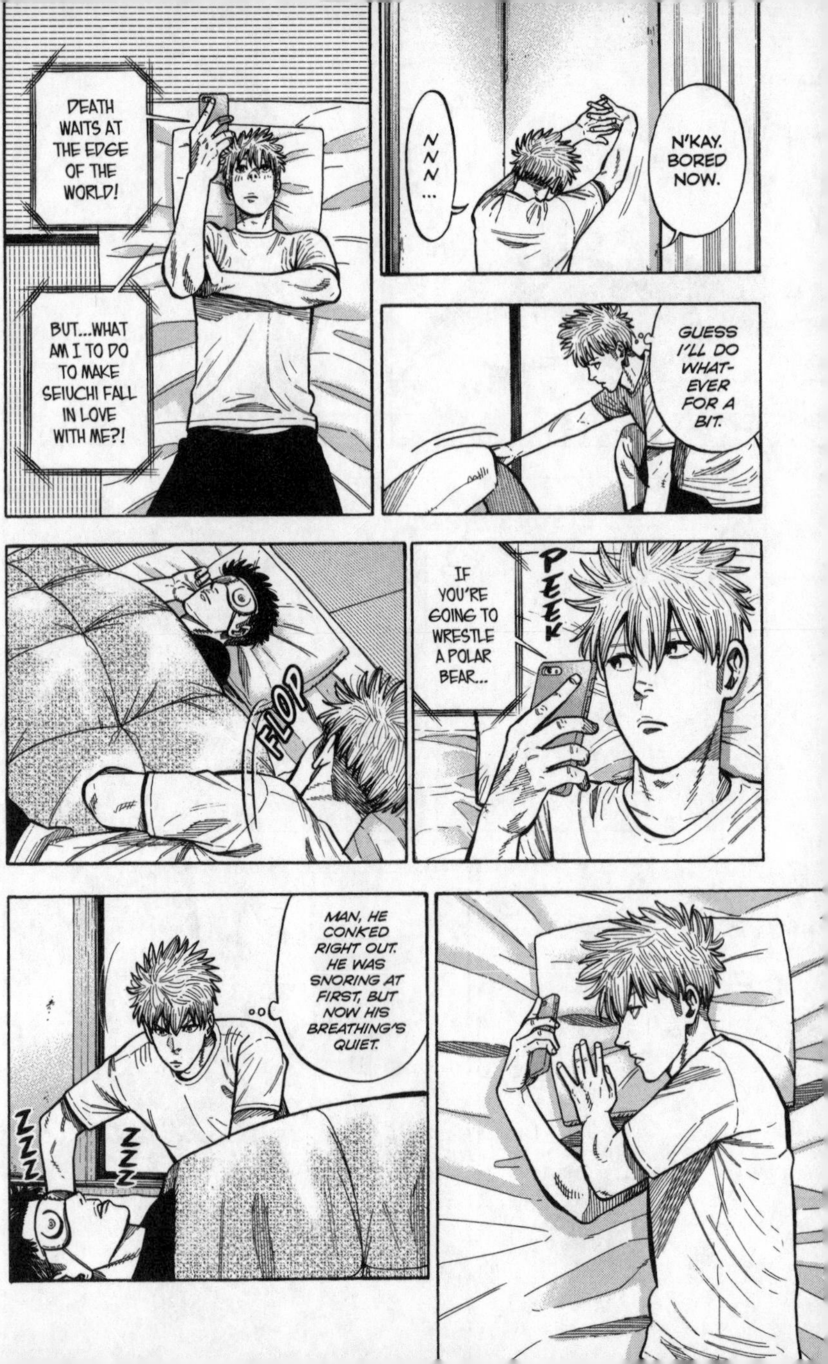
NNN...
N'KAY. BORED NOW.
GUESS I'LL DO WHAT-EVER FOR A BIT.
DEATH WAITS AT THE EDGE OF THE WORLD!
BUT...WHAT AM I TO DO TO MAKE SEIUCHI FALL IN LOVE WITH ME?!
PEEK
IF YOU'RE GOING TO WRESTLE A POLAR BEAR...
FLOP
MAN, HE CONKED RIGHT OUT. HE WAS SNORING AT FIRST, BUT NOW HIS BREATHING'S QUIET.
ZZZ
ZZZ

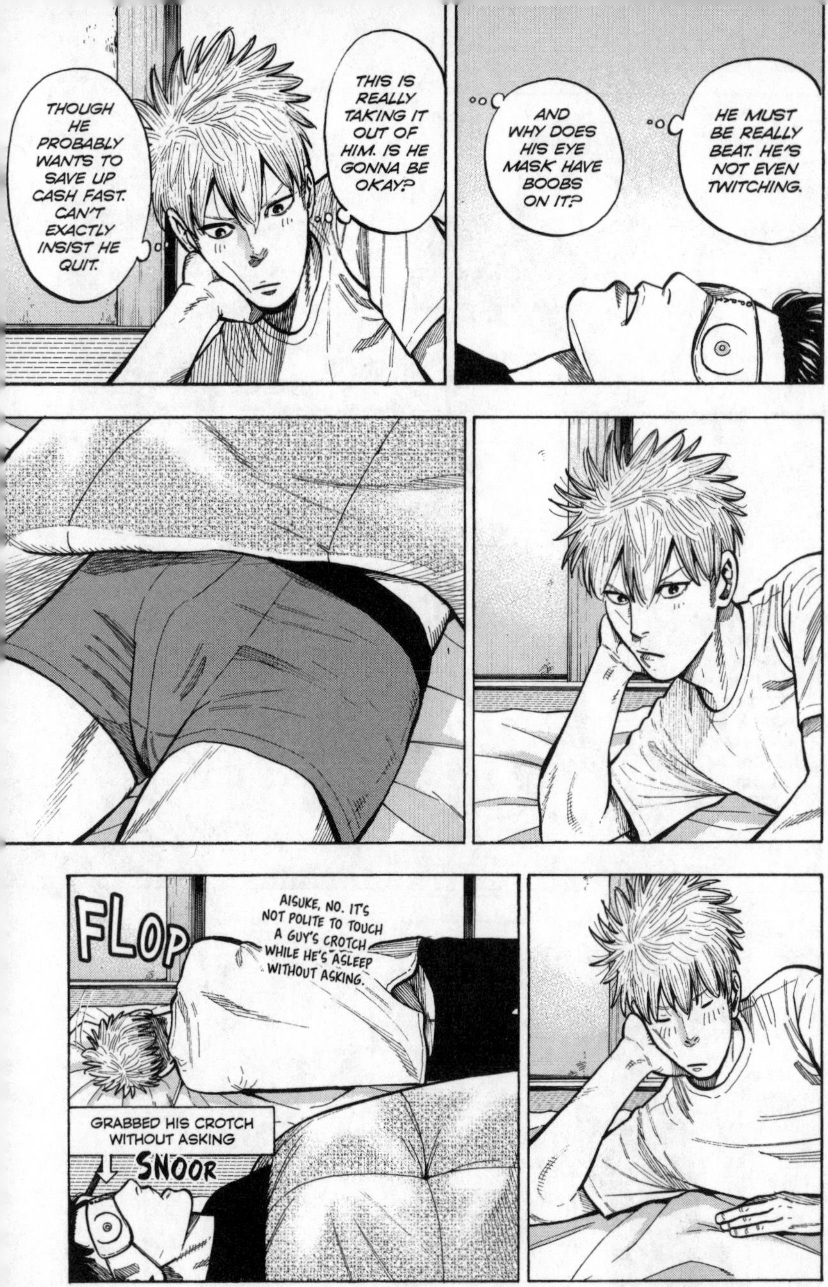
HE MUST BE REALLY BEAT. HE'S NOT EVEN TWITCHING.
AND WHY DOES HIS EYE MASK HAVE BOOBS ON IT?
THIS IS REALLY TAKING IT OUT OF HIM. IS HE GONNA BE OKAY?
THOUGH HE PROBABLY WANTS TO SAVE UP CASH FAST. CAN'T EXACTLY INSIST HE QUIT.
AISUKE, NO. IT'S NOT POLITE TO TOUCH A GUY'S CROTCH WHILE HE'S ASLEEP WITHOUT ASKING.
FLOP
GRABBED HIS CROTCH WITHOUT ASKING
SNOOR

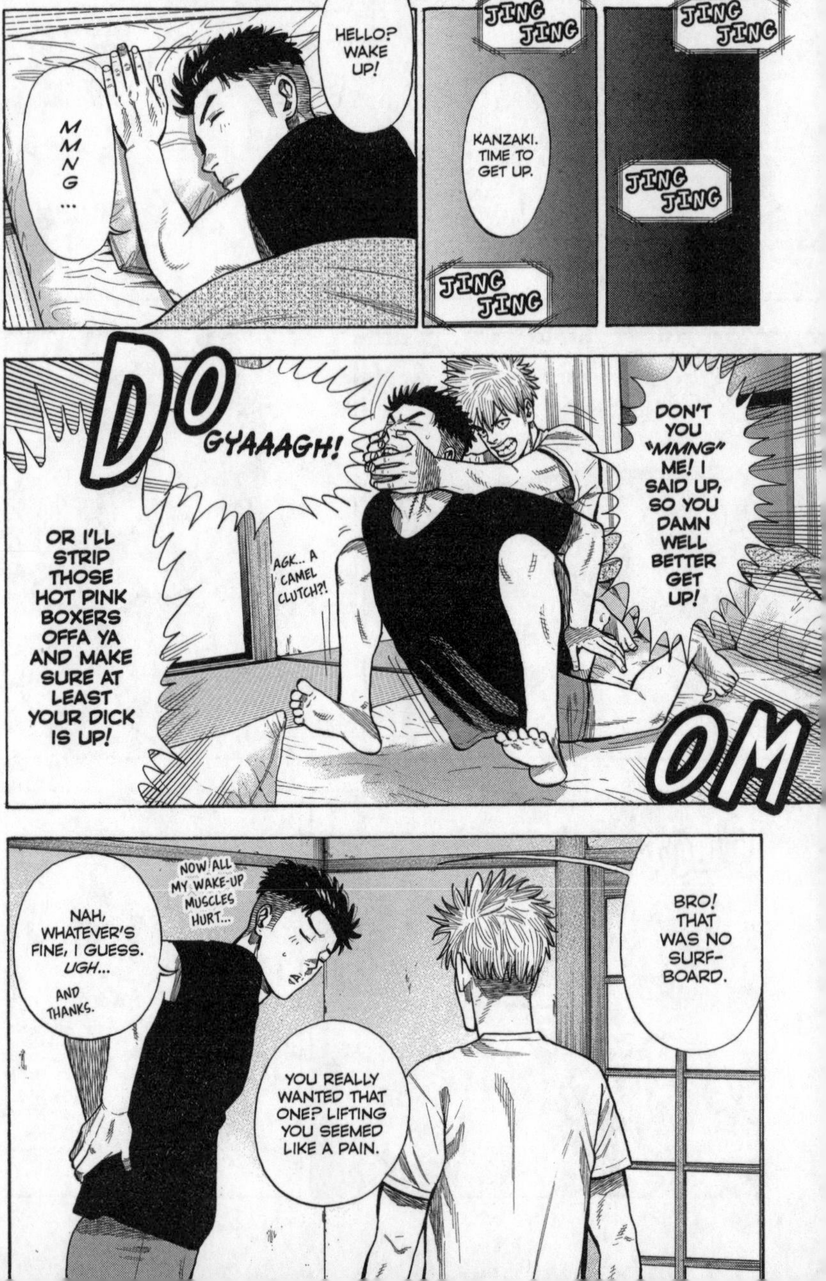
JING JING
JING JING
JING JING
KANZAKI. TIME TO GET UP.
JING JING
HELLO? WAKE UP!
MMNG...
DO
OM
DON'T YOU "MMNG" ME! I SAID UP, SO YOU DAMN WELL BETTER GET UP!
GYAAAGH!
AGK... A CAMEL CLUTCH?!
OR I'LL STRIP THOSE HOT PINK BOXERS OFFA YA AND MAKE SURE AT LEAST YOUR DICK IS UP!
BRO! THAT WAS NO SURF-BOARD.
YOU REALLY WANTED THAT ONE? LIFTING YOU SEEMED LIKE A PAIN.
NOW ALL MY WAKE-UP MUSCLES HURT...
NAH, WHATEVER'S FINE, I GUESS. UGH...
AND THANKS.

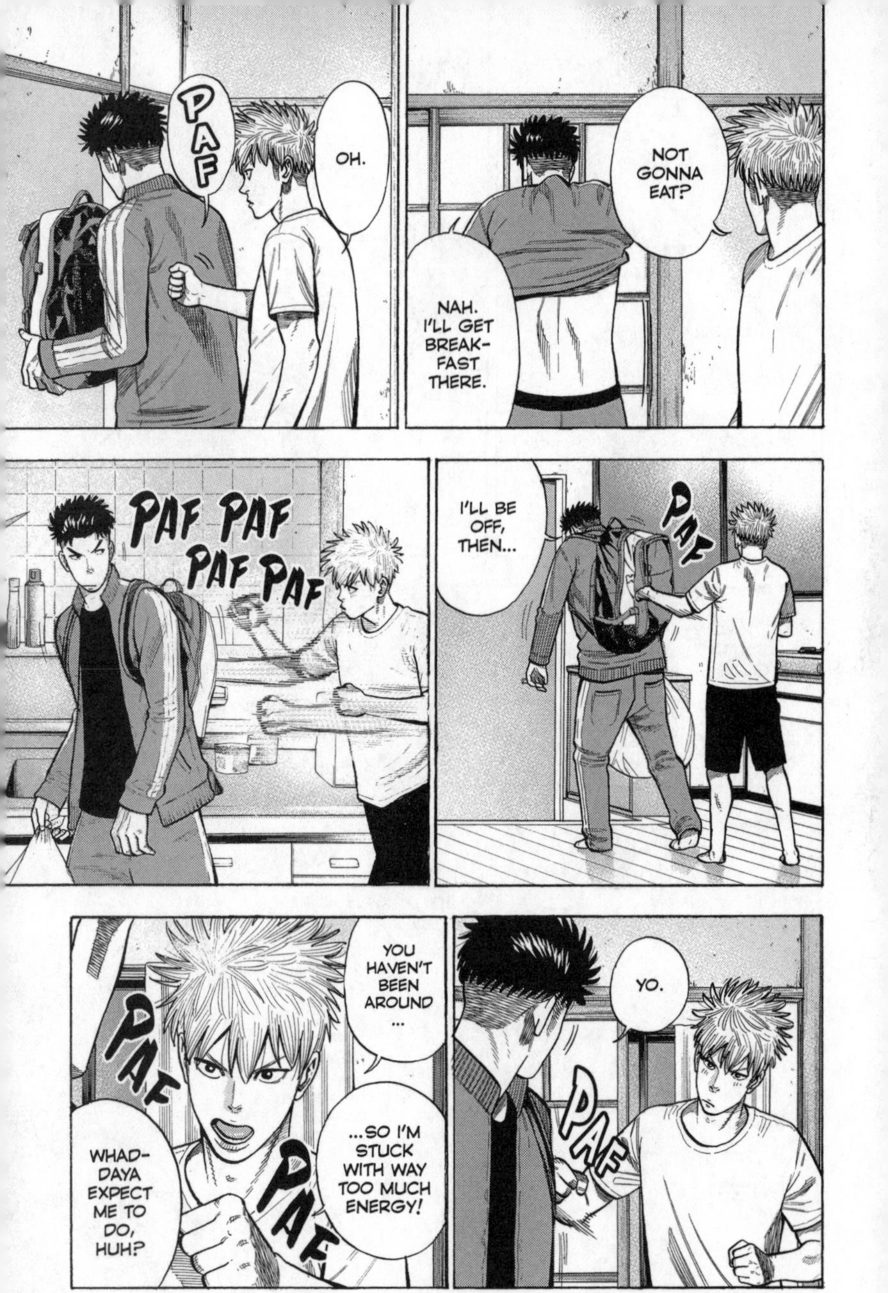
NOT GONNA EAT?
NAH. I'LL GET BREAK-FAST THERE.
OH.
PAF
I'LL BE OFF, THEN...
PAF
PAF PAF PAF PAF
YO.
PAF
YOU HAVEN'T BEEN AROUND ...
...SO I'M STUCK WITH WAY TOO MUCH ENERGY!
PAF
WHAD-DAYA EXPECT ME TO DO, HUH?
PAF
PAF

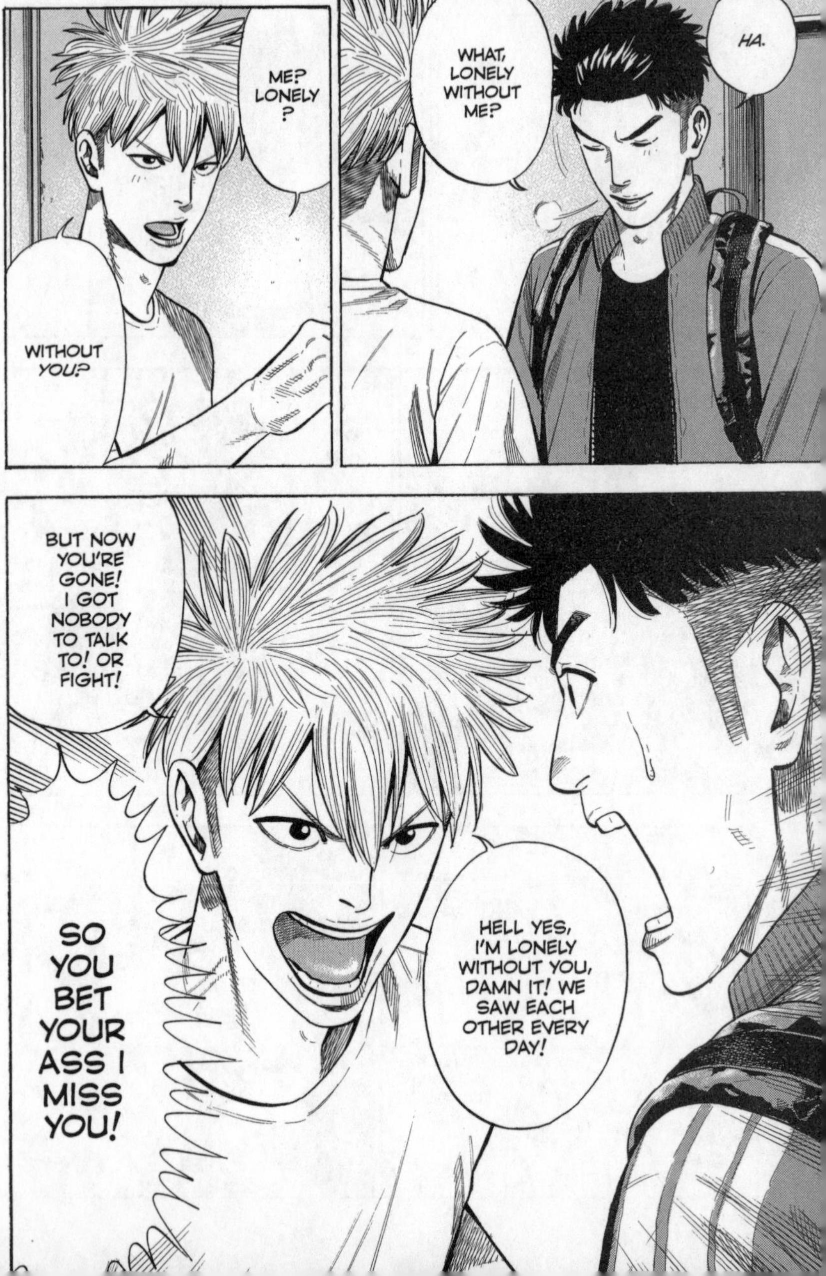
HA.
WHAT, LONELY WITHOUT ME?
ME? LONELY?
WITHOUT YOU?
HELL YES, I'M LONELY WITHOUT YOU, DAMN IT! WE SAW EACH OTHER EVERY DAY!
BUT NOW YOU'RE GONE! I GOT NOBODY TO TALK TO! OR FIGHT!
SO YOU BET YOUR ASS I MISS YOU!

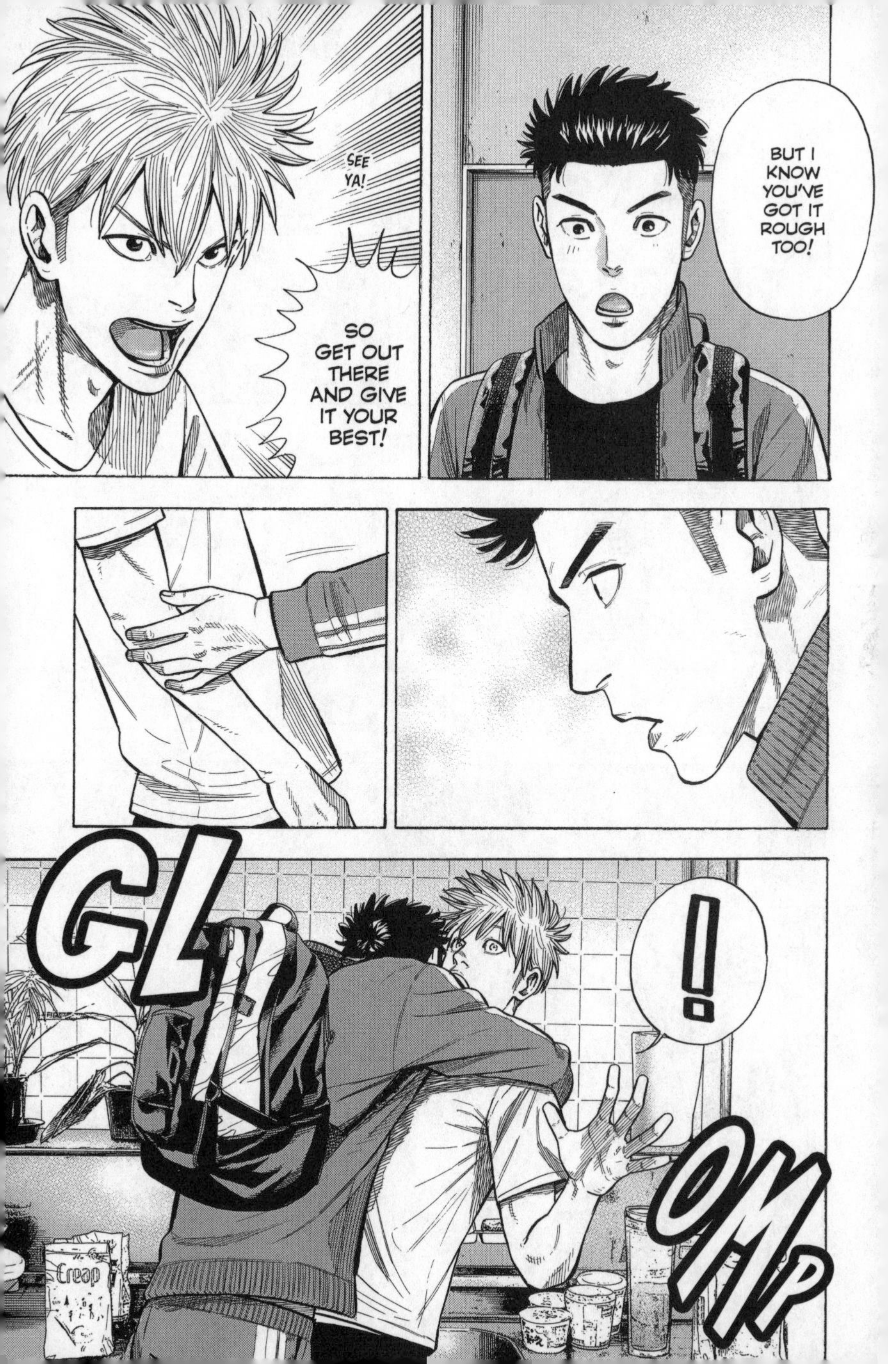
BUT I KNOW YOU'VE GOT IT ROUGH TOO!
SEE YA!
SO GET OUT THERE AND GIVE IT YOUR BEST!
!
GLOMP

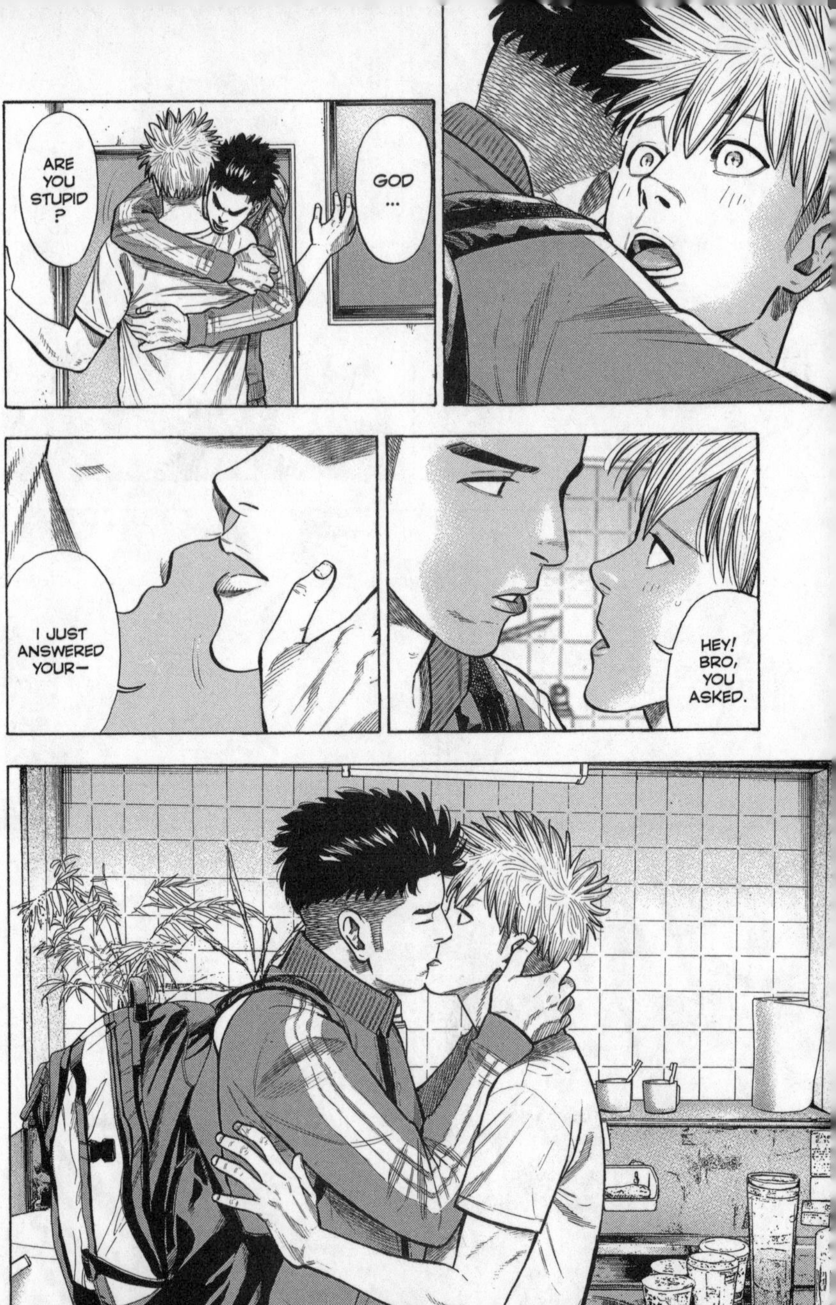
GOD ...
ARE YOU STUPID ?
HEY! BRO, YOU ASKED.
I JUST ANSWERED YOUR—

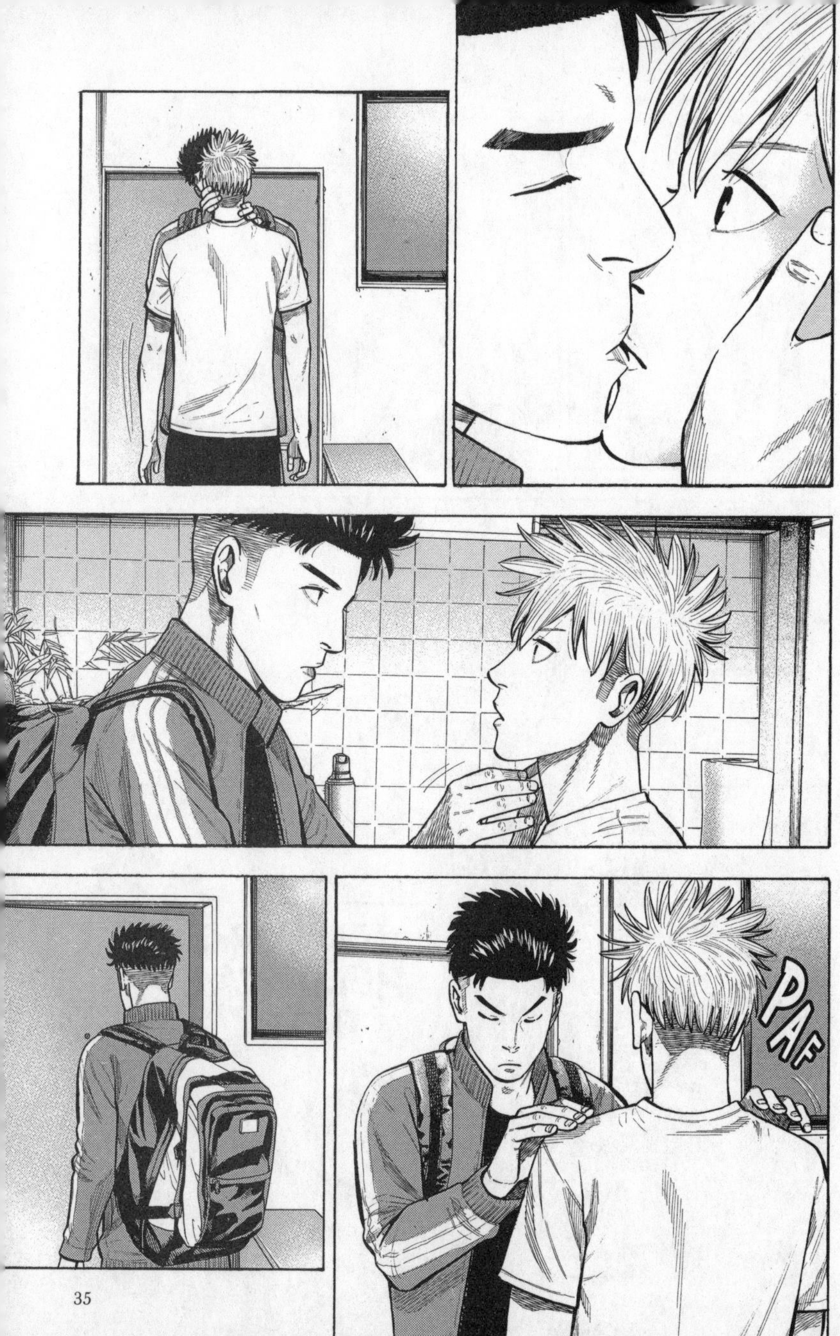
PAF

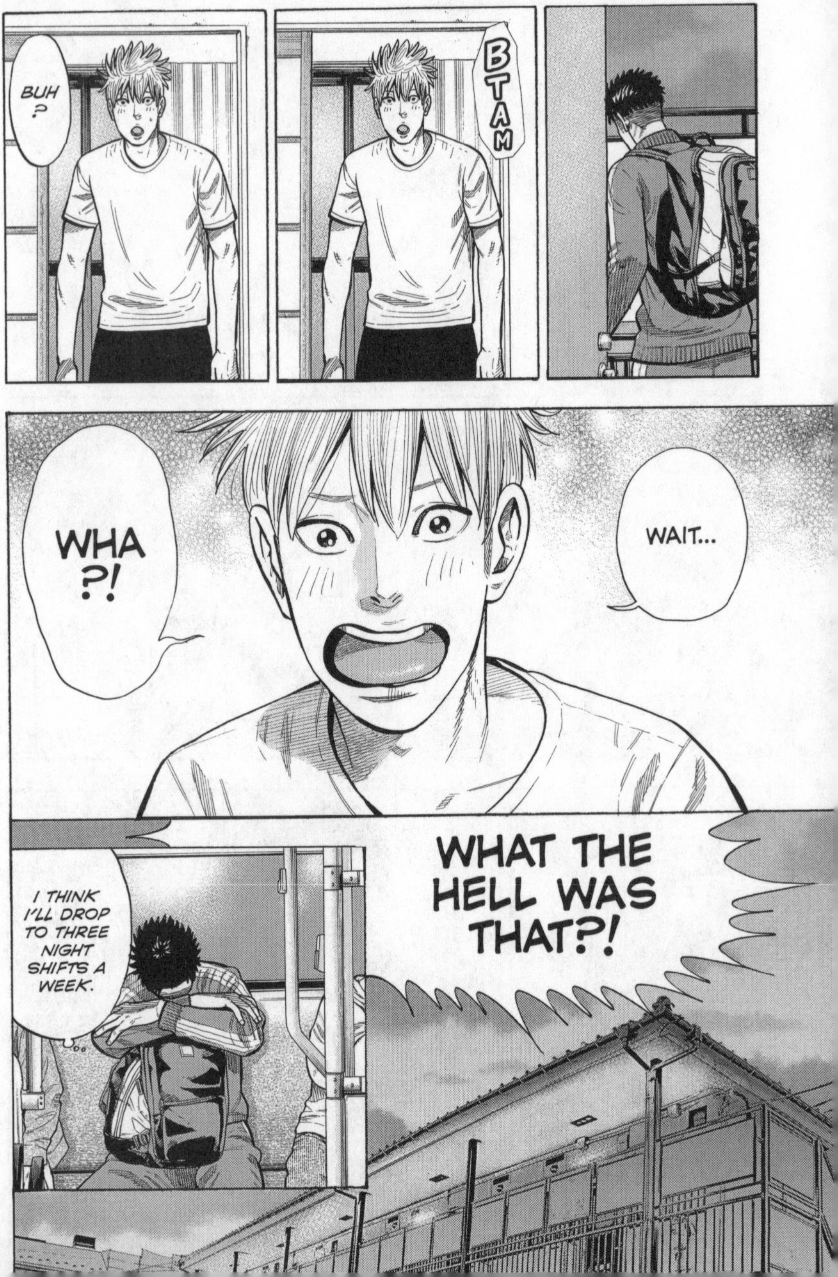
BTAM
BUH?
WAIT...
WHA?!
WHAT THE HELL WAS THAT?!
I THINK I'LL DROP TO THREE NIGHT SHIFTS A WEEK.

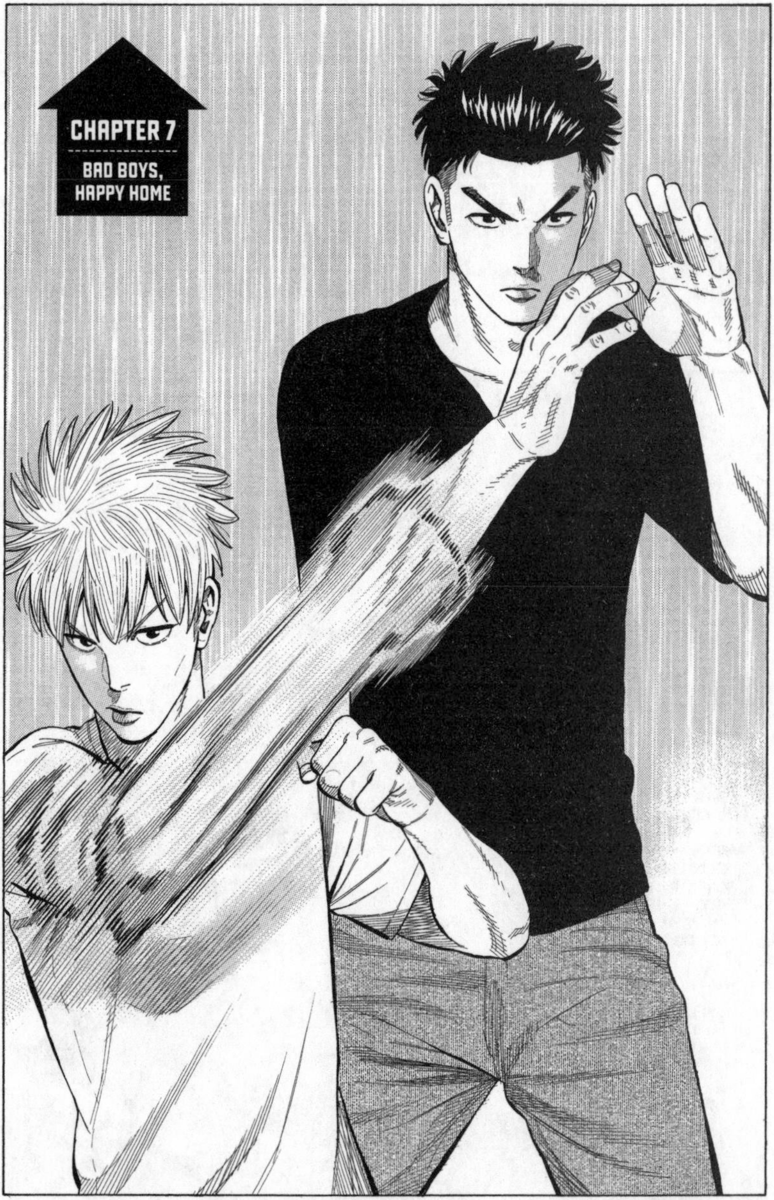
CHAPTER 7
BAD BOYS, HAPPY HOME

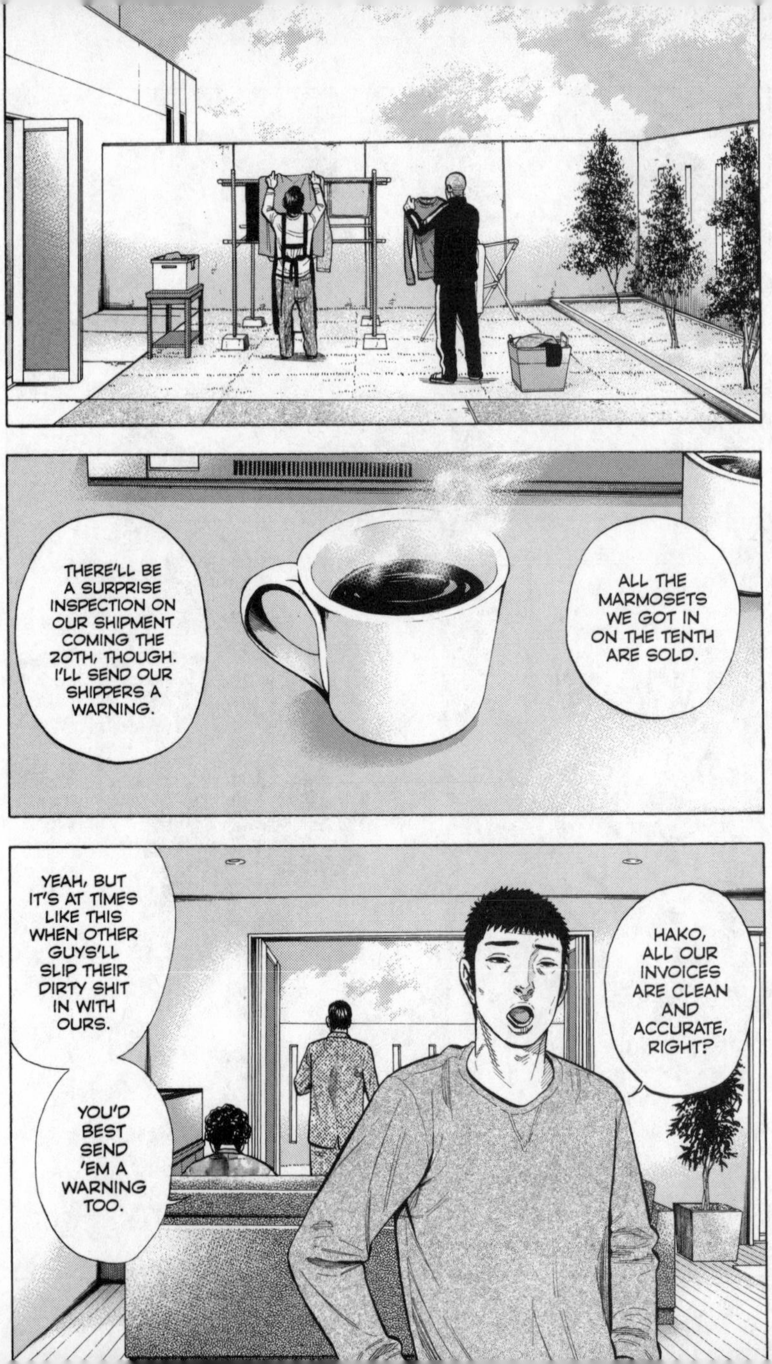
ALL THE MARMOSETS WE GOT IN ON THE TENTH ARE SOLD.
THERE'LL BE A SURPRISE INSPECTION ON OUR SHIPMENT COMING THE 20TH, THOUGH. I'LL SEND OUR SHIPPERS A WARNING.
HAKO, ALL OUR INVOICES ARE CLEAN AND ACCURATE, RIGHT?
YEAH, BUT IT'S AT TIMES LIKE THIS WHEN OTHER GUYS'LL SLIP THEIR DIRTY SHIT IN WITH OURS.
YOU'D BEST SEND 'EM A WARNING TOO.

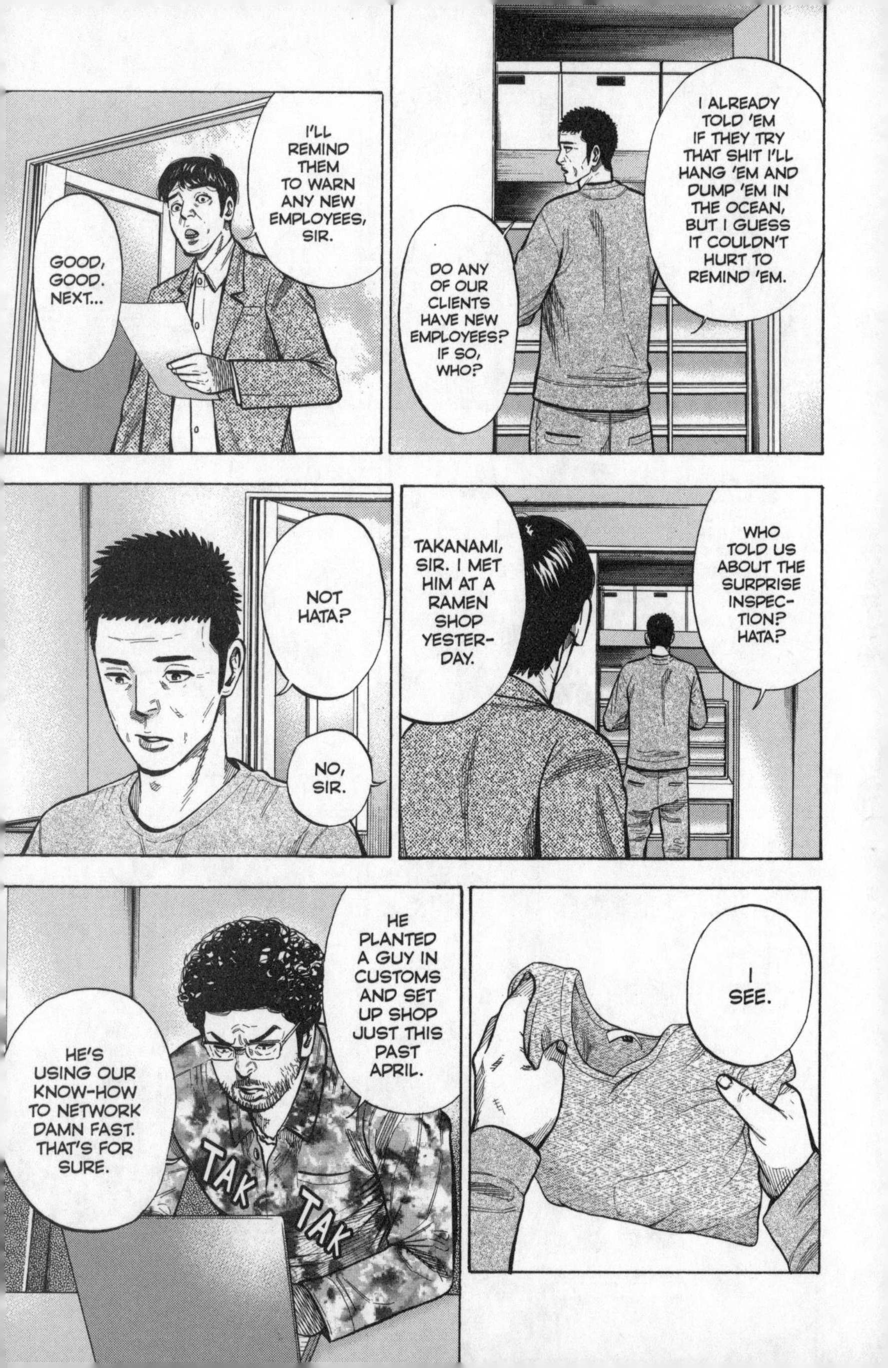
I ALREADY TOLD 'EM IF THEY TRY THAT SHIT I'LL HANG 'EM AND DUMP 'EM IN THE OCEAN, BUT I GUESS IT COULDN'T HURT TO REMIND 'EM.
DO ANY OF OUR CLIENTS HAVE NEW EMPLOYEES? IF SO, WHO?
I'LL REMIND THEM TO WARN ANY NEW EMPLOYEES, SIR.
GOOD, GOOD. NEXT...
WHO TOLD US ABOUT THE SURPRISE INSPEC-TION? HATA?
TAKANAMI, SIR. I MET HIM AT A RAMEN SHOP YESTER-DAY.
NOT HATA?
NO, SIR.
I SEE.
HE PLANTED A GUY IN CUSTOMS AND SET UP SHOP JUST THIS PAST APRIL.
HE'S USING OUR KNOW-HOW TO NETWORK DAMN FAST. THAT'S FOR SURE.
TAK
TAK

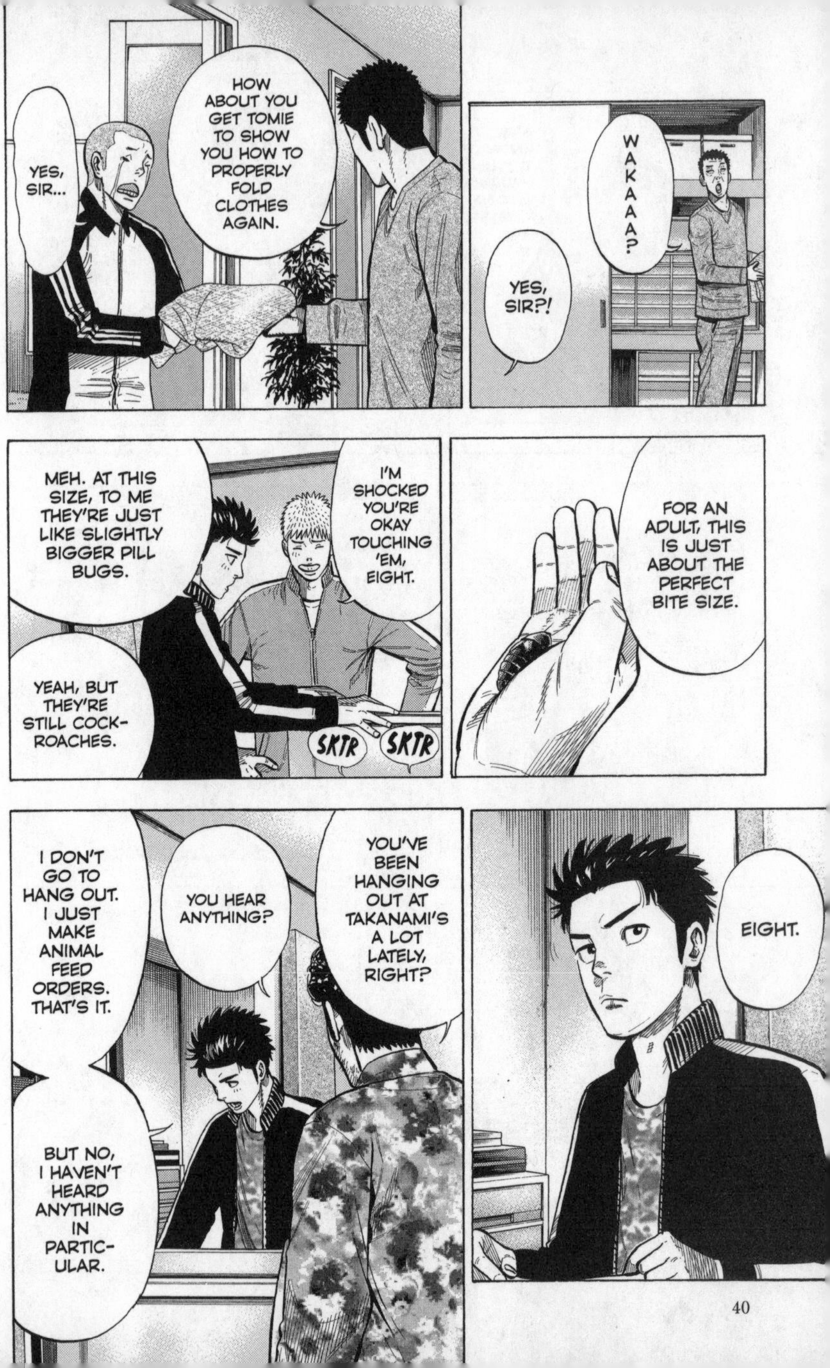
WAKAAAA?
YES, SIR?!
HOW ABOUT YOU GET TOMIE TO SHOW YOU HOW TO PROPERLY FOLD CLOTHES AGAIN.
YES, SIR...
FOR AN ADULT, THIS IS JUST ABOUT THE PERFECT BITE SIZE.
I'M SHOCKED YOU'RE OKAY TOUCHING 'EM, EIGHT.
MEH. AT THIS SIZE, TO ME THEY'RE JUST LIKE SLIGHTLY BIGGER PILL BUGS.
SKTR
SKTR
YEAH, BUT THEY'RE STILL COCK-ROACHES.
EIGHT.
YOU'VE BEEN HANGING OUT AT TAKANAMI'S A LOT LATELY, RIGHT?
YOU HEAR ANYTHING?
I DON'T GO TO HANG OUT. I JUST MAKE ANIMAL FEED ORDERS. THAT'S IT.
BUT NO, I HAVEN'T HEARD ANYTHING IN PARTIC-ULAR.

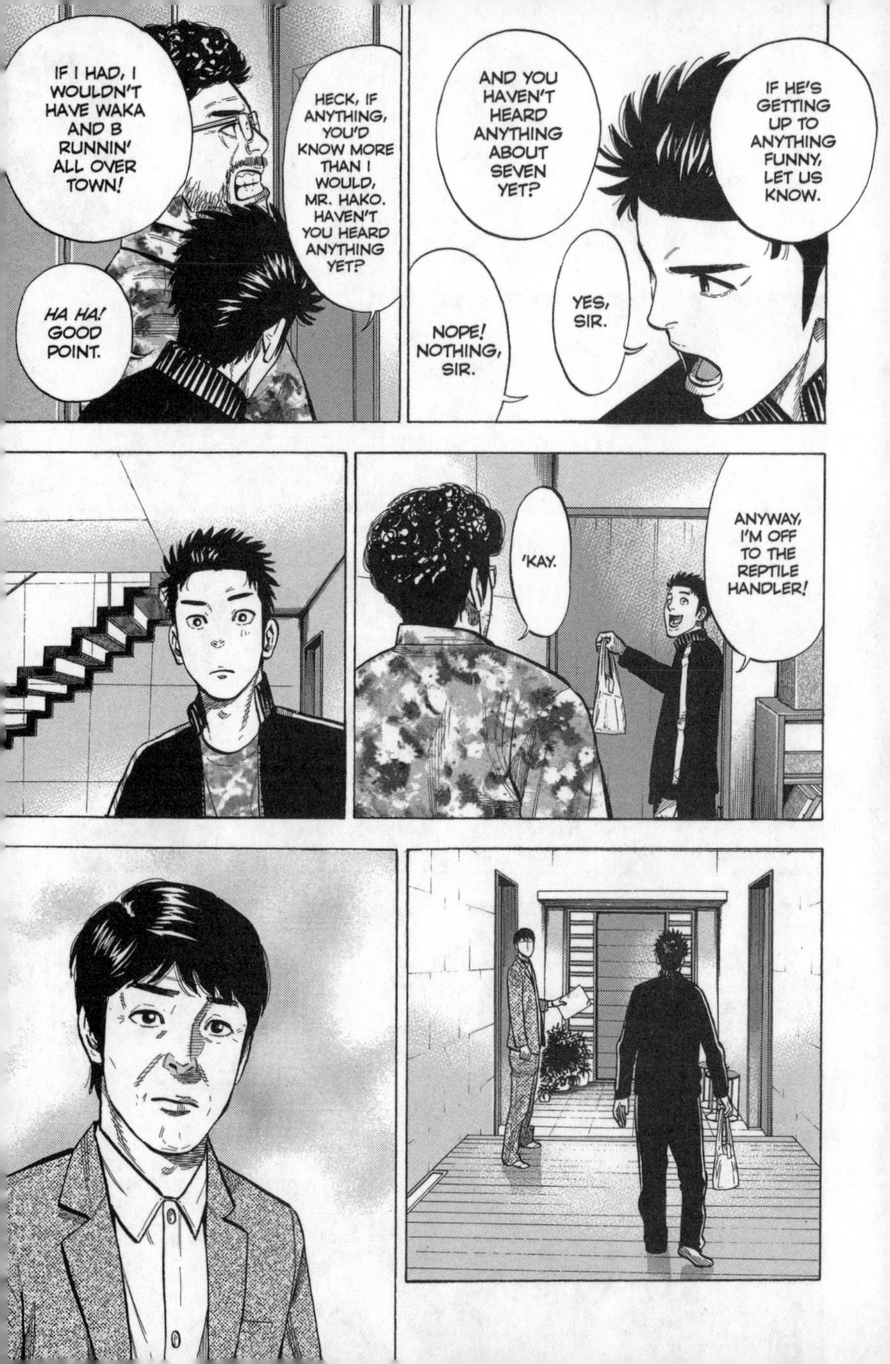
IF HE'S GETTING UP TO ANYTHING FUNNY, LET US KNOW.
AND YOU HAVEN'T HEARD ANYTHING ABOUT SEVEN YET?
YES, SIR.
NOPE! NOTHING, SIR.
HECK, IF ANYTHING, YOU'D KNOW MORE THAN I WOULD, MR. HAKO. HAVEN'T YOU HEARD ANYTHING YET?
IF I HAD, I WOULDN'T HAVE WAKA AND B RUNNIN' ALL OVER TOWN!
HA HA! GOOD POINT.
ANYWAY, I'M OFF TO THE REPTILE HANDLER!
'KAY.

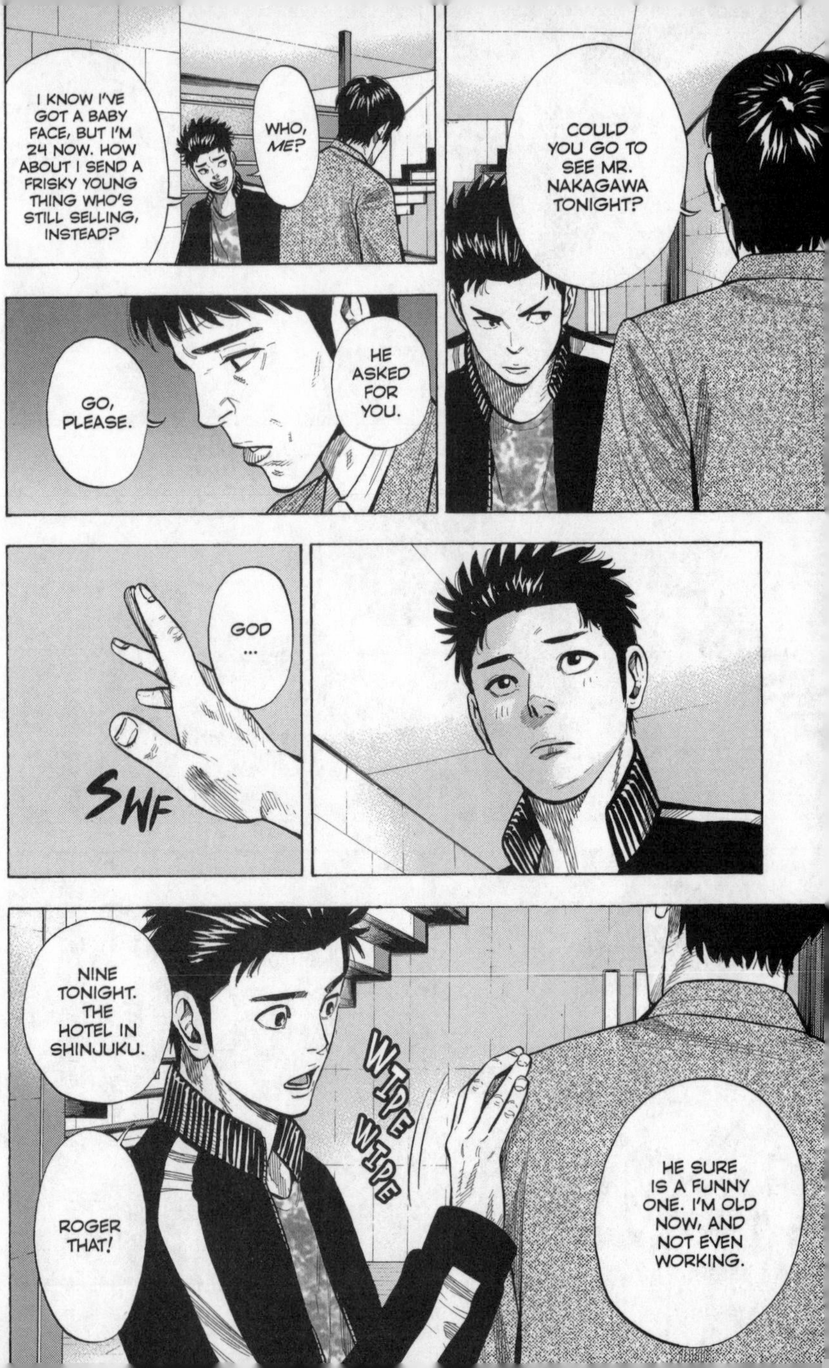
COULD YOU GO TO SEE MR. NAKAGAWA TONIGHT?
WHO, *ME?*
I KNOW I'VE GOT A BABY FACE, BUT I'M 24 NOW. HOW ABOUT I SEND A FRISKY YOUNG THING WHO'S STILL SELLING, INSTEAD?
HE ASKED FOR YOU.
GO, PLEASE.
GOD ...
SWF
HE SURE IS A FUNNY ONE. I'M OLD NOW, AND NOT EVEN WORKING.
WIPE WIPE
NINE TONIGHT. THE HOTEL IN SHINJUKU.
ROGER THAT!

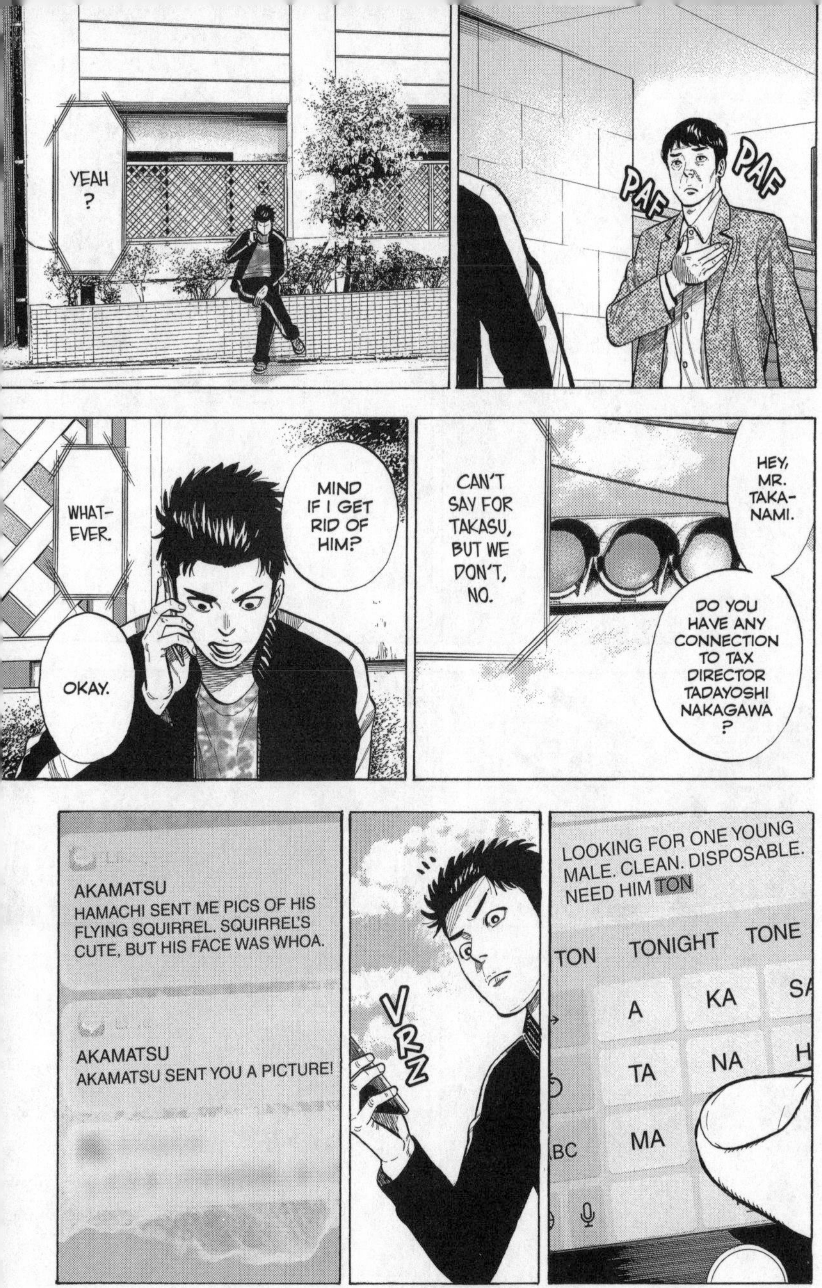
PAF
PAF
YEAH
?
HEY, MR. TAKA-NAMI.
DO YOU HAVE ANY CONNECTION TO TAX DIRECTOR TADAYOSHI NAKAGAWA
?
CAN'T SAY FOR TAKASU, BUT WE DON'T, NO.
MIND IF I GET RID OF HIM?
WHAT-EVER.
OKAY.
LOOKING FOR ONE YOUNG MALE. CLEAN. DISPOSABLE. NEED HIM TON
TON
TONIGHT
TONE
A
KA
TA
NA
MA
VRZ
AKAMATSU
HAMACHI SENT ME PICS OF HIS FLYING SQUIRREL. SQUIRREL'S CUTE, BUT HIS FACE WAS WHOA.
AKAMATSU
AKAMATSU SENT YOU A PICTURE!

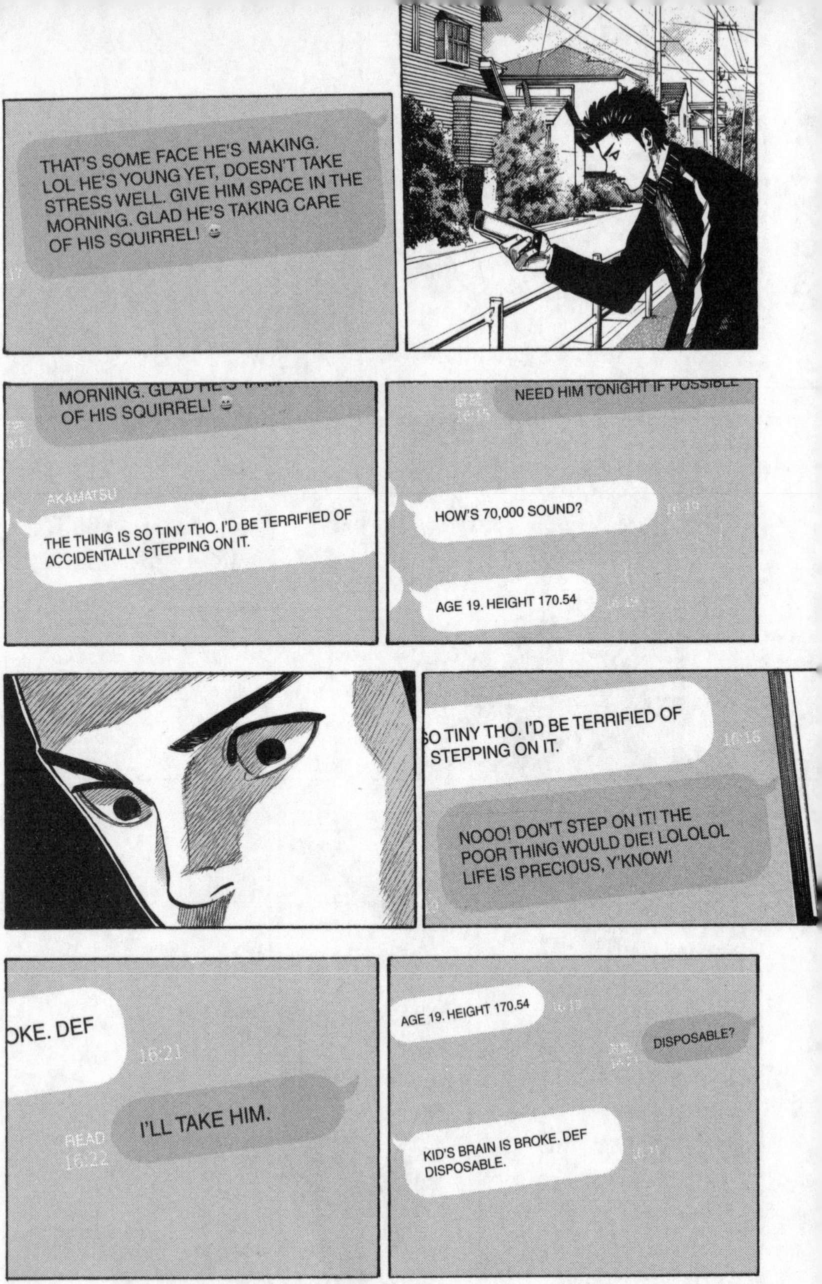
THAT'S SOME FACE HE'S MAKING. LOL HE'S YOUNG YET, DOESN'T TAKE STRESS WELL. GIVE HIM SPACE IN THE MORNING. GLAD HE'S TAKING CARE OF HIS SQUIRREL! 😄
NEED HIM TONIGHT IF POSSIBLE
HOW'S 70,000 SOUND?
AGE 19. HEIGHT 170.54
MORNING. GLAD HE'S TAKING CARE OF HIS SQUIRREL! 😄
AKAMATSU
THE THING IS SO TINY THO. I'D BE TERRIFIED OF ACCIDENTALLY STEPPING ON IT.
SO TINY THO. I'D BE TERRIFIED OF STEPPING ON IT.
NOOO! DON'T STEP ON IT! THE POOR THING WOULD DIE! LOLOLOL LIFE IS PRECIOUS, Y'KNOW!
AGE 19. HEIGHT 170.54
DISPOSABLE?
KID'S BRAIN IS BROKE. DEF DISPOSABLE.
OKE. DEF
16:21
I'LL TAKE HIM.
READ
16:22

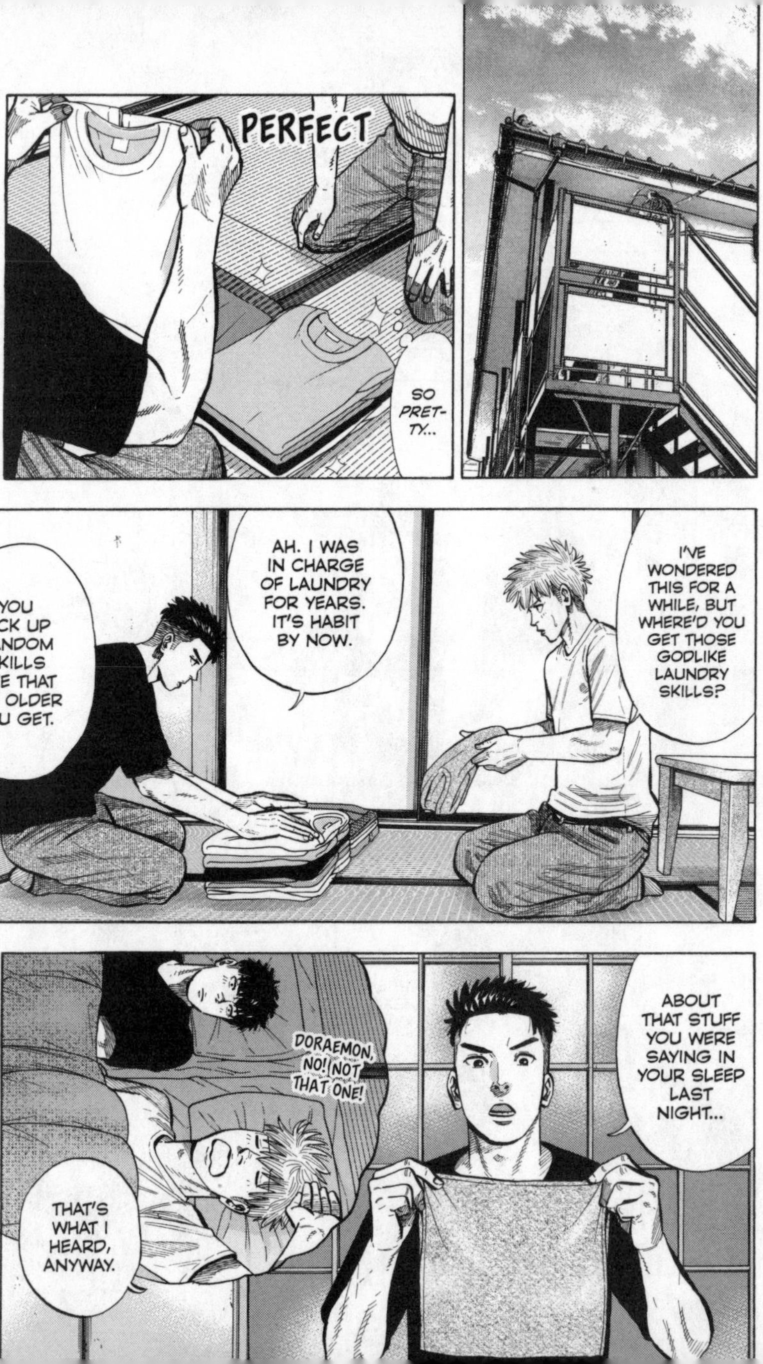
PERFECT
SO PRETTY...
I'VE WONDERED THIS FOR A WHILE, BUT WHERE'D YOU GET THOSE GODLIKE LAUNDRY SKILLS?
AH. I WAS IN CHARGE OF LAUNDRY FOR YEARS. IT'S HABIT BY NOW.
YOU PICK UP RANDOM SKILLS LIKE THAT THE OLDER YOU GET.
ABOUT THAT STUFF YOU WERE SAYING IN YOUR SLEEP LAST NIGHT...
DORAEMON, NO! NOT THAT ONE!
THAT'S WHAT I HEARD, ANYWAY.

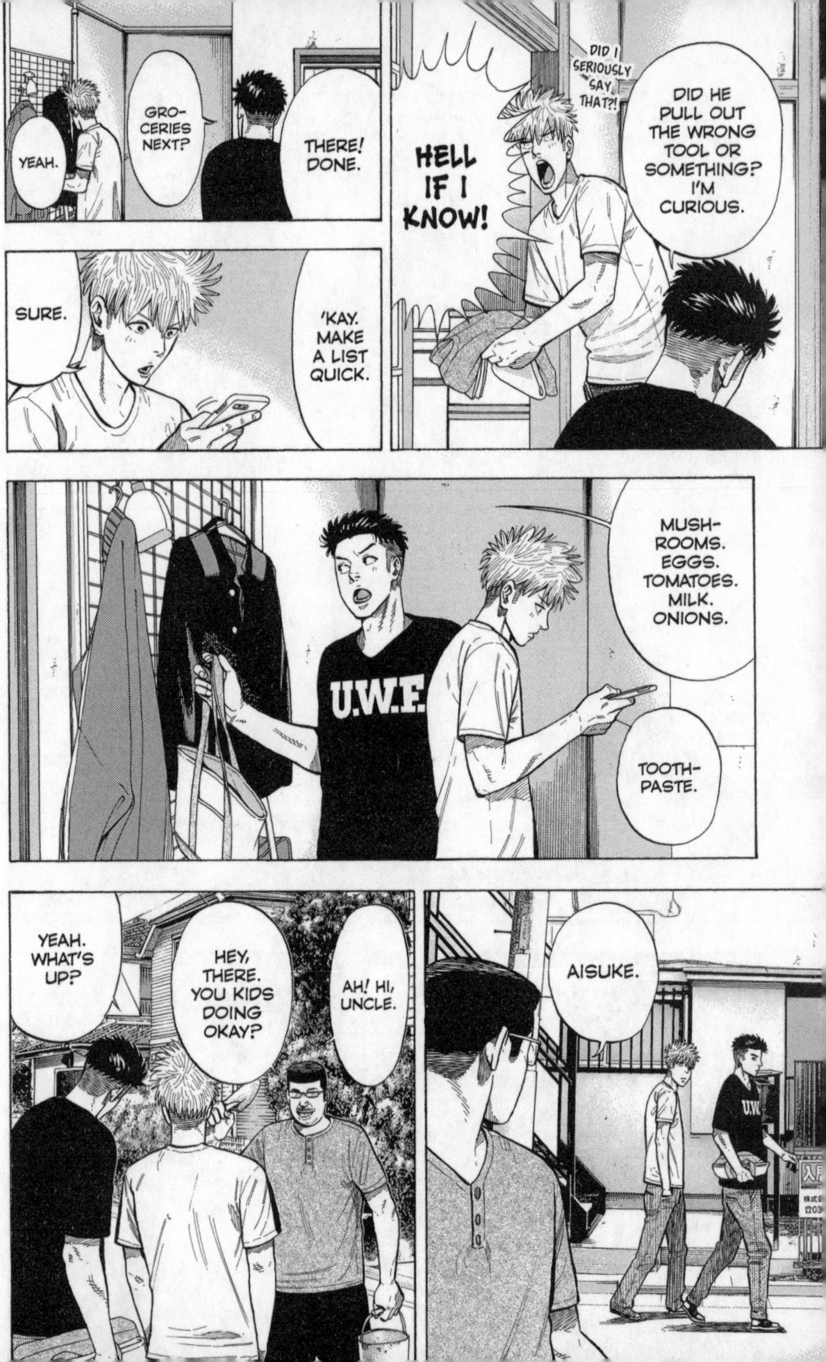
DID HE PULL OUT THE WRONG TOOL OR SOMETHING? I'M CURIOUS.
DID I SERIOUSLY SAY THAT?!
HELL IF I KNOW!
THERE! DONE.
GRO-CERIES NEXT?
YEAH.
'KAY. MAKE A LIST QUICK.
SURE.
MUSH-ROOMS. EGGS. TOMATOES. MILK. ONIONS.
TOOTH-PASTE.
AISUKE.
AH! HI, UNCLE.
HEY, THERE. YOU KIDS DOING OKAY?
YEAH. WHAT'S UP?

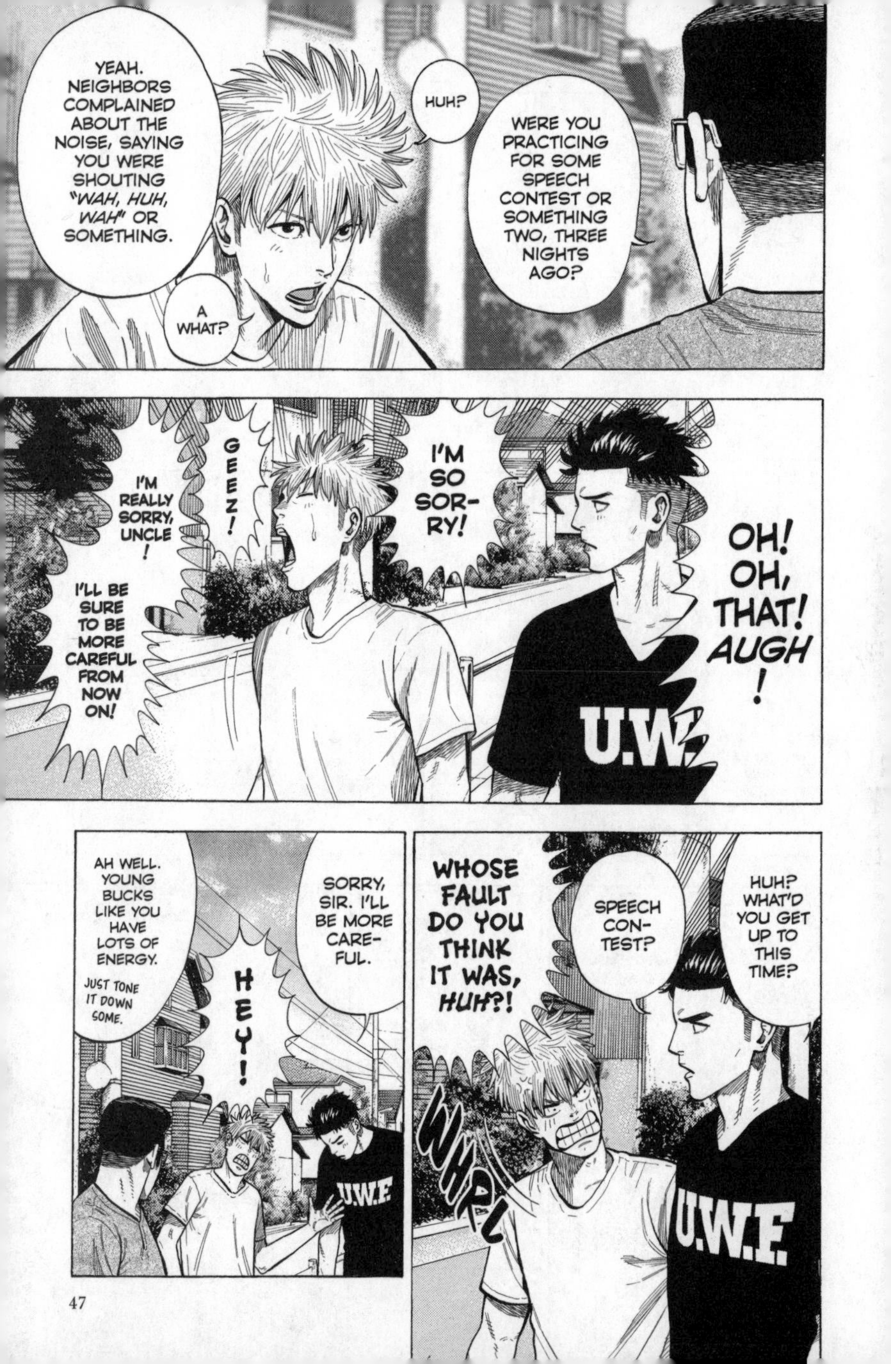
WERE YOU PRACTICING FOR SOME SPEECH CONTEST OR SOMETHING TWO, THREE NIGHTS AGO?
HUH?
A WHAT?
YEAH. NEIGHBORS COMPLAINED ABOUT THE NOISE, SAYING YOU WERE SHOUTING "WAH, HUH, WAH" OR SOMETHING.
OH! OH, THAT! AUGH!
I'M SO SORRY!
GEEZ!
I'M REALLY SORRY, UNCLE!
I'LL BE SURE TO BE MORE CAREFUL FROM NOW ON!
HUH? WHAT'D YOU GET UP TO THIS TIME?
SPEECH CONTEST?
WHOSE FAULT DO YOU THINK IT WAS, HUH?!
WHMPL
SORRY, SIR. I'LL BE MORE CAREFUL.
HEY!
AH WELL. YOUNG BUCKS LIKE YOU HAVE LOTS OF ENERGY.
JUST TONE IT DOWN SOME.

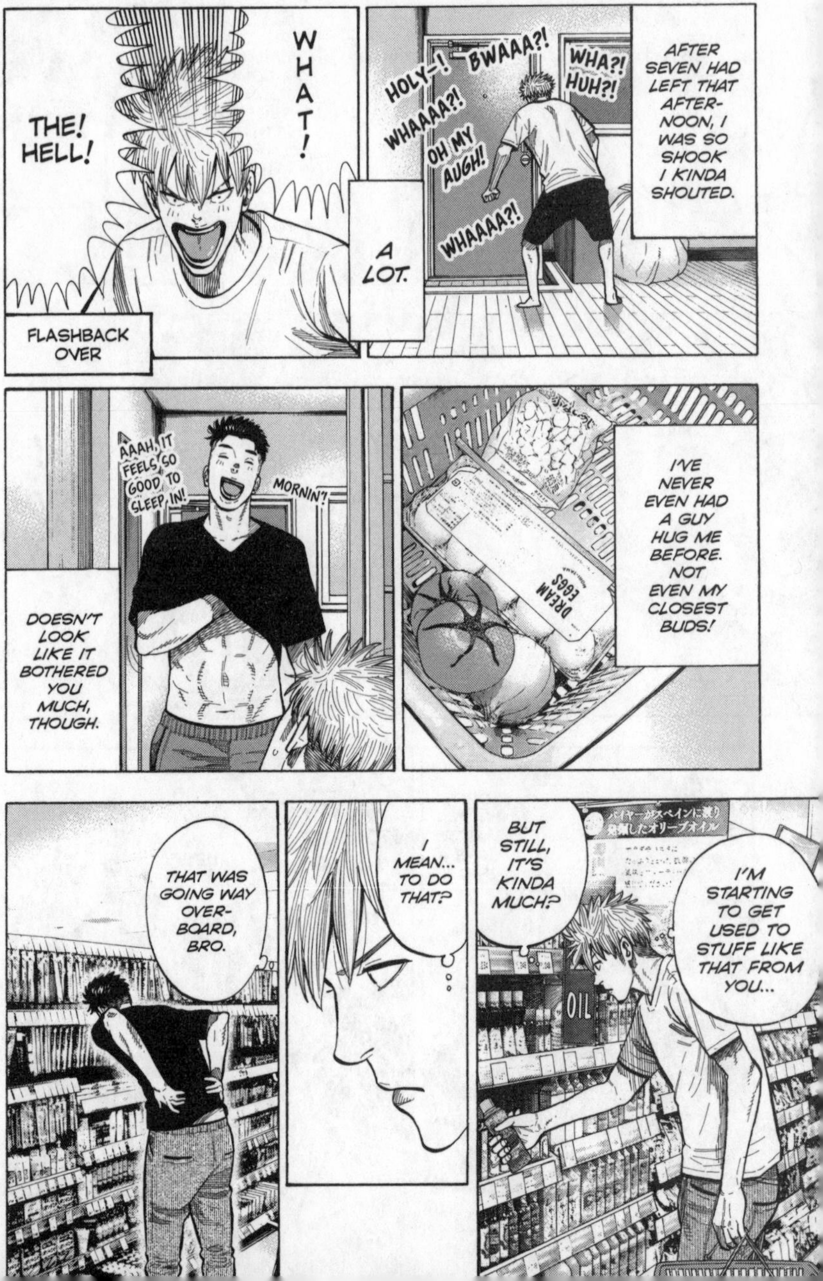
AFTER SEVEN HAD LEFT THAT AFTERNOON, I WAS SO SHOOK I KINDA SHOUTED.
WHA?! HUH?!
BWAAA?!
HOLY-!
WHAAAA?!
OH MY AUGH!
WHAAAA?!
A LOT.
WHAT!
THE! HELL!
FLASHBACK OVER
I'VE NEVER EVEN HAD A GUY HUG ME BEFORE. NOT EVEN MY CLOSEST BUDS!
DREAM EGGS
MORNIN'!
AAAH, IT FEELS SO GOOD TO SLEEP IN!
DOESN'T LOOK LIKE IT BOTHERED YOU MUCH, THOUGH.
バイヤーがスペインに渡り発掘したオリーブオイル
I'M STARTING TO GET USED TO STUFF LIKE THAT FROM YOU...
BUT STILL, IT'S KINDA MUCH?
OIL
I MEAN... TO DO THAT?
THAT WAS GOING WAY OVERBOARD, BRO.

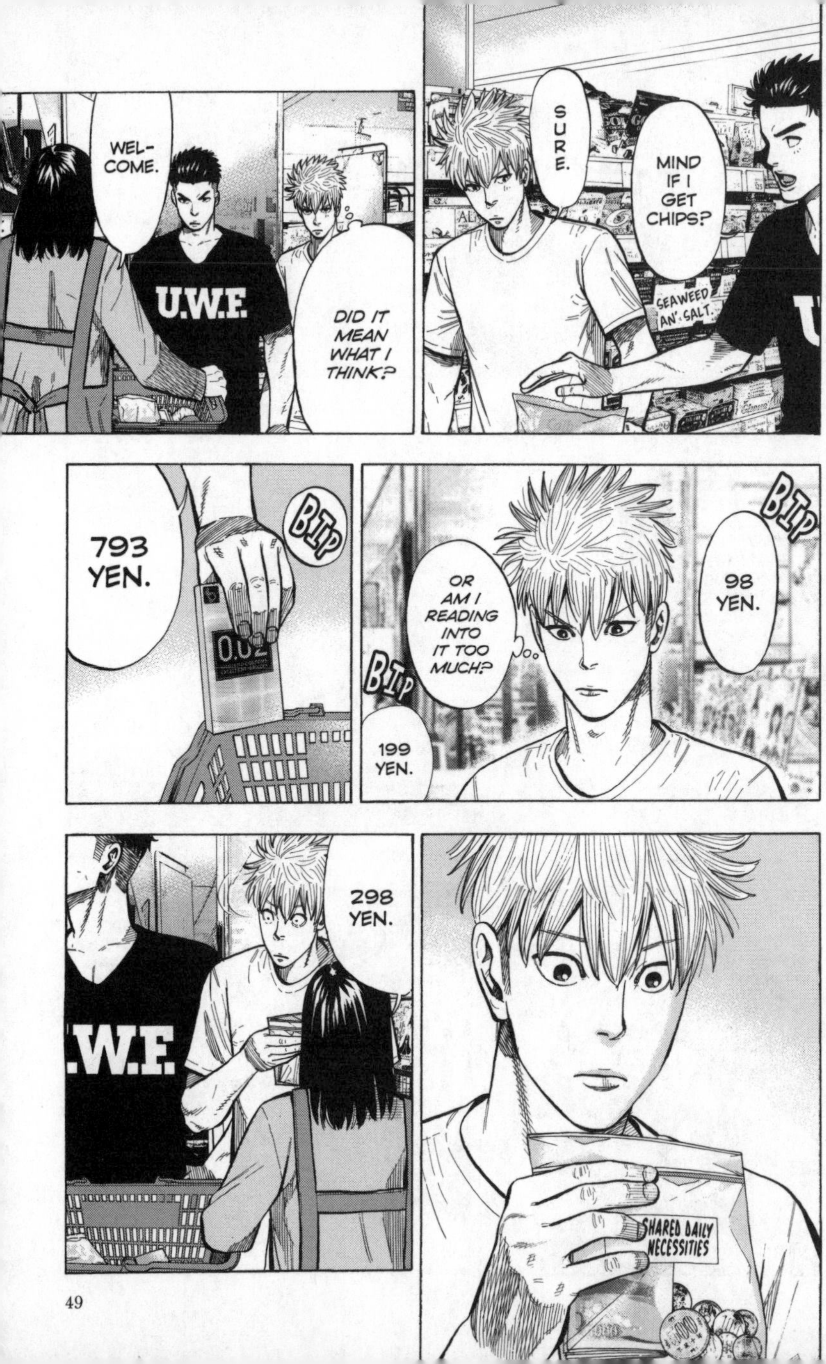
MIND IF I GET CHIPS?
SURE.
SEAWEED AN' SALT.
WEL-COME.
DID IT MEAN WHAT I THINK?
BIP
98 YEN.
OR AM I READING INTO IT TOO MUCH?
BIP
199 YEN.
BIP
793 YEN.
0.02
SHARED DAILY NECESSITIES
298 YEN.

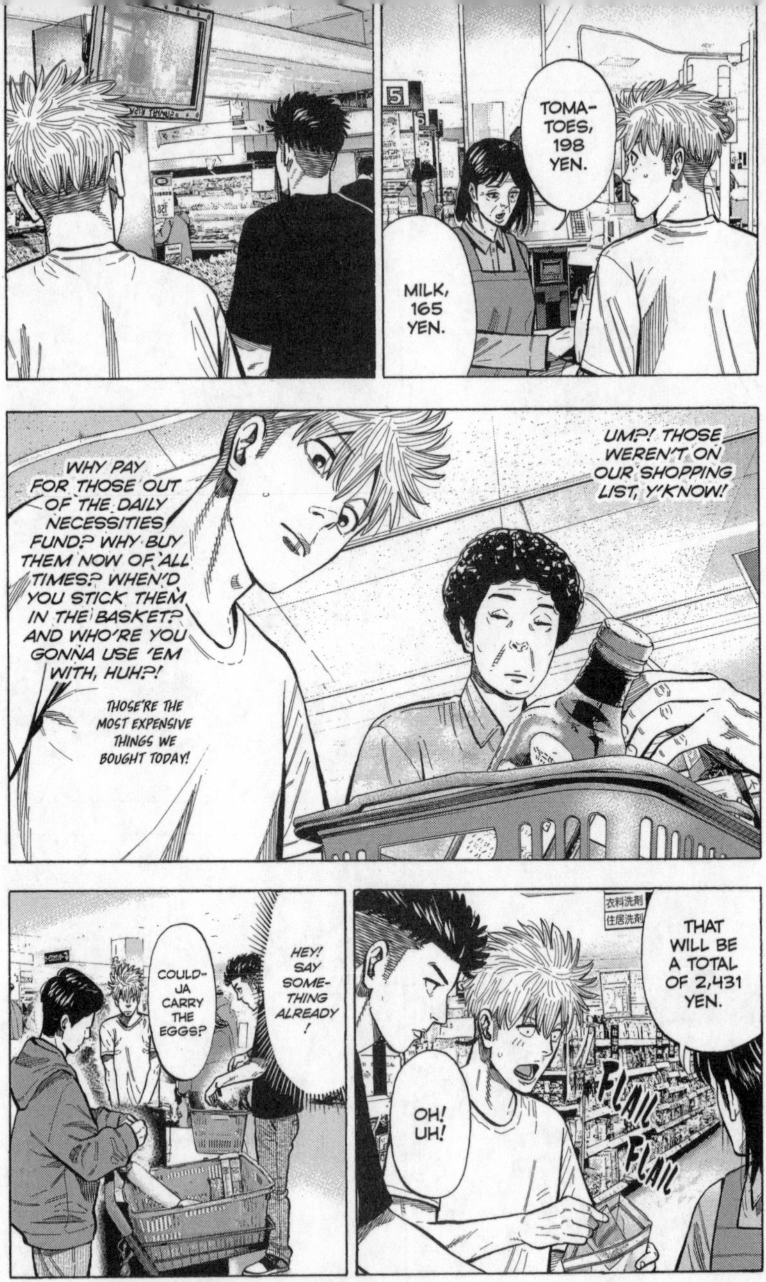
TOMA-TOES, 198 YEN.
MILK, 165 YEN.
UM?! THOSE WEREN'T ON OUR SHOPPING LIST, Y'KNOW!
WHY PAY FOR THOSE OUT OF THE DAILY NECESSITIES FUND? WHY BUY THEM NOW OF ALL TIMES? WHEN'D YOU STICK THEM IN THE BASKET? AND WHO'RE YOU GONNA USE 'EM WITH, HUH?!
THOSE'RE THE MOST EXPENSIVE THINGS WE BOUGHT TODAY!
衣料洗剤
住居洗剤
THAT WILL BE A TOTAL OF 2,431 YEN.
FLAIL FLAIL
OH! UH!
HEY! SAY SOME-THING ALREADY!
COULD-JA CARRY THE EGGS?

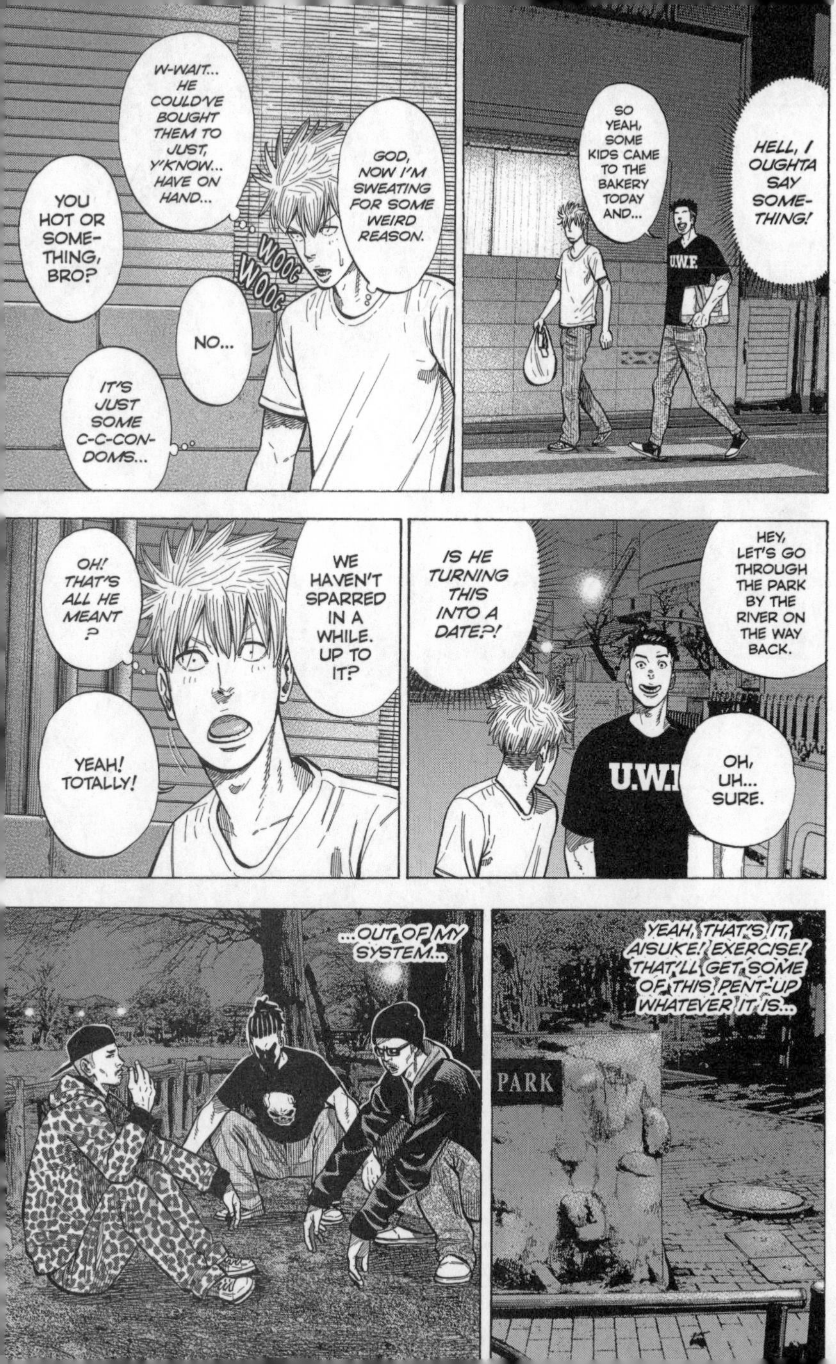
HELL, I OUGHTA SAY SOME-THING!
SO YEAH, SOME KIDS CAME TO THE BAKERY TODAY AND...
U.W.F.
GOD, NOW I'M SWEATING FOR SOME WEIRD REASON.
W-WAIT... HE COULD'VE BOUGHT THEM TO JUST, Y'KNOW... HAVE ON HAND...
YOU HOT OR SOME-THING, BRO?
WOOG WOOG
NO...
IT'S JUST SOME C-C-CON-DOMS...
HEY, LET'S GO THROUGH THE PARK BY THE RIVER ON THE WAY BACK.
IS HE TURNING THIS INTO A DATE?!
OH, UH... SURE.
WE HAVEN'T SPARRED IN A WHILE. UP TO IT?
OH! THAT'S ALL HE MEANT?
YEAH! TOTALLY!
YEAH, THAT'S IT, AISUKE! EXERCISE! THAT'LL GET SOME OF THIS PENT-UP WHATEVER IT IS...
PARK
...OUT OF MY SYSTEM...

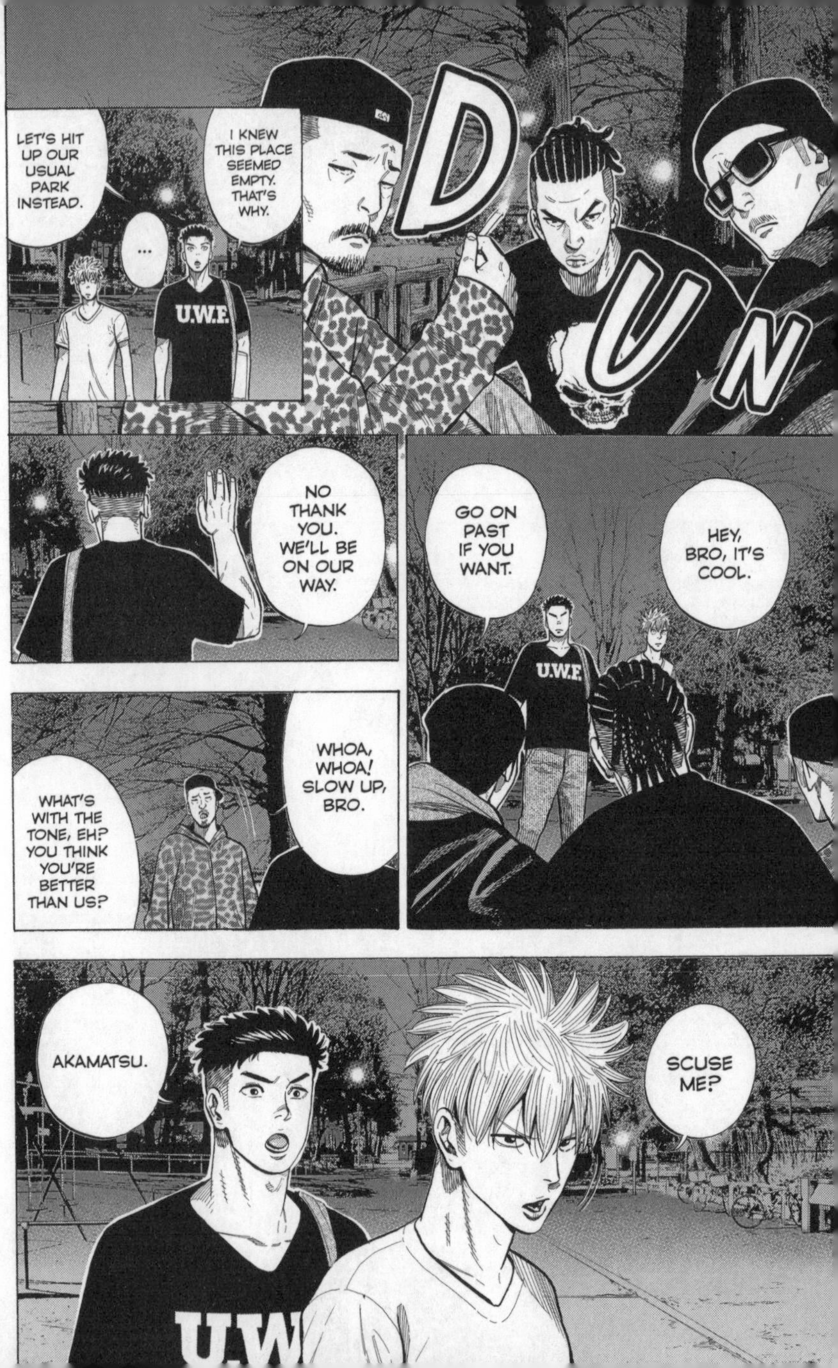
DUN
I KNEW THIS PLACE SEEMED EMPTY. THAT'S WHY.
...
LET'S HIT UP OUR USUAL PARK INSTEAD.
U.W.F.
HEY, BRO, IT'S COOL.
GO ON PAST IF YOU WANT.
U.W.F.
NO THANK YOU. WE'LL BE ON OUR WAY.
WHOA, WHOA! SLOW UP, BRO.
WHAT'S WITH THE TONE, EH? YOU THINK YOU'RE BETTER THAN US?
SCUSE ME?
AKAMATSU.
U.W

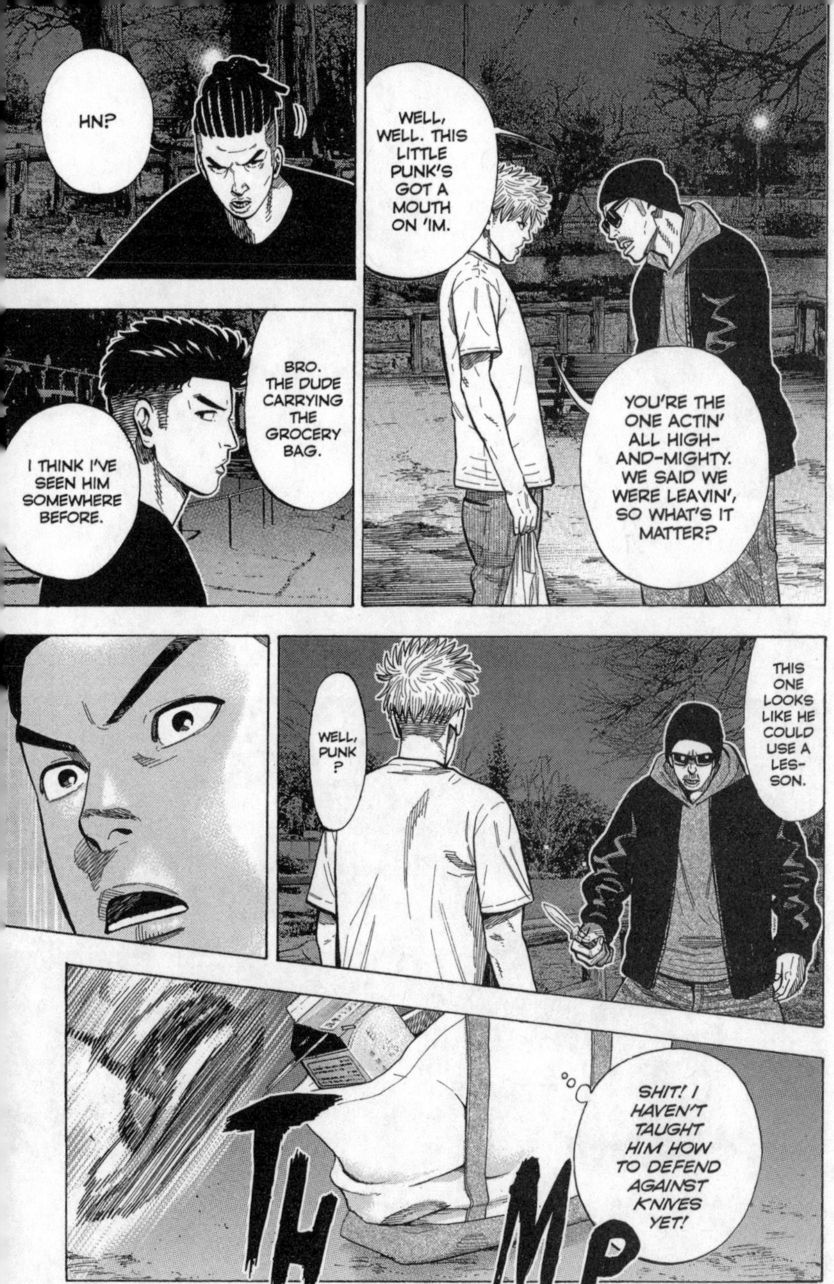
WELL, WELL. THIS LITTLE PUNK'S GOT A MOUTH ON 'IM.
YOU'RE THE ONE ACTIN' ALL HIGH-AND-MIGHTY. WE SAID WE WERE LEAVIN', SO WHAT'S IT MATTER?
HN?
BRO. THE DUDE CARRYING THE GROCERY BAG.
I THINK I'VE SEEN HIM SOMEWHERE BEFORE.
THIS ONE LOOKS LIKE HE COULD USE A LES-SON.
WELL, PUNK?
SHIT! I HAVEN'T TAUGHT HIM HOW TO DEFEND AGAINST KNIVES YET!
THMP

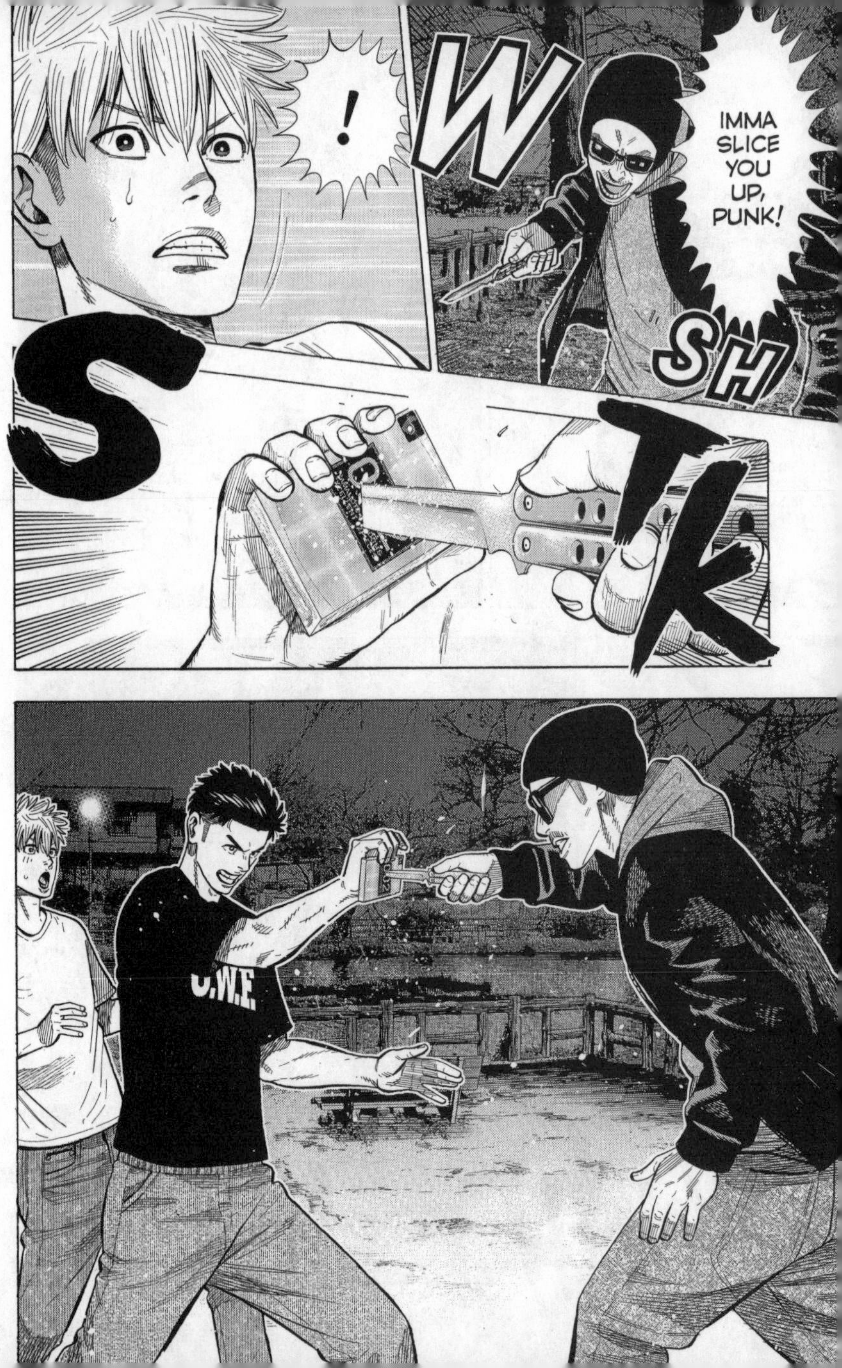
WSH
IMMA SLICE YOU UP, PUNK!
!
STK

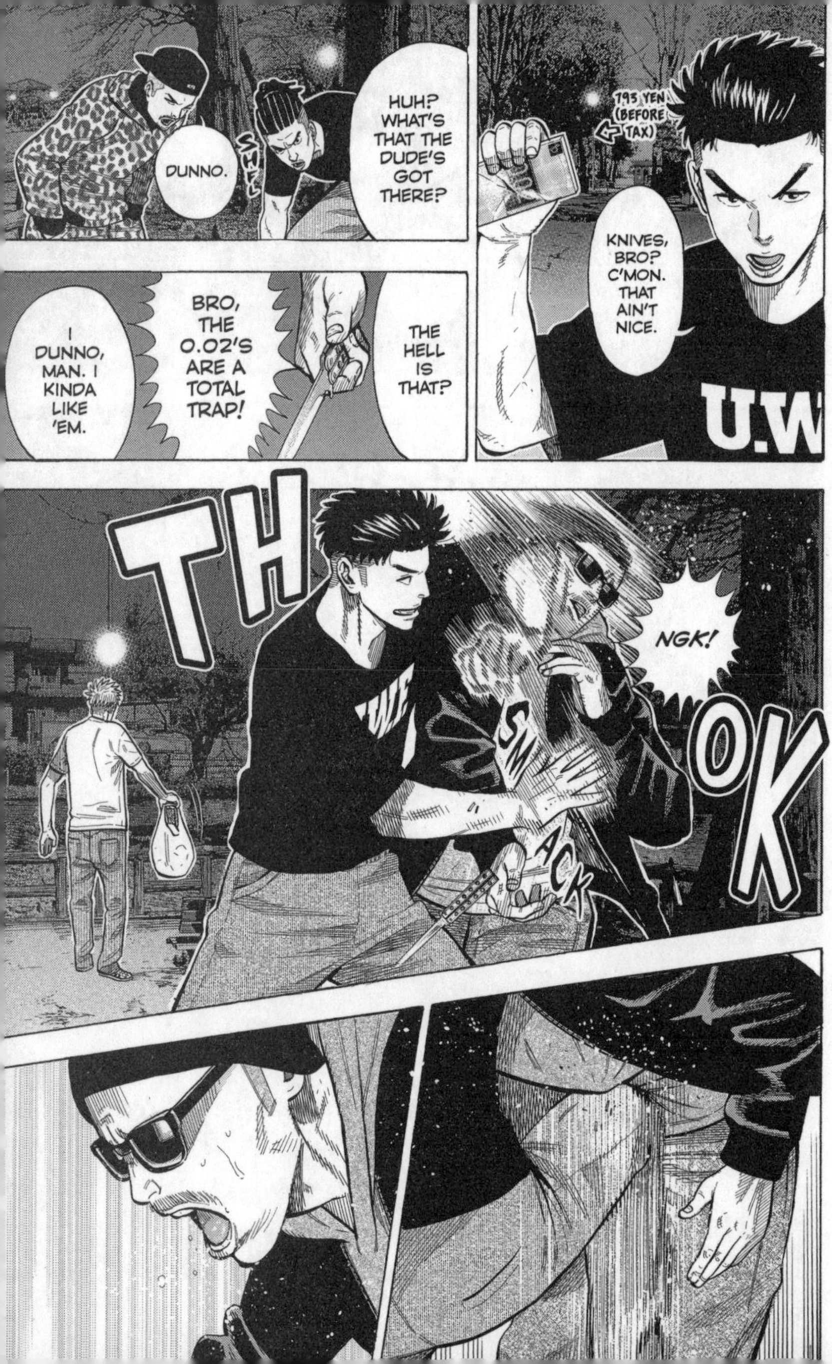
793 YEN (BEFORE TAX)
KNIVES, BRO? C'MON. THAT AIN'T NICE.
U.W
HUH? WHAT'S THAT THE DUDE'S GOT THERE?
SHFL
DUNNO.
THE HELL IS THAT?
BRO, THE 0.02'S ARE A TOTAL TRAP!
I DUNNO, MAN. I KINDA LIKE 'EM.
THOK
NGK!
SMACK

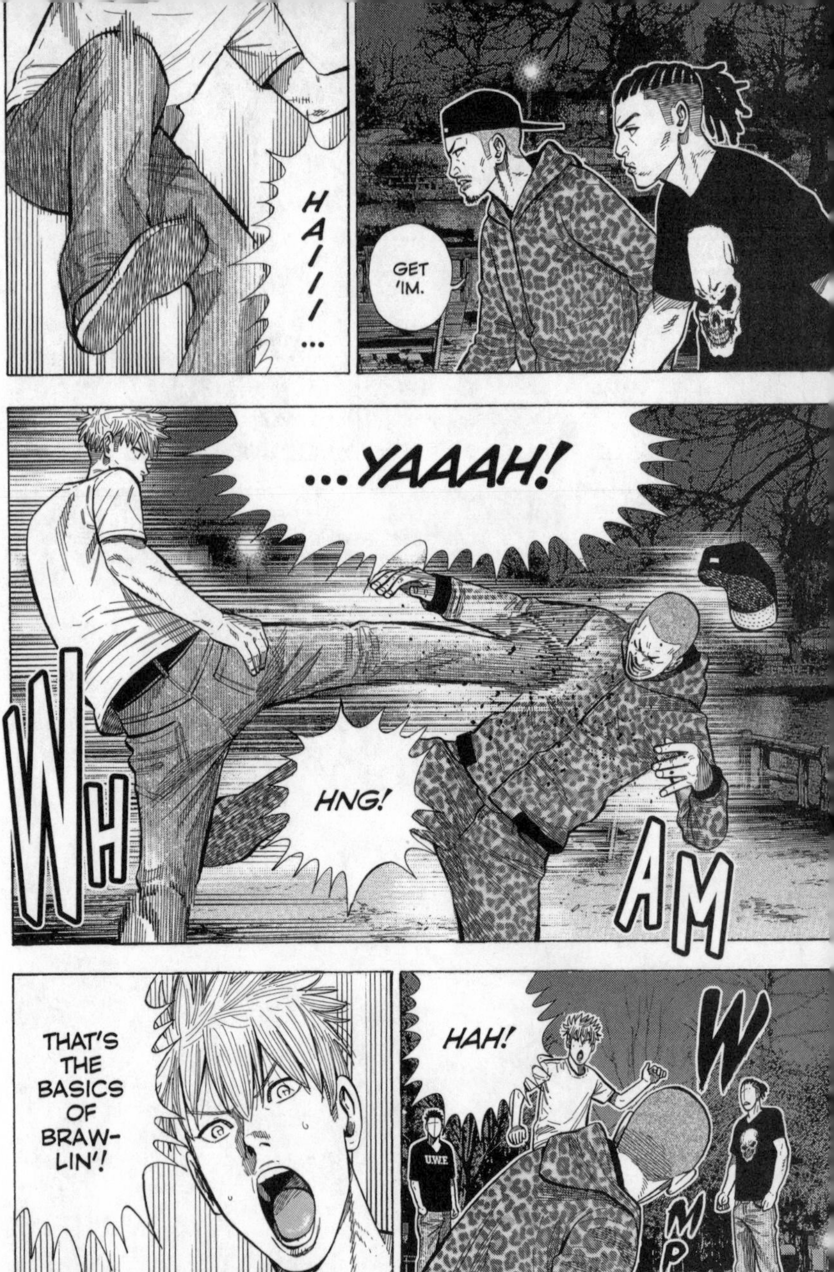
GET 'IM.
HAIII...
...YAAAH!
WHAM
HNG!
HAH!
WMP
THAT'S THE BASICS OF BRAWLIN'!

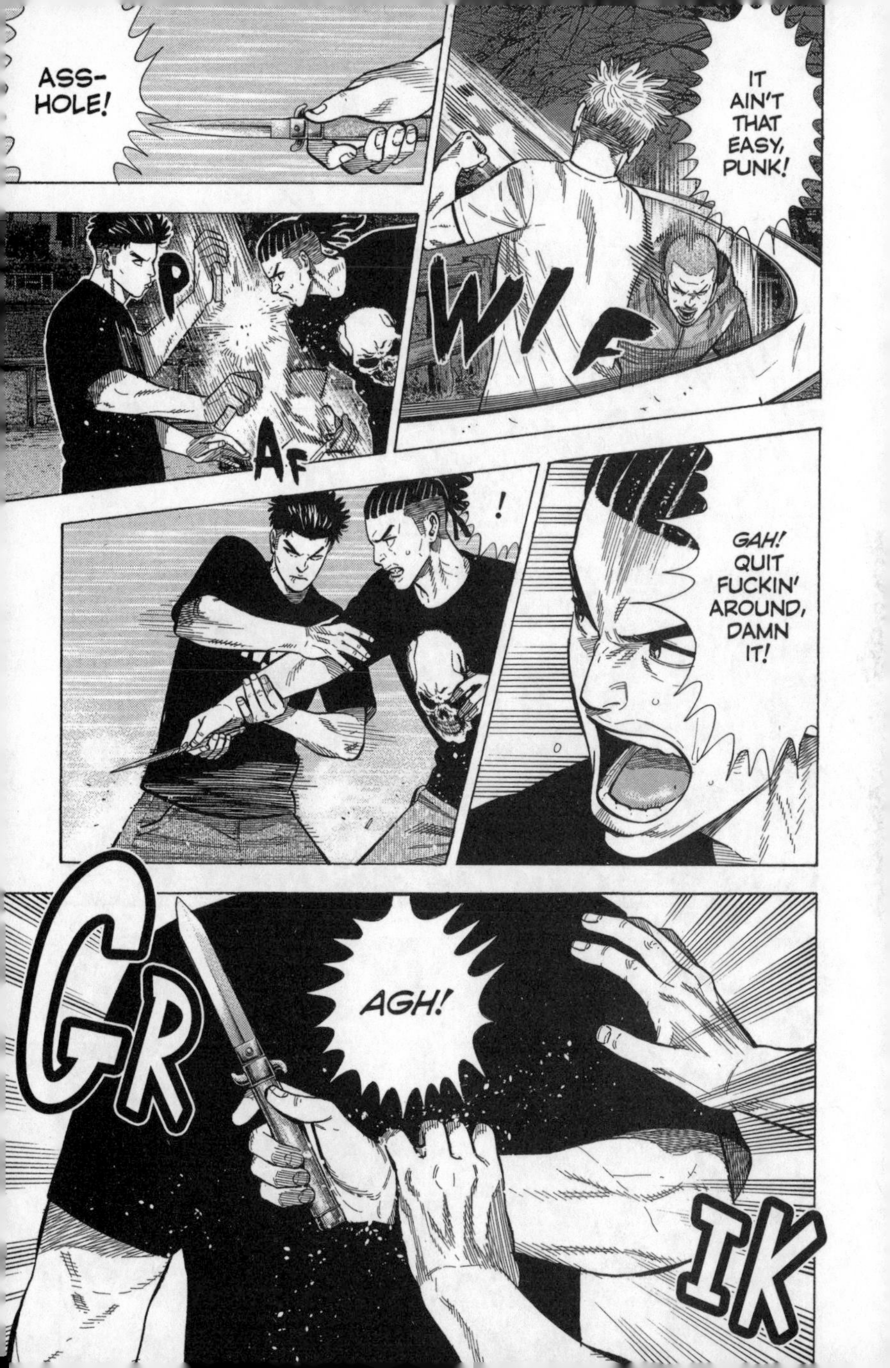
IT AIN'T THAT EASY, PUNK!
WI
F
ASS-HOLE!
P
AF
GAH! QUIT FUCKIN' AROUND, DAMN IT!
!
AGH!
GR
IK

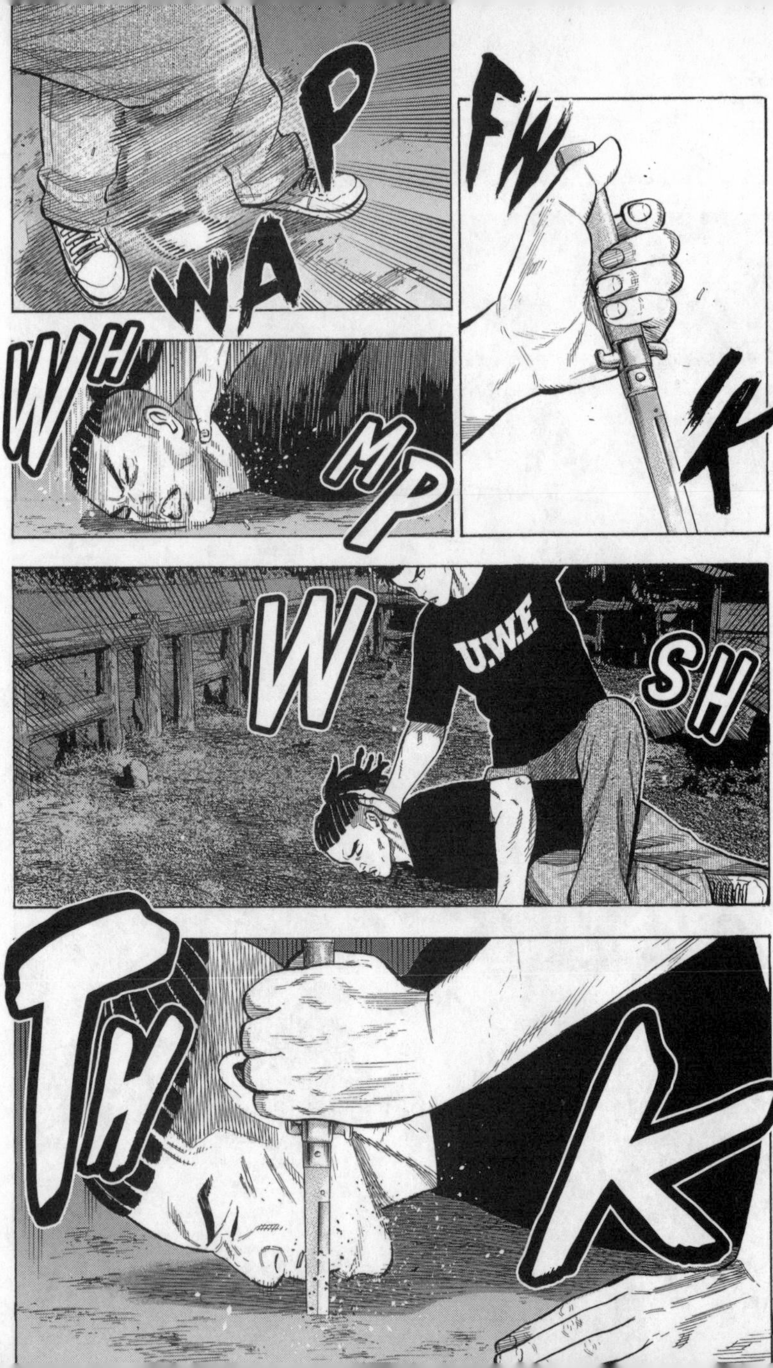
FWK
WAP
WHMP
WSH
THK

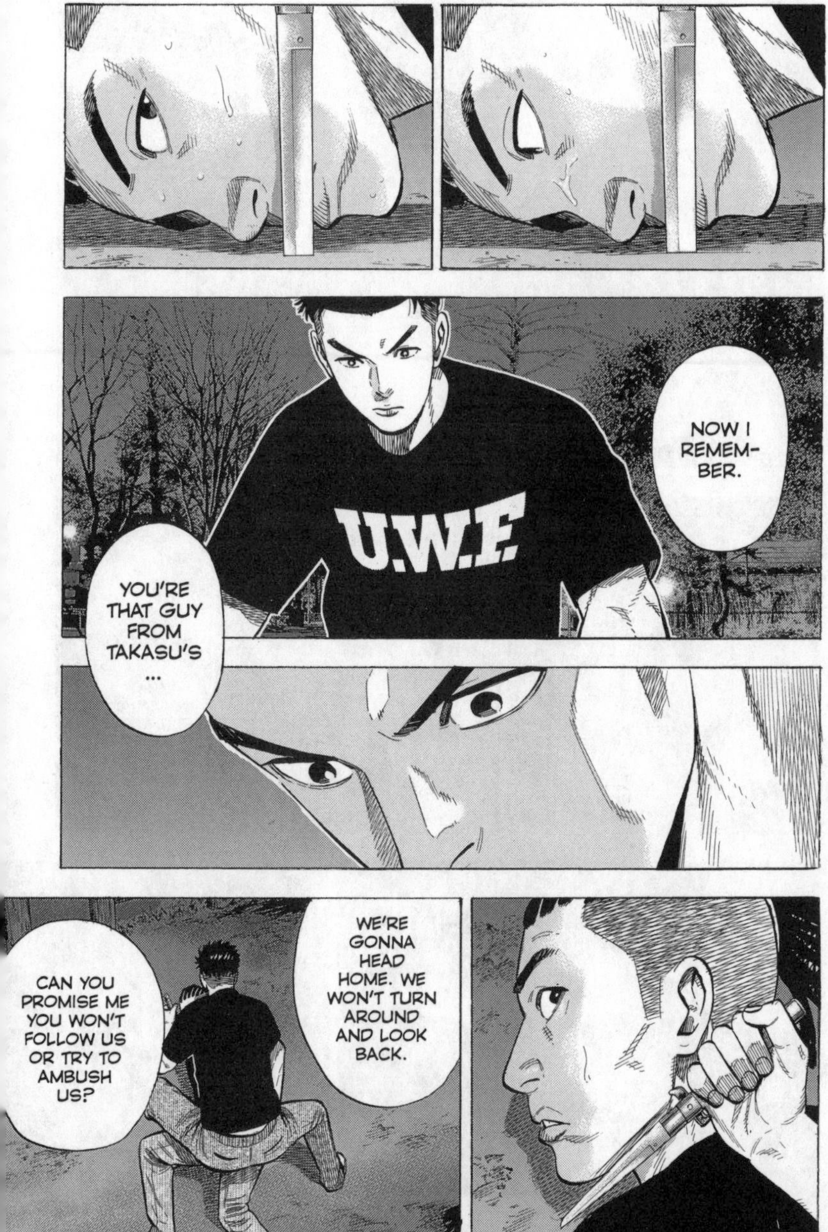
NOW I REMEMBER.
YOU'RE THAT GUY FROM TAKASU'S ...
WE'RE GONNA HEAD HOME. WE WON'T TURN AROUND AND LOOK BACK.
CAN YOU PROMISE ME YOU WON'T FOLLOW US OR TRY TO AMBUSH US?

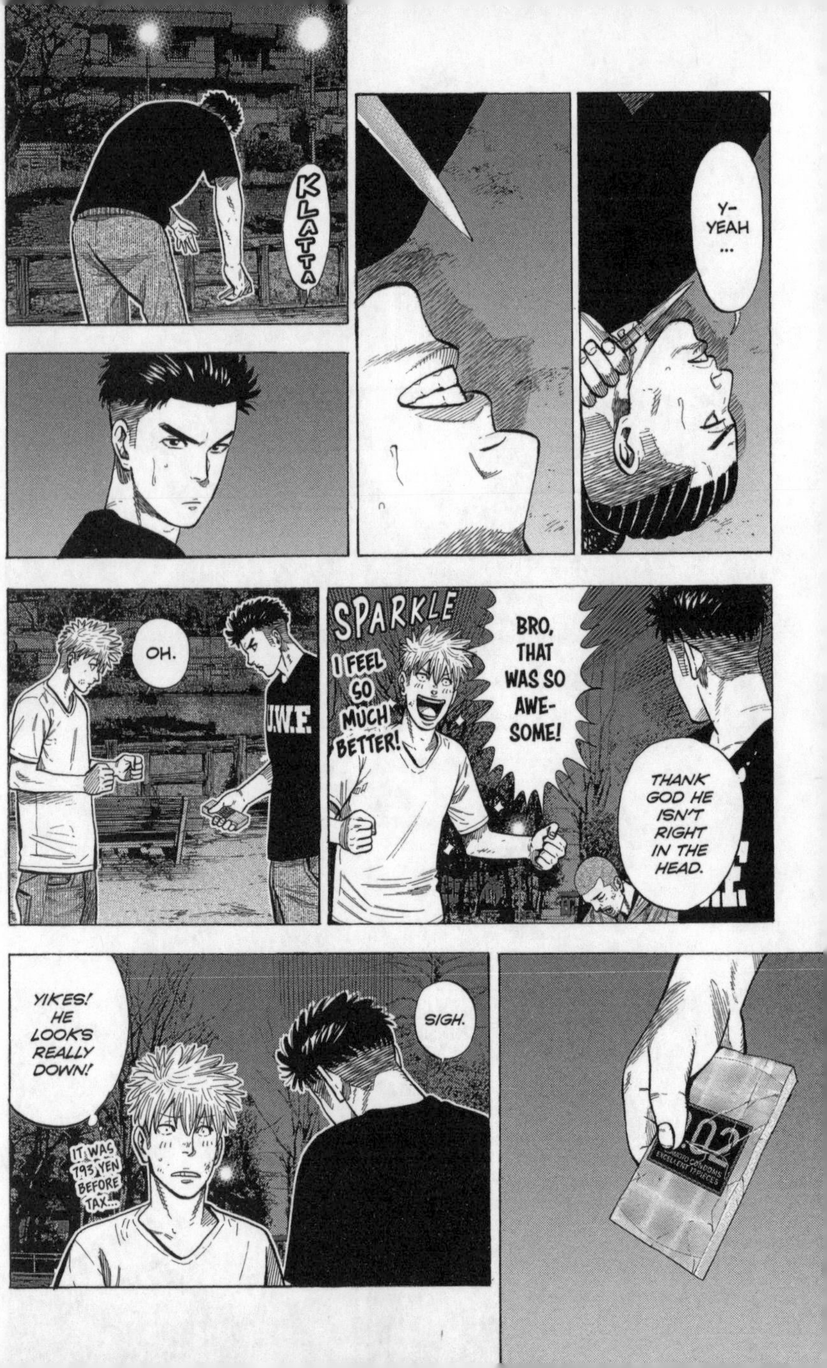
Y-YEAH...
KLATTA
BRO, THAT WAS SO AWESOME!
SPARKLE
I FEEL SO MUCH BETTER!
THANK GOD HE ISN'T RIGHT IN THE HEAD.
OH.
SIGH.
YIKES! HE LOOKS REALLY DOWN!
IT WAS 793 YEN BEFORE TAX...

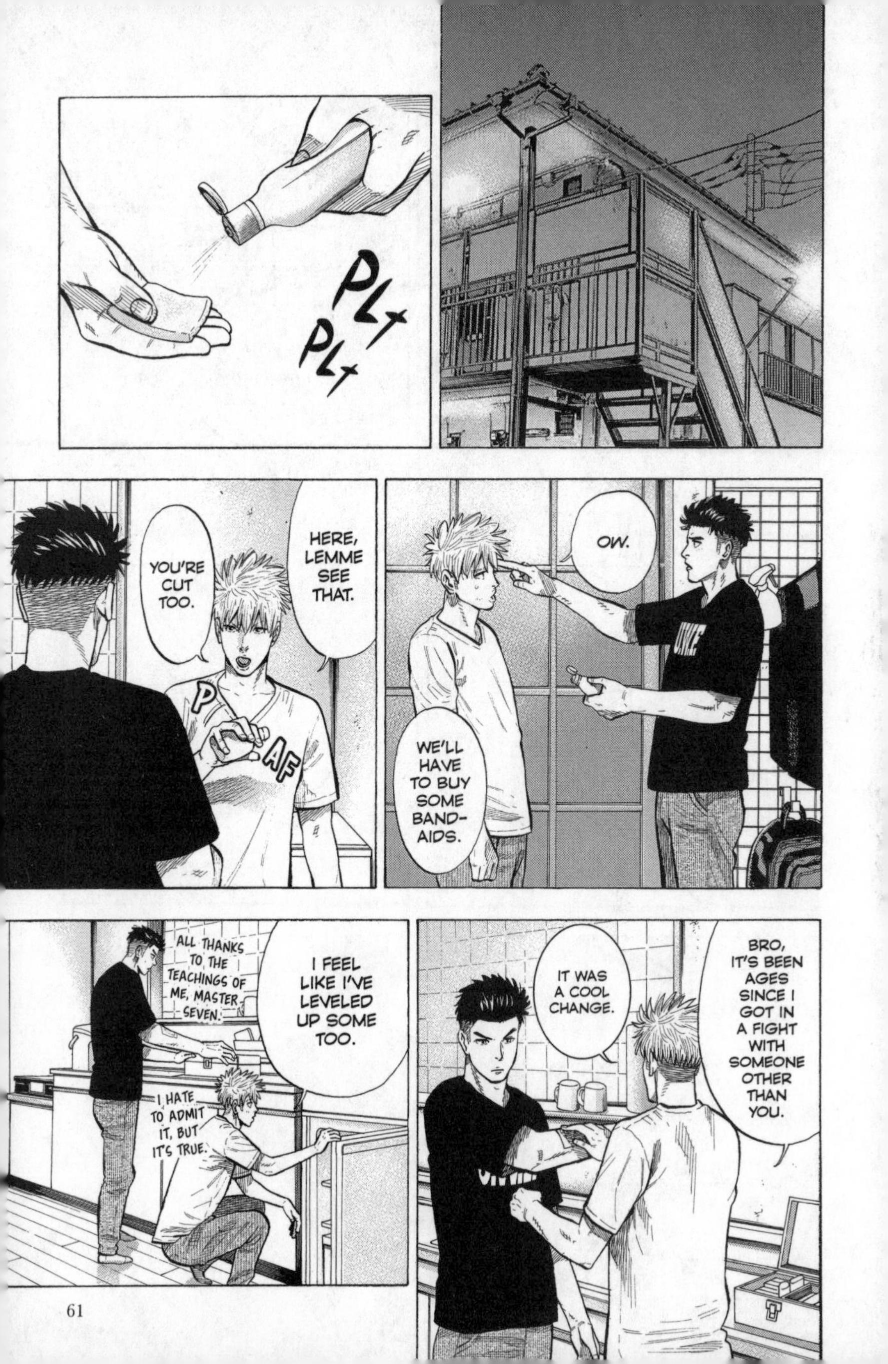
PLT PLT
OW.
WE'LL HAVE TO BUY SOME BAND-AIDS.
HERE, LEMME SEE THAT.
YOU'RE CUT TOO.
BRO, IT'S BEEN AGES SINCE I GOT IN A FIGHT WITH SOMEONE OTHER THAN YOU.
IT WAS A COOL CHANGE.
I FEEL LIKE I'VE LEVELED UP SOME TOO.
ALL THANKS TO THE TEACHINGS OF ME, MASTER SEVEN.
I HATE TO ADMIT IT, BUT IT'S TRUE.

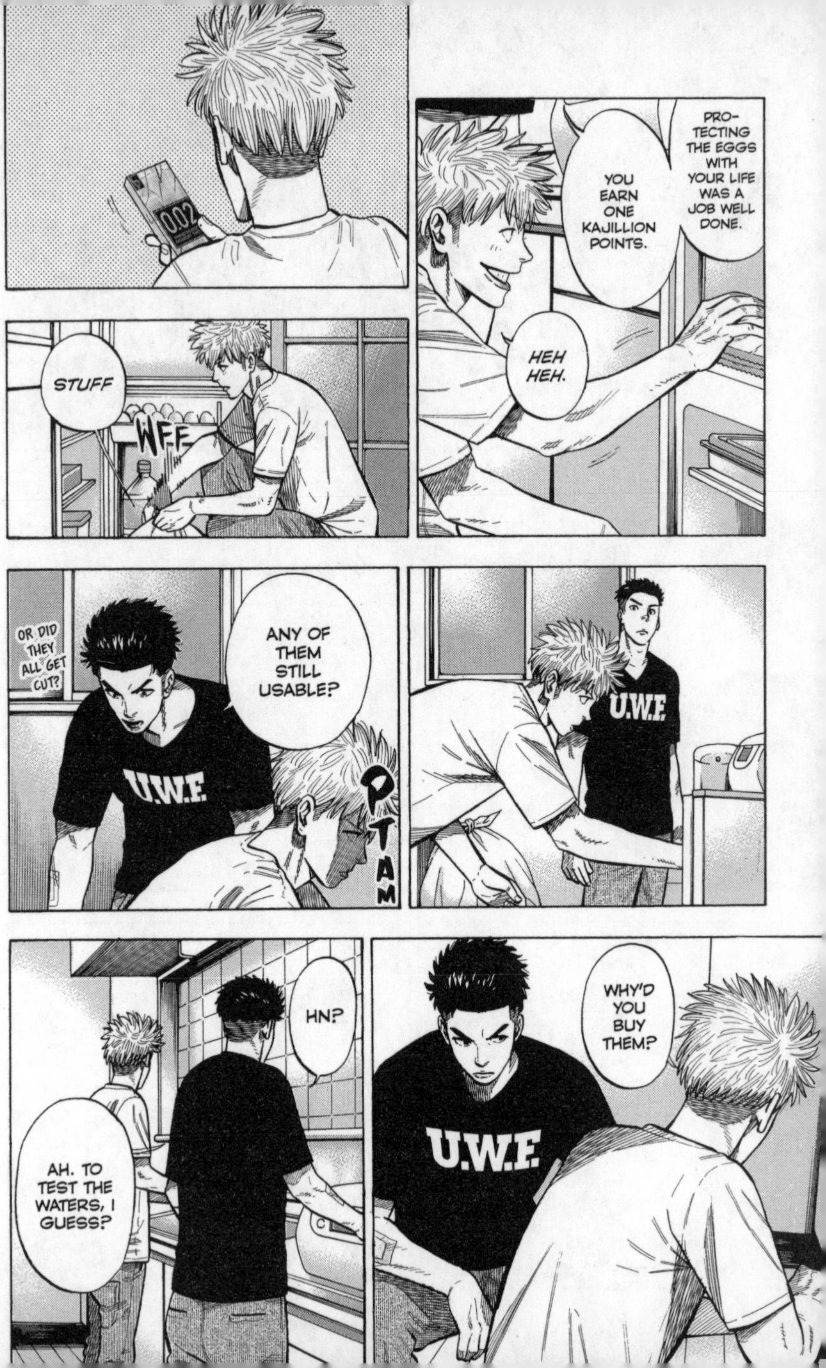
PRO-TECTING THE EGGS WITH YOUR LIFE WAS A JOB WELL DONE.
YOU EARN ONE KAJILLION POINTS.
HEH HEH.
STUFF
WFF
ANY OF THEM STILL USABLE?
OR DID THEY ALL GET CUT?
PTAM
WHY'D YOU BUY THEM?
HN?
AH. TO TEST THE WATERS, I GUESS?

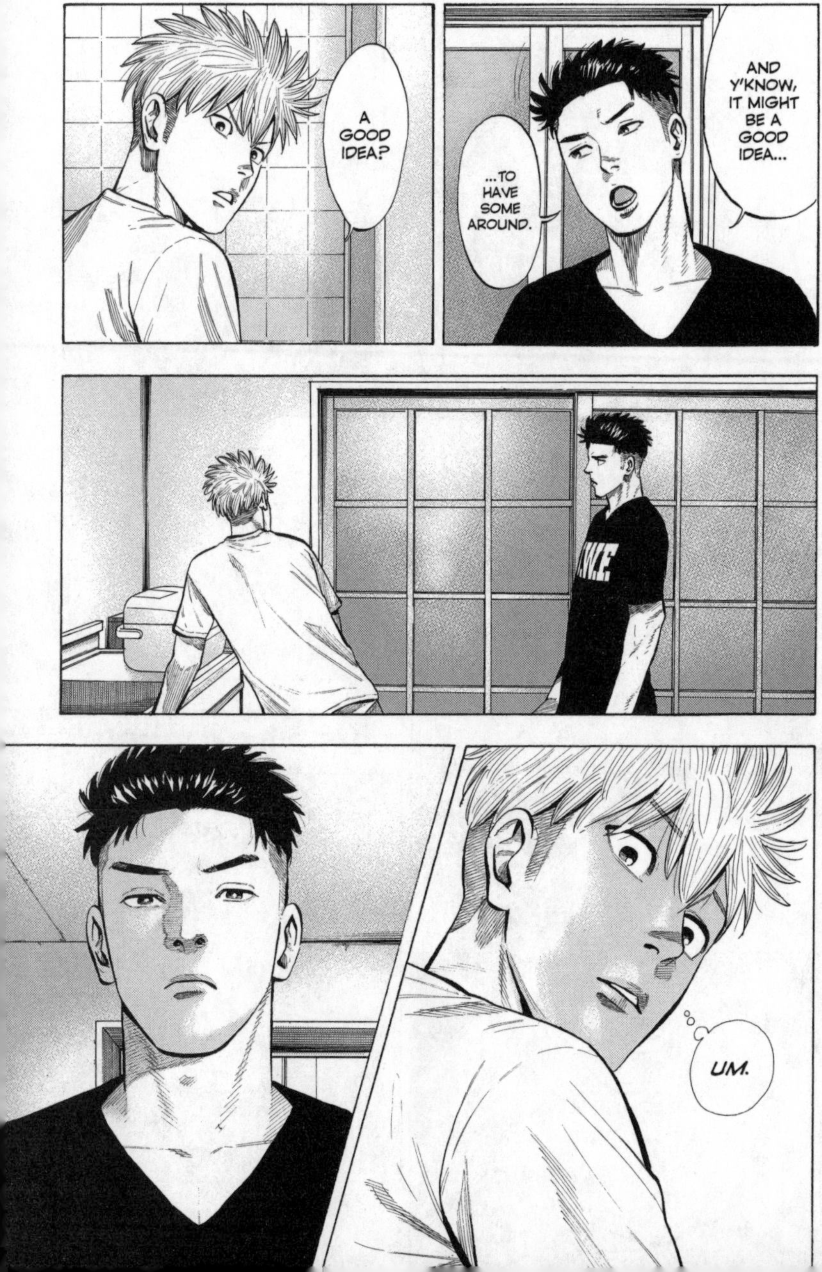
AND Y'KNOW, IT MIGHT BE A GOOD IDEA...
...TO HAVE SOME AROUND.
A GOOD IDEA?
UM.

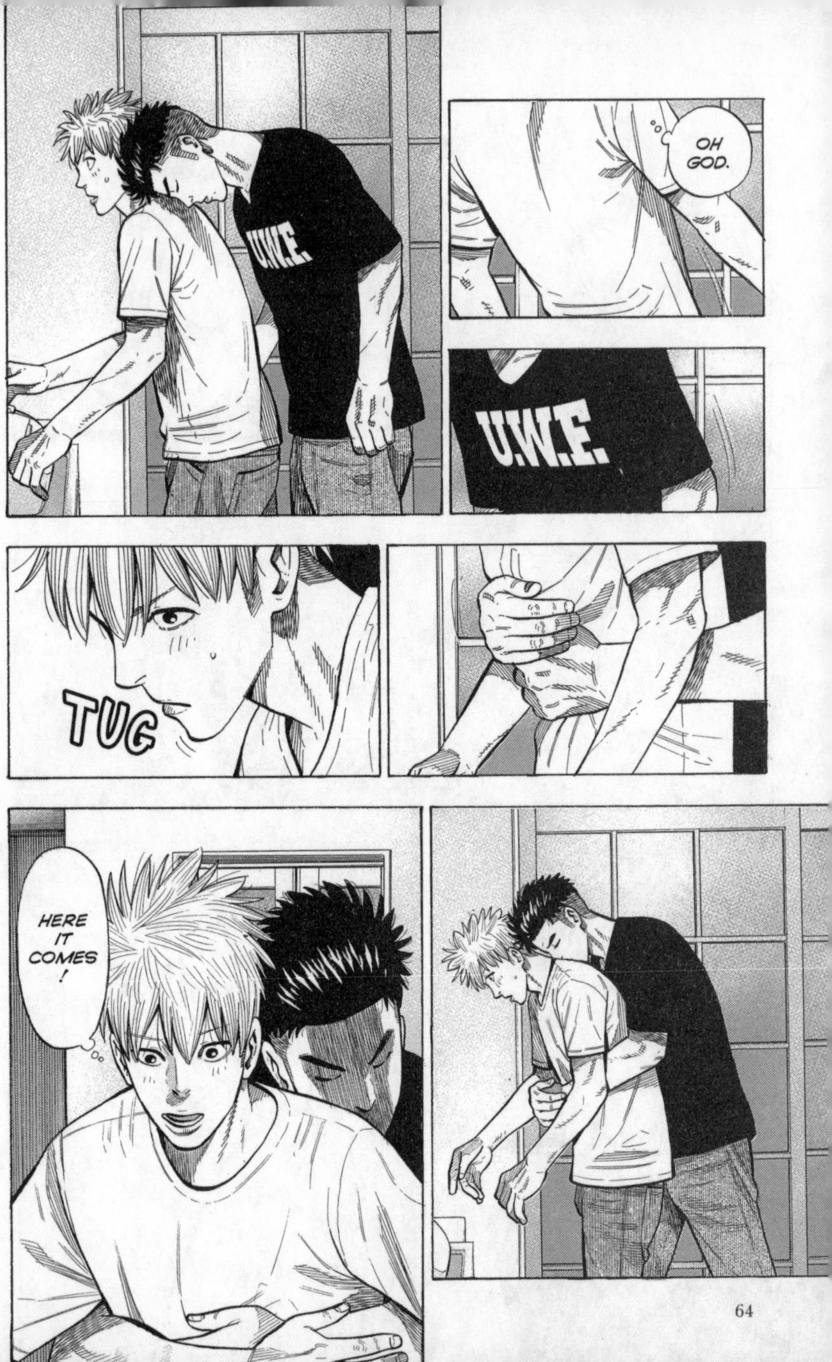
OH GOD.
TUG
HERE IT COMES!

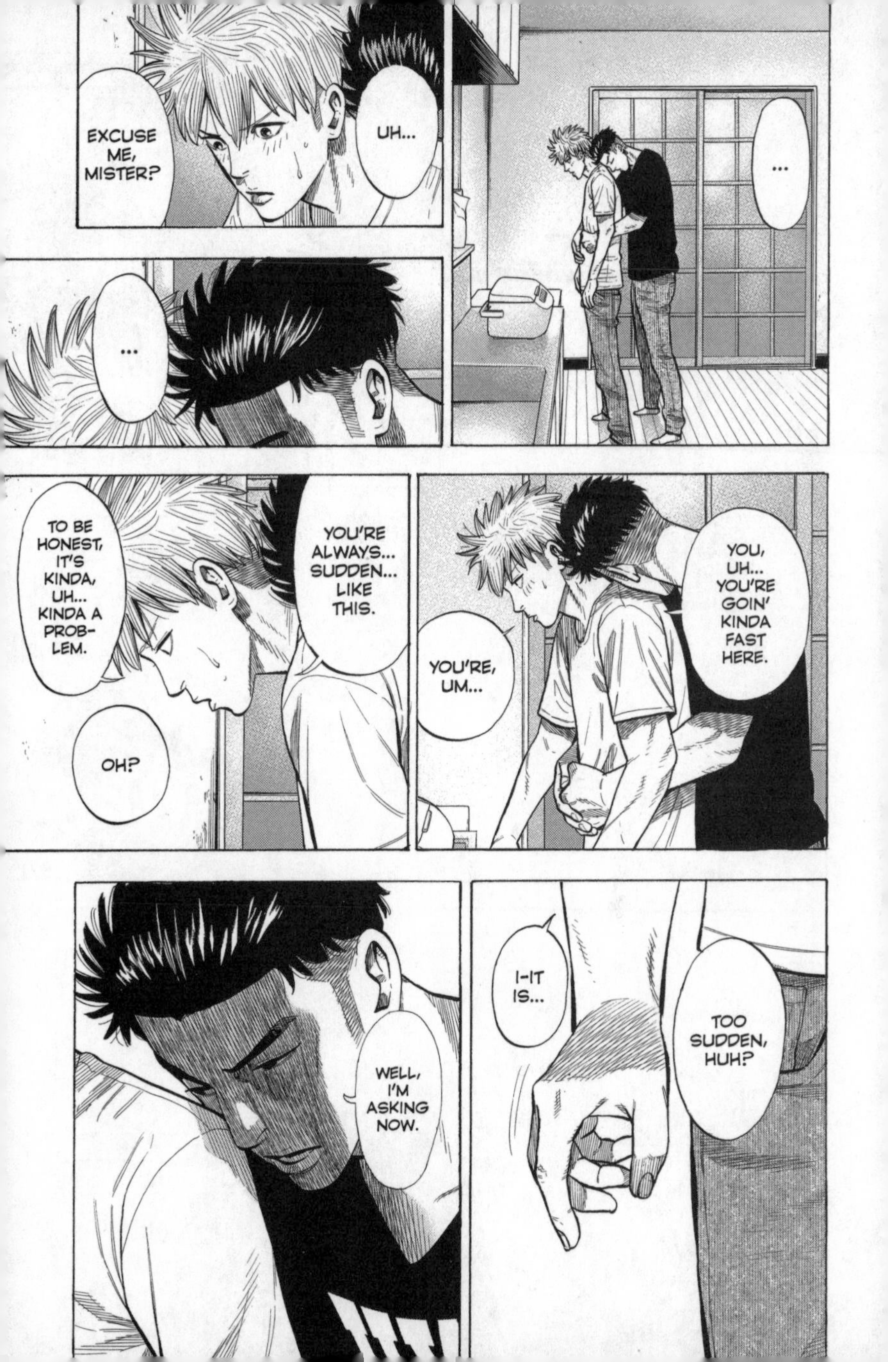
...
UH...
EXCUSE ME, MISTER?
...
YOU, UH... YOU'RE GOIN' KINDA FAST HERE.
YOU'RE, UM...
YOU'RE ALWAYS... SUDDEN... LIKE THIS.
TO BE HONEST, IT'S KINDA, UH... KINDA A PROB-LEM.
OH?
TOO SUDDEN, HUH?
I-IT IS...
WELL, I'M ASKING NOW.

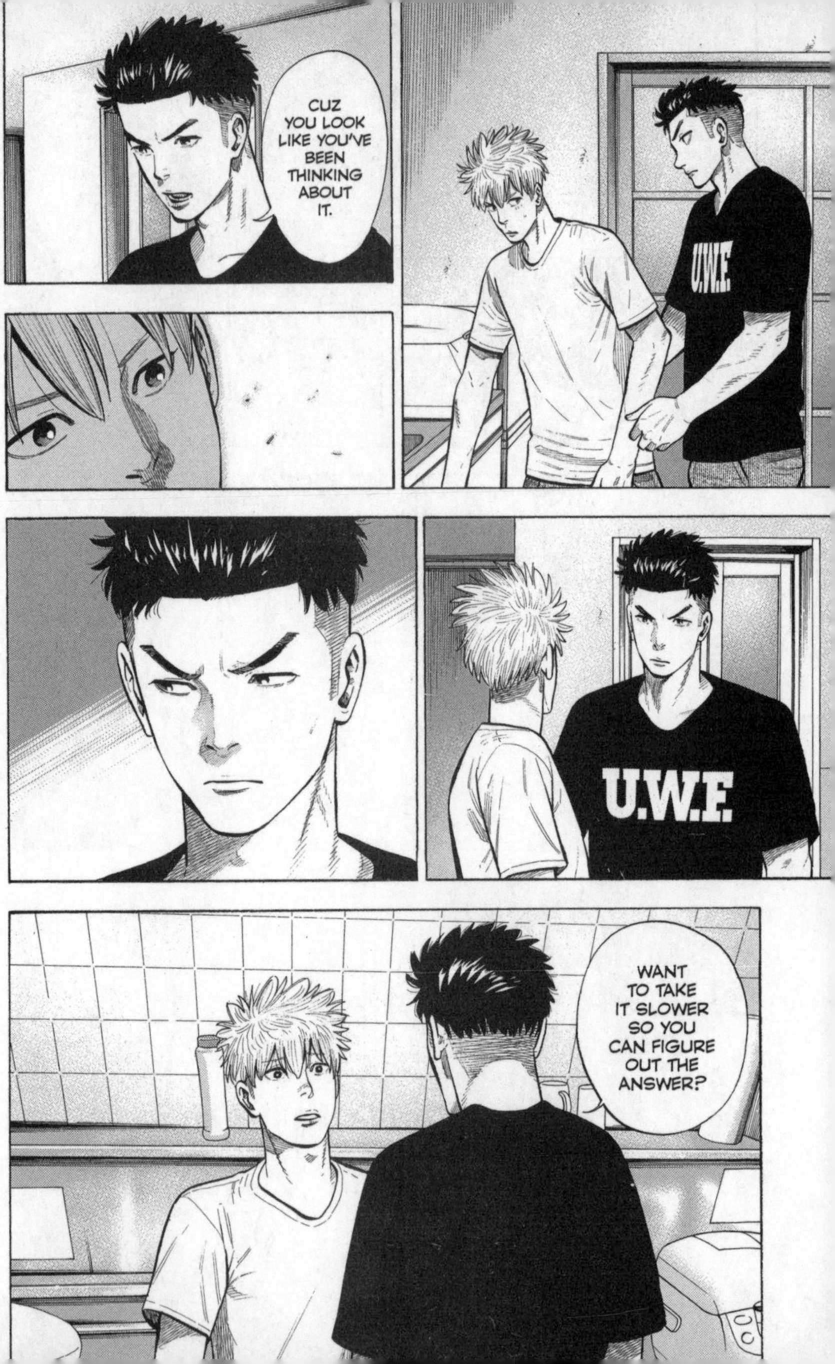
U.W.F.
CUZ YOU LOOK LIKE YOU'VE BEEN THINKING ABOUT IT.
U.W.F.
WANT TO TAKE IT SLOWER SO YOU CAN FIGURE OUT THE ANSWER?

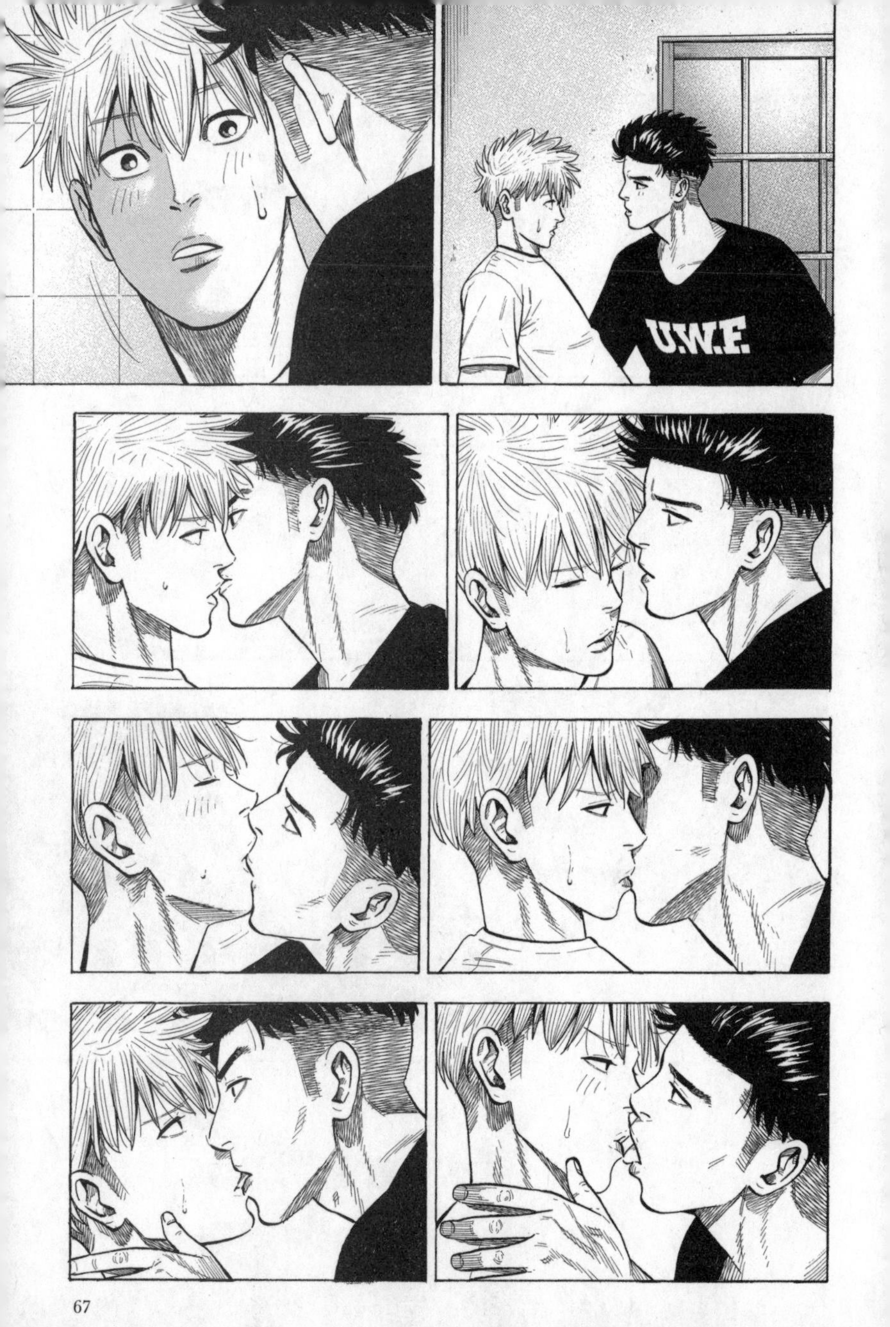
U.W.F.

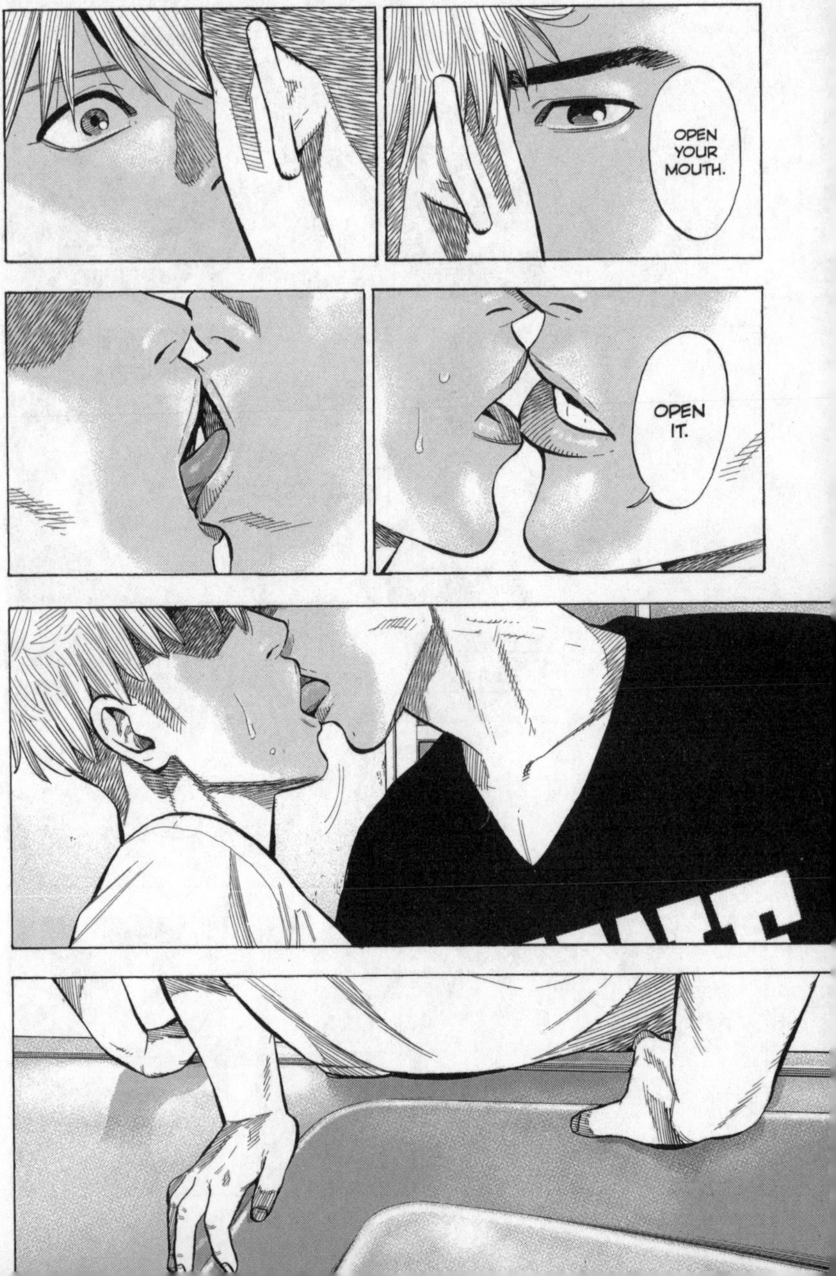
OPEN YOUR MOUTH.
OPEN IT.

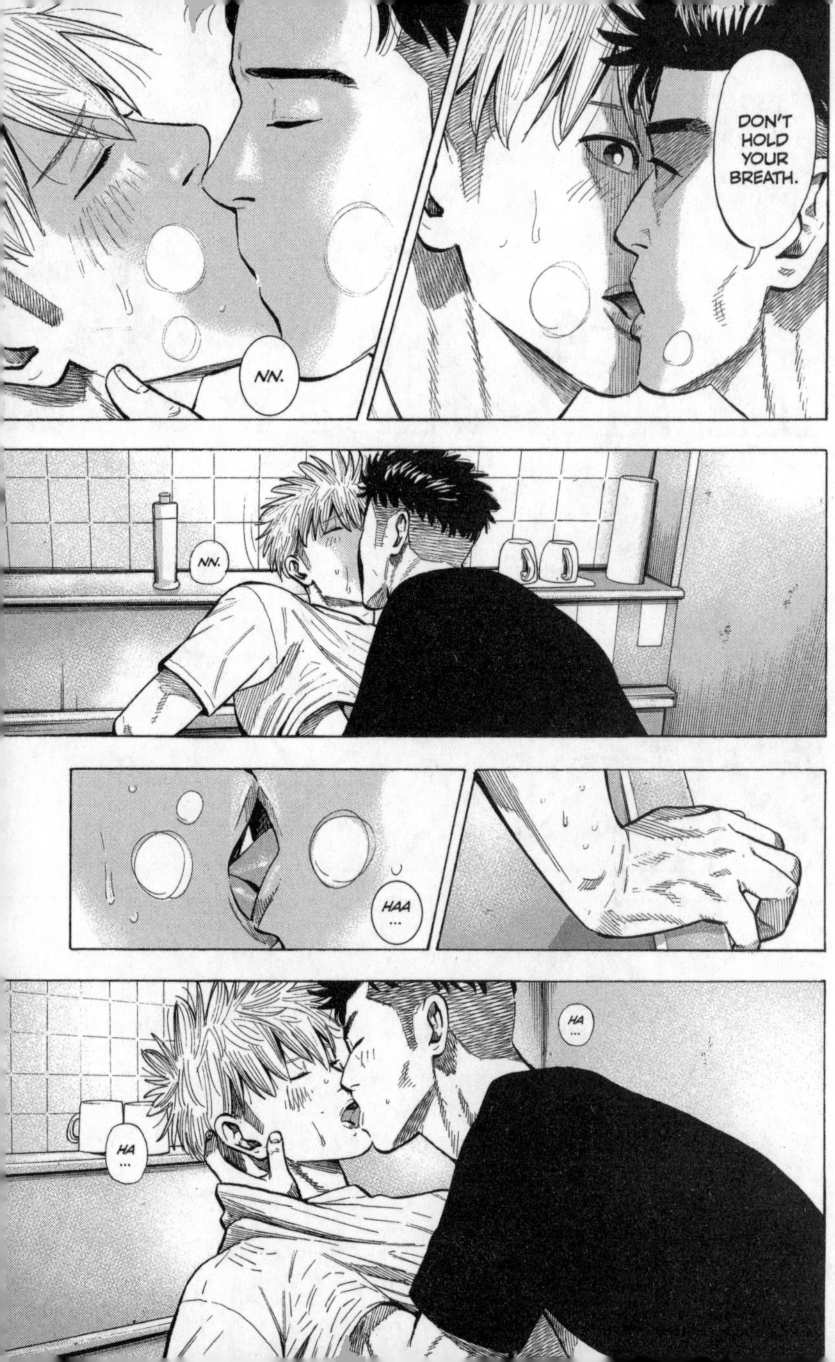
DON'T HOLD YOUR BREATH.
NN.
NN.
HAA ...
HA ...
HA ...

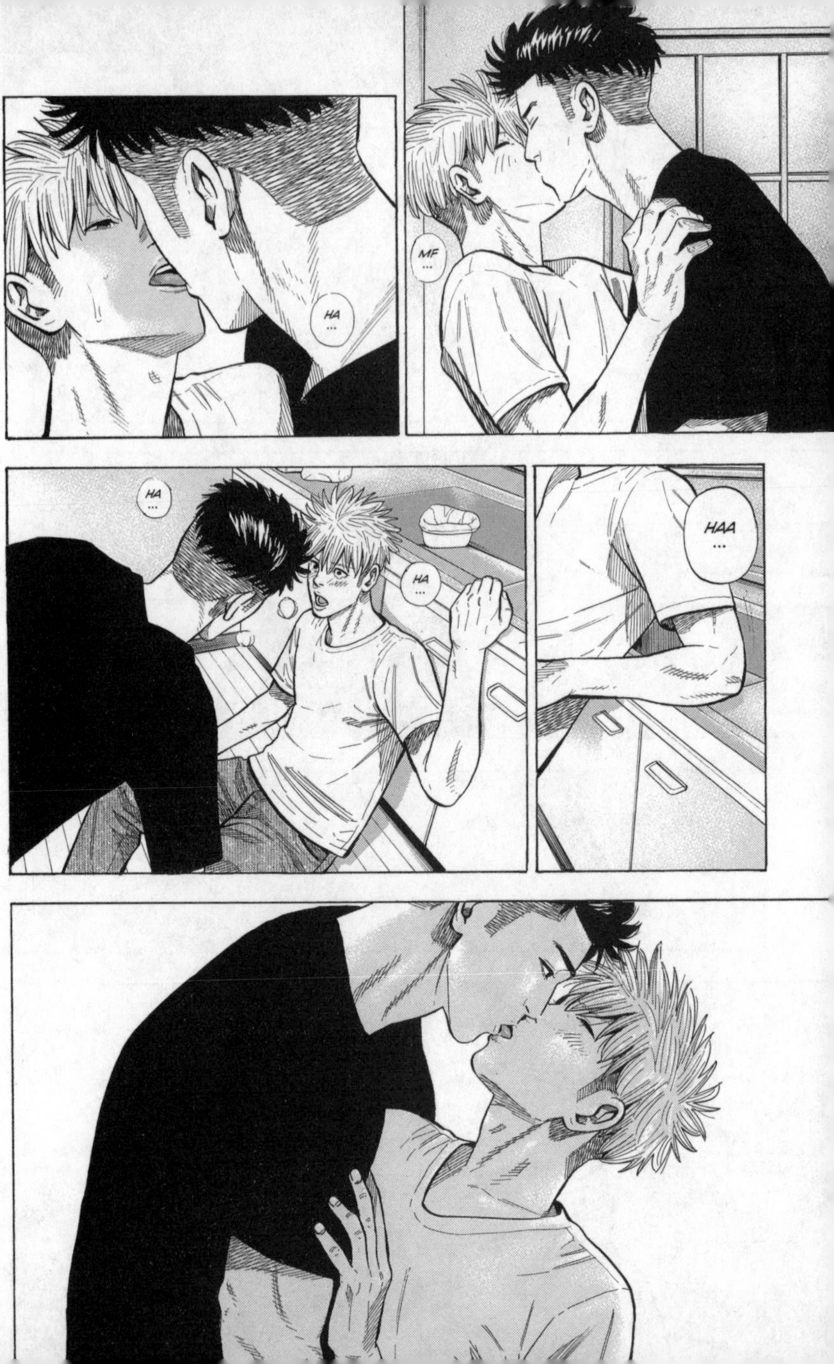
MF ...
HA ...
HAA ...
HA ...
HA ...

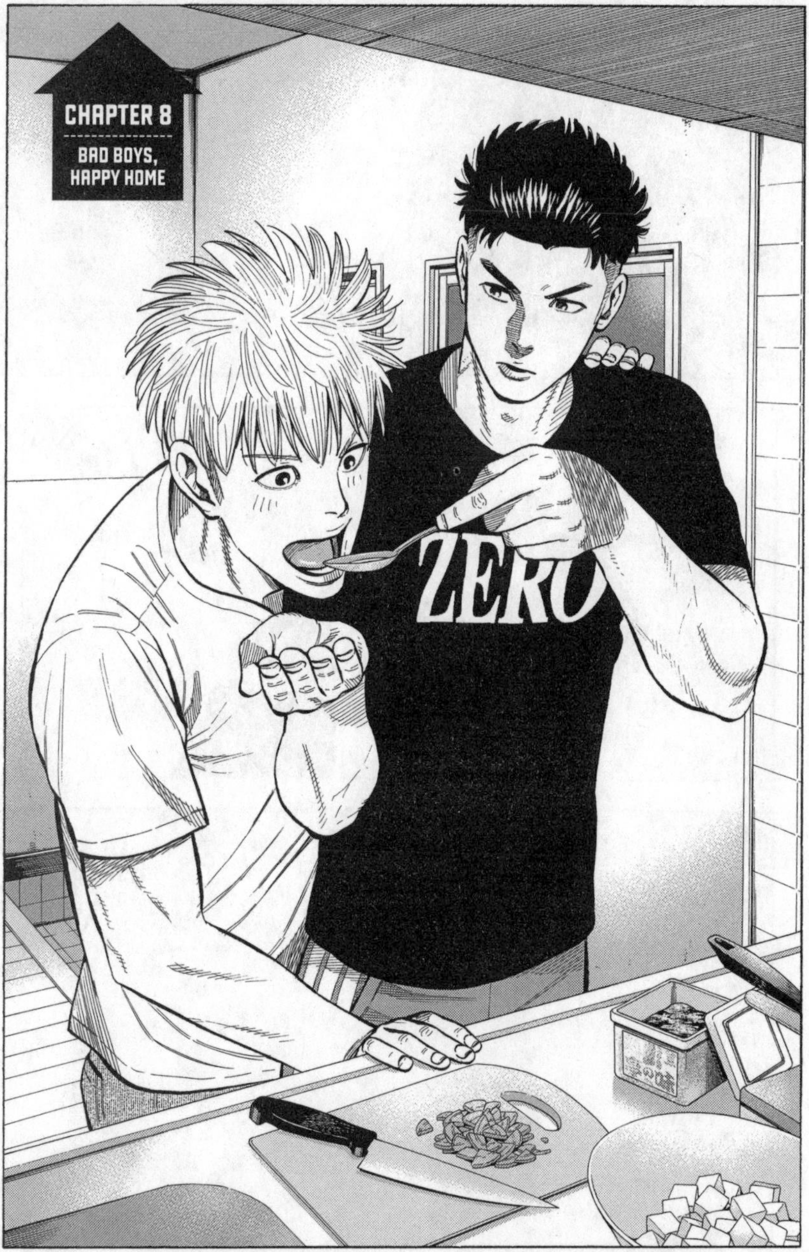
CHAPTER 8
BAD BOYS, HAPPY HOME
ZERO

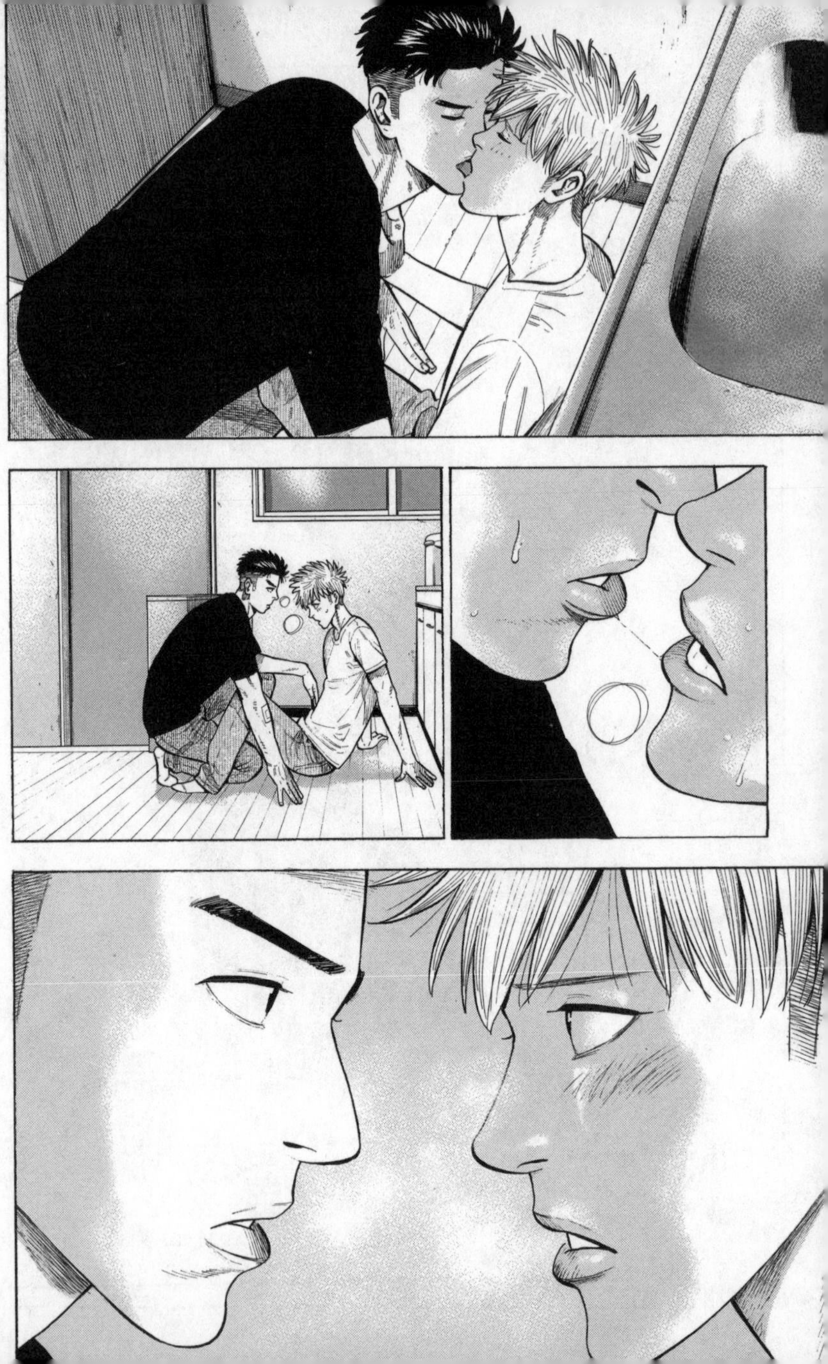

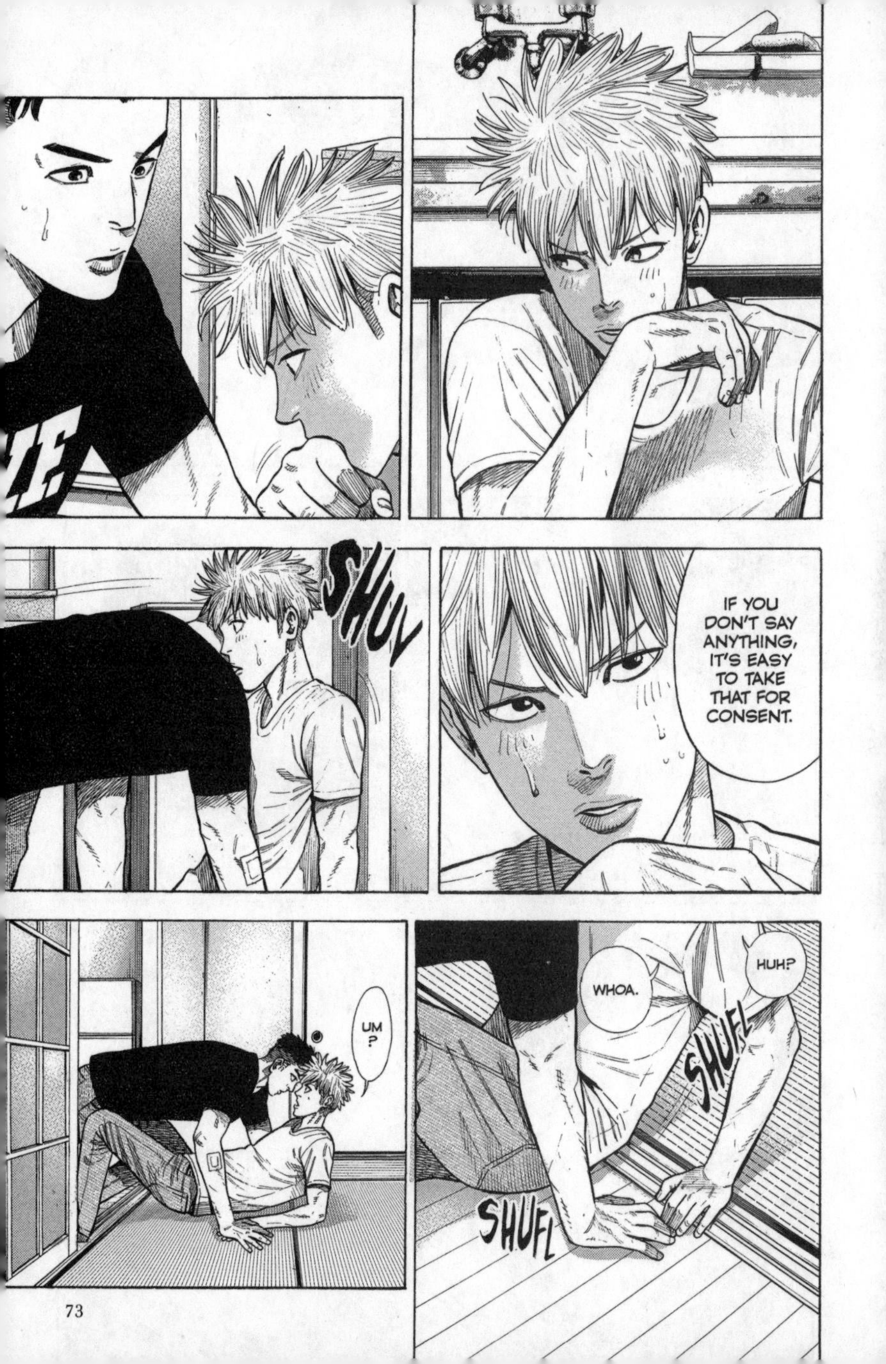
IF YOU DON'T SAY ANYTHING, IT'S EASY TO TAKE THAT FOR CONSENT.
SHUV
HUH?
WHOA.
SHUFL
SHUFL
UM ?

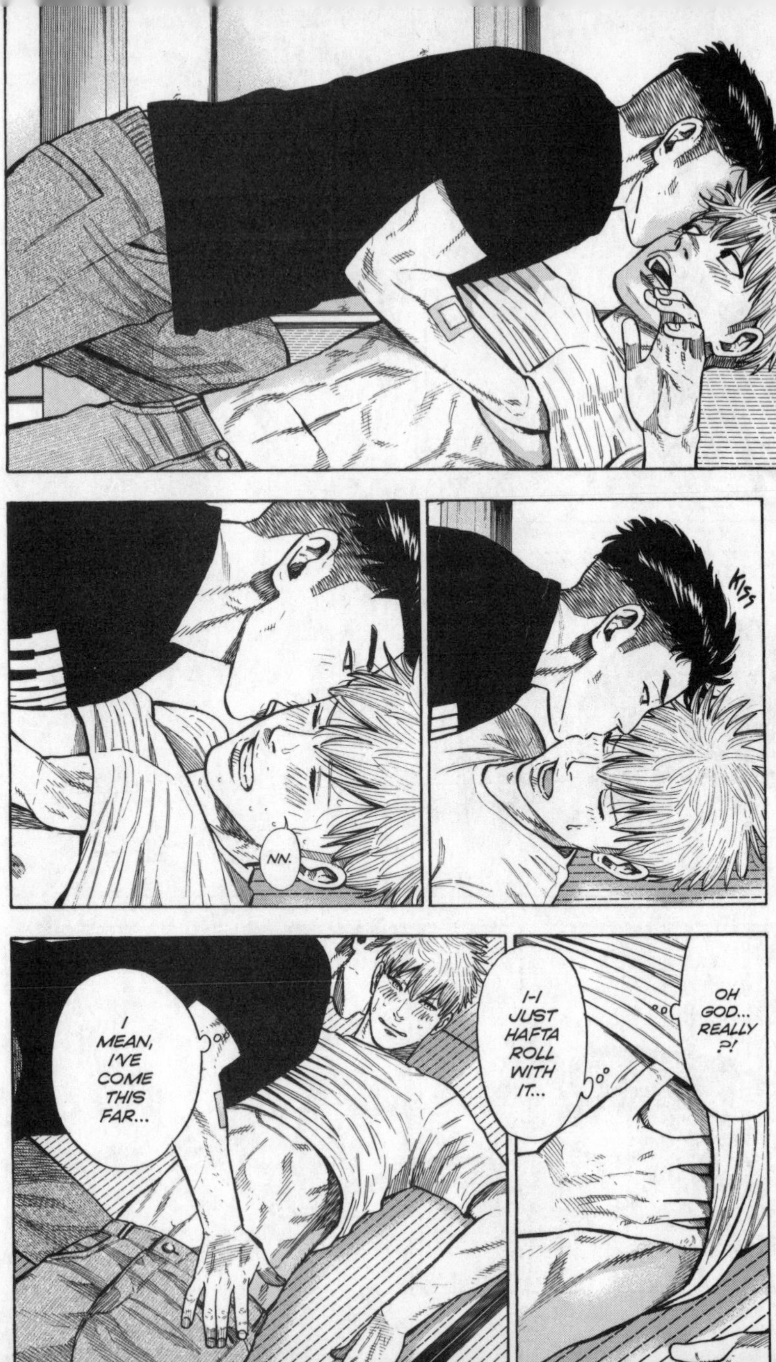
KISS
NN.
OH GOD... REALLY?!
I-I JUST HAFTA ROLL WITH IT...
I MEAN, I'VE COME THIS FAR...

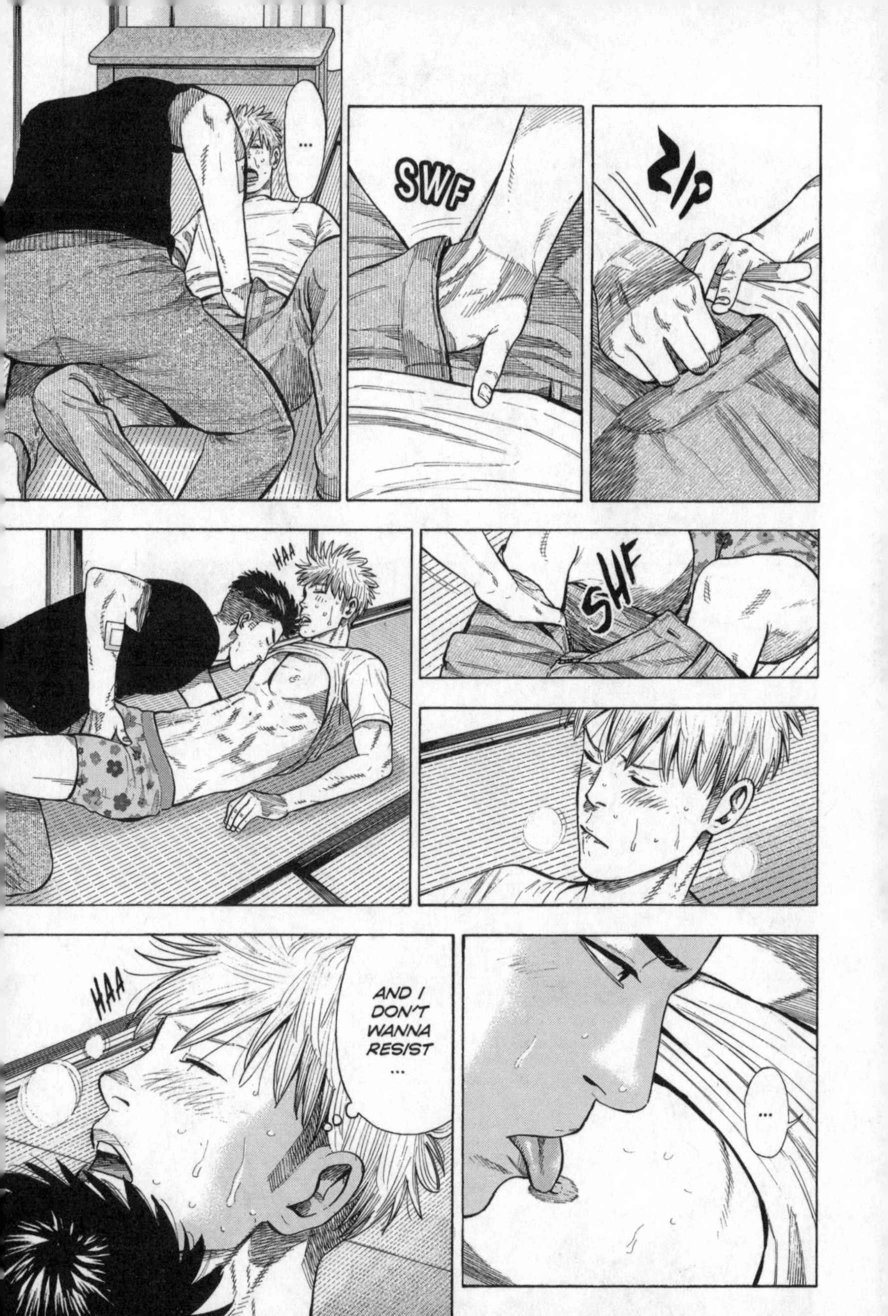
ZIP
SWF
...
SHF
HAA
...
AND I DON'T WANNA RESIST ...
HAA

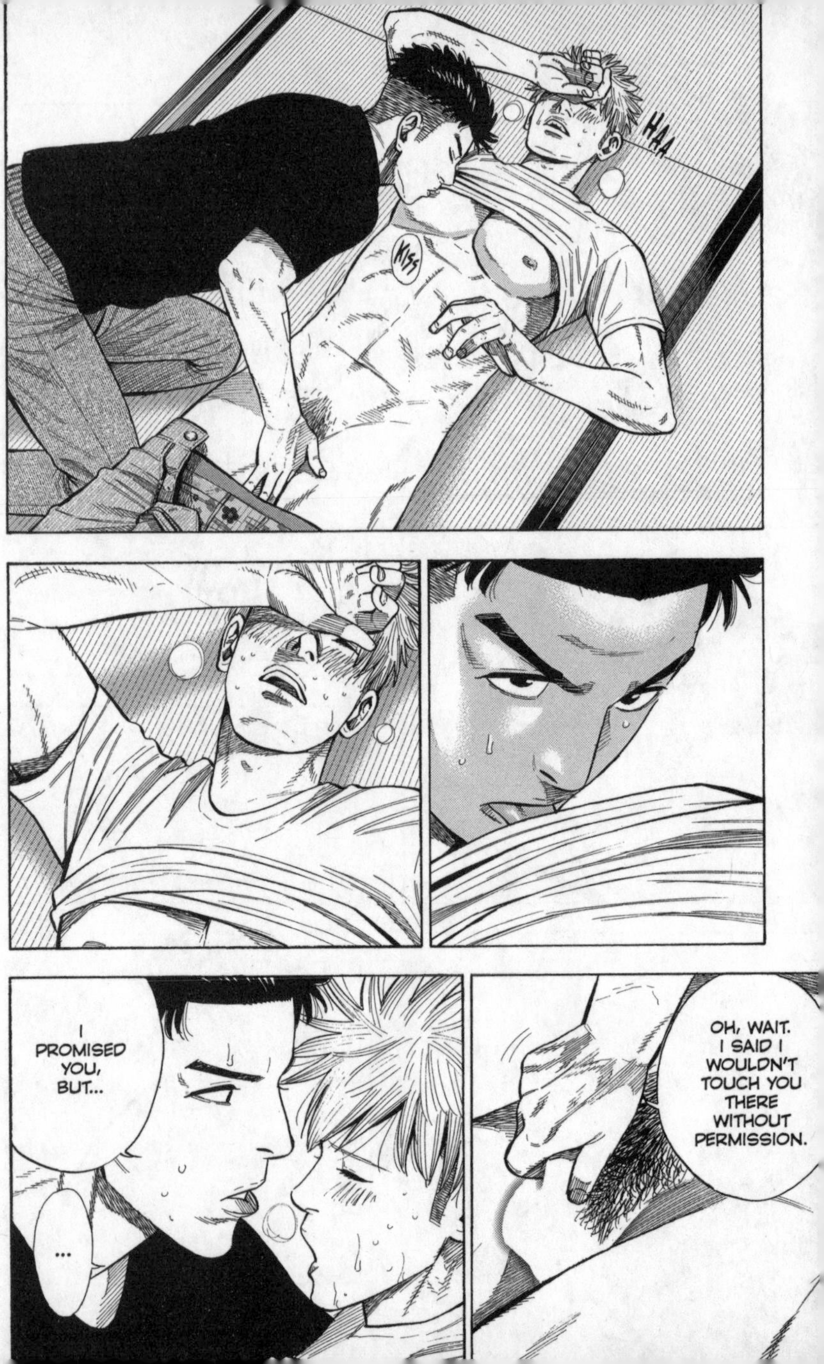
HAA
OH, WAIT. I SAID I WOULDN'T TOUCH YOU THERE WITHOUT PERMISSION.
I PROMISED YOU, BUT...
...

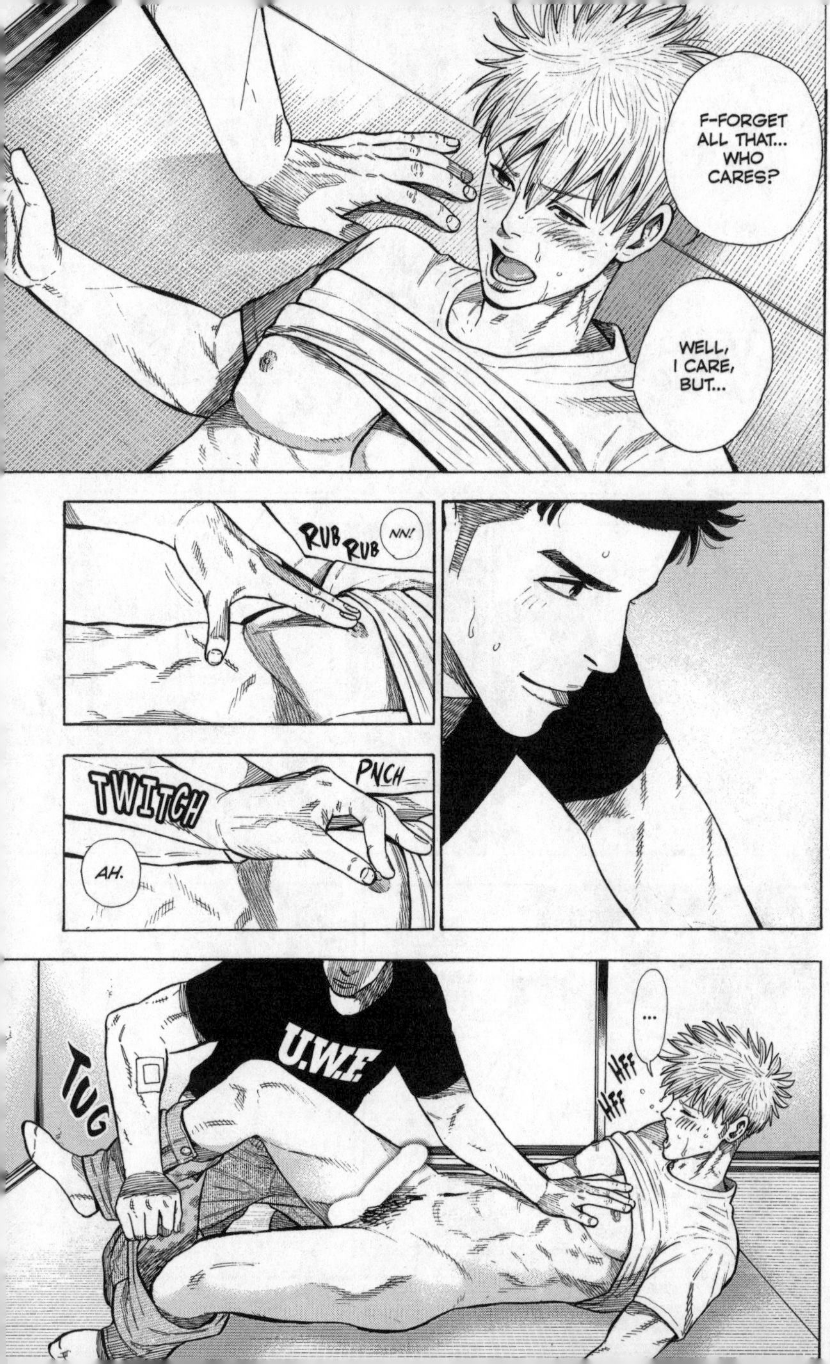
F-FORGET ALL THAT... WHO CARES?
WELL, I CARE, BUT...
NN!
RUB RUB
PNCH
TWITCH
AH.
...
HFF HFF
TUG

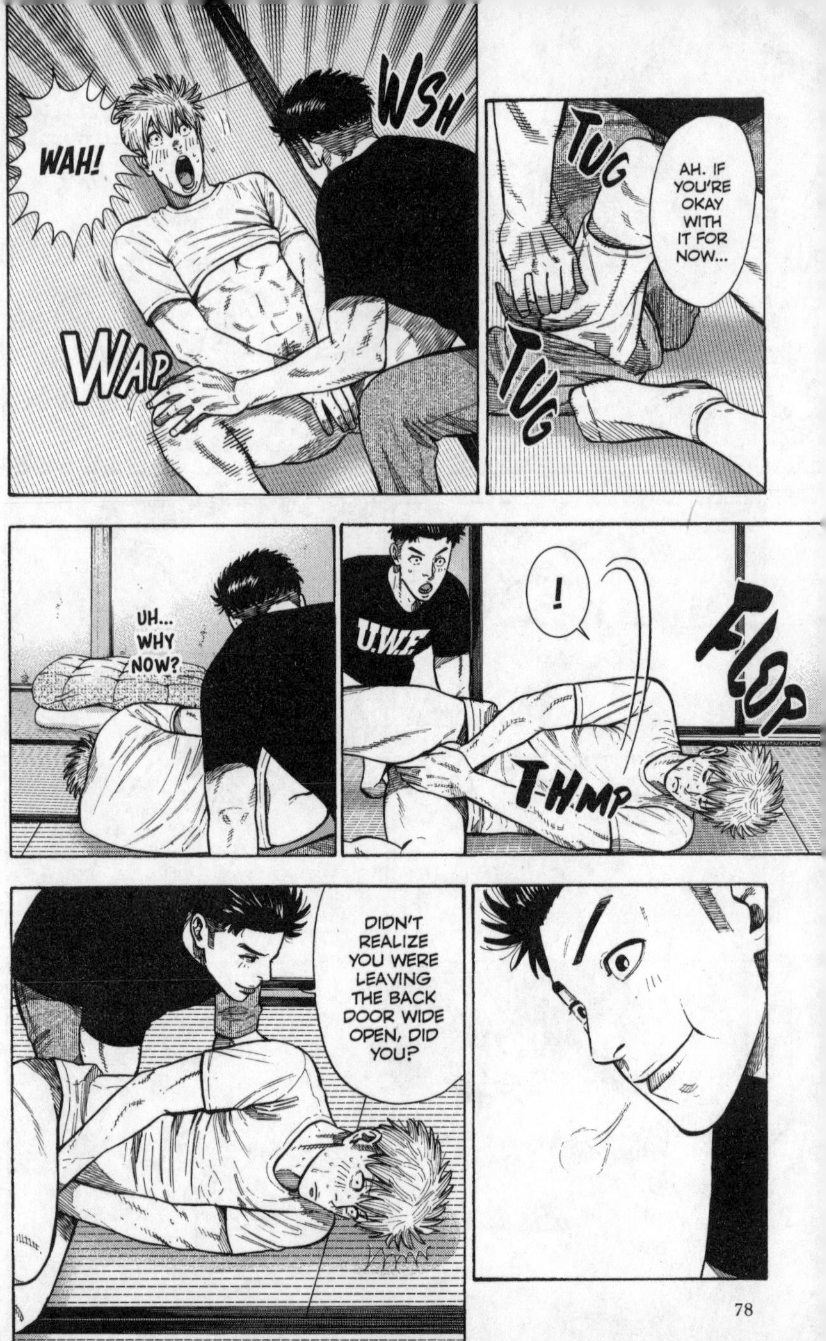
AH. IF YOU'RE OKAY WITH IT FOR NOW...
TUG
TUG
WSH
WAH!
WAP
!
FLOP
THMP
UH... WHY NOW?
DIDN'T REALIZE YOU WERE LEAVING THE BACK DOOR WIDE OPEN, DID YOU?

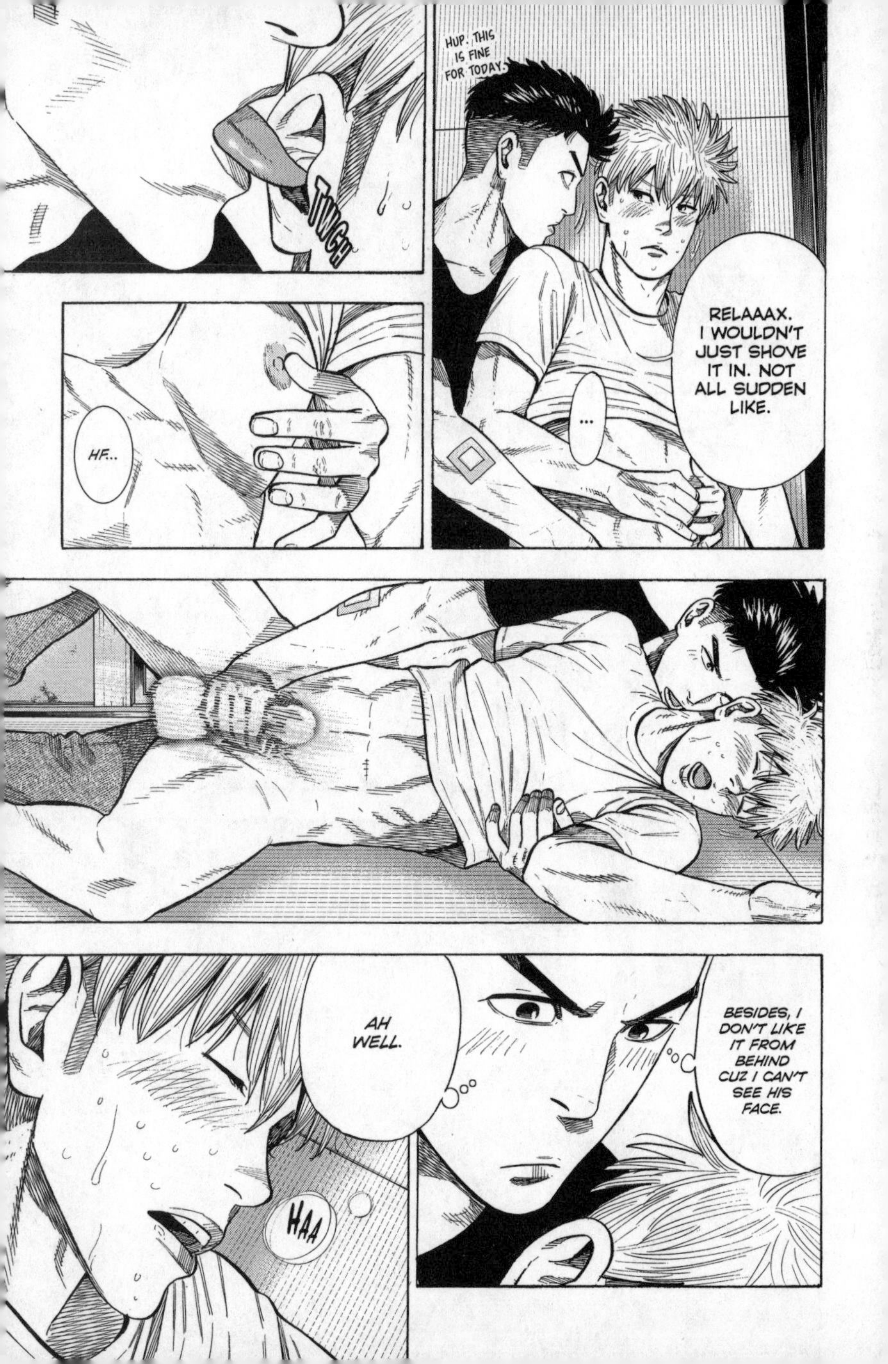
HUP. THIS IS FINE FOR TODAY.
RELAAAX. I WOULDN'T JUST SHOVE IT IN. NOT ALL SUDDEN LIKE.
...
TWCH
HF...
AH WELL.
BESIDES, I DON'T LIKE IT FROM BEHIND CUZ I CAN'T SEE HIS FACE.
HAA

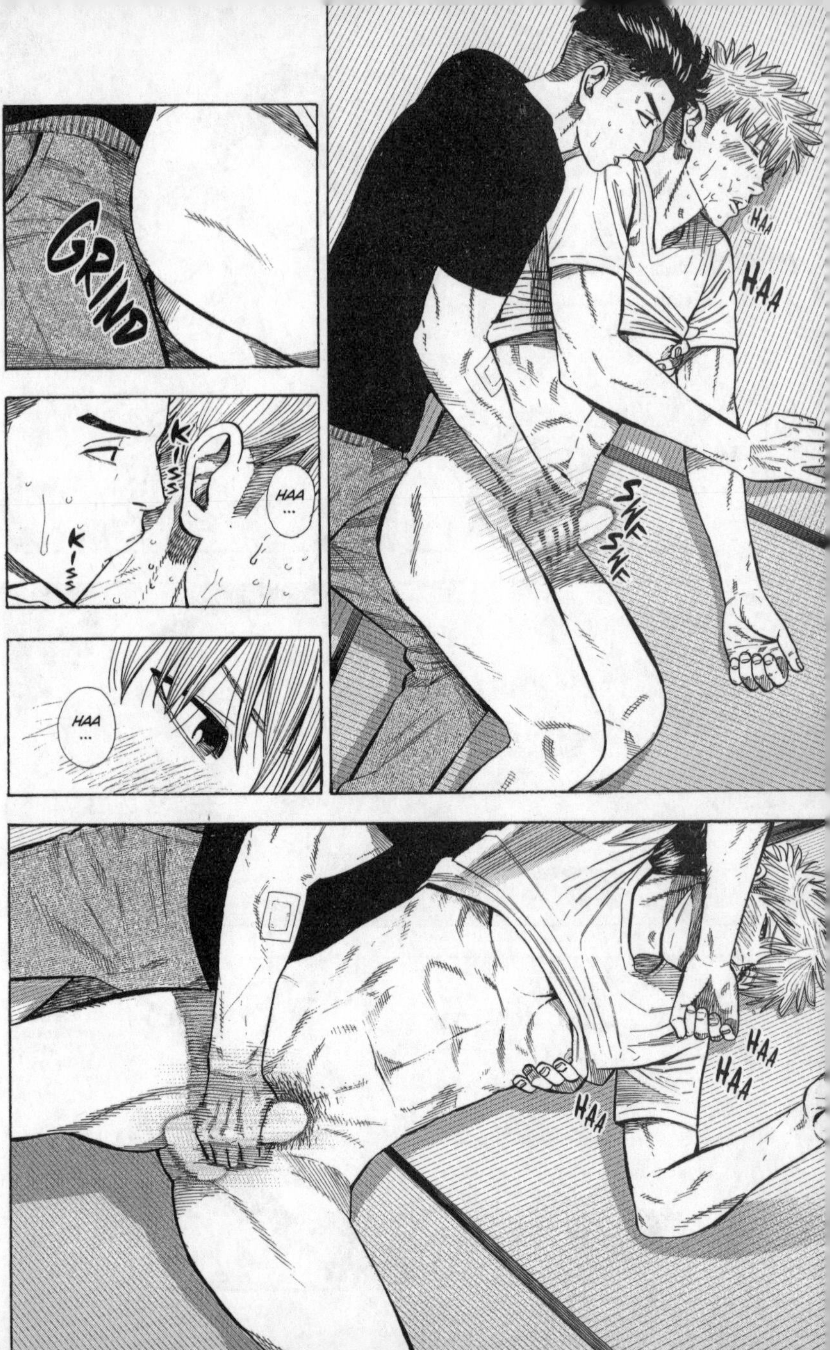
HAA
HAA
SWF SWF
GRIND
K-ISS
HAA...
K-ISS
HAA...
HAA
HAA
HAA

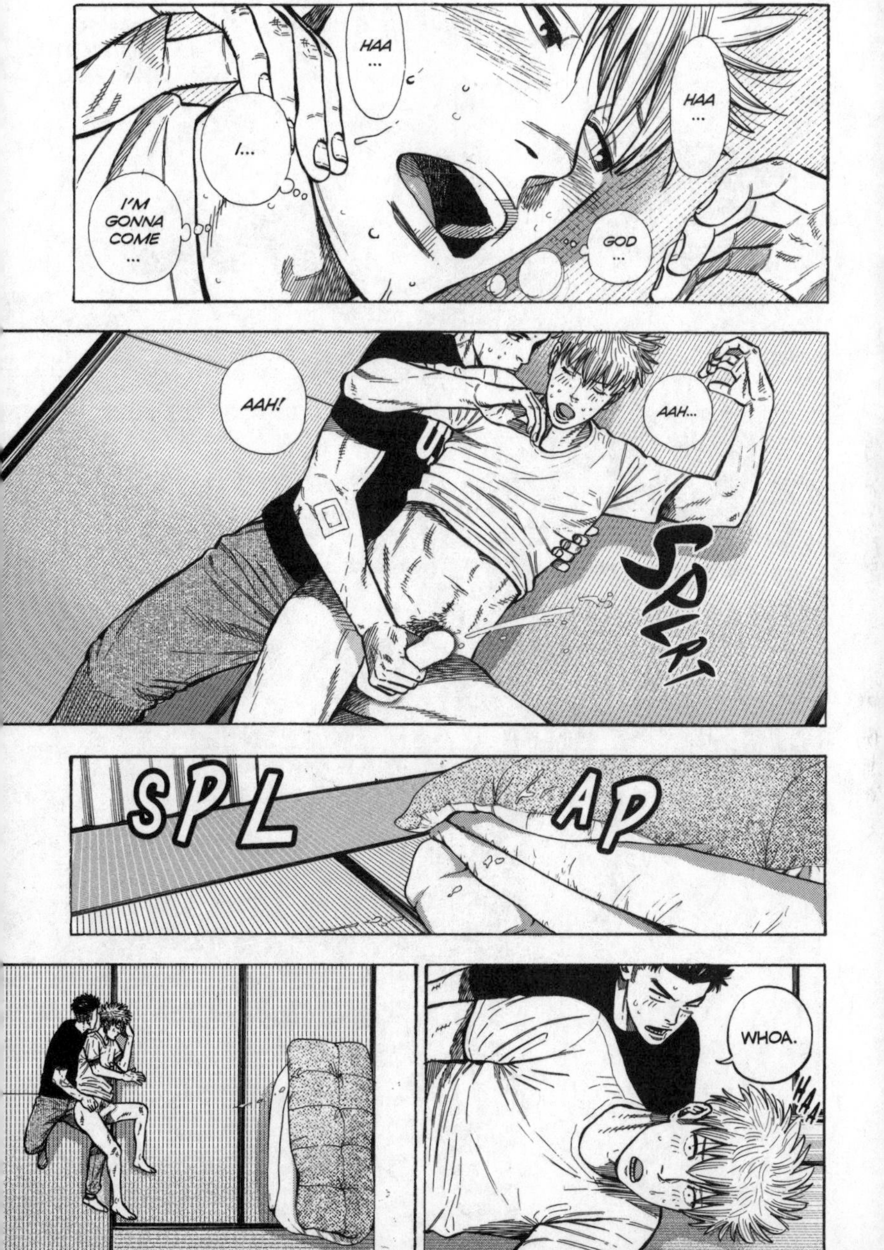
HAA...
GOD...
HAA...
I...
I'M GONNA COME...
AAH...
AAH!
SPLRT
SPL AP
WHOA.
HAA

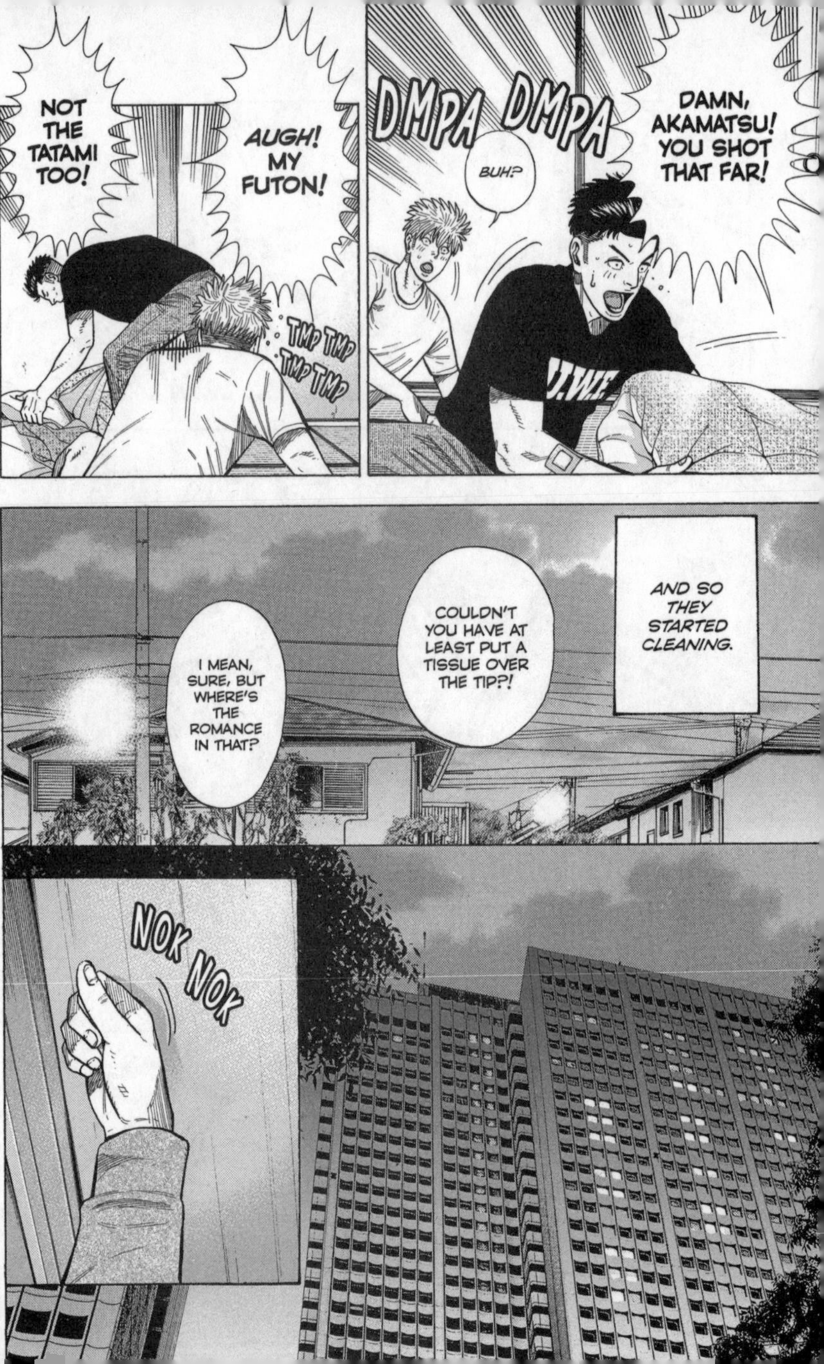
DAMN, AKAMATSU! YOU SHOT THAT FAR!
DMPA DMPA
BUH?
AUGH! MY FUTON!
NOT THE TATAMI TOO!
TMP TMP TMP TMP
AND SO THEY STARTED CLEANING.
COULDN'T YOU HAVE AT LEAST PUT A TISSUE OVER THE TIP?!
I MEAN, SURE, BUT WHERE'S THE ROMANCE IN THAT?
NOK NOK

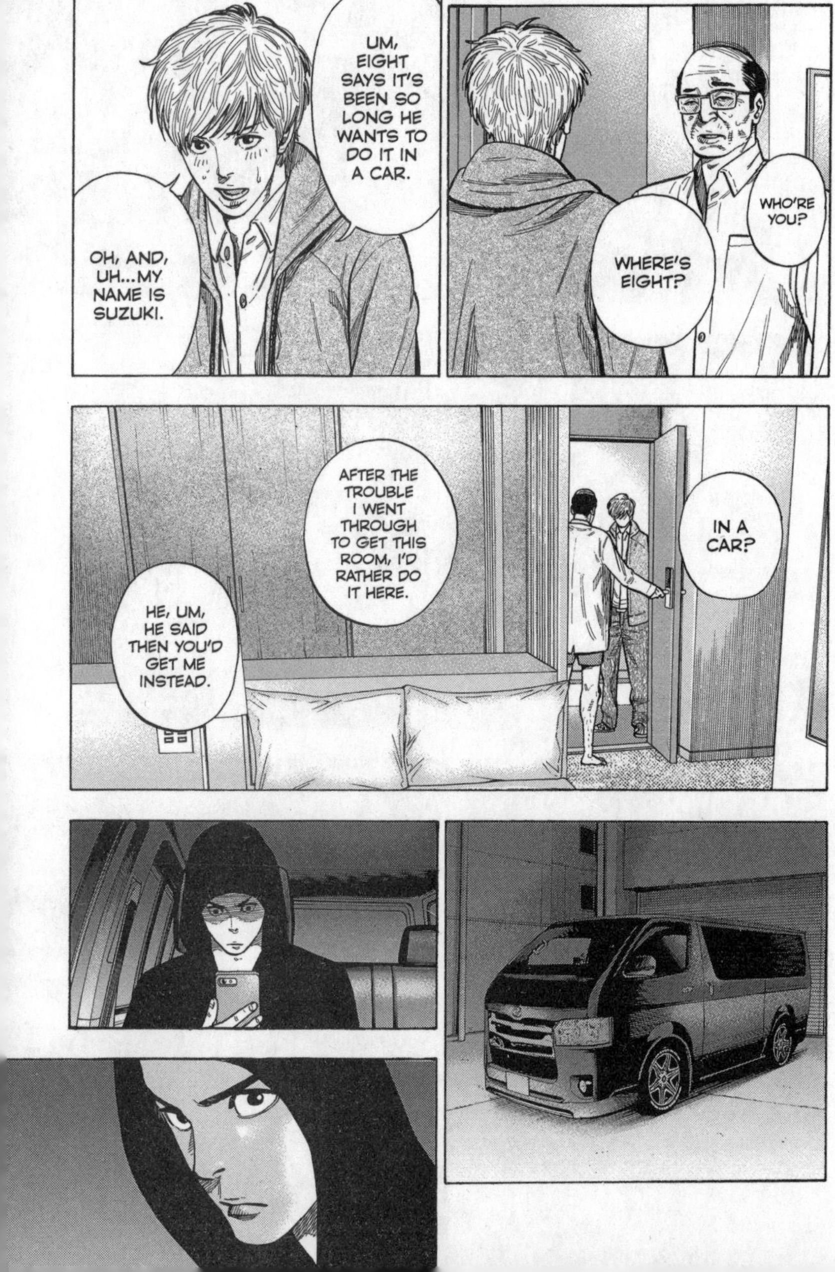
WHO'RE YOU?
WHERE'S EIGHT?
UM, EIGHT SAYS IT'S BEEN SO LONG HE WANTS TO DO IT IN A CAR.
OH, AND, UH...MY NAME IS SUZUKI.
IN A CAR?
AFTER THE TROUBLE I WENT THROUGH TO GET THIS ROOM, I'D RATHER DO IT HERE.
HE, UM, HE SAID THEN YOU'D GET ME INSTEAD.

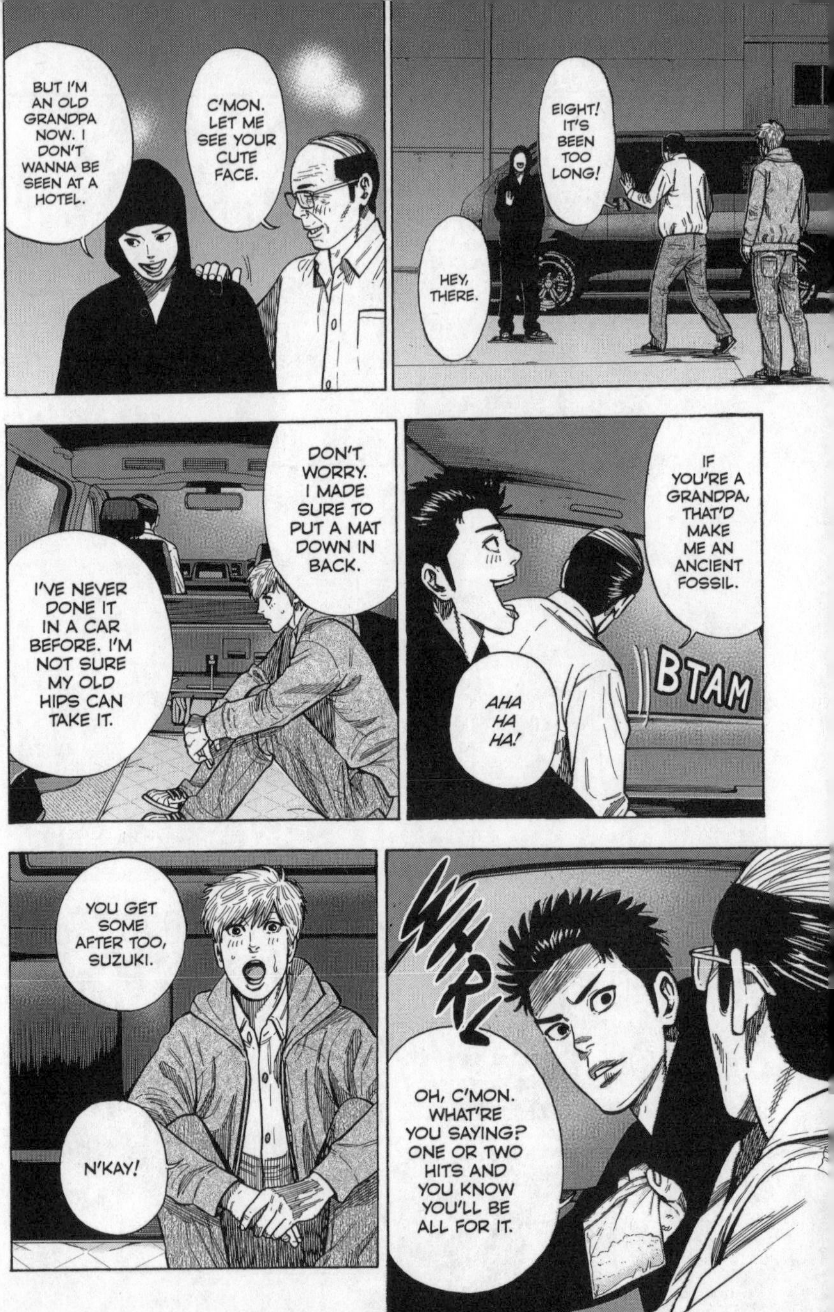
EIGHT! IT'S BEEN TOO LONG!
HEY, THERE.
C'MON. LET ME SEE YOUR CUTE FACE.
BUT I'M AN OLD GRANDPA NOW. I DON'T WANNA BE SEEN AT A HOTEL.
IF YOU'RE A GRANDPA, THAT'D MAKE ME AN ANCIENT FOSSIL.
BTAM
AHA HA HA!
DON'T WORRY. I MADE SURE TO PUT A MAT DOWN IN BACK.
I'VE NEVER DONE IT IN A CAR BEFORE. I'M NOT SURE MY OLD HIPS CAN TAKE IT.
WHRL
OH, C'MON. WHAT'RE YOU SAYING? ONE OR TWO HITS AND YOU KNOW YOU'LL BE ALL FOR IT.
YOU GET SOME AFTER TOO, SUZUKI.
N'KAY!

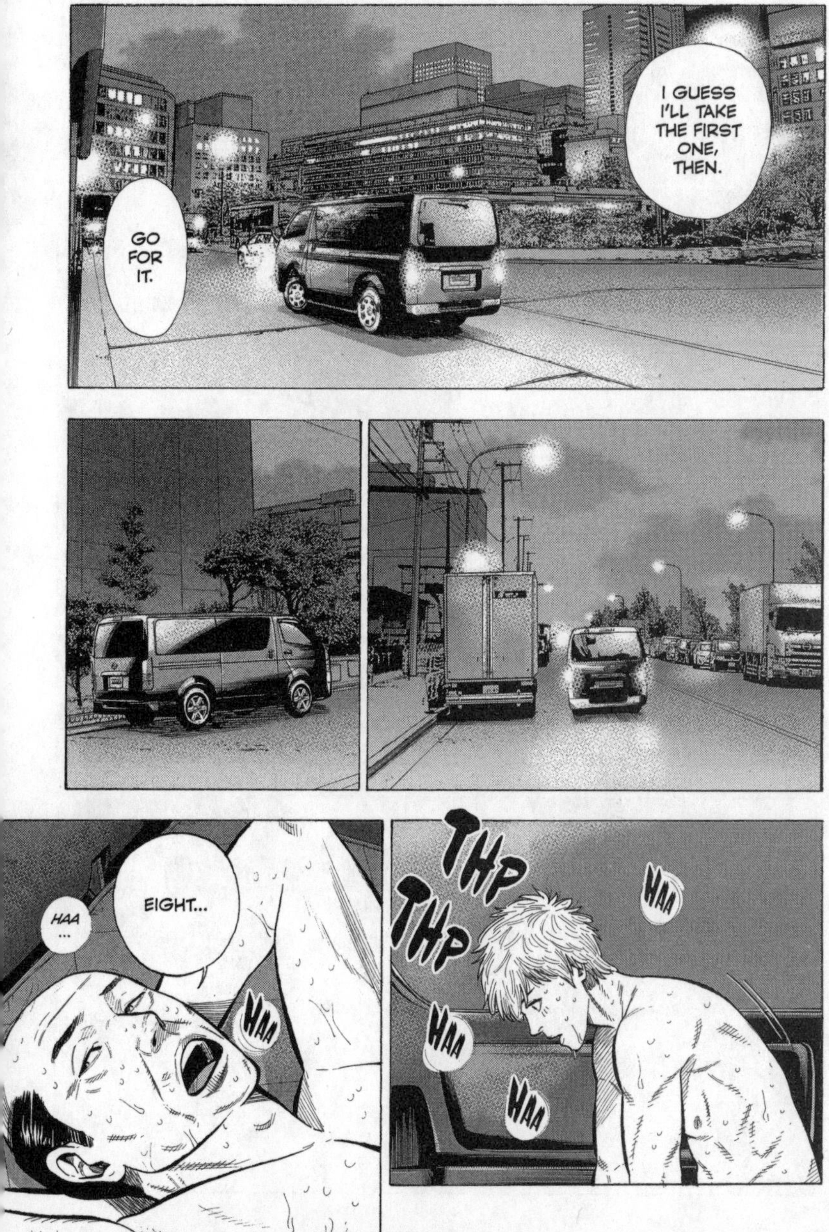
I GUESS I'LL TAKE THE FIRST ONE, THEN.
GO FOR IT.
THP THP
HAA
HAA
HAA
EIGHT...
HAA ...
HAA

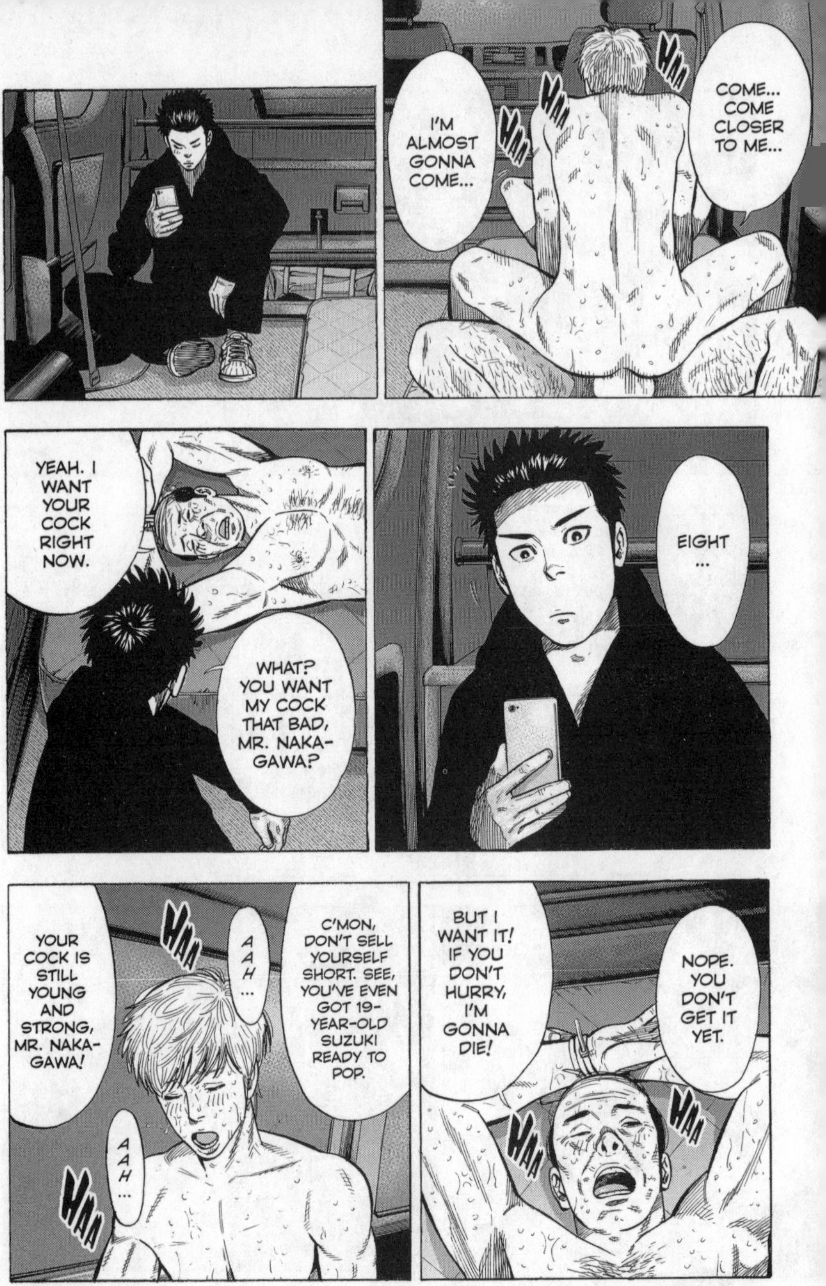
HAA
HAA
HAA
COME... COME CLOSER TO ME...
I'M ALMOST GONNA COME...
EIGHT ...
WHAT? YOU WANT MY COCK THAT BAD, MR. NAKA-GAWA?
YEAH. I WANT YOUR COCK RIGHT NOW.
NOPE. YOU DON'T GET IT YET.
BUT I WANT IT! IF YOU DON'T HURRY, I'M GONNA DIE!
HAA
HAA
C'MON, DON'T SELL YOURSELF SHORT. SEE, YOU'VE EVEN GOT 19-YEAR-OLD SUZUKI READY TO POP.
AAH ...
HAA
YOUR COCK IS STILL YOUNG AND STRONG, MR. NAKA-GAWA!
AAH ...
HAA

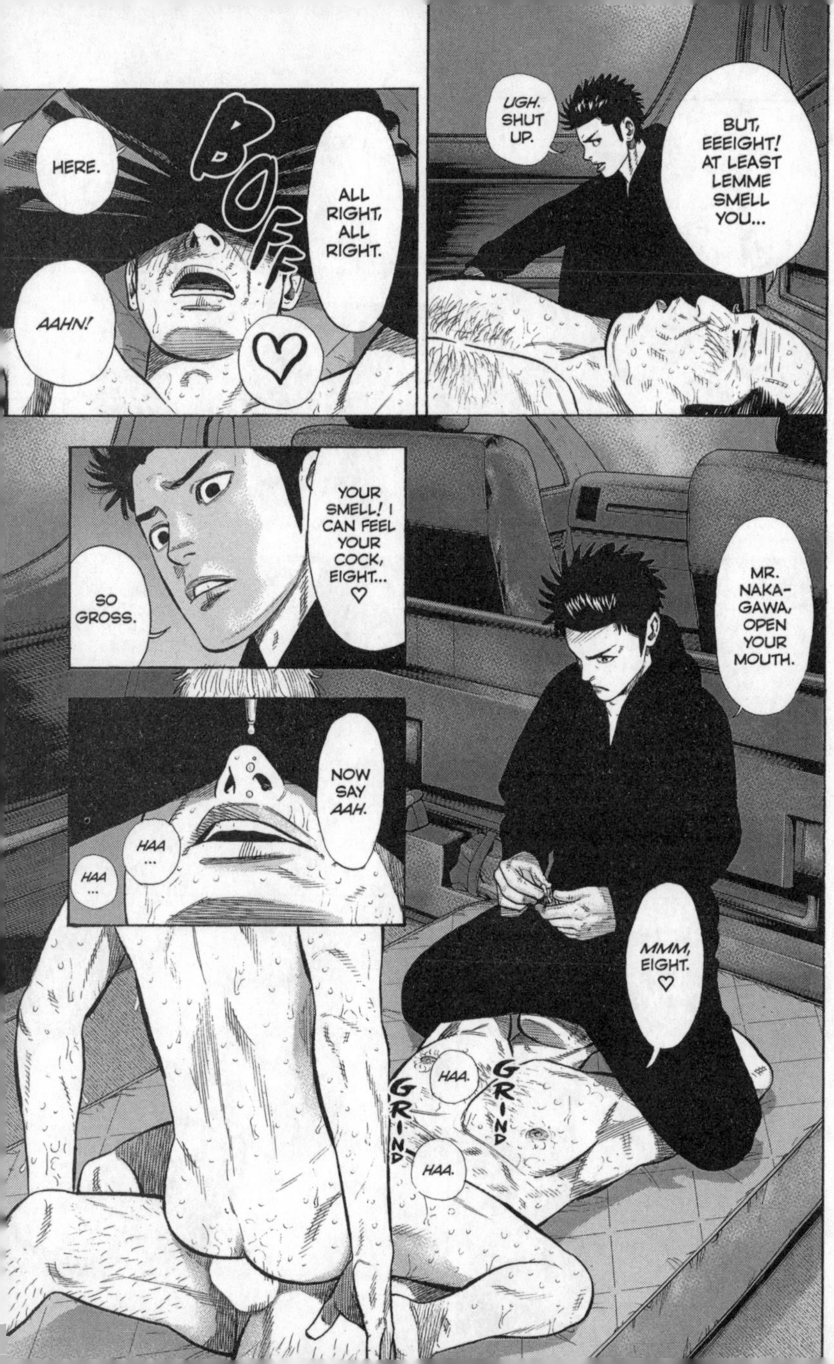
BUT, EEEIGHT! AT LEAST LEMME SMELL YOU...
UGH. SHUT UP.
ALL RIGHT, ALL RIGHT.
BOFF
HERE.
AAHN!
♡
MR. NAKAGAWA, OPEN YOUR MOUTH.
YOUR SMELL! I CAN FEEL YOUR COCK, EIGHT... ♡
SO GROSS.
NOW SAY *AAH.*
HAA...
HAA...
MMM, EIGHT. ♡
GRIND
HAA.
GRIND
HAA.

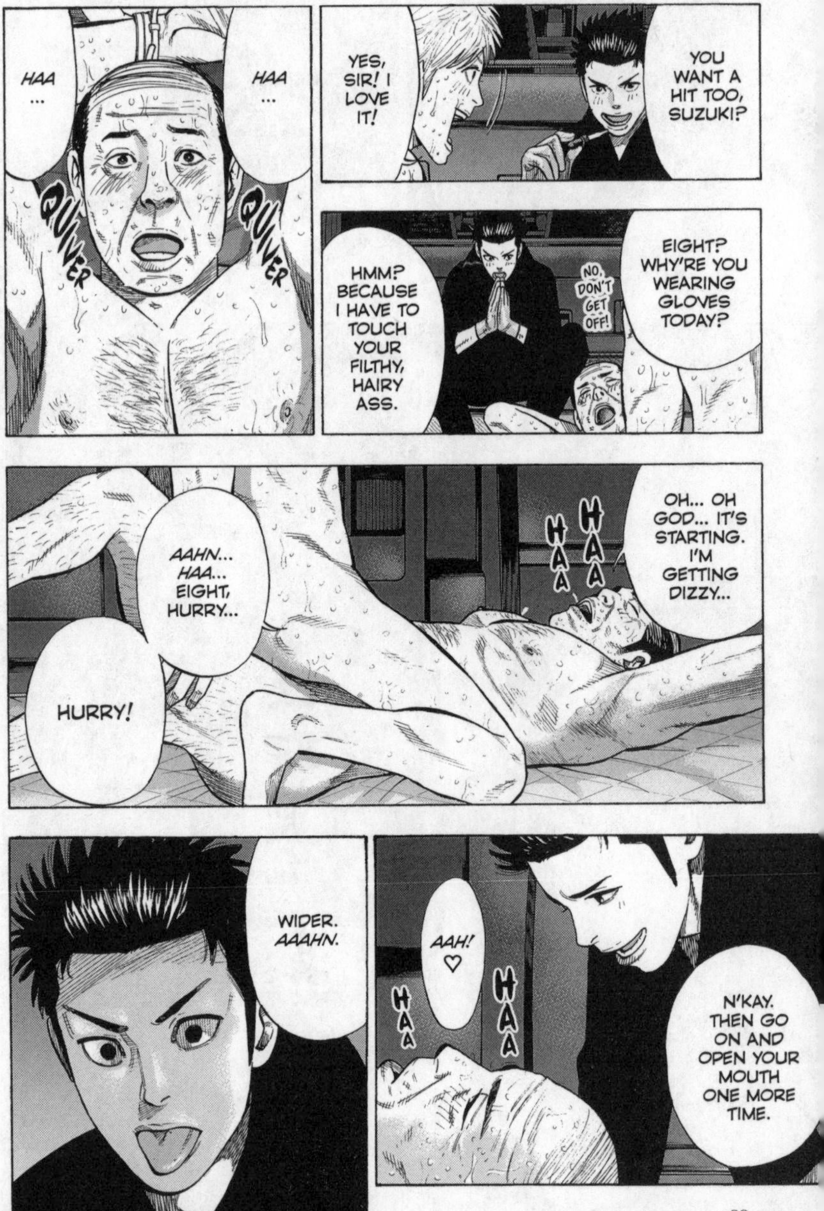
YOU WANT A HIT TOO, SUZUKI?
YES, SIR! I LOVE IT!
EIGHT? WHY'RE YOU WEARING GLOVES TODAY?
NO, DON'T GET OFF!
HMM? BECAUSE I HAVE TO TOUCH YOUR FILTHY, HAIRY ASS.
HAA ...
HAA ...
QUIVER
QUIVER
OH... OH GOD... IT'S STARTING. I'M GETTING DIZZY...
HAA
HAA
AAHN... HAA... EIGHT, HURRY...
HURRY!
N'KAY. THEN GO ON AND OPEN YOUR MOUTH ONE MORE TIME.
HAA
AAH! ♡
HAA
WIDER. AAAHN.

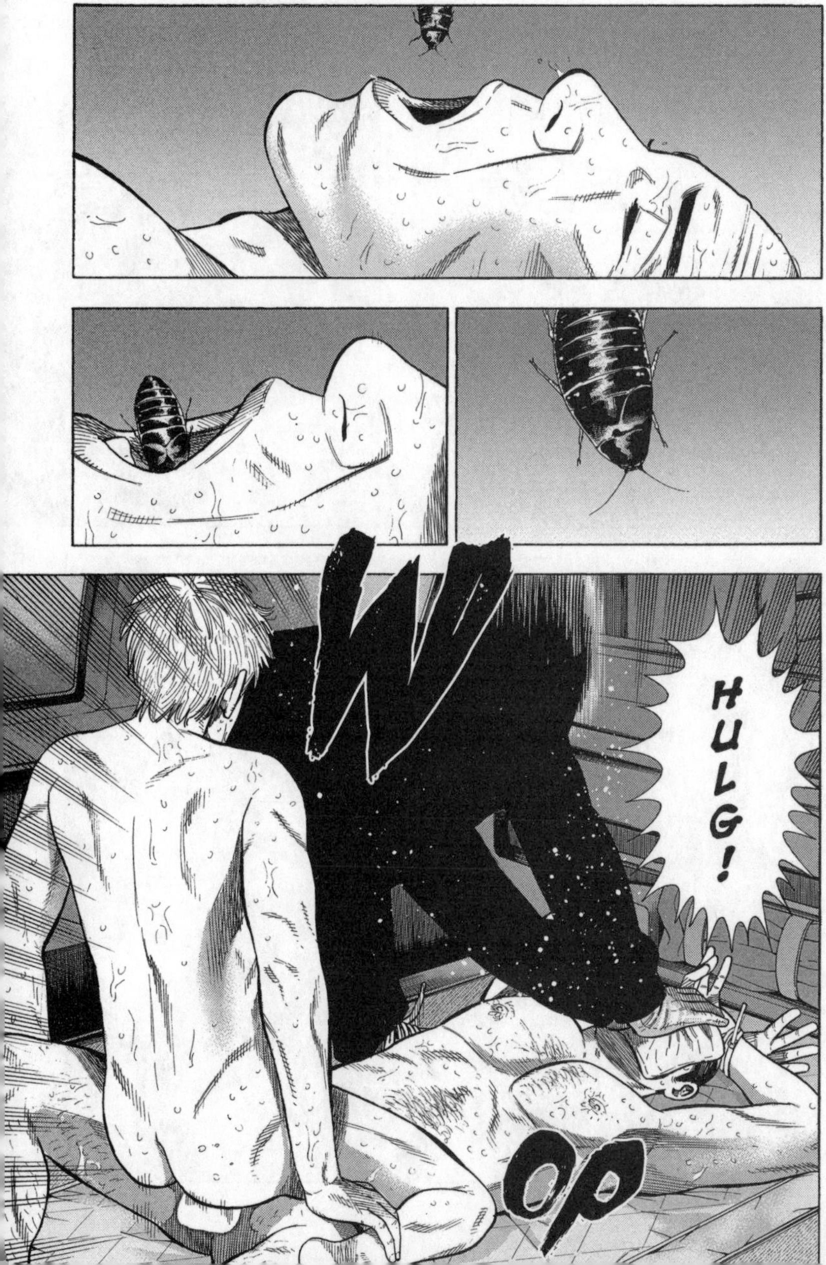
HULG!
W
OP

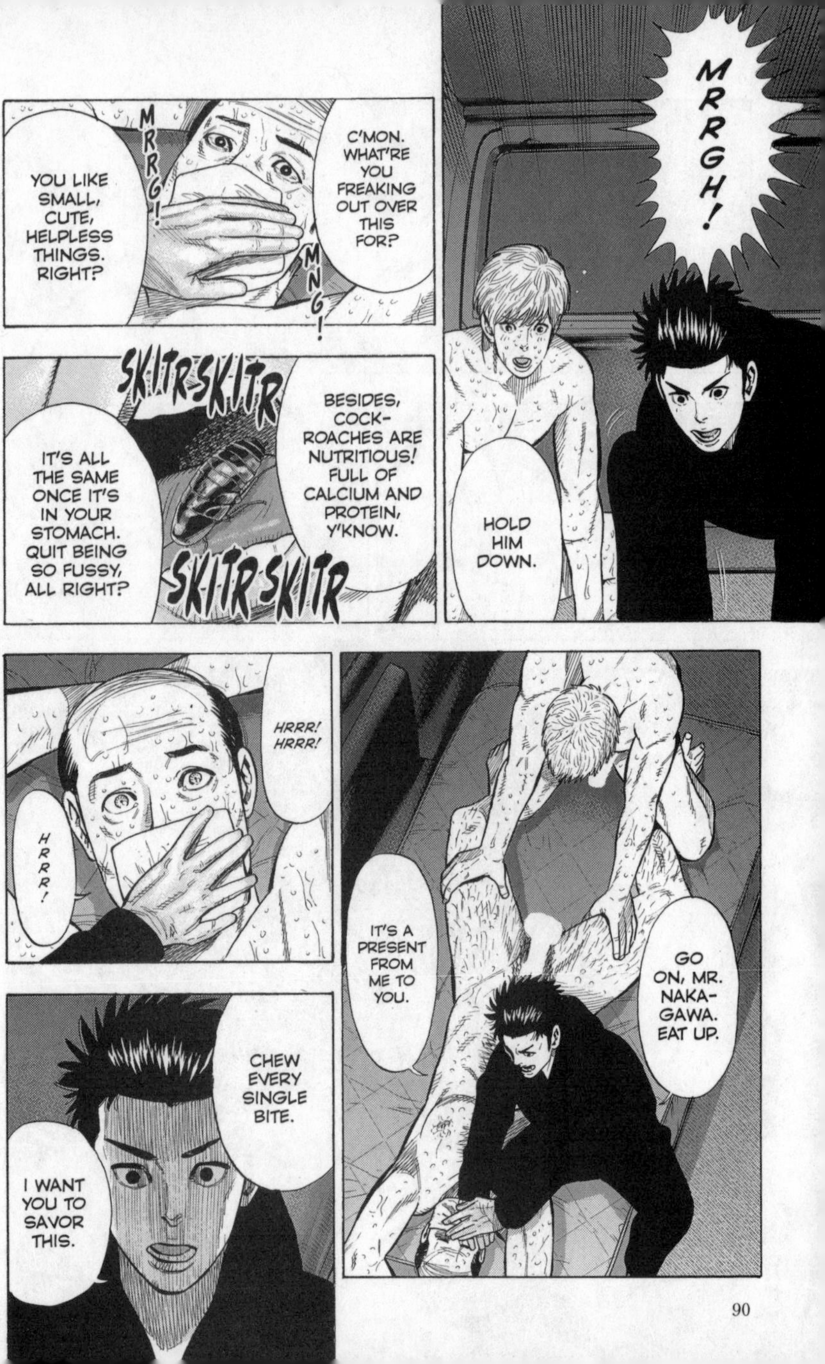
MRRGH!
HOLD HIM DOWN.
C'MON. WHAT'RE YOU FREAKING OUT OVER THIS FOR?
MRRG!
MNG!
YOU LIKE SMALL, CUTE, HELPLESS THINGS. RIGHT?
SKITR SKITR
BESIDES, COCK-ROACHES ARE NUTRITIOUS! FULL OF CALCIUM AND PROTEIN, Y'KNOW.
IT'S ALL THE SAME ONCE IT'S IN YOUR STOMACH. QUIT BEING SO FUSSY, ALL RIGHT?
SKITR SKITR
GO ON, MR. NAKA-GAWA. EAT UP.
IT'S A PRESENT FROM ME TO YOU.
HRRR! HRRR!
HRRR!
CHEW EVERY SINGLE BITE.
I WANT YOU TO SAVOR THIS.

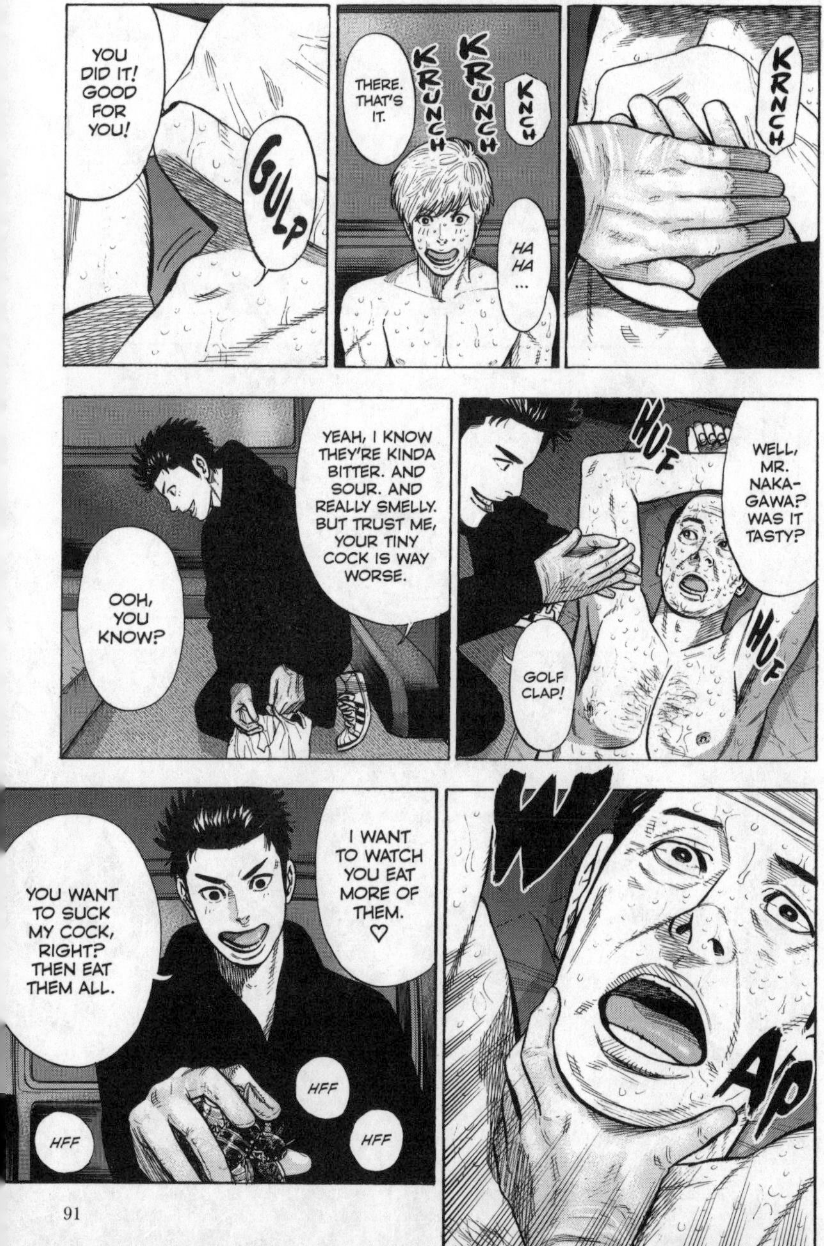
KRNCH
KNCH
KRUNCH
KRUNCH
THERE. THAT'S IT.
HA HA ...
YOU DID IT! GOOD FOR YOU!
GULP
HUF
WELL, MR. NAKAGAWA? WAS IT TASTY?
HUF
GOLF CLAP!
YEAH, I KNOW THEY'RE KINDA BITTER. AND SOUR. AND REALLY SMELLY. BUT TRUST ME, YOUR TINY COCK IS WAY WORSE.
OOH, YOU KNOW?
W
AP
I WANT TO WATCH YOU EAT MORE OF THEM. ♡
YOU WANT TO SUCK MY COCK, RIGHT? THEN EAT THEM ALL.
HFF
HFF
HFF

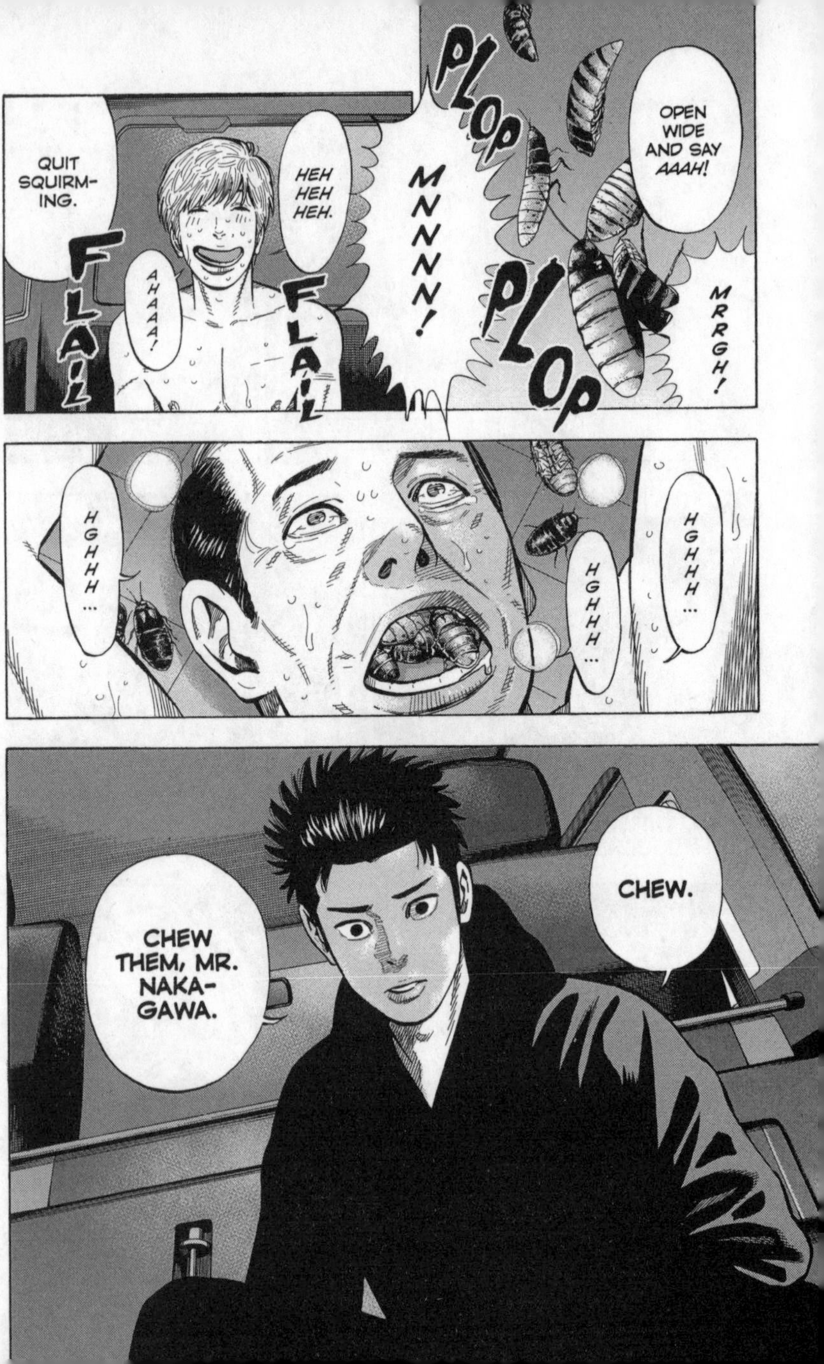
OPEN WIDE AND SAY AAAH!
PLOP
PLOP
PLOP
MRRGH!
MNNNNN!
HEH HEH HEH.
QUIT SQUIRMING.
FLAIL
FLAIL
AHAAAA!
HGHHH...
HGHHH...
HGHHH...
HGHHH...
CHEW.
CHEW THEM, MR. NAKAGAWA.

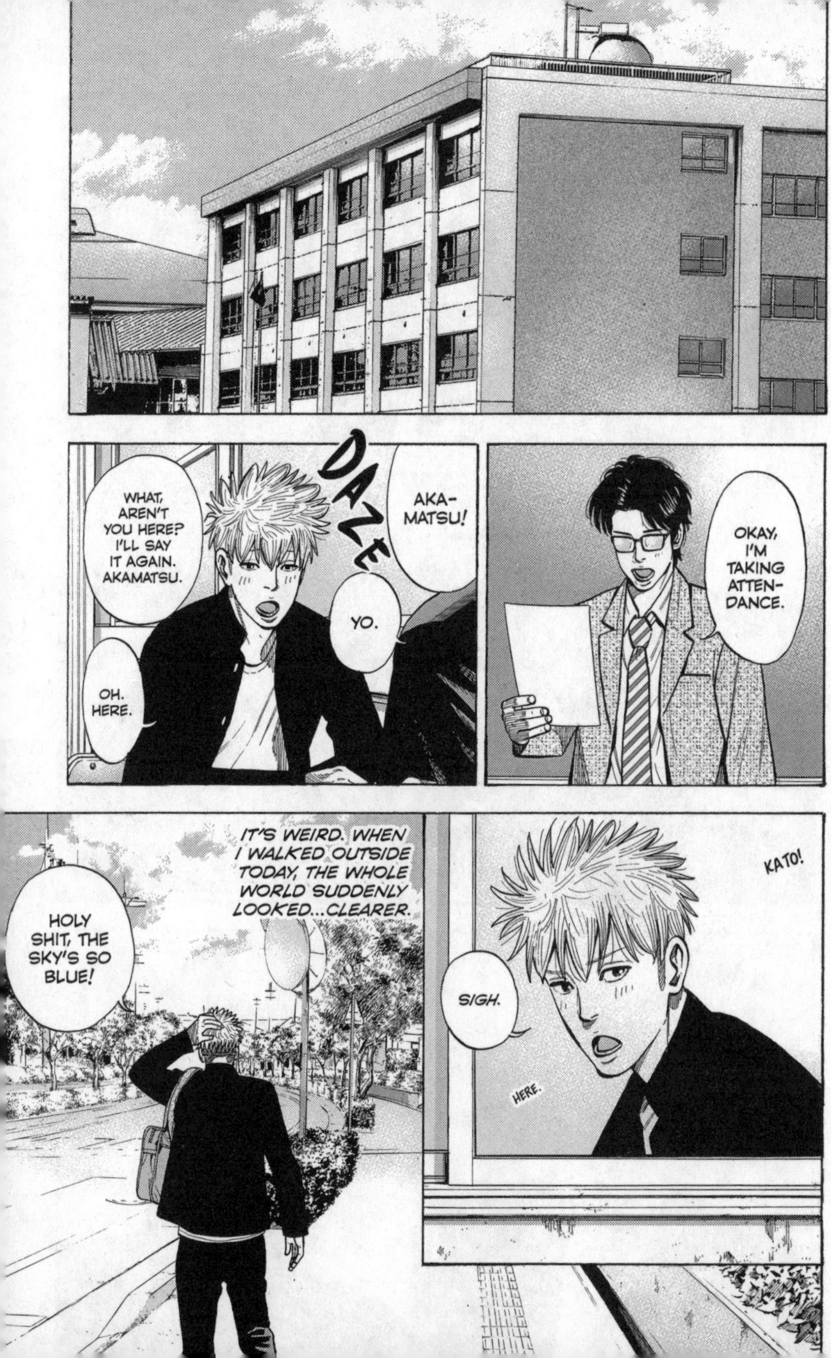
OKAY, I'M TAKING ATTEN-DANCE.
AKA-MATSU!
DAZE
YO.
WHAT, AREN'T YOU HERE? I'LL SAY IT AGAIN. AKAMATSU.
OH. HERE.
KATO!
SIGH.
HERE.
IT'S WEIRD. WHEN I WALKED OUTSIDE TODAY, THE WHOLE WORLD SUDDENLY LOOKED...CLEARER.
HOLY SHIT, THE SKY'S SO BLUE!

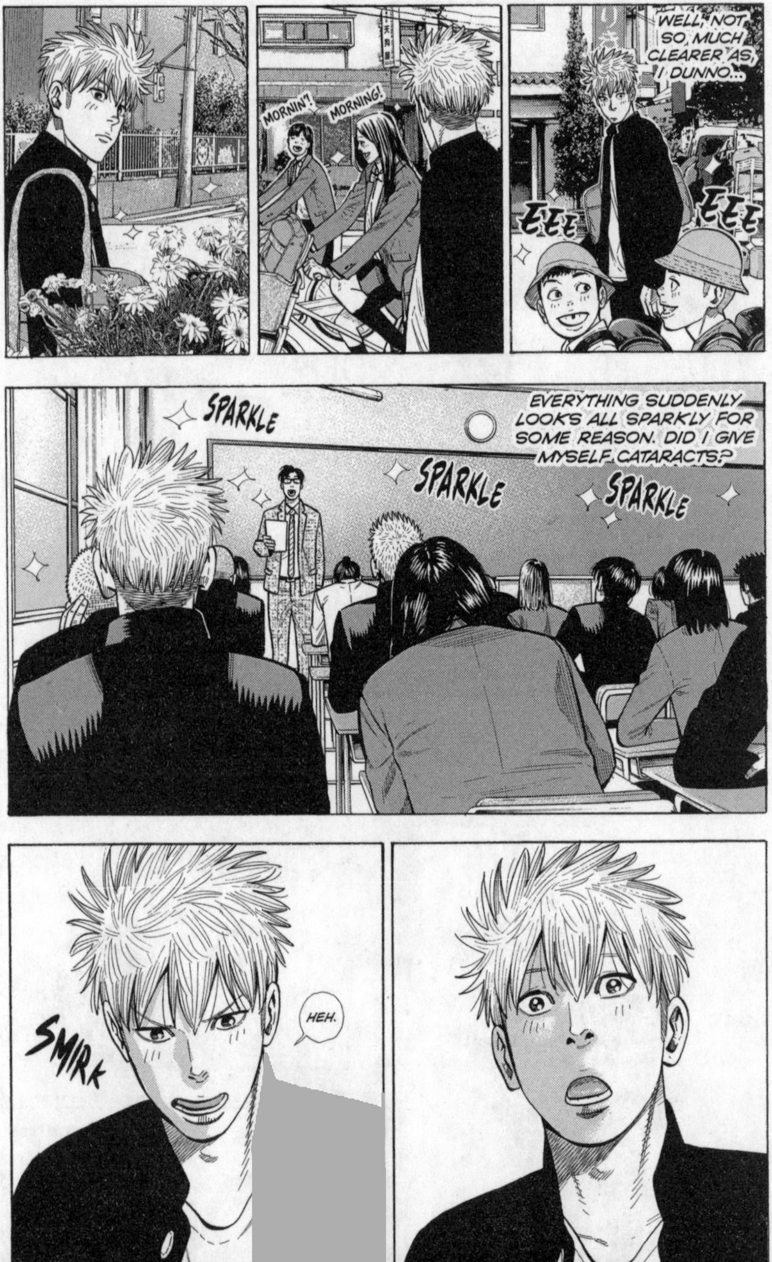
WELL, NOT SO MUCH CLEARER AS, I DUNNO...
EEE
EEE
MORNING!
MORNIN'!
EVERYTHING SUDDENLY LOOKS ALL SPARKLY FOR SOME REASON. DID I GIVE MYSELF CATARACTS?
SPARKLE
SPARKLE
SPARKLE
HEH.
SMIRK

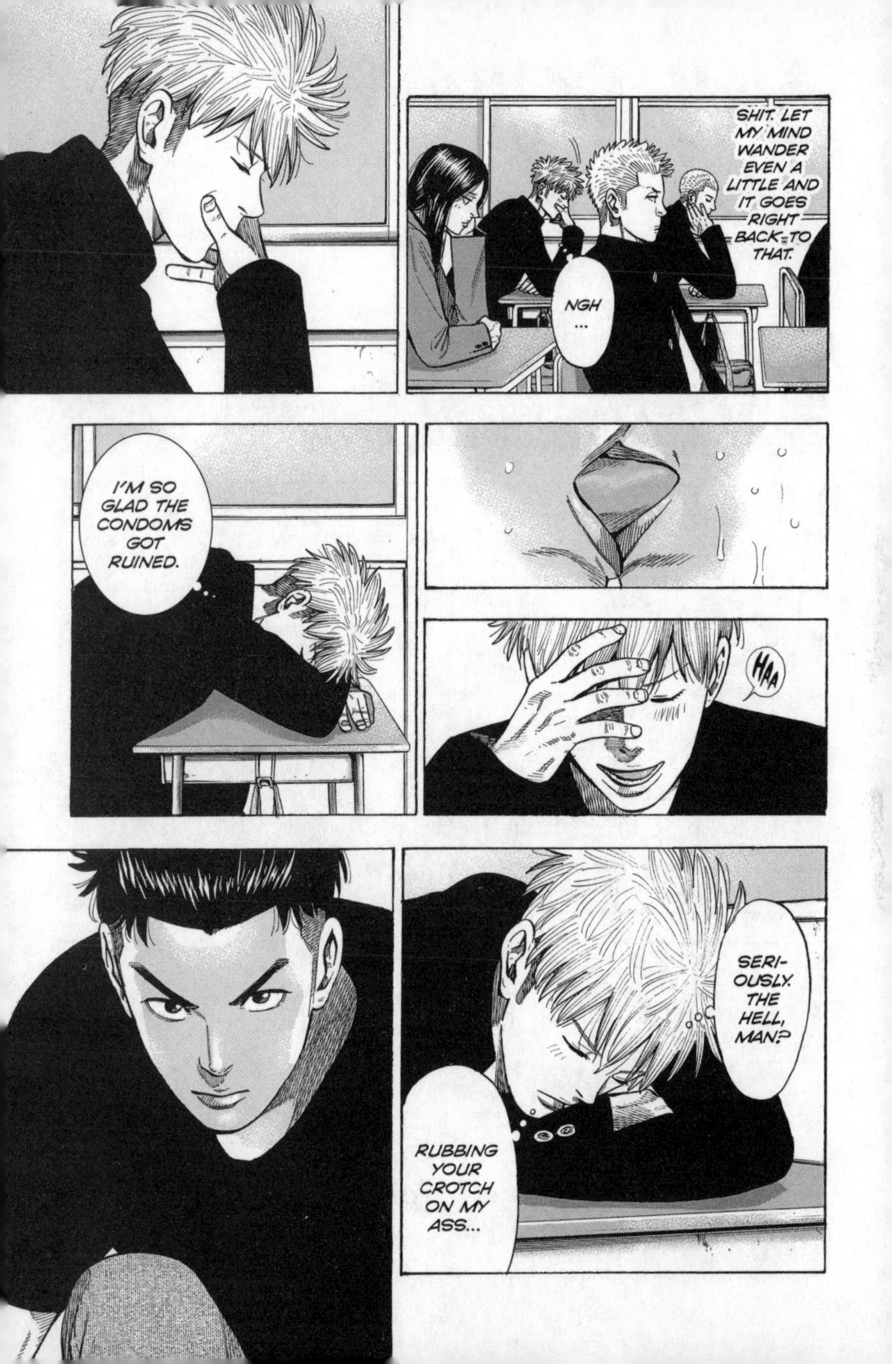
SHIT. LET MY MIND WANDER EVEN A LITTLE AND IT GOES RIGHT BACK TO THAT.
NGH...
HAA
I'M SO GLAD THE CONDOMS GOT RUINED.
SERI-OUSLY. THE HELL, MAN?
RUBBING YOUR CROTCH ON MY ASS...

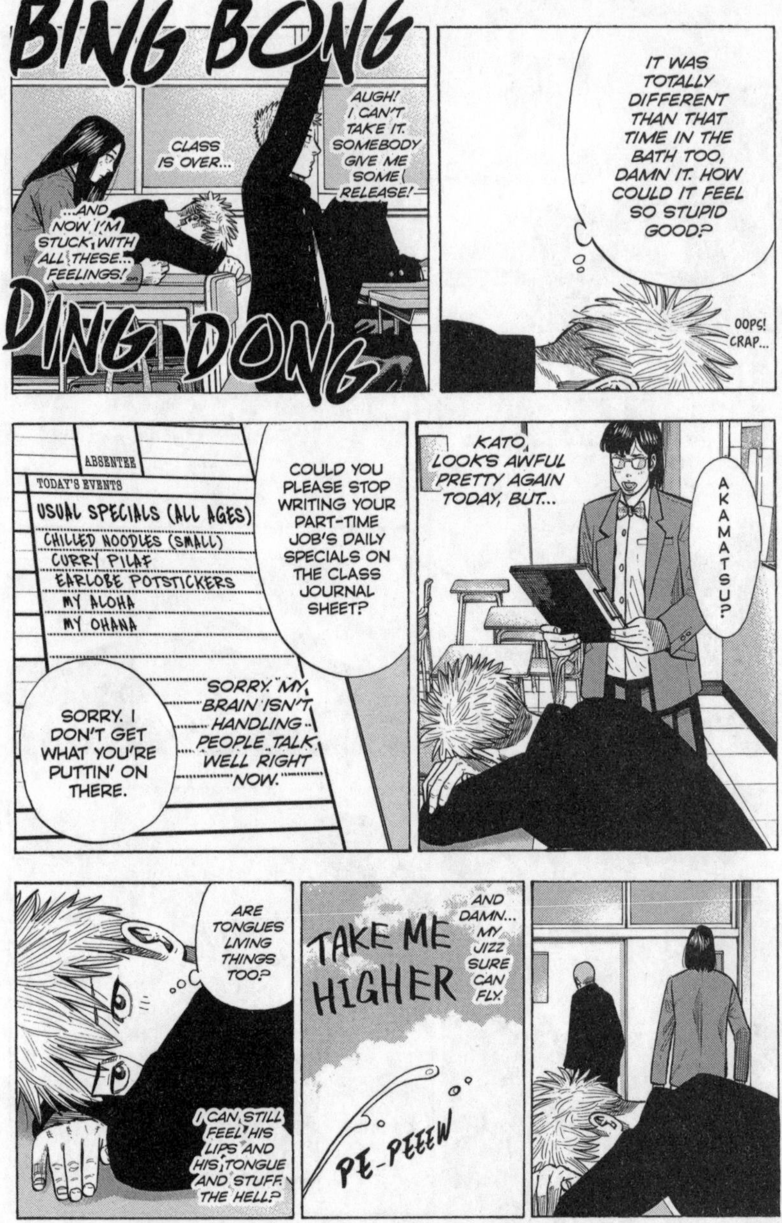
IT WAS TOTALLY DIFFERENT THAN THAT TIME IN THE BATH TOO, DAMN IT. HOW COULD IT FEEL SO STUPID GOOD?
OOPS! CRAP...
BING BONG
AUGH! I CAN'T TAKE IT. SOMEBODY GIVE ME SOME RELEASE!
CLASS IS OVER...
...AND NOW I'M STUCK WITH ALL THESE... FEELINGS!
DING DONG
AKAMATSU?
KATO, LOOKS AWFUL PRETTY AGAIN TODAY, BUT...
ABSENTEE
TODAY'S EVENTS
USUAL SPECIALS (ALL AGES)
CHILLED NOODLES (SMALL)
CURRY PILAF
EARLOBE POTSTICKERS
MY ALOHA
MY OHANA
COULD YOU PLEASE STOP WRITING YOUR PART-TIME JOB'S DAILY SPECIALS ON THE CLASS JOURNAL SHEET?
SORRY. MY BRAIN ISN'T HANDLING PEOPLE TALK WELL RIGHT NOW.
SORRY. I DON'T GET WHAT YOU'RE PUTTIN' ON THERE.
AND DAMN... MY JIZZ SURE CAN FLY.
TAKE ME HIGHER
PE-PEEEW
ARE TONGUES LIVING THINGS TOO?
I CAN STILL FEEL HIS LIPS AND HIS TONGUE AND STUFF. THE HELL?

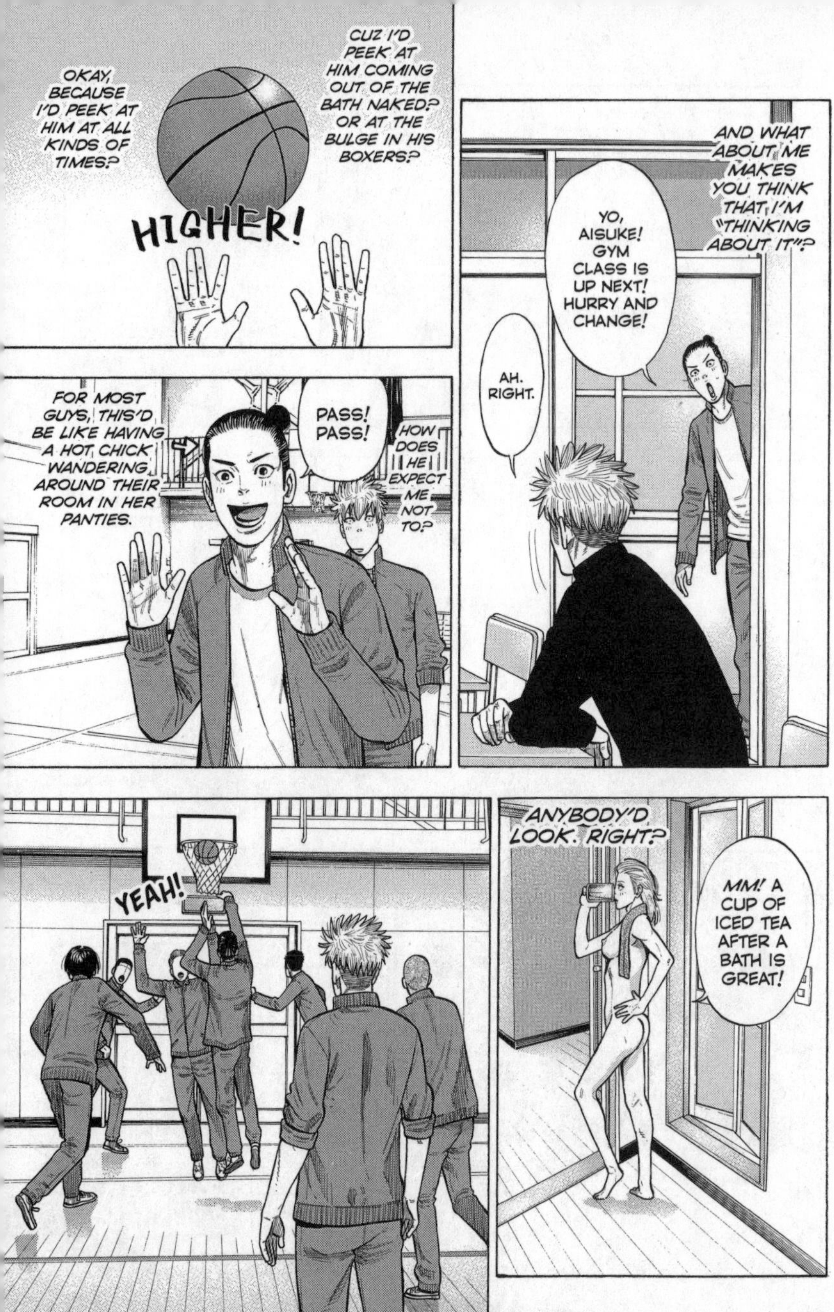
AND WHAT ABOUT ME MAKES YOU THINK THAT I'M "THINKING ABOUT IT"?
YO, AISUKE! GYM CLASS IS UP NEXT! HURRY AND CHANGE!
AH. RIGHT.
CUZ I'D PEEK AT HIM COMING OUT OF THE BATH NAKED? OR AT THE BULGE IN HIS BOXERS?
OKAY, BECAUSE I'D PEEK AT HIM AT ALL KINDS OF TIMES?
HIGHER!
HOW DOES HE EXPECT ME NOT TO?
PASS! PASS!
FOR MOST GUYS, THIS'D BE LIKE HAVING A HOT CHICK WANDERING AROUND THEIR ROOM IN HER PANTIES.
ANYBODY'D LOOK. RIGHT?
MM! A CUP OF ICED TEA AFTER A BATH IS GREAT!
YEAH!

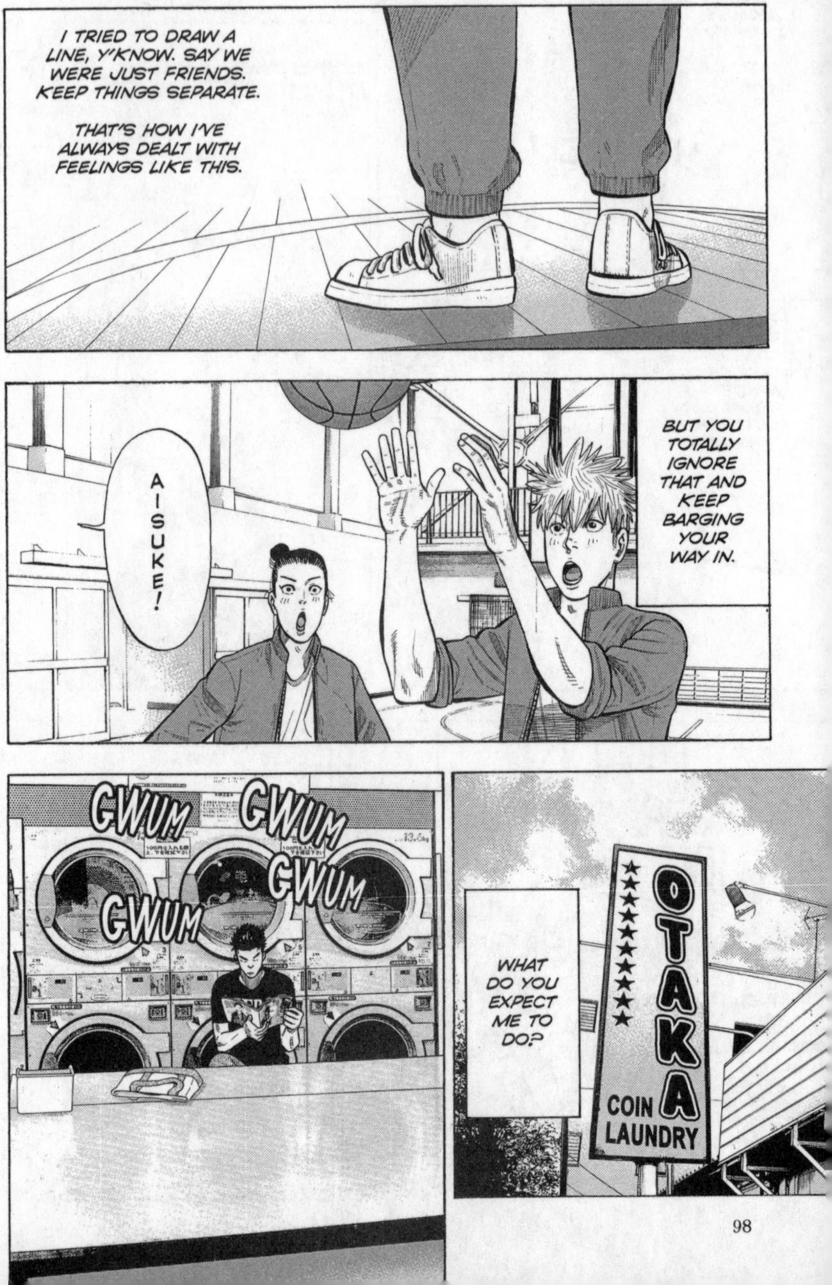
I TRIED TO DRAW A LINE, Y'KNOW. SAY WE WERE JUST FRIENDS. KEEP THINGS SEPARATE.
THAT'S HOW I'VE ALWAYS DEALT WITH FEELINGS LIKE THIS.
BUT YOU TOTALLY IGNORE THAT AND KEEP BARGING YOUR WAY IN.
AISUKE!
OTAKA
COIN LAUNDRY
WHAT DO YOU EXPECT ME TO DO?
GWUM
GWUM
GWUM
GWUM

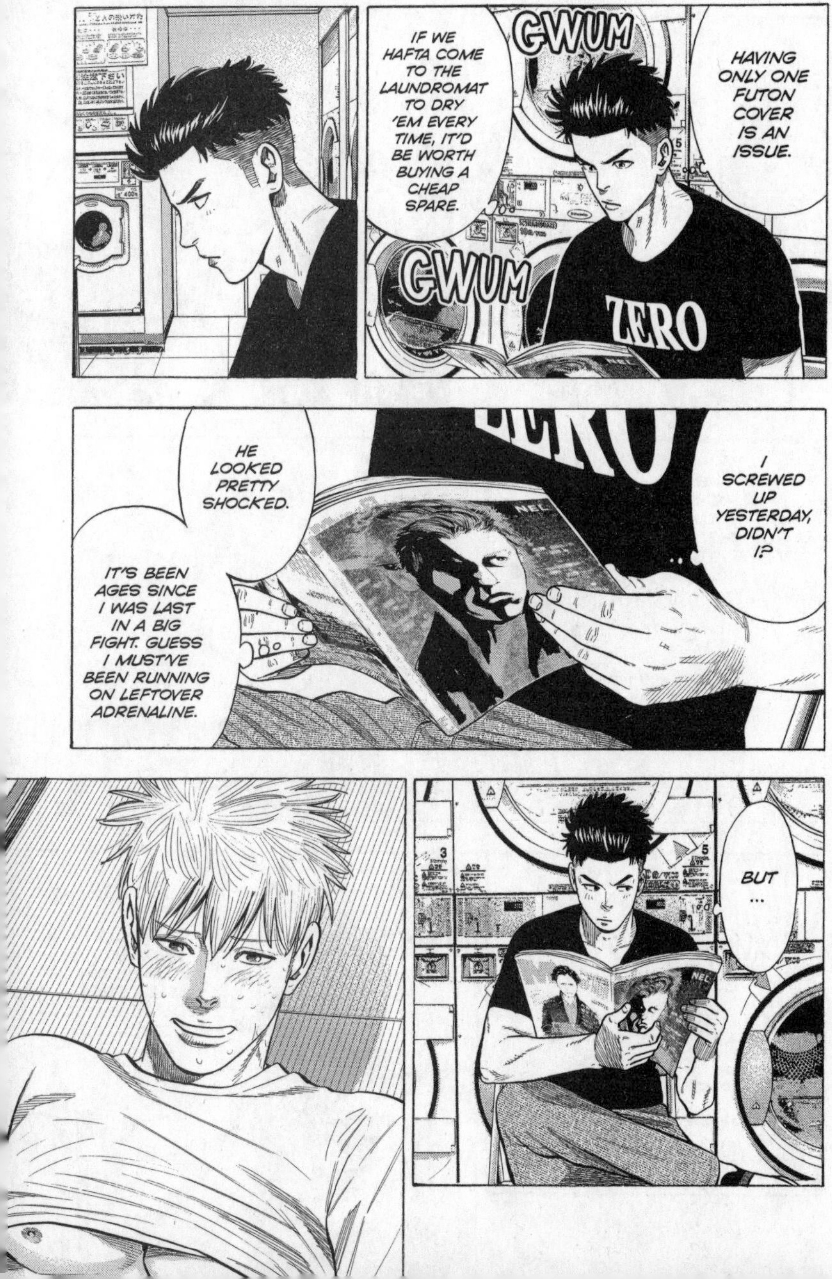
HAVING ONLY ONE FUTON COVER IS AN ISSUE.
GWUM
IF WE HAFTA COME TO THE LAUNDROMAT TO DRY 'EM EVERY TIME, IT'D BE WORTH BUYING A CHEAP SPARE.
ZERO
GWUM
I SCREWED UP YESTERDAY, DIDN'T I?
HE LOOKED PRETTY SHOCKED.
IT'S BEEN AGES SINCE I WAS LAST IN A BIG FIGHT. GUESS I MUST'VE BEEN RUNNING ON LEFTOVER ADRENALINE.
BUT ...

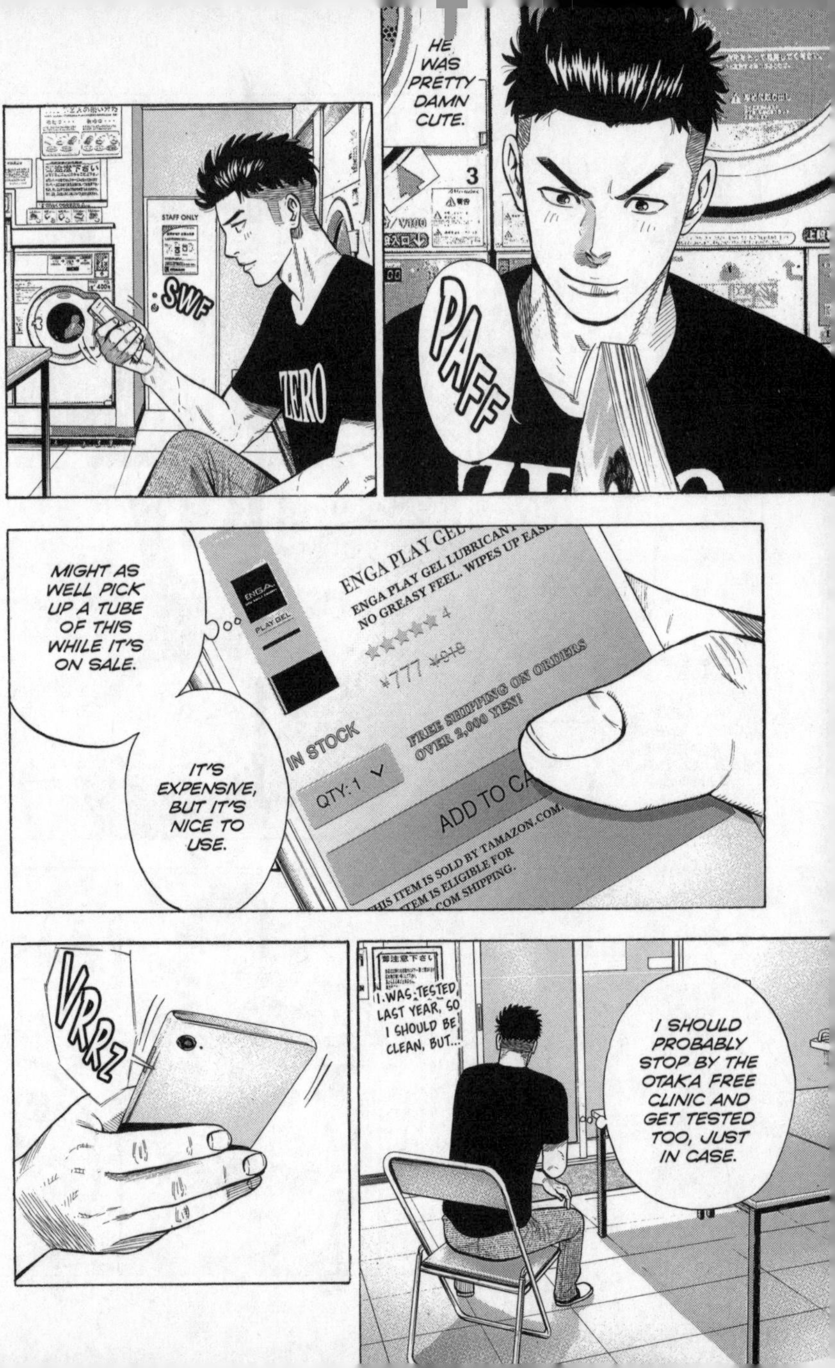
HE WAS PRETTY DAMN CUTE.
PAFF
SWF
MIGHT AS WELL PICK UP A TUBE OF THIS WHILE IT'S ON SALE.
ENGA PLAY GEL
ENGA PLAY GEL LUBRICANT
NO GREASY FEEL. WIPES UP EASI
¥777 ¥918
FREE SHIPPING ON ORDERS OVER 2,000 YEN!
IN STOCK
QTY: 1
ADD TO CA
TAMAZON.COM.
THIS ITEM IS SOLD BY TAMAZON.COM
ITEM IS ELIGIBLE FOR
.COM SHIPPING.
IT'S EXPENSIVE, BUT IT'S NICE TO USE.
I WAS TESTED LAST YEAR, SO I SHOULD BE CLEAN, BUT...
I SHOULD PROBABLY STOP BY THE OTAKA FREE CLINIC AND GET TESTED TOO, JUST IN CASE.
VRRZ

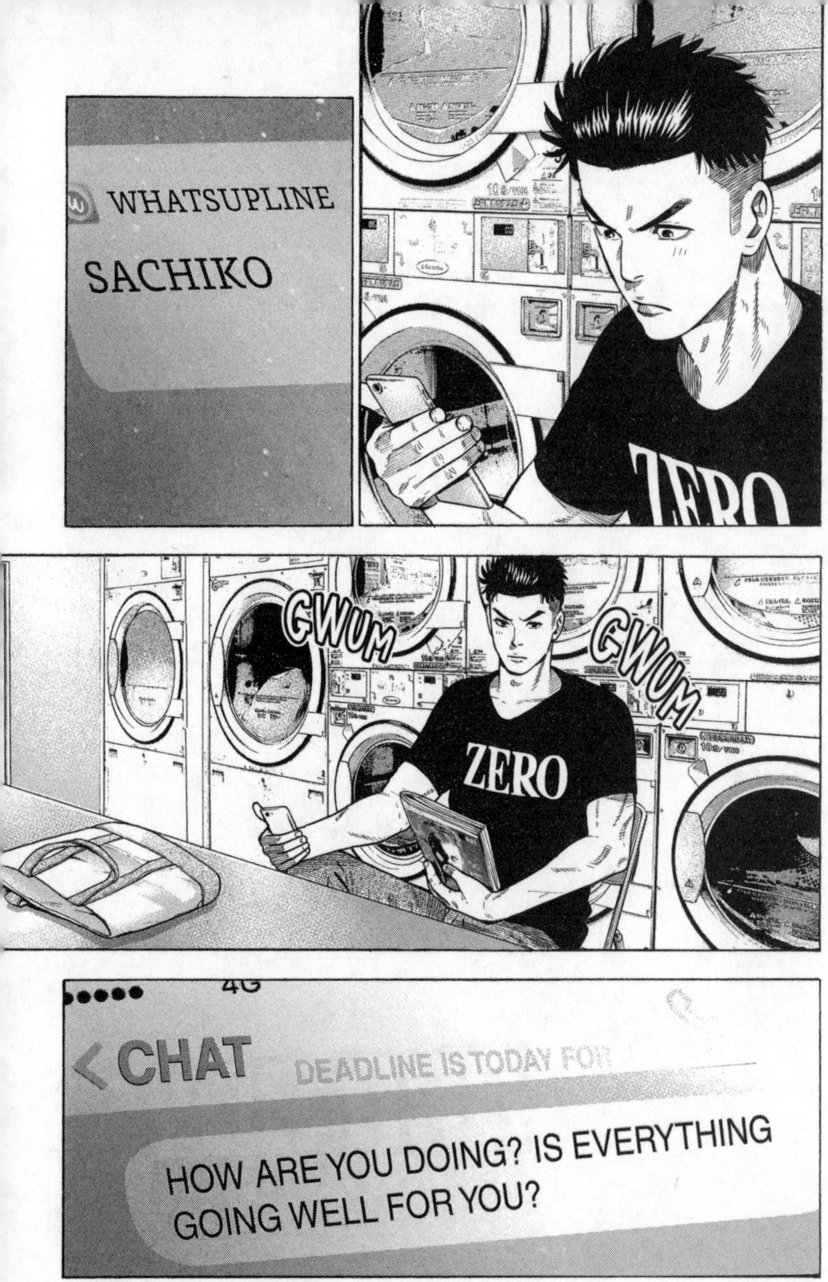
WHATSUPLINE
SACHIKO
GWUM
GWUM
4G
CHAT
DEADLINE IS TODAY FOR
HOW ARE YOU DOING? IS EVERYTHING GOING WELL FOR YOU?

BAD BOYS
HAPPY HOME

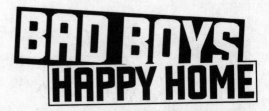

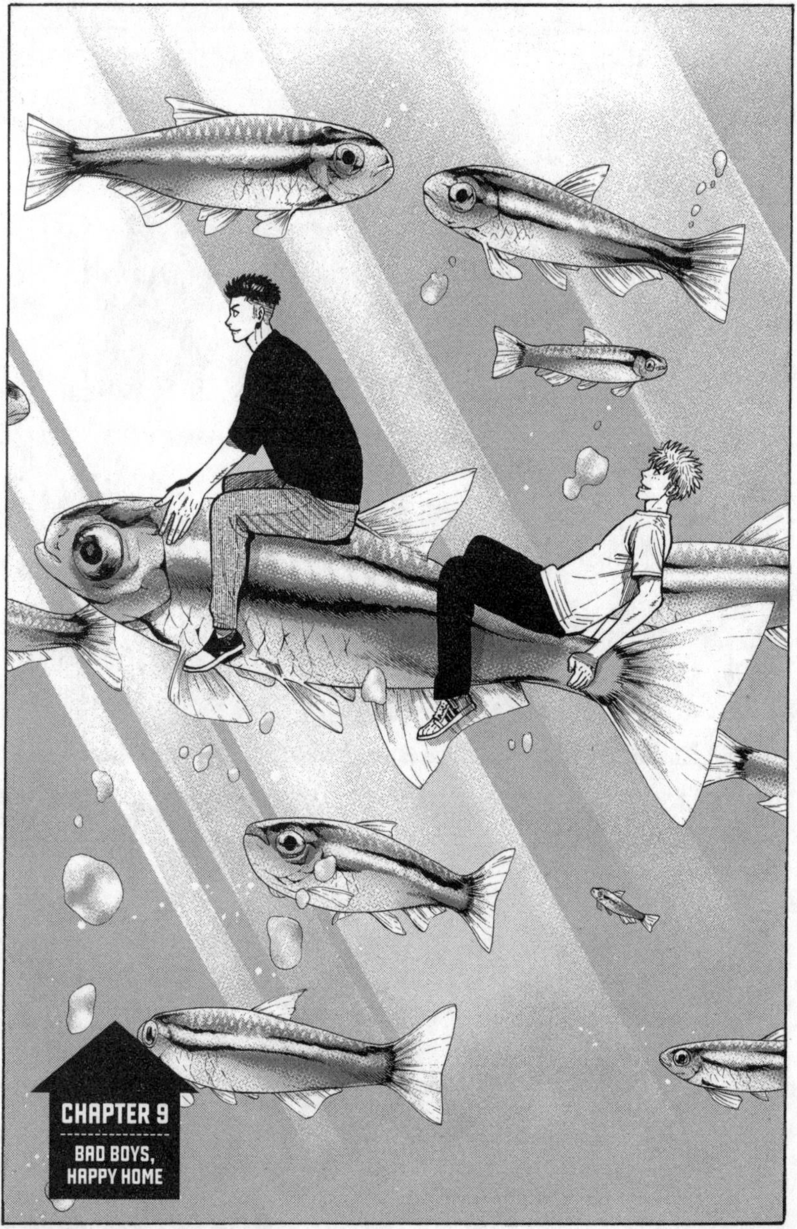
CHAPTER 9
BAD BOYS,
HAPPY HOME

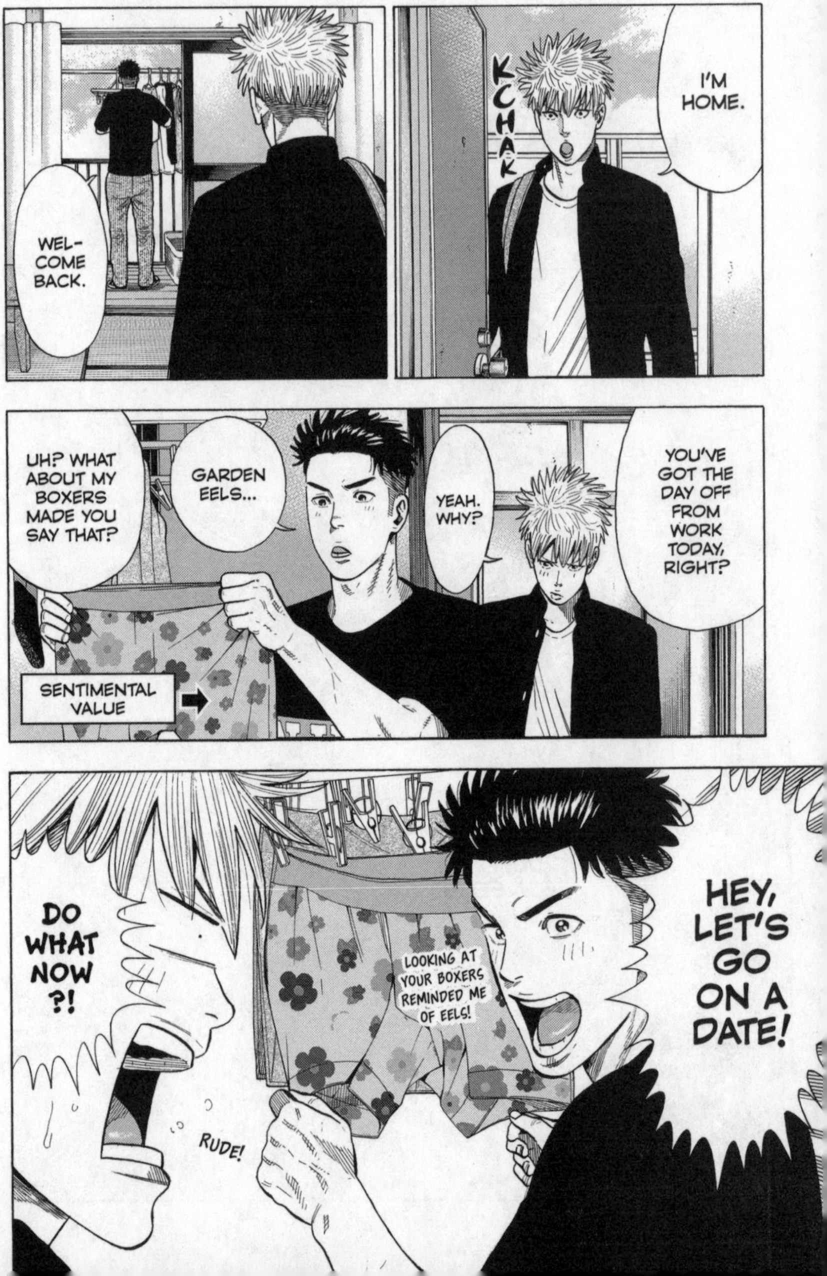
KCHAK
I'M HOME.
WEL-COME BACK.
YOU'VE GOT THE DAY OFF FROM WORK TODAY, RIGHT?
YEAH. WHY?
GARDEN EELS...
UH? WHAT ABOUT MY BOXERS MADE YOU SAY THAT?
SENTIMENTAL VALUE
HEY, LET'S GO ON A DATE!
LOOKING AT YOUR BOXERS REMINDED ME OF EELS!
DO WHAT NOW?!
RUDE!

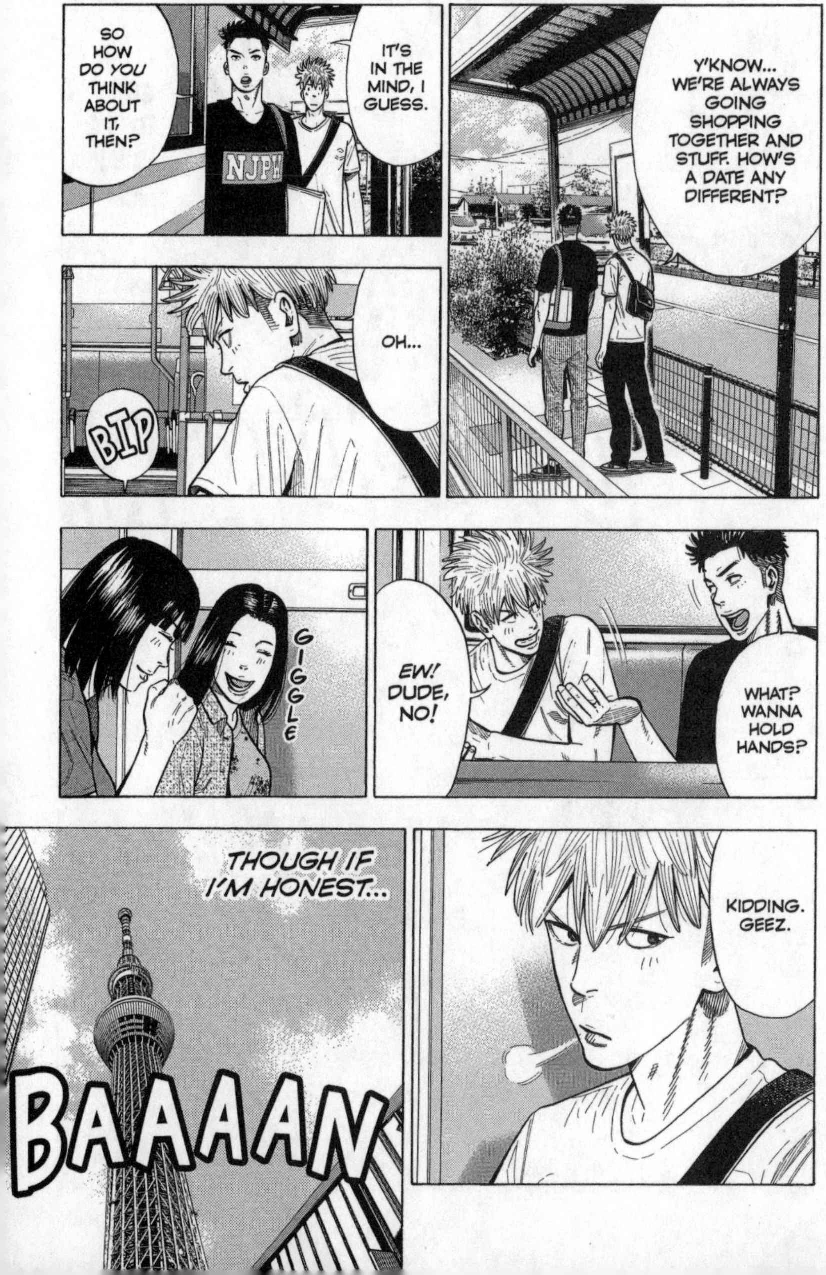
Y'KNOW... WE'RE ALWAYS GOING SHOPPING TOGETHER AND STUFF. HOW'S A DATE ANY DIFFERENT?
IT'S IN THE MIND, I GUESS.
SO HOW DO *YOU* THINK ABOUT IT, THEN?
NJPW
OH...
BIP
WHAT? WANNA HOLD HANDS?
EW! DUDE, NO!
GIGGLE
KIDDING. GEEZ.
THOUGH IF I'M HONEST...
BAAAAN

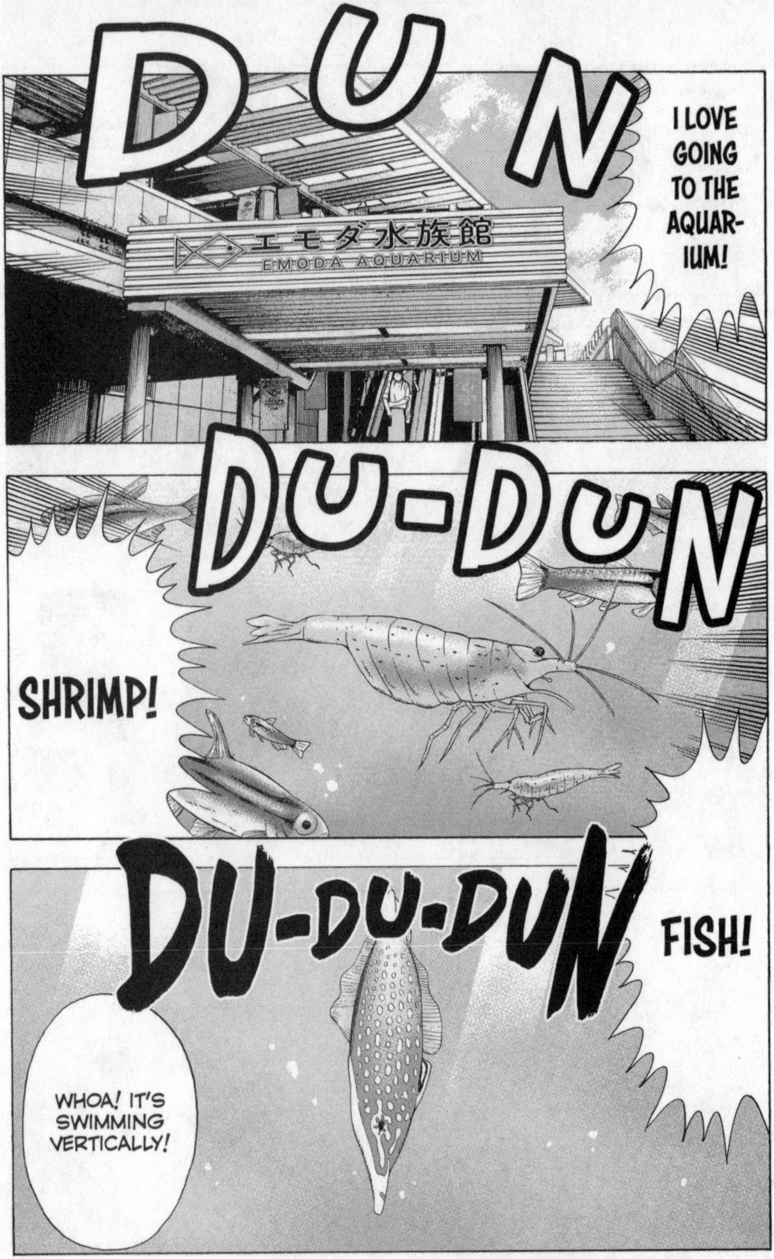
DUN
I LOVE GOING TO THE AQUARIUM!
エモダ水族館
EMODA AQUARIUM
DU-DUN
SHRIMP!
DU-DU-DUN
FISH!
WHOA! IT'S SWIMMING VERTICALLY!

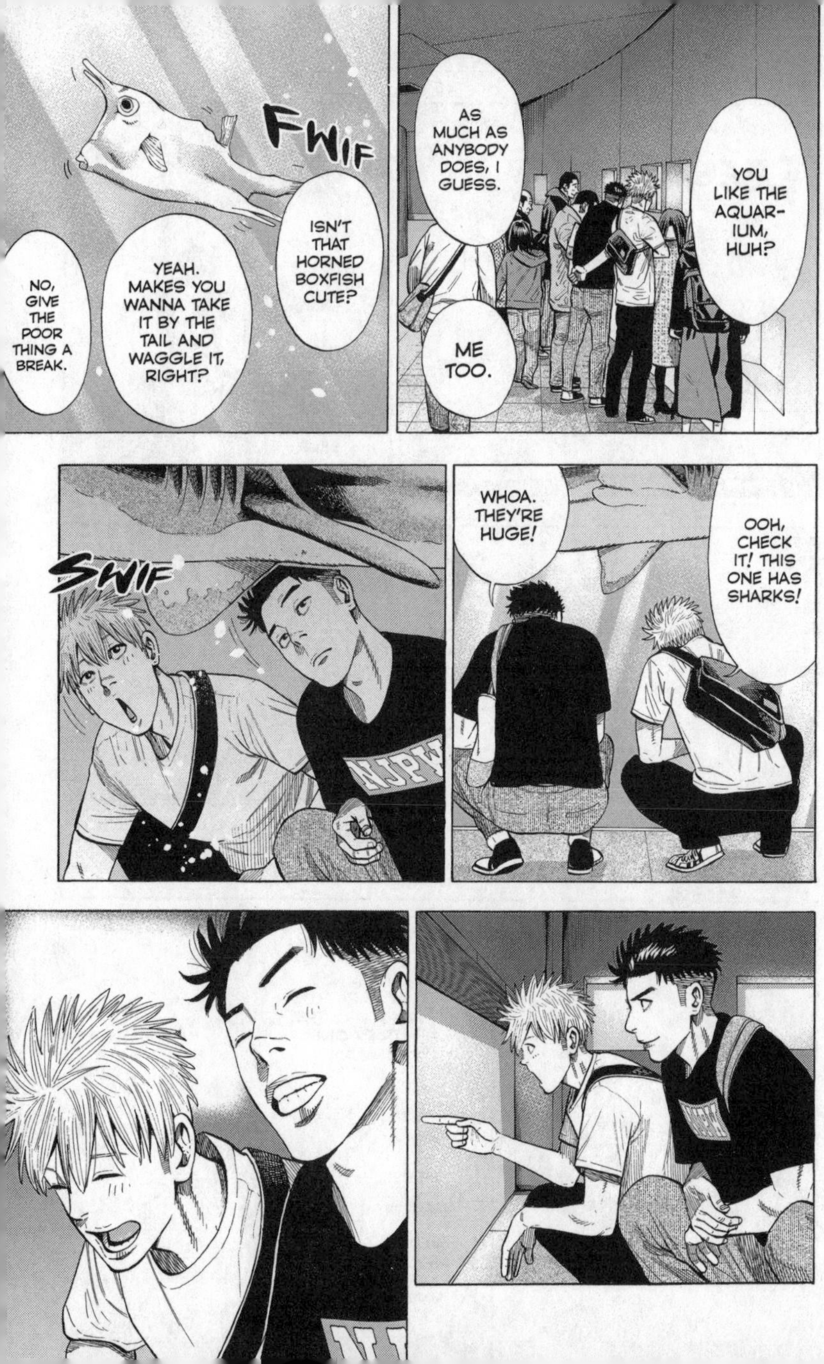
YOU LIKE THE AQUAR-IUM, HUH?
AS MUCH AS ANYBODY DOES, I GUESS.
ME TOO.
FWIF
ISN'T THAT HORNED BOXFISH CUTE?
YEAH. MAKES YOU WANNA TAKE IT BY THE TAIL AND WAGGLE IT, RIGHT?
NO, GIVE THE POOR THING A BREAK.
OOH, CHECK IT! THIS ONE HAS SHARKS!
WHOA. THEY'RE HUGE!
SWIF

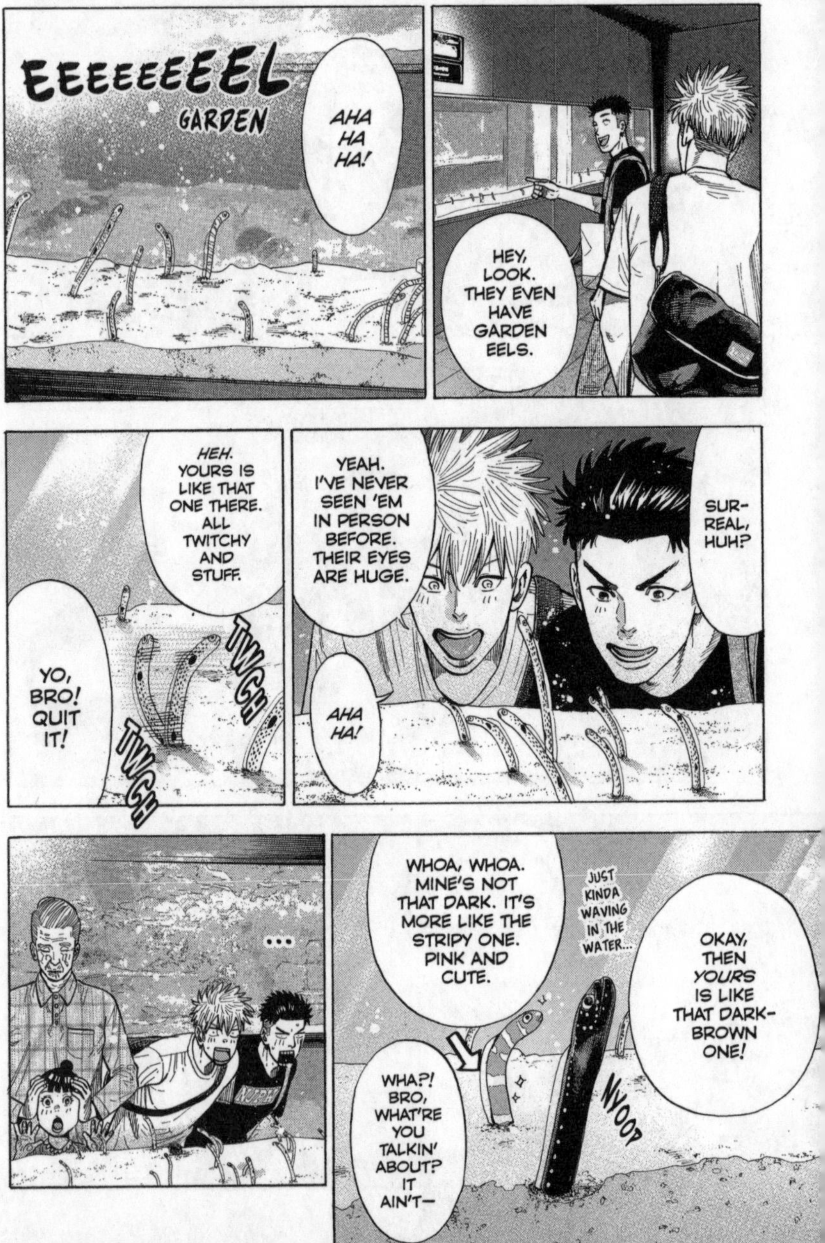
HEY, LOOK. THEY EVEN HAVE GARDEN EELS.
AHA HA HA!
EEEEEEEEL
GARDEN
SUR-REAL, HUH?
YEAH. I'VE NEVER SEEN 'EM IN PERSON BEFORE. THEIR EYES ARE HUGE.
AHA HA!
HEH. YOURS IS LIKE THAT ONE THERE. ALL TWITCHY AND STUFF.
YO, BRO! QUIT IT!
TWICH
TWICH
OKAY, THEN YOURS IS LIKE THAT DARK-BROWN ONE!
JUST KINDA WAVING IN THE WATER...
WHOA, WHOA. MINE'S NOT THAT DARK. IT'S MORE LIKE THE STRIPY ONE. PINK AND CUTE.
NYOOP
WHA?! BRO, WHAT'RE YOU TALKIN' ABOUT? IT AIN'T—
...

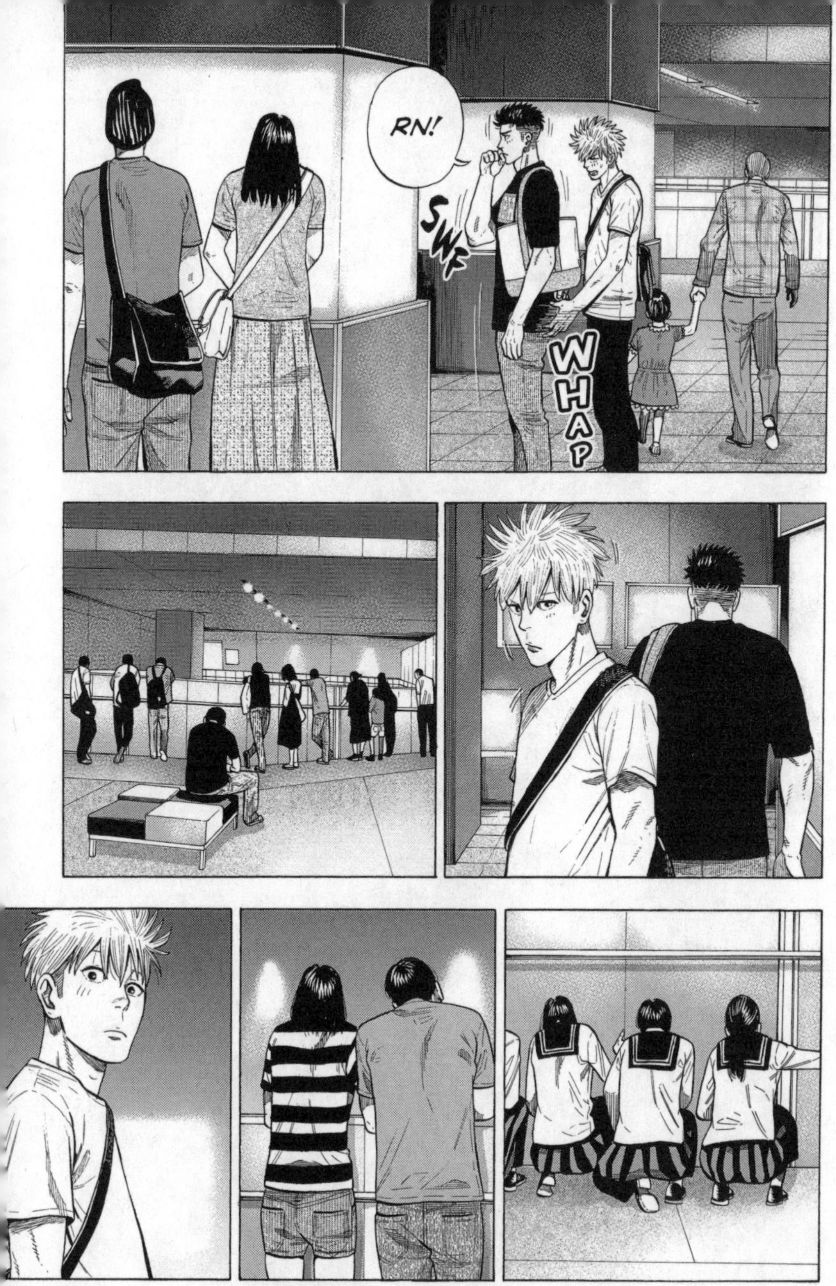
WHAP
RN!
SWF

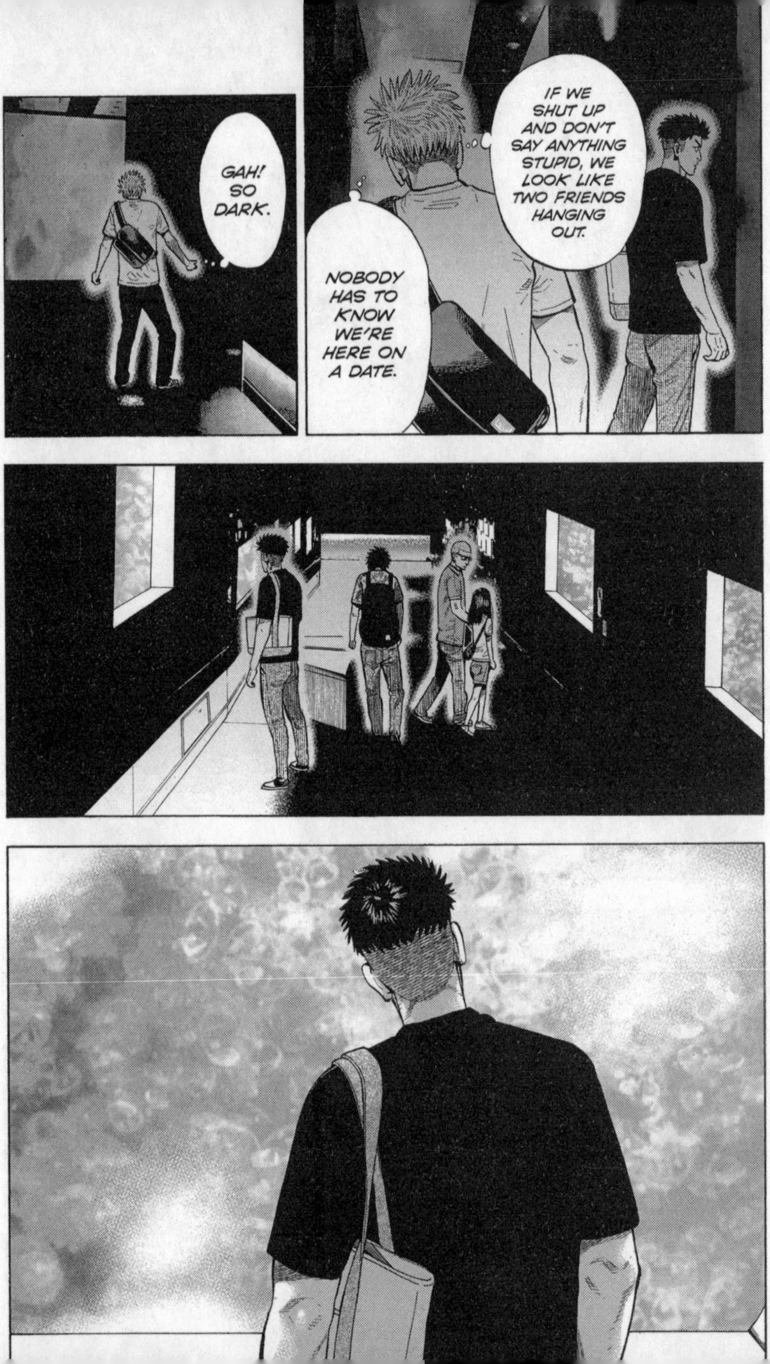
IF WE SHUT UP AND DON'T SAY ANYTHING STUPID, WE LOOK LIKE TWO FRIENDS HANGING OUT.
NOBODY HAS TO KNOW WE'RE HERE ON A DATE.
GAH! SO DARK.

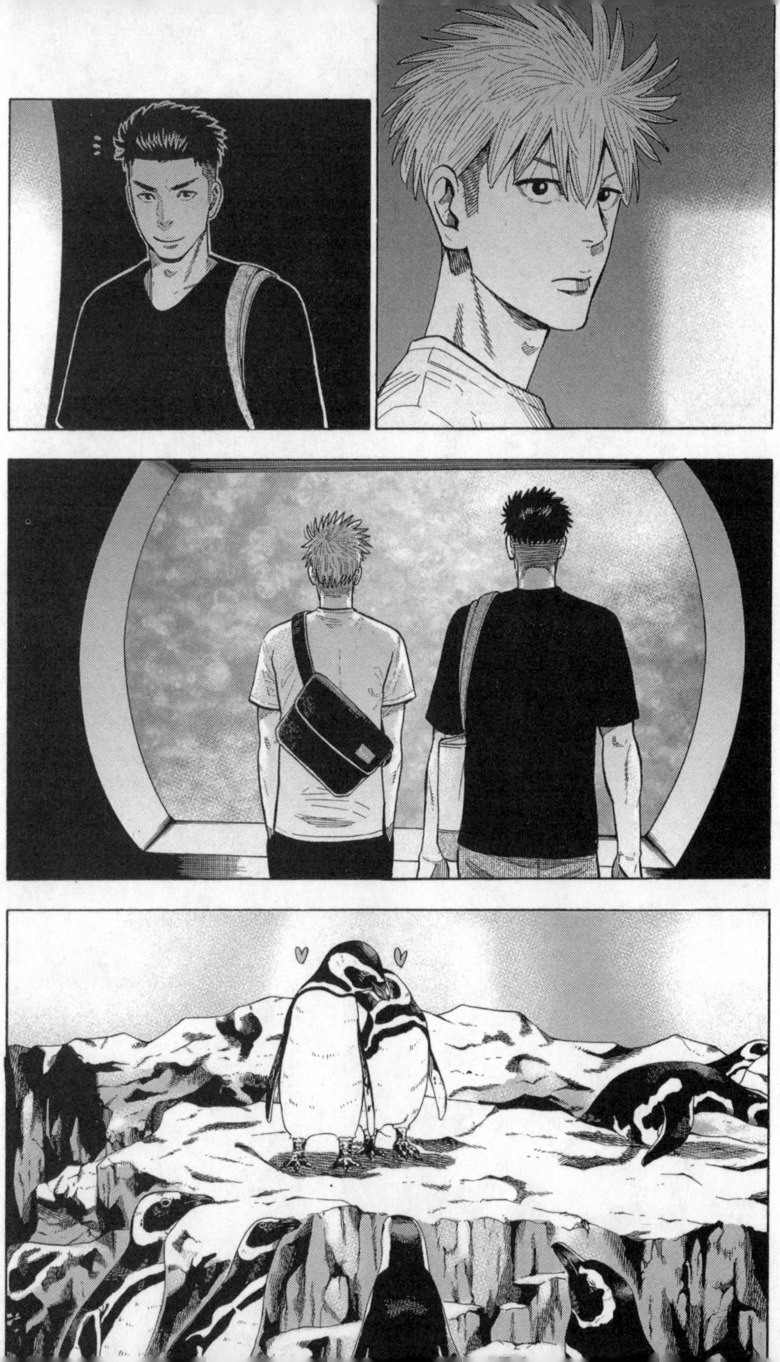

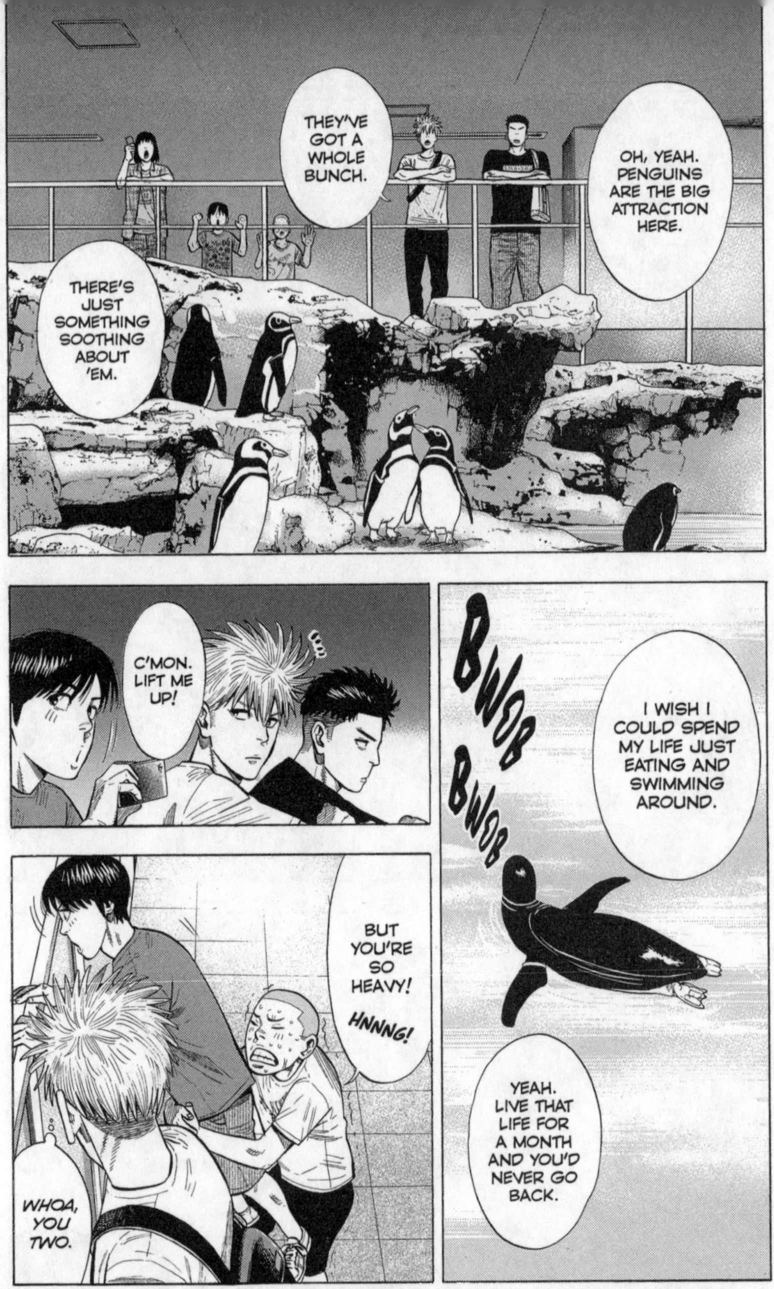
OH, YEAH. PENGUINS ARE THE BIG ATTRACTION HERE.
THEY'VE GOT A WHOLE BUNCH.
THERE'S JUST SOMETHING SOOTHING ABOUT 'EM.
BWOB
BWOB
I WISH I COULD SPEND MY LIFE JUST EATING AND SWIMMING AROUND.
YEAH. LIVE THAT LIFE FOR A MONTH AND YOU'D NEVER GO BACK.
C'MON. LIFT ME UP!
BUT YOU'RE SO HEAVY!
HNNNG!
WHOA, YOU TWO.

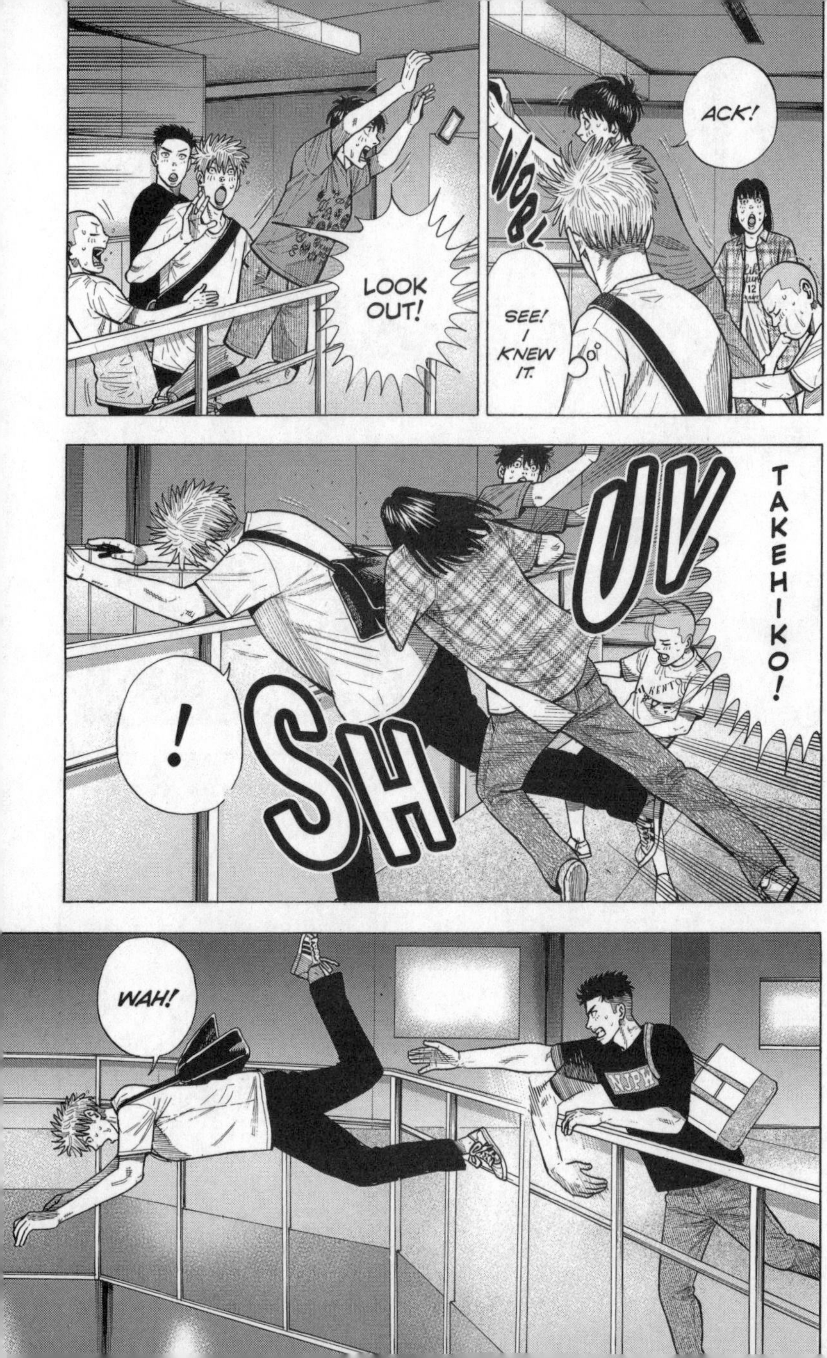
ACK!
WOBL
SEE! I KNEW IT.
LOOK OUT!
TAKEHIKO!
UV
!
SH
WAH!

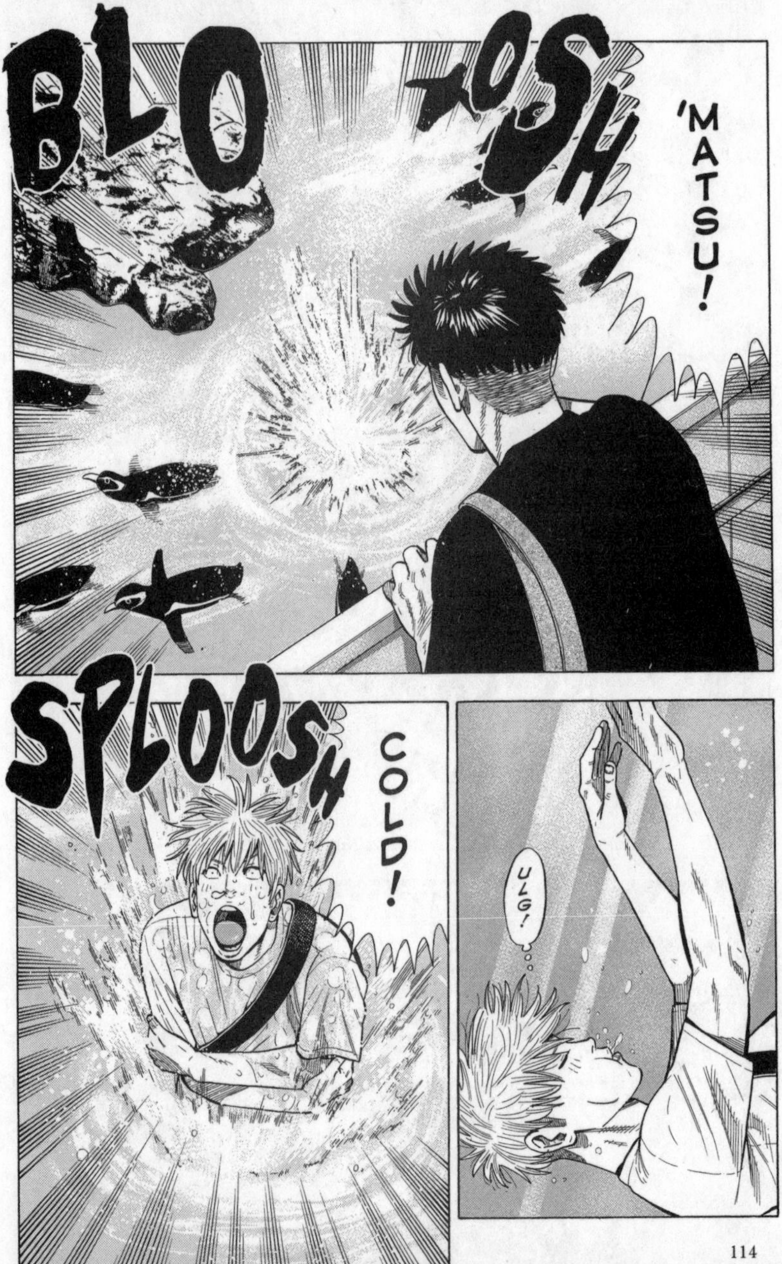
BLOOSH
'MATSU!
ULG!
SPLOOSH
COLD!

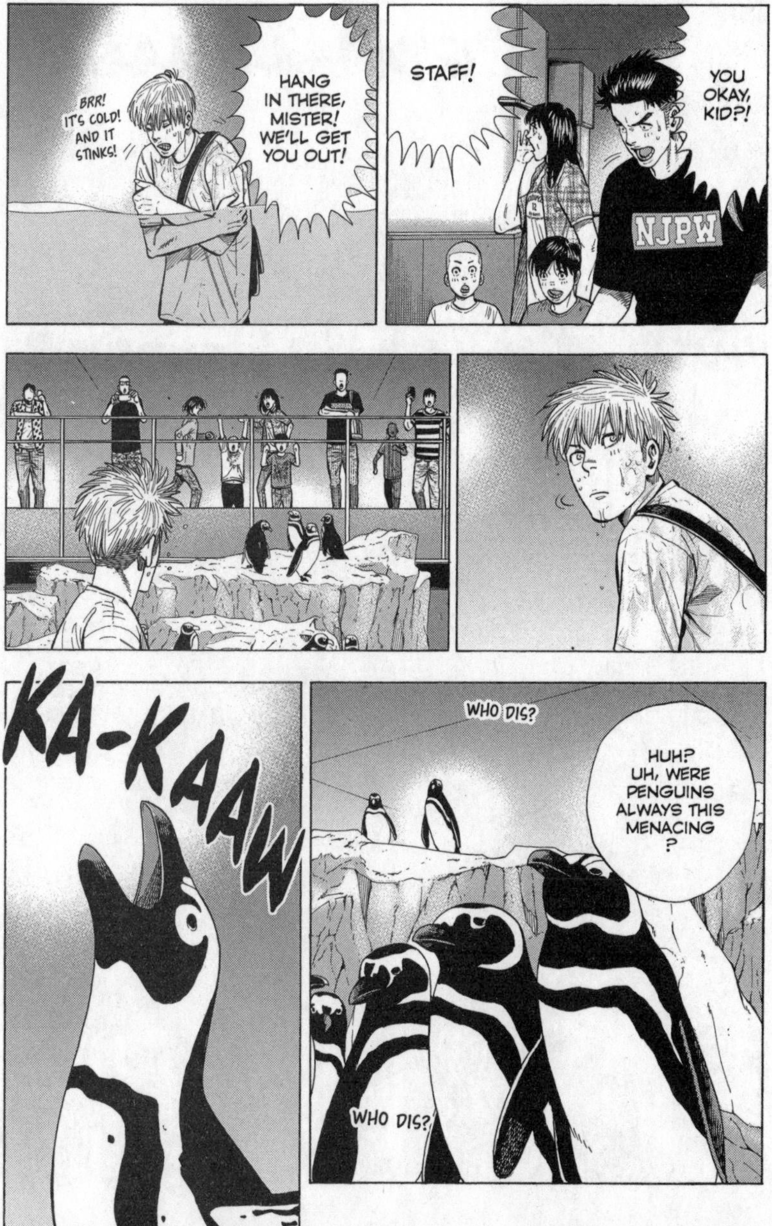
YOU OKAY, KID?!
STAFF!
HANG IN THERE, MISTER! WE'LL GET YOU OUT!
BRR! IT'S COLD! AND IT STINKS!
HUH? UH, WERE PENGUINS ALWAYS THIS MENACING?
WHO DIS?
WHO DIS?
KA-KAAAW

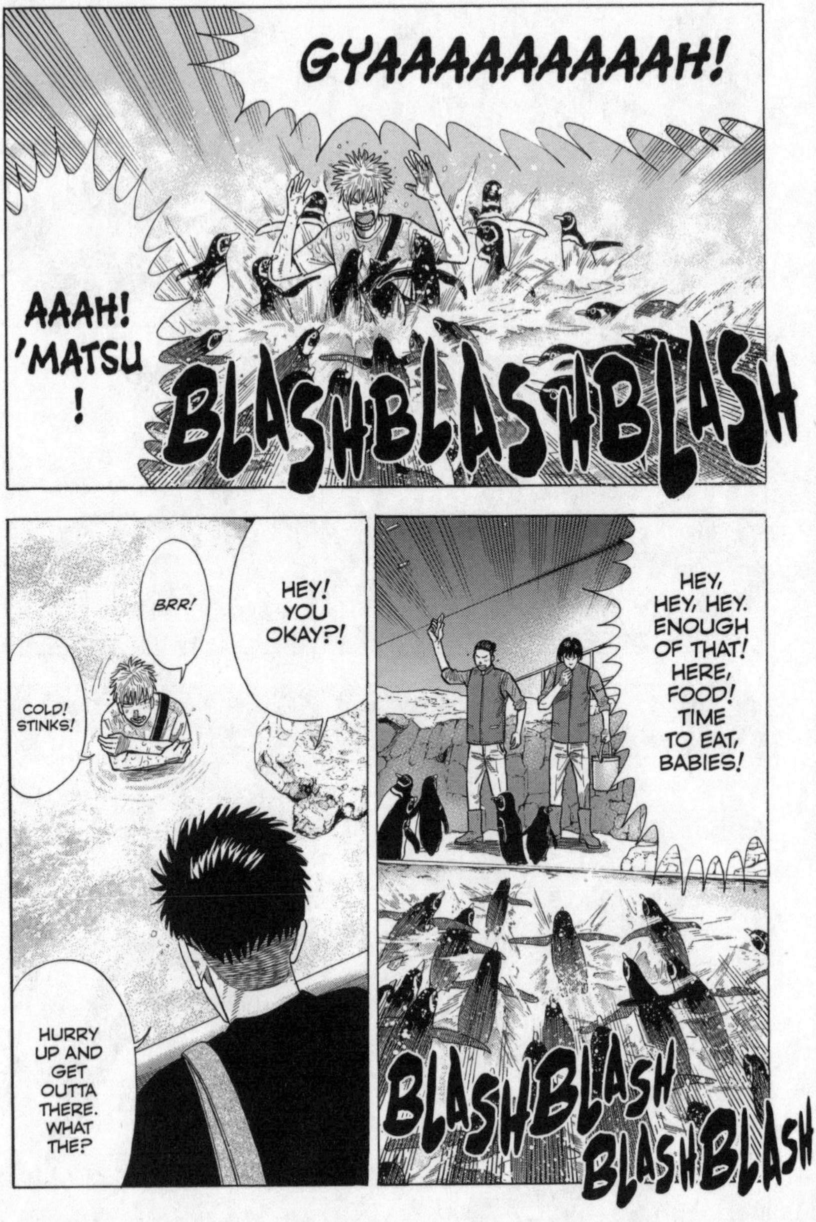
GYAAAAAAAAAH!
BLASHBLASHBLASH
AAAH! 'MATSU!
HEY, HEY, HEY. ENOUGH OF THAT! HERE, FOOD! TIME TO EAT, BABIES!
BLASHBLASH
BLASHBLASH
HEY! YOU OKAY?!
BRR!
COLD! STINKS!
HURRY UP AND GET OUTTA THERE. WHAT THE?

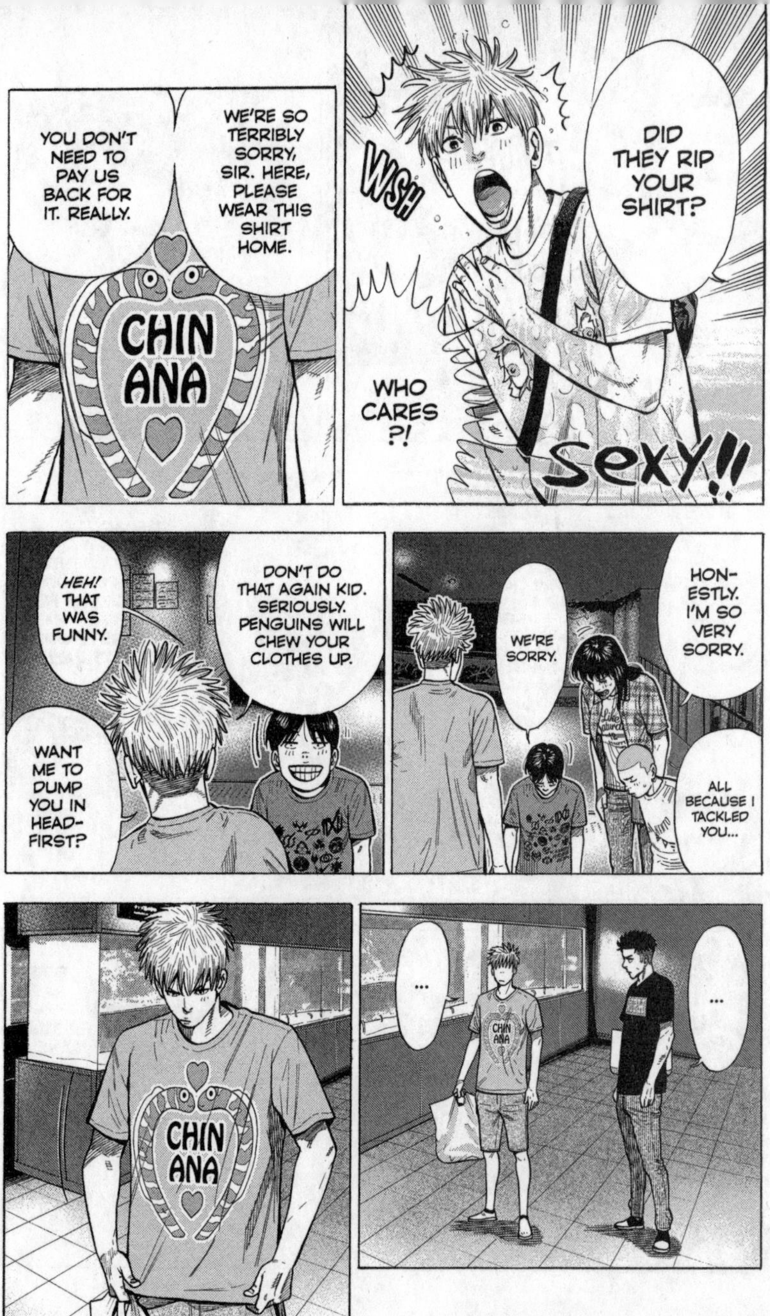
DID THEY RIP YOUR SHIRT?
WSH
WHO CARES?!
SEXY!!
WE'RE SO TERRIBLY SORRY, SIR. HERE, PLEASE WEAR THIS SHIRT HOME.
YOU DON'T NEED TO PAY US BACK FOR IT. REALLY.
CHIN ANA
HON-ESTLY. I'M SO VERY SORRY.
WE'RE SORRY.
ALL BECAUSE I TACKLED YOU...
DON'T DO THAT AGAIN KID. SERIOUSLY. PENGUINS WILL CHEW YOUR CLOTHES UP.
HEH! THAT WAS FUNNY.
WANT ME TO DUMP YOU IN HEAD-FIRST?
...
...
CHIN ANA
CHIN ANA

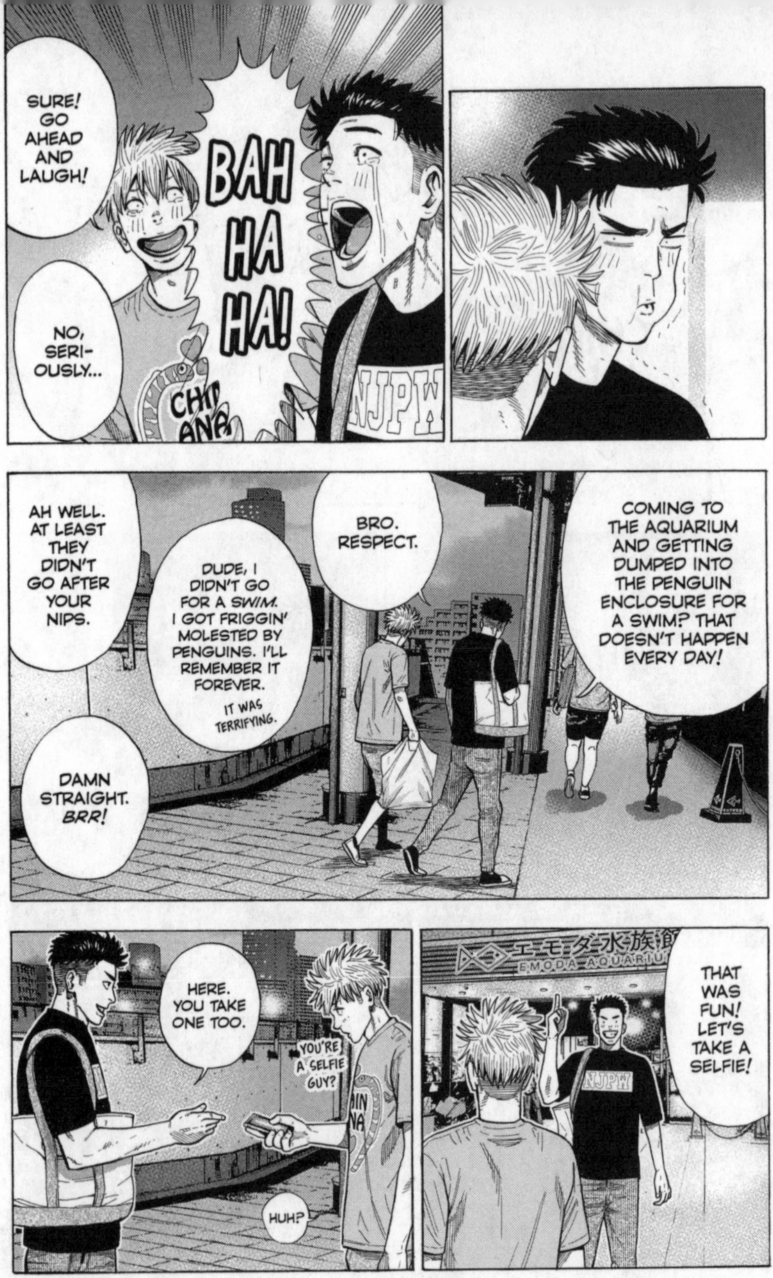
BAH HA HA!
SURE! GO AHEAD AND LAUGH!
NO, SERIOUSLY...
COMING TO THE AQUARIUM AND GETTING DUMPED INTO THE PENGUIN ENCLOSURE FOR A SWIM? THAT DOESN'T HAPPEN EVERY DAY!
BRO. RESPECT.
DUDE, I DIDN'T GO FOR A *SWIM*. I GOT FRIGGIN' MOLESTED BY PENGUINS. I'LL REMEMBER IT FOREVER.
IT WAS TERRIFYING.
AH WELL. AT LEAST THEY DIDN'T GO AFTER YOUR NIPS.
DAMN STRAIGHT. *BRR!*
エモダ水族館
THAT WAS FUN! LET'S TAKE A SELFIE!
HERE. YOU TAKE ONE TOO.
YOU'RE A SELFIE GUY?
HUH?

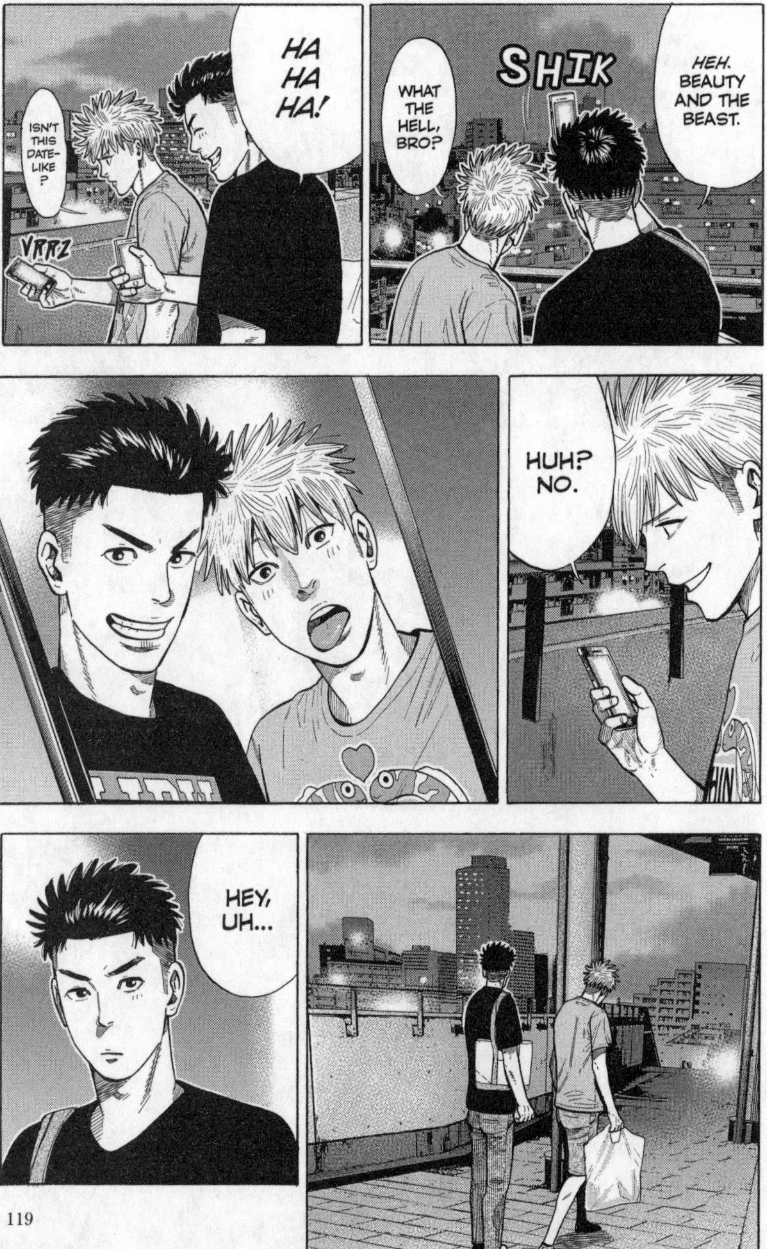
HEH. BEAUTY AND THE BEAST.
SHIK
WHAT THE HELL, BRO?
HA HA HA!
ISN'T THIS DATE-LIKE?
VRRZ
HUH? NO.
HEY, UH...

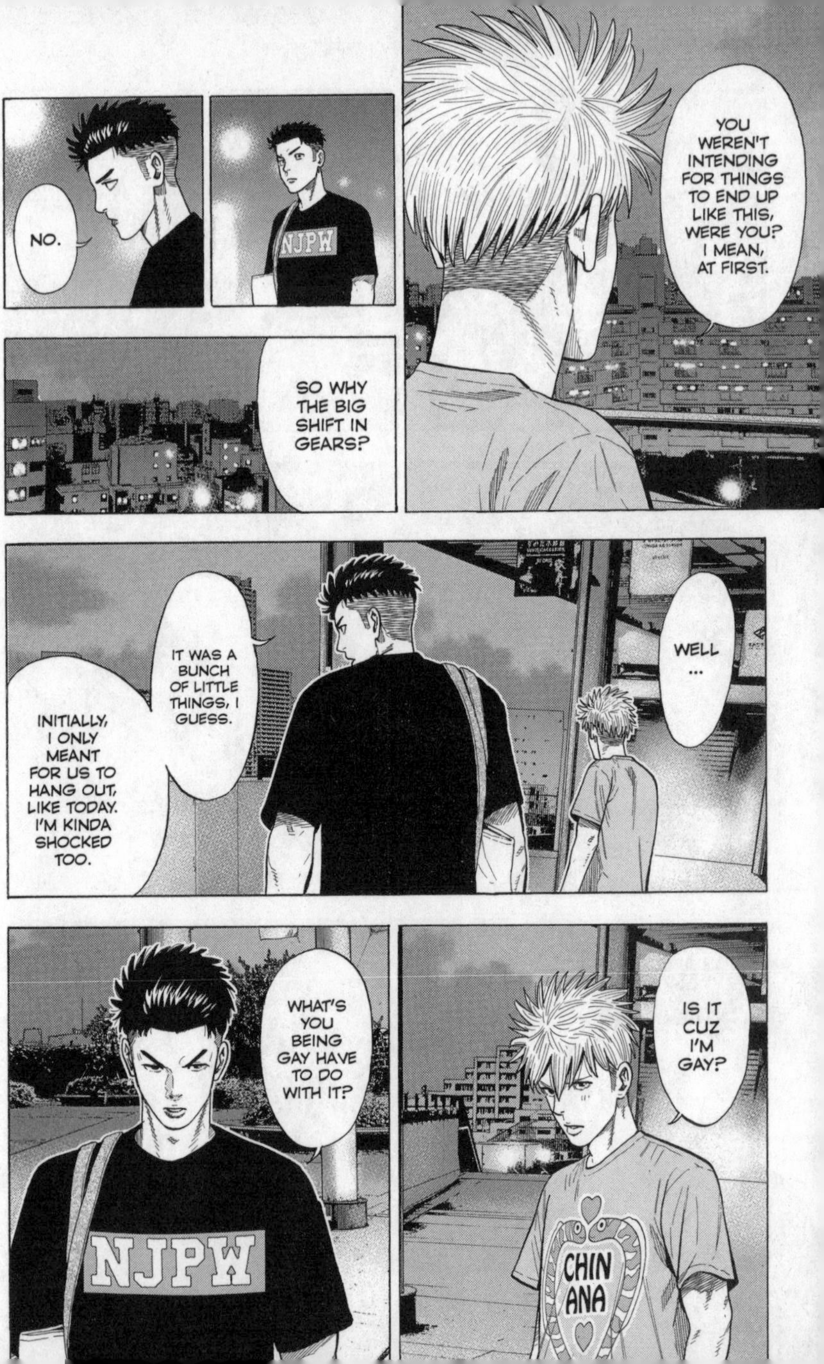
YOU WEREN'T INTENDING FOR THINGS TO END UP LIKE THIS, WERE YOU? I MEAN, AT FIRST.
NJPW
NO.
SO WHY THE BIG SHIFT IN GEARS?
WELL ...
IT WAS A BUNCH OF LITTLE THINGS, I GUESS.
INITIALLY, I ONLY MEANT FOR US TO HANG OUT, LIKE TODAY. I'M KINDA SHOCKED TOO.
IS IT CUZ I'M GAY?
CHIN ANA
WHAT'S YOU BEING GAY HAVE TO DO WITH IT?
NJPW

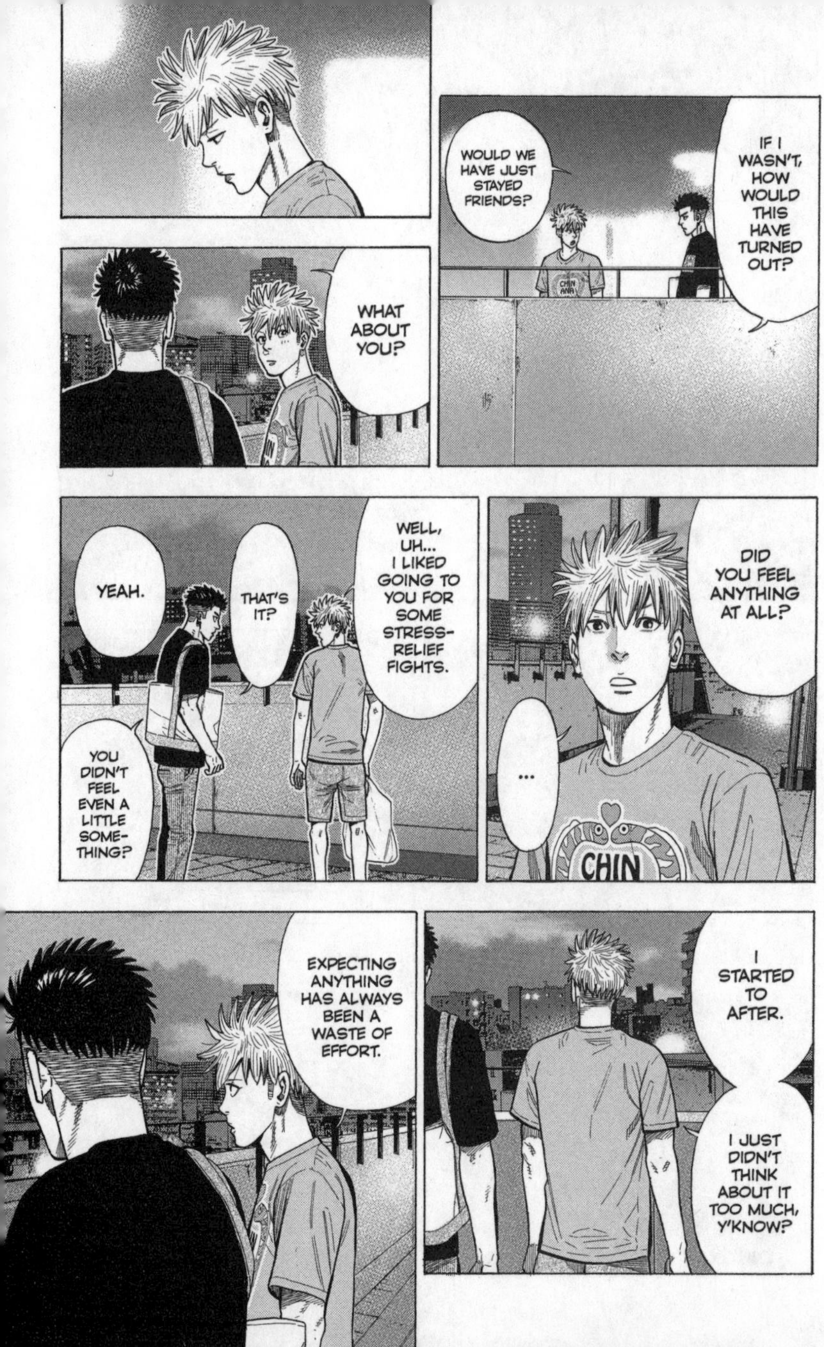
IF I WASN'T, HOW WOULD THIS HAVE TURNED OUT?
WOULD WE HAVE JUST STAYED FRIENDS?
WHAT ABOUT YOU?
DID YOU FEEL ANYTHING AT ALL?
...
CHIN
WELL, UH... I LIKED GOING TO YOU FOR SOME STRESS-RELIEF FIGHTS.
THAT'S IT?
YEAH.
YOU DIDN'T FEEL EVEN A LITTLE SOMETHING?
I STARTED TO AFTER.
I JUST DIDN'T THINK ABOUT IT TOO MUCH, Y'KNOW?
EXPECTING ANYTHING HAS ALWAYS BEEN A WASTE OF EFFORT.

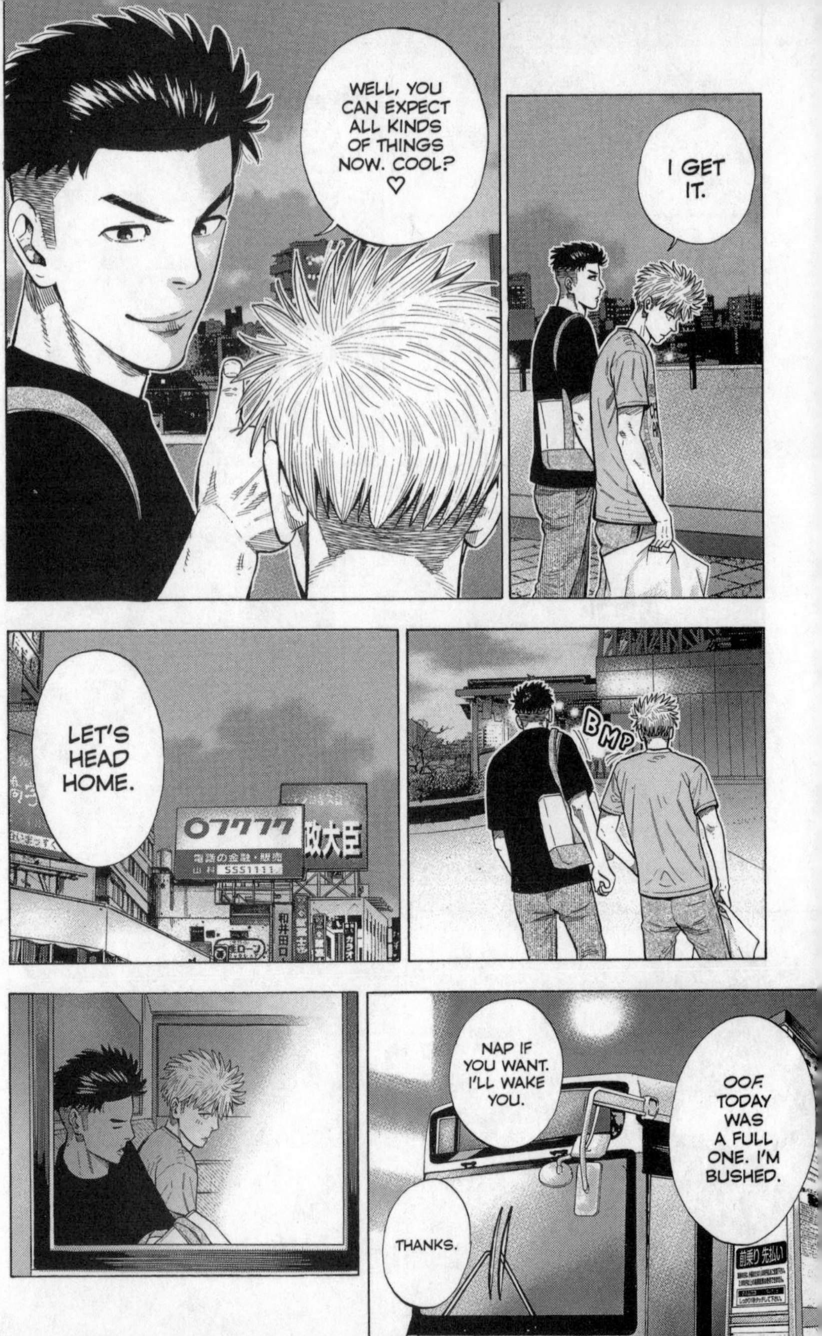
WELL, YOU CAN EXPECT ALL KINDS OF THINGS NOW. COOL? ♡
I GET IT.
BMP
LET'S HEAD HOME.
OOF. TODAY WAS A FULL ONE. I'M BUSHED.
NAP IF YOU WANT. I'LL WAKE YOU.
THANKS.
前乗り 先払い

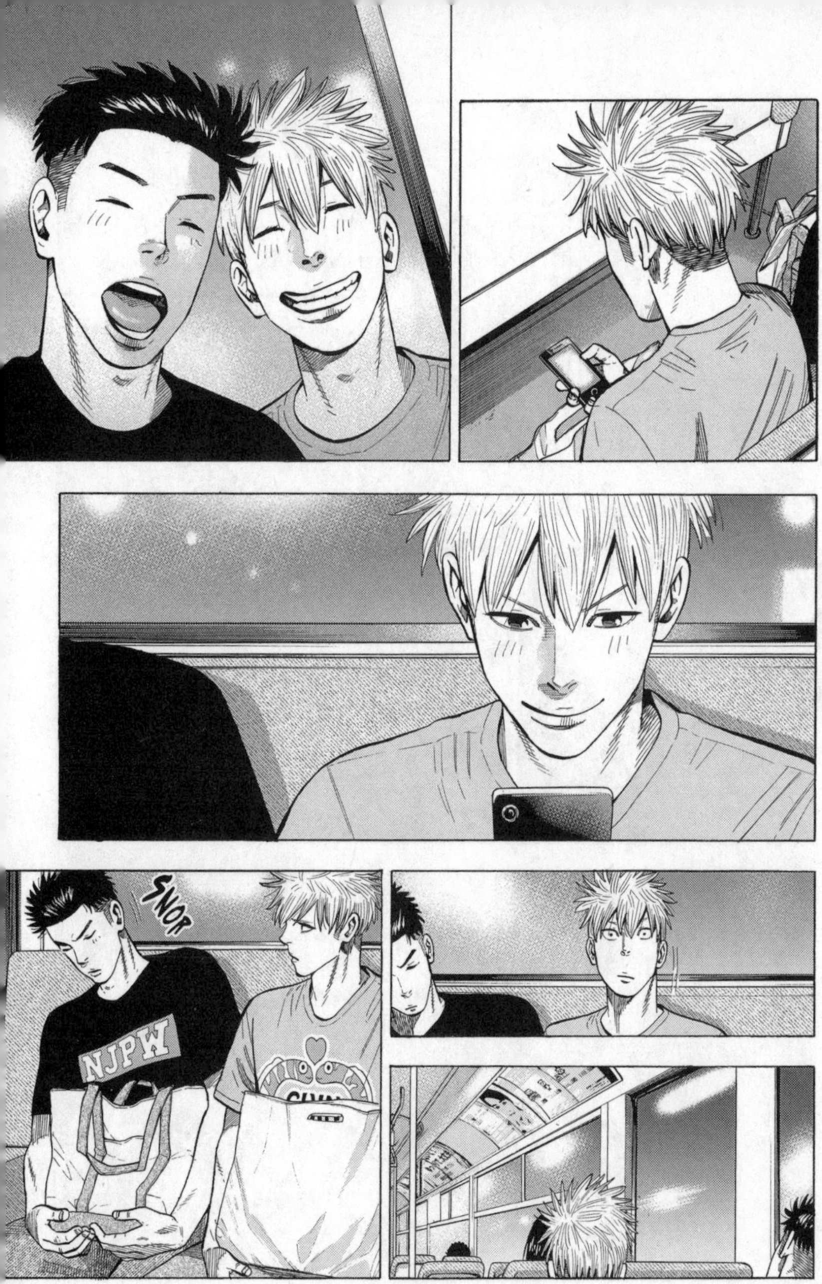
SNOR
NJPW

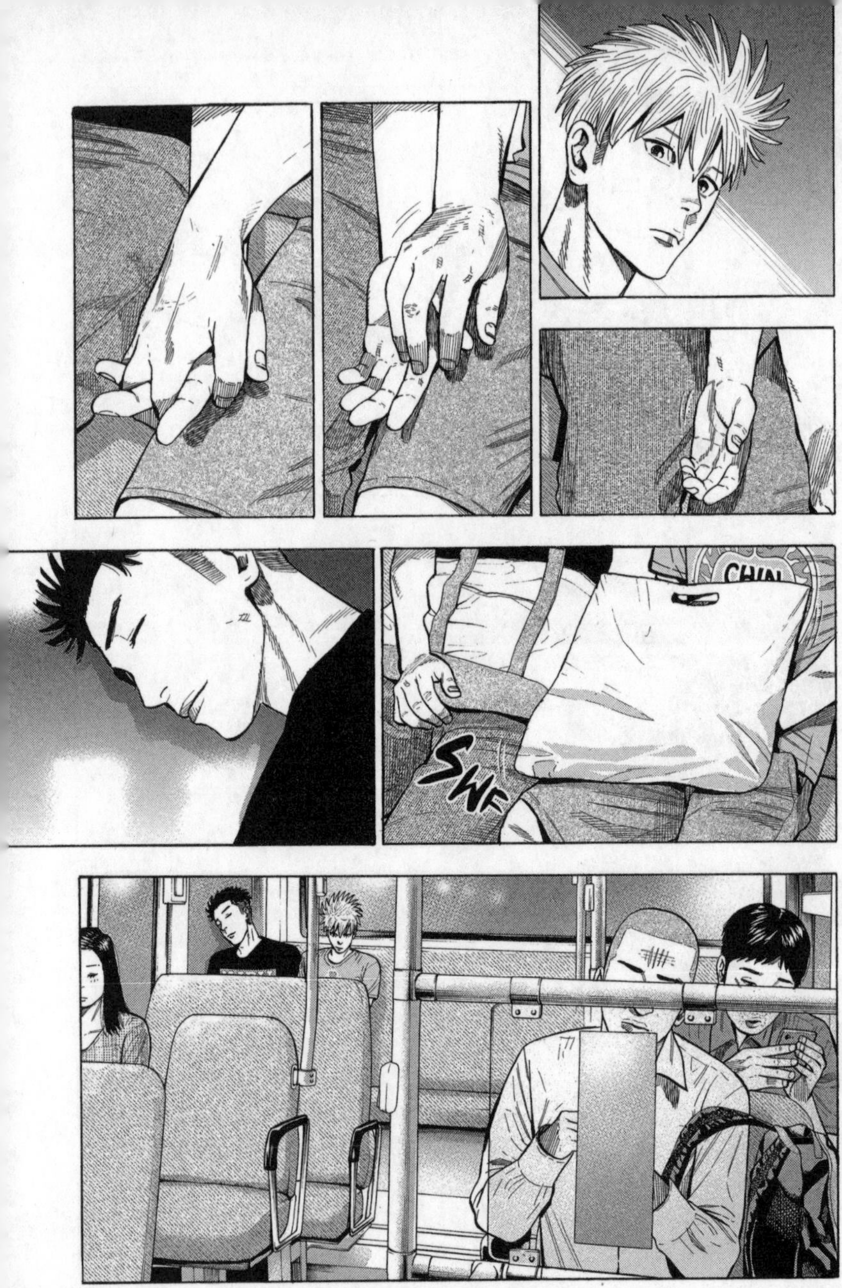
CHIN
SWF

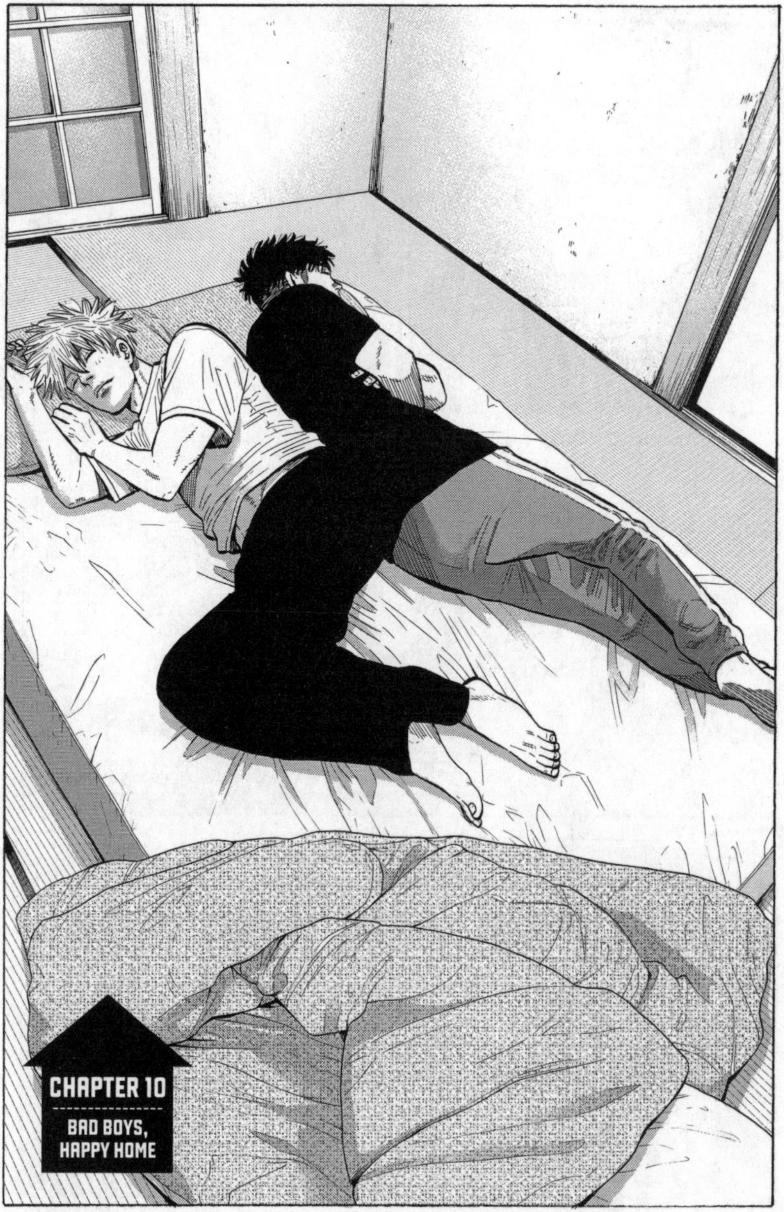
CHAPTER 10
BAD BOYS, HAPPY HOME

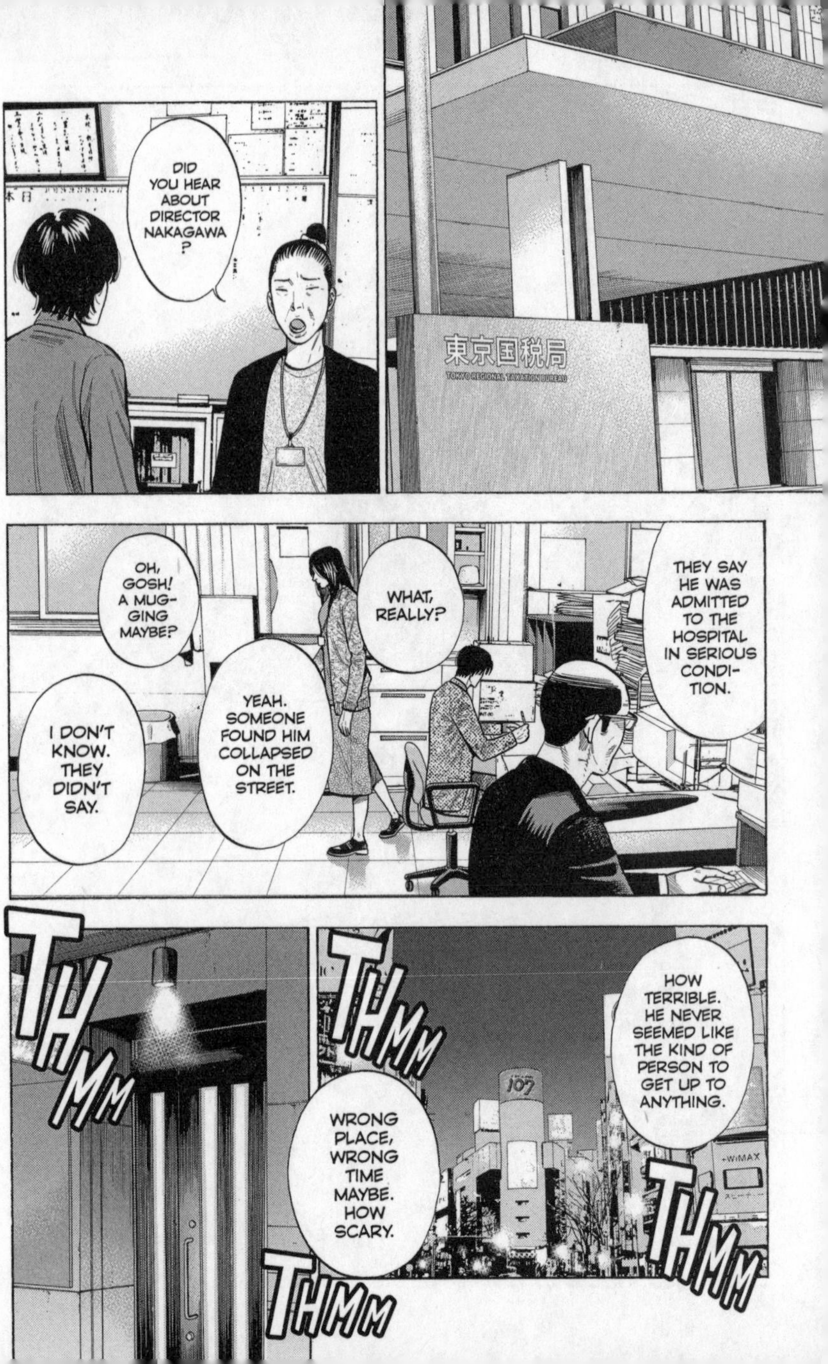
東京国税局
TOKYO REGIONAL TAXATION BUREAU
DID YOU HEAR ABOUT DIRECTOR NAKAGAWA?
THEY SAY HE WAS ADMITTED TO THE HOSPITAL IN SERIOUS CONDITION.
WHAT, REALLY?
OH, GOSH! A MUGGING MAYBE?
YEAH. SOMEONE FOUND HIM COLLAPSED ON THE STREET.
I DON'T KNOW. THEY DIDN'T SAY.
HOW TERRIBLE. HE NEVER SEEMED LIKE THE KIND OF PERSON TO GET UP TO ANYTHING.
THMM
107
+WiMAX
THMM
WRONG PLACE, WRONG TIME MAYBE. HOW SCARY.
THMM
THMM

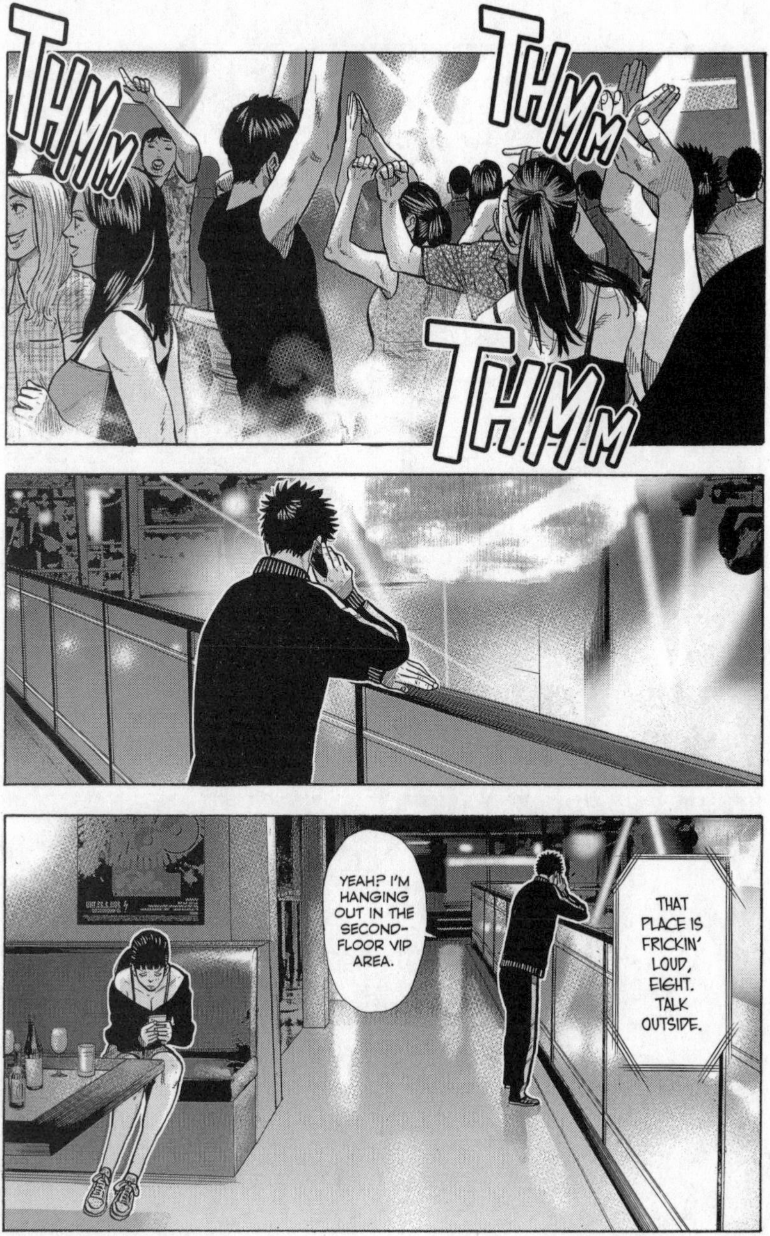
THMM
THMM
THMM
THAT PLACE IS FRICKIN' LOUD, EIGHT. TALK OUTSIDE.
YEAH? I'M HANGING OUT IN THE SECOND-FLOOR VIP AREA.

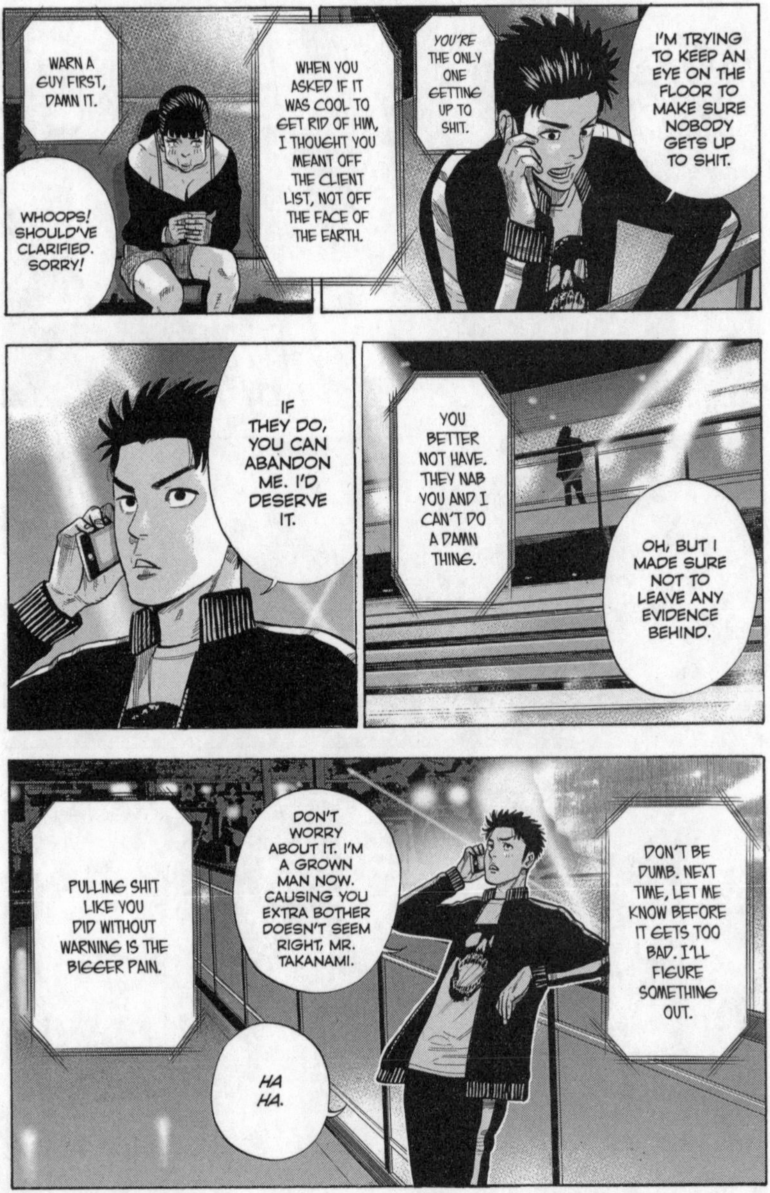
I'M TRYING TO KEEP AN EYE ON THE FLOOR TO MAKE SURE NOBODY GETS UP TO SHIT.
YOU'RE THE ONLY ONE GETTING UP TO SHIT.
WHEN YOU ASKED IF IT WAS COOL TO GET RID OF HIM, I THOUGHT YOU MEANT OFF THE CLIENT LIST, NOT OFF THE FACE OF THE EARTH.
WARN A GUY FIRST, DAMN IT.
WHOOPS! SHOULD'VE CLARIFIED. SORRY!
OH, BUT I MADE SURE NOT TO LEAVE ANY EVIDENCE BEHIND.
YOU BETTER NOT HAVE. THEY NAB YOU AND I CAN'T DO A DAMN THING.
IF THEY DO, YOU CAN ABANDON ME. I'D DESERVE IT.
DON'T WORRY ABOUT IT. I'M A GROWN MAN NOW. CAUSING YOU EXTRA BOTHER DOESN'T SEEM RIGHT, MR. TAKANAMI.
DON'T BE DUMB. NEXT TIME, LET ME KNOW BEFORE IT GETS TOO BAD. I'LL FIGURE SOMETHING OUT.
PULLING SHIT LIKE YOU DID WITHOUT WARNING IS THE BIGGER PAIN.
HA HA.

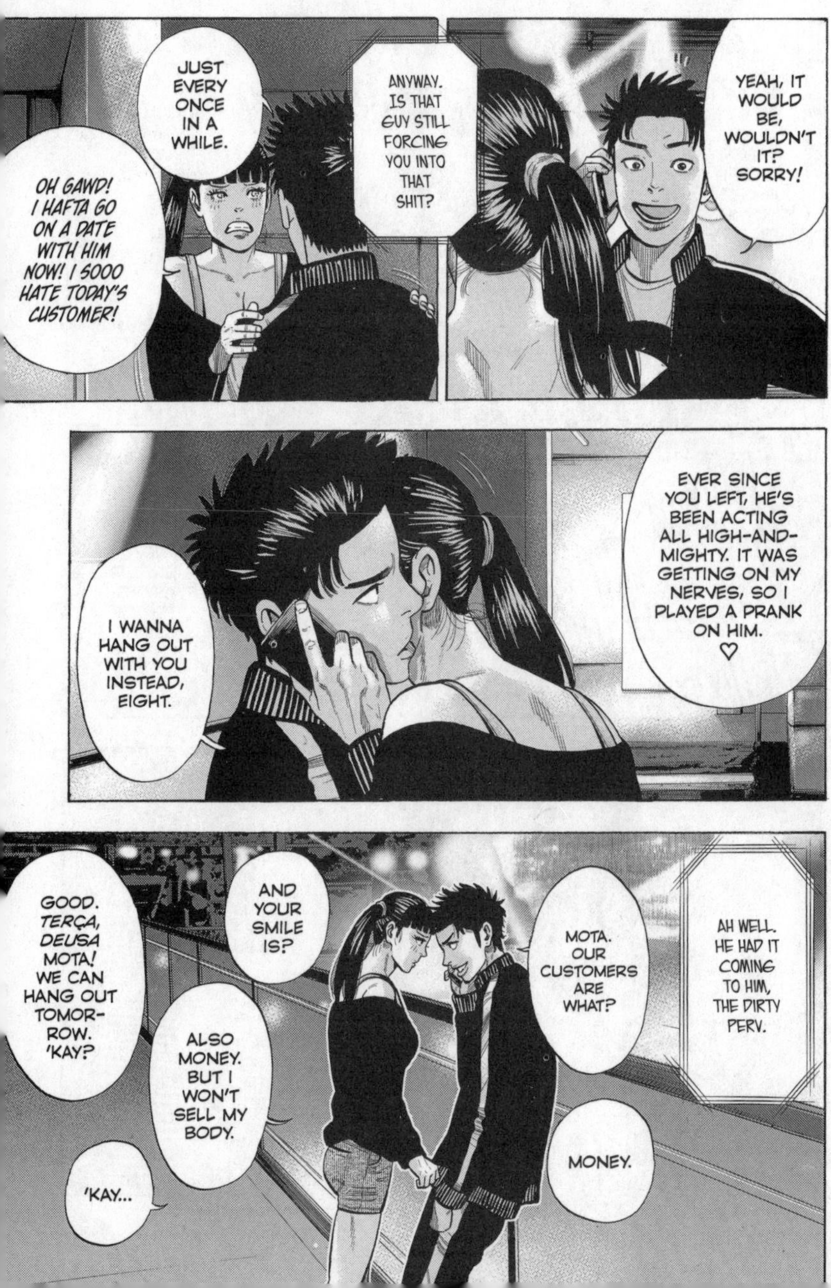

YEAH, IT WOULD BE, WOULDN'T IT? SORRY!
ANYWAY. IS THAT GUY STILL FORCING YOU INTO THAT SHIT?
JUST EVERY ONCE IN A WHILE.
OH GAWD! I HAFTA GO ON A DATE WITH HIM NOW! I SOOO HATE TODAY'S CUSTOMER!
EVER SINCE YOU LEFT, HE'S BEEN ACTING ALL HIGH-AND-MIGHTY. IT WAS GETTING ON MY NERVES, SO I PLAYED A PRANK ON HIM. ♡
I WANNA HANG OUT WITH YOU INSTEAD, EIGHT.
AH WELL. HE HAD IT COMING TO HIM, THE DIRTY PERV.
MOTA. OUR CUSTOMERS ARE WHAT?
MONEY.
AND YOUR SMILE IS?
ALSO MONEY. BUT I WON'T SELL MY BODY.
GOOD. TERÇA, DEUSA MOTA! WE CAN HANG OUT TOMORROW. 'KAY?
'KAY...

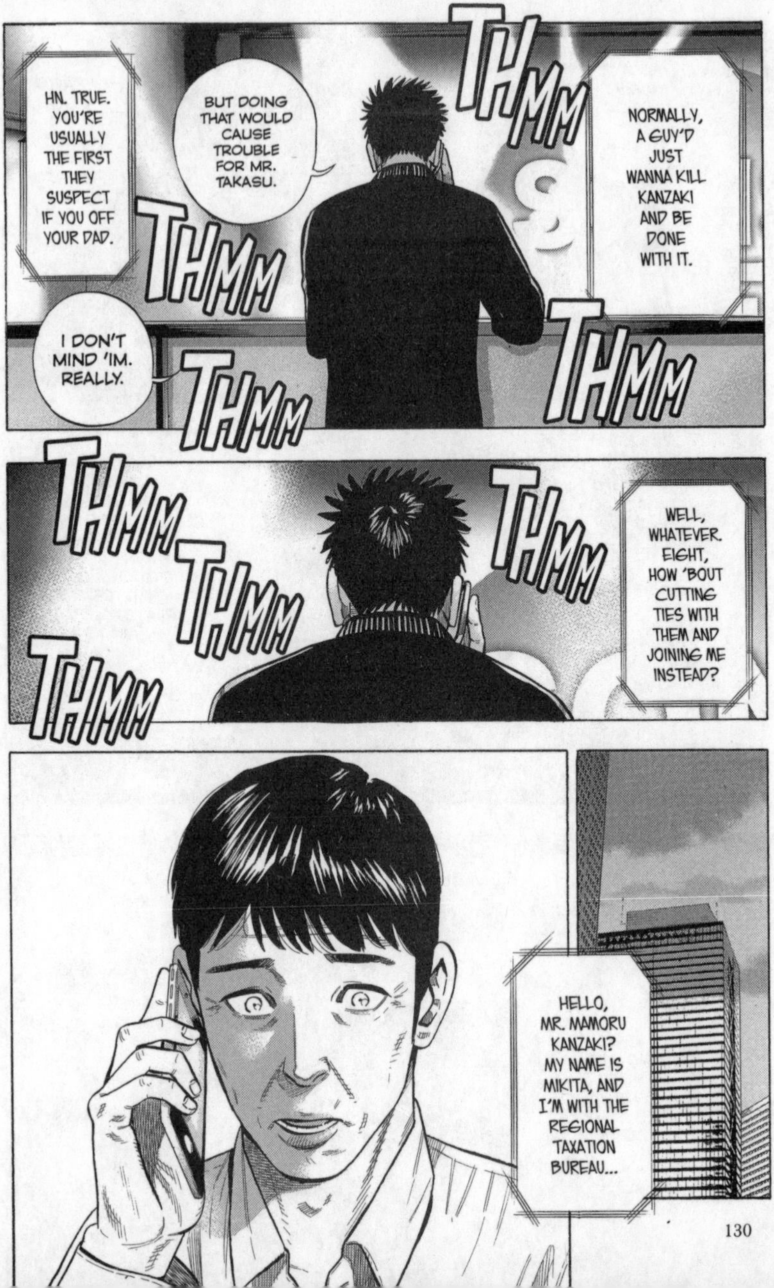
THMM
NORMALLY, A GUY'D JUST WANNA KILL KANZAKI AND BE DONE WITH IT.
BUT DOING THAT WOULD CAUSE TROUBLE FOR MR. TAKASU.
HN. TRUE. YOU'RE USUALLY THE FIRST THEY SUSPECT IF YOU OFF YOUR DAD.
THMM
THMM
I DON'T MIND 'IM. REALLY.
THMM
WELL, WHATEVER. EIGHT, HOW 'BOUT CUTTING TIES WITH THEM AND JOINING ME INSTEAD?
THMM
THMM-THMM
THMM
HELLO, MR. MAMORU KANZAKI? MY NAME IS MIKITA, AND I'M WITH THE REGIONAL TAXATION BUREAU...

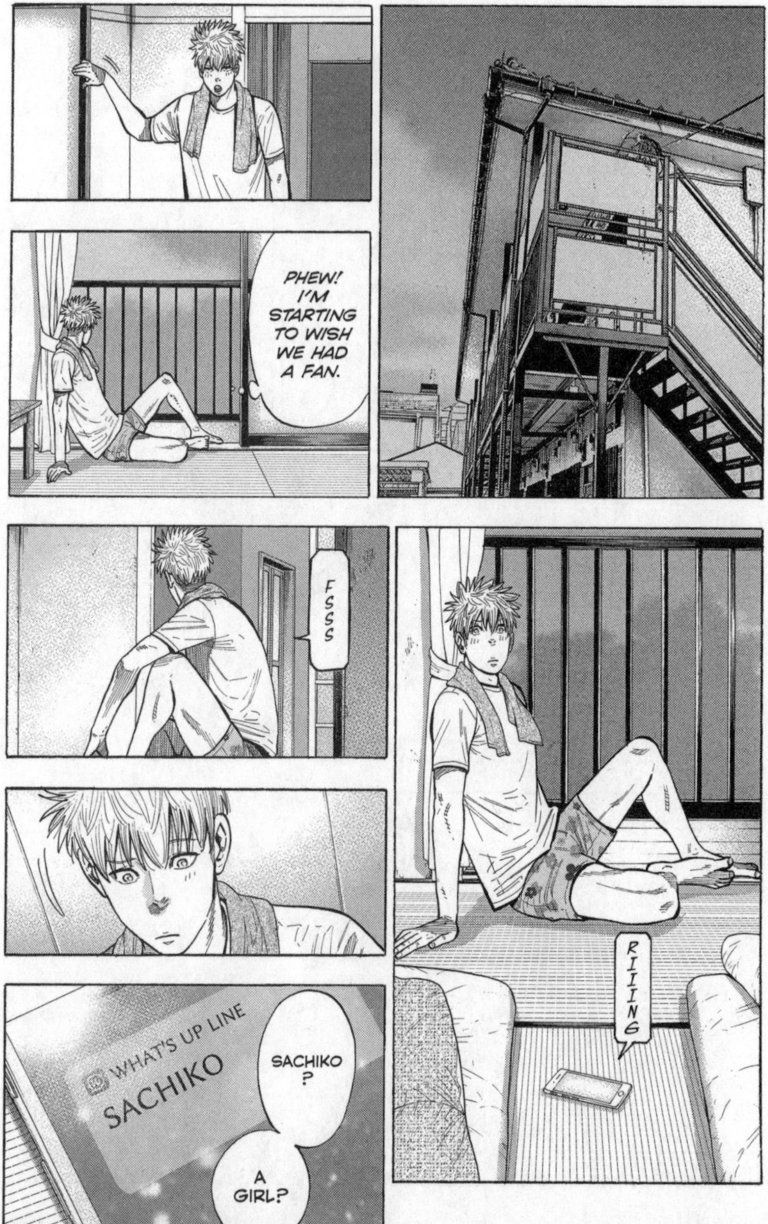
PHEW! I'M STARTING TO WISH WE HAD A FAN.
RIIING
FSSS
WHAT'S UP LINE
SACHIKO
SACHIKO?
A GIRL?

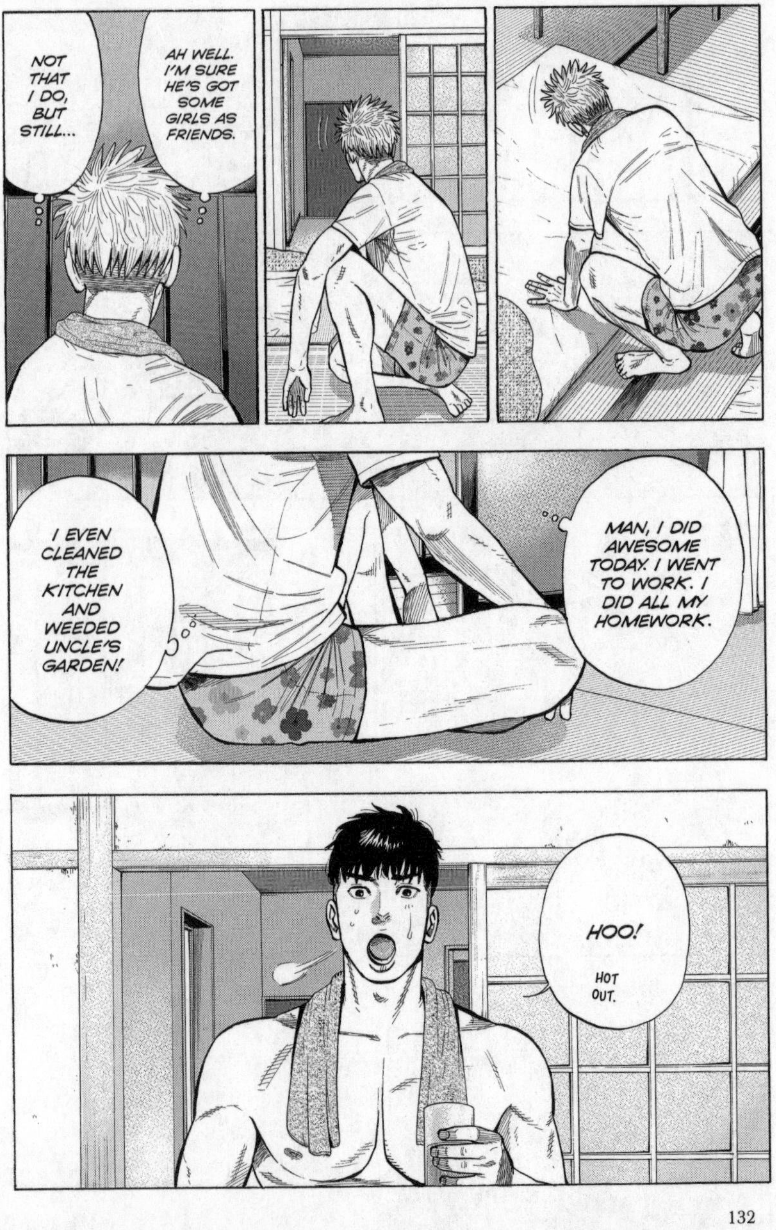
AH WELL. I'M SURE HE'S GOT SOME GIRLS AS FRIENDS.
NOT THAT I DO, BUT STILL...
MAN, I DID AWESOME TODAY. I WENT TO WORK. I DID ALL MY HOMEWORK.
I EVEN CLEANED THE KITCHEN AND WEEDED UNCLE'S GARDEN!
HOO!
HOT OUT.

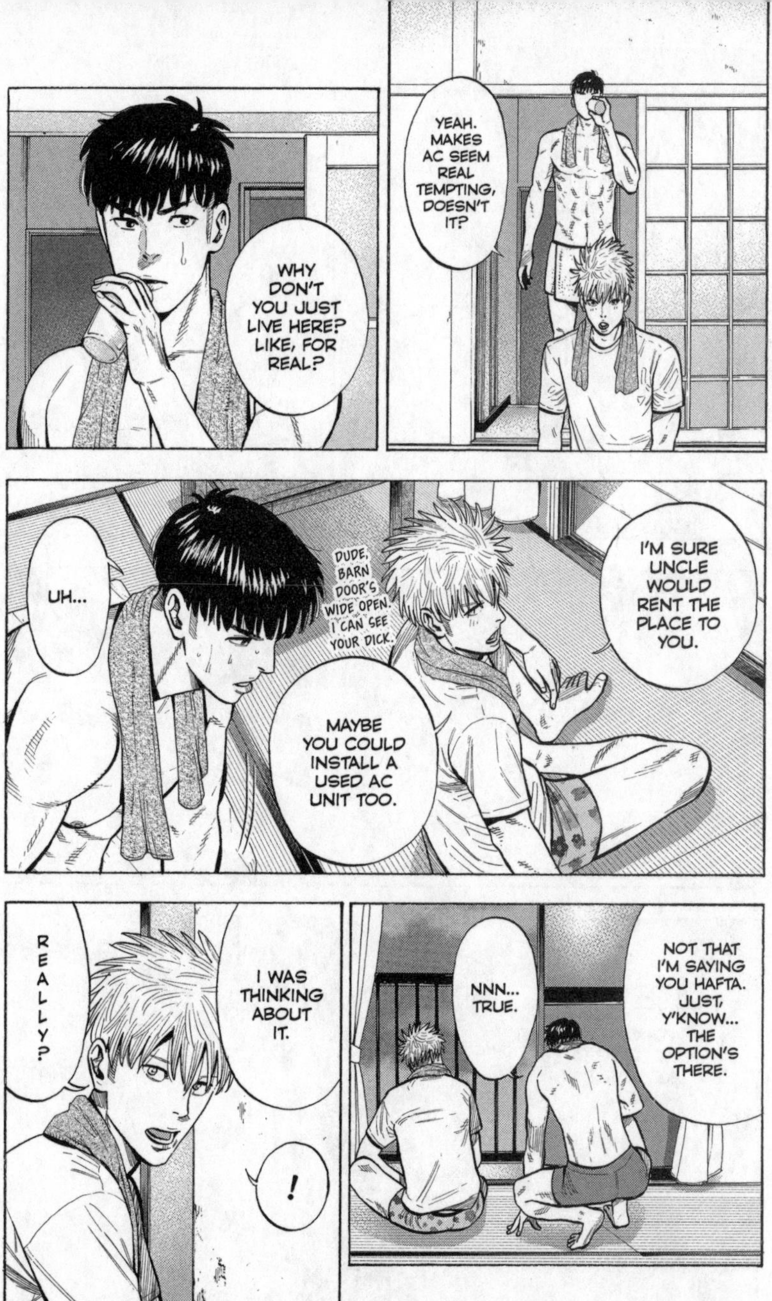
YEAH. MAKES AC SEEM REAL TEMPTING, DOESN'T IT?
WHY DON'T YOU JUST LIVE HERE? LIKE, FOR REAL?
I'M SURE UNCLE WOULD RENT THE PLACE TO YOU.
DUDE, BARN DOOR'S WIDE OPEN. I CAN SEE YOUR DICK.
MAYBE YOU COULD INSTALL A USED AC UNIT TOO.
UH...
NOT THAT I'M SAYING YOU HAFTA. JUST, Y'KNOW... THE OPTION'S THERE.
NNN... TRUE.
I WAS THINKING ABOUT IT.
REALLY?
!

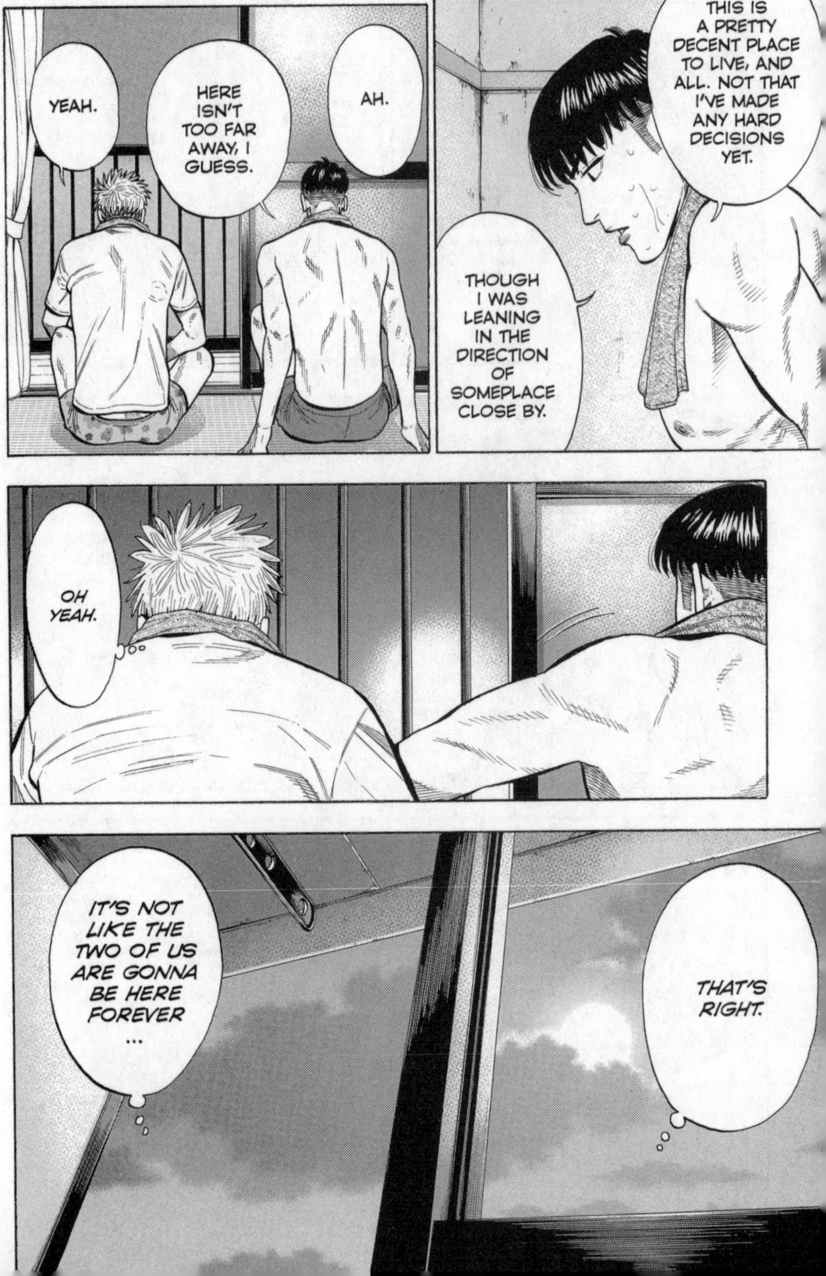
THIS IS A PRETTY DECENT PLACE TO LIVE, AND ALL. NOT THAT I'VE MADE ANY HARD DECISIONS YET.
THOUGH I WAS LEANING IN THE DIRECTION OF SOMEPLACE CLOSE BY.
AH.
HERE ISN'T TOO FAR AWAY, I GUESS.
YEAH.
OH YEAH.
THAT'S RIGHT.
IT'S NOT LIKE THE TWO OF US ARE GONNA BE HERE FOREVER ...

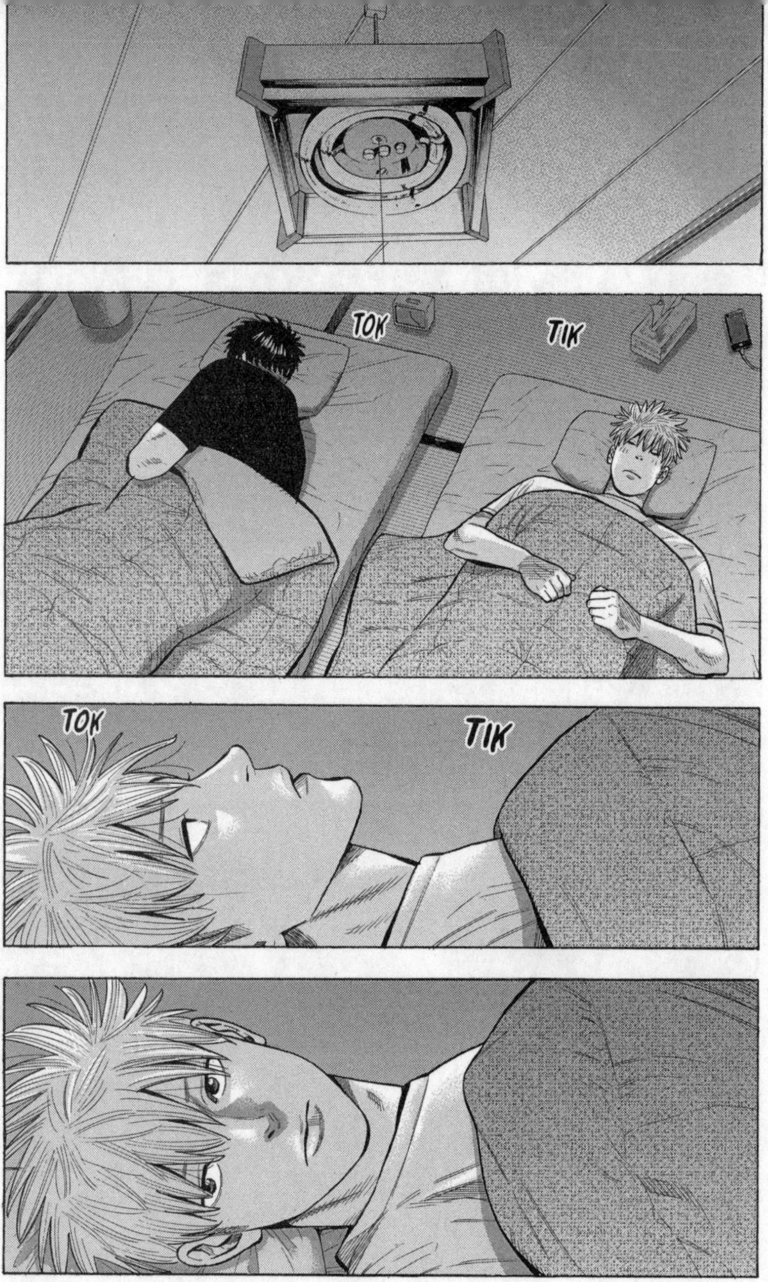
TIK
TOK
TIK
TOK

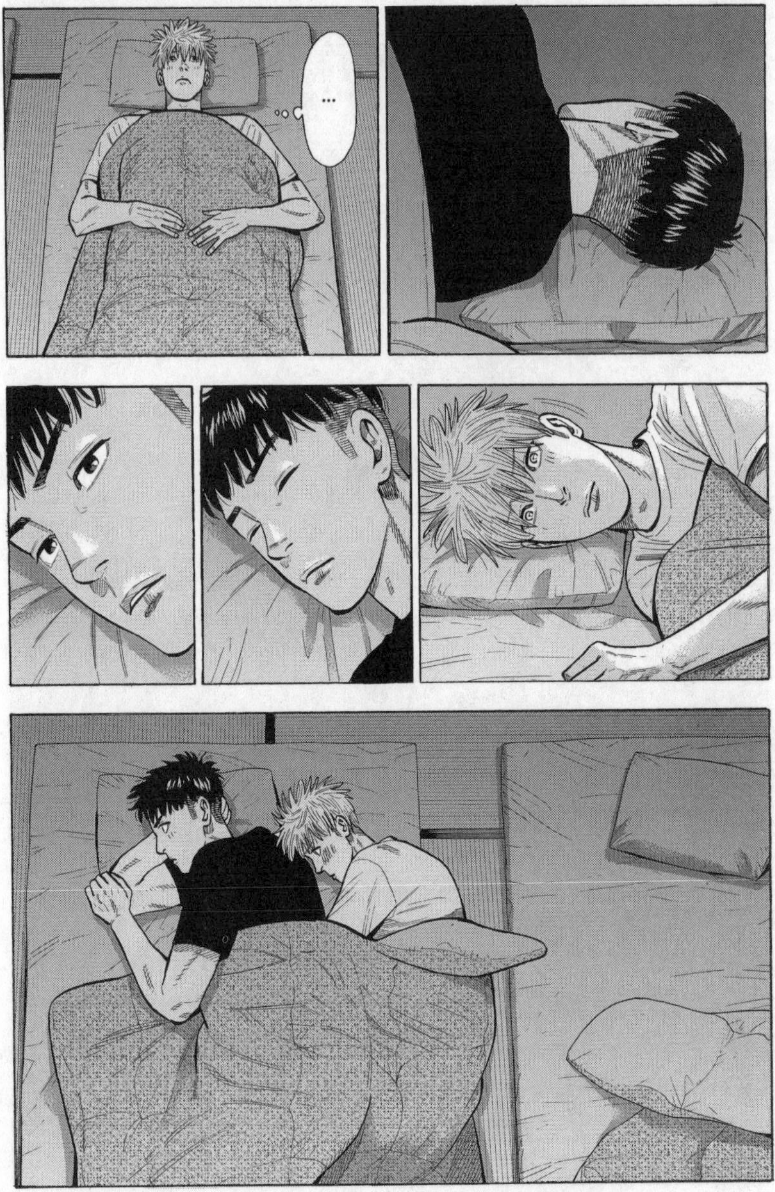
...

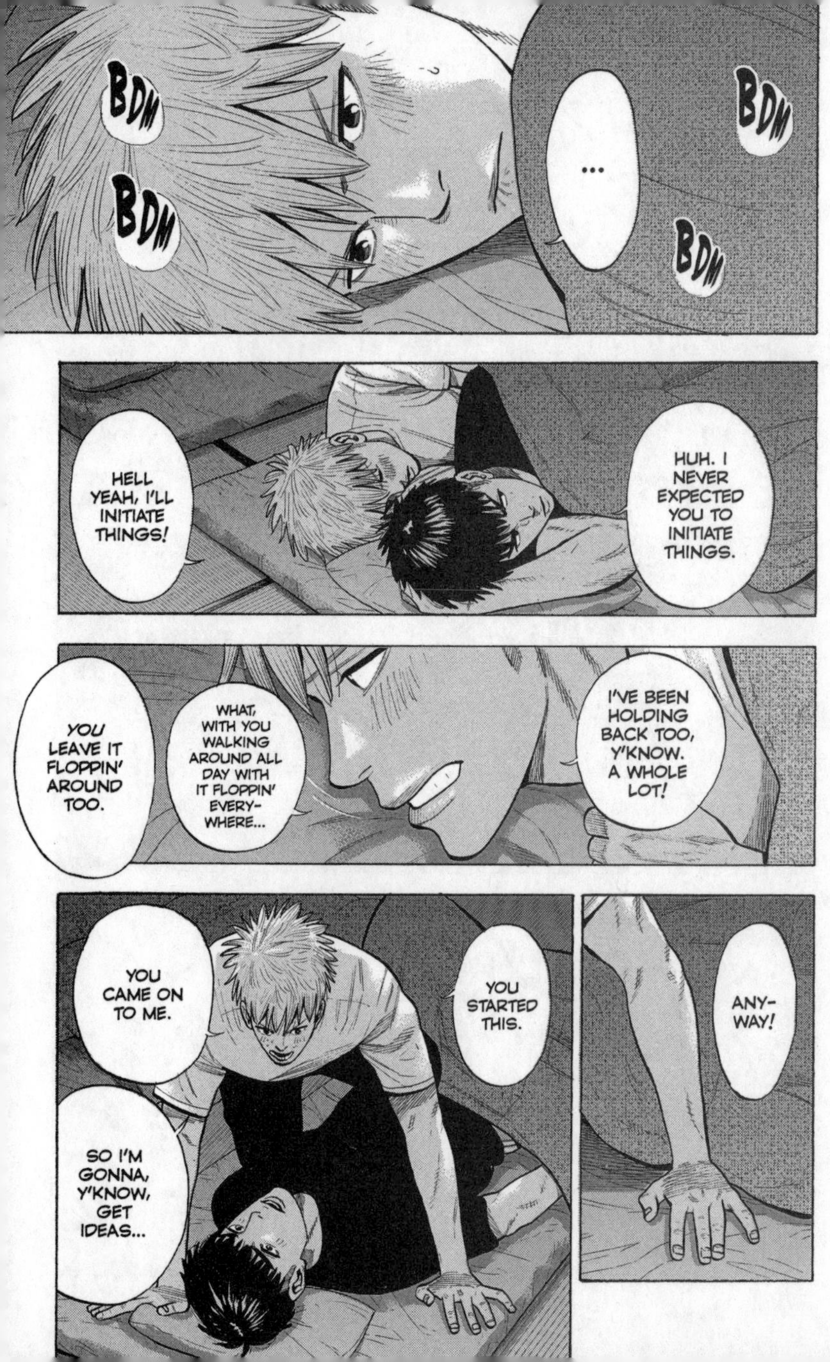
BDM
...
BDM
BDM
BDM
HUH. I NEVER EXPECTED YOU TO INITIATE THINGS.
HELL YEAH, I'LL INITIATE THINGS!
I'VE BEEN HOLDING BACK TOO, Y'KNOW. A WHOLE LOT!
WHAT, WITH YOU WALKING AROUND ALL DAY WITH IT FLOPPIN' EVERY-WHERE...
YOU LEAVE IT FLOPPIN' AROUND TOO.
ANY-WAY!
YOU STARTED THIS.
YOU CAME ON TO ME.
SO I'M GONNA, Y'KNOW, GET IDEAS...

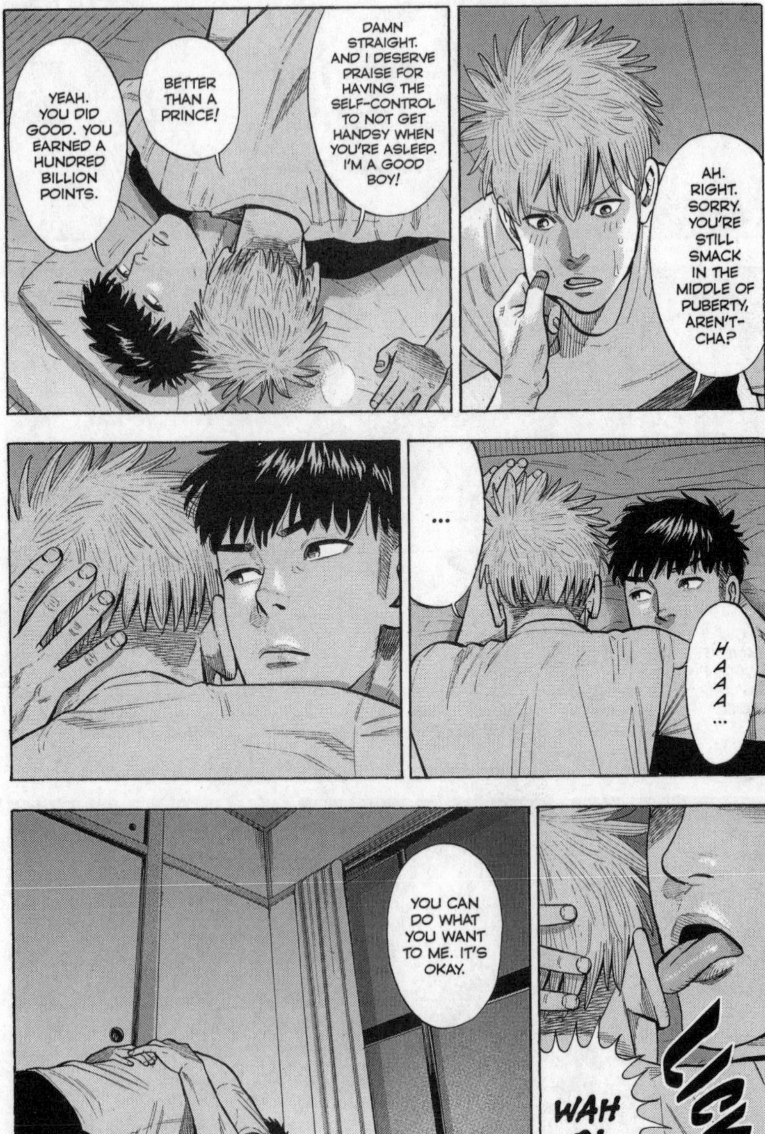
AH. RIGHT. SORRY. YOU'RE STILL SMACK IN THE MIDDLE OF PUBERTY, AREN'T-CHA?
DAMN STRAIGHT. AND I DESERVE PRAISE FOR HAVING THE SELF-CONTROL TO NOT GET HANDSY WHEN YOU'RE ASLEEP. I'M A GOOD BOY!
BETTER THAN A PRINCE!
YEAH. YOU DID GOOD. YOU EARNED A HUNDRED BILLION POINTS.
HAAAA...
...
LICK
WAH ?!
YOU CAN DO WHAT YOU WANT TO ME. IT'S OKAY.

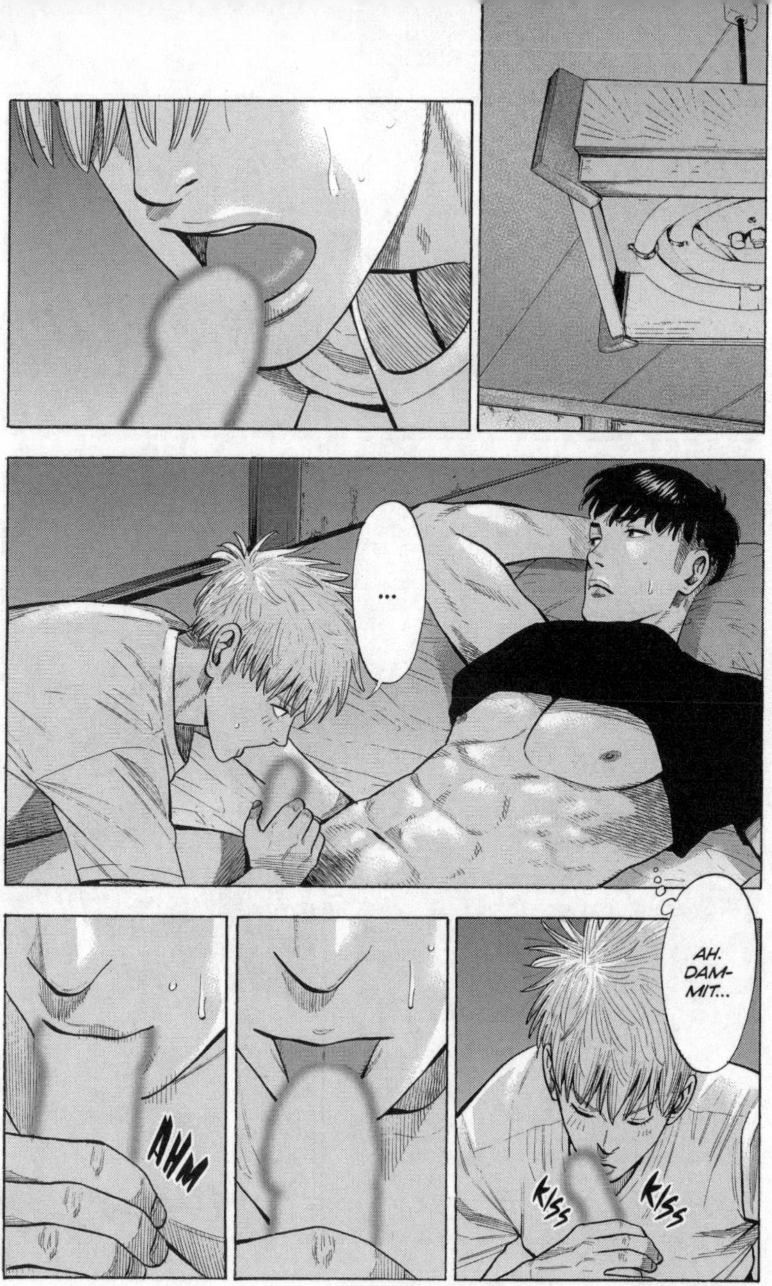
...
AH. DAMMIT...
KISS
KISS
AHM

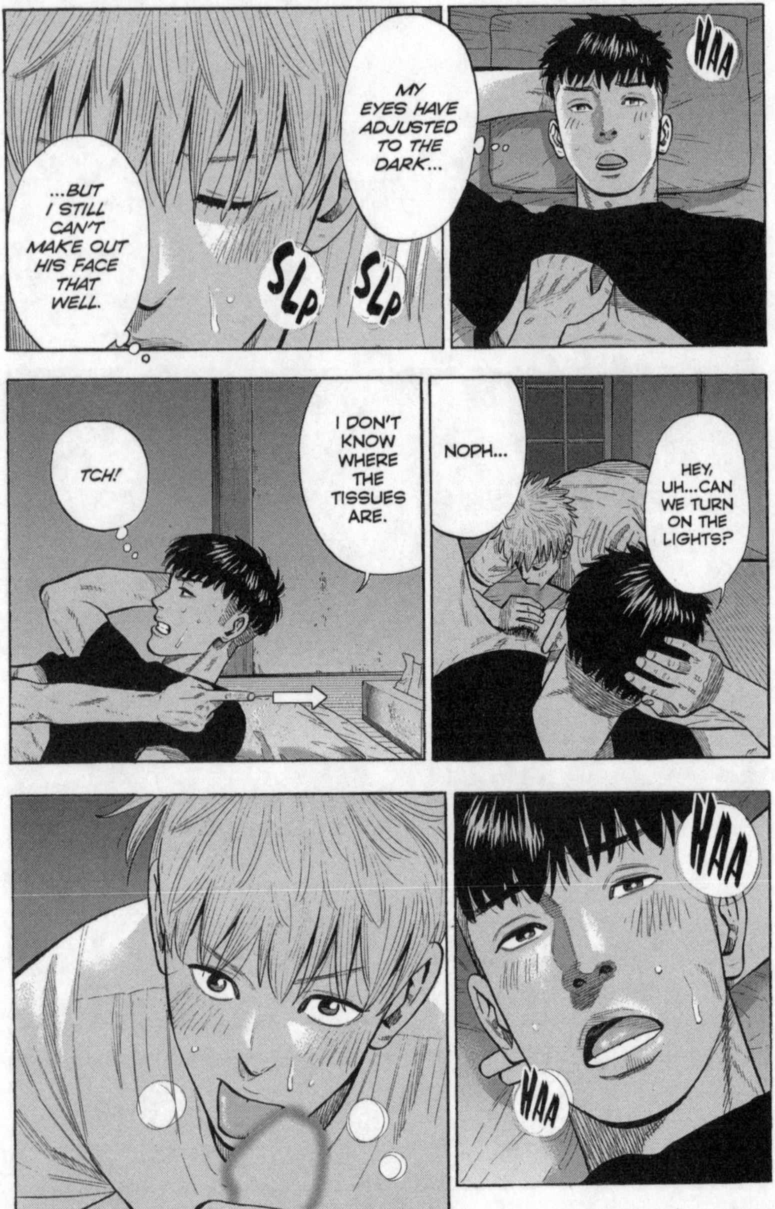
HAA
MY EYES HAVE ADJUSTED TO THE DARK...
...BUT I STILL CAN'T MAKE OUT HIS FACE THAT WELL.
SLP
SLP
HEY, UH...CAN WE TURN ON THE LIGHTS?
NOPH...
I DON'T KNOW WHERE THE TISSUES ARE.
TCH!
HAA
HAA

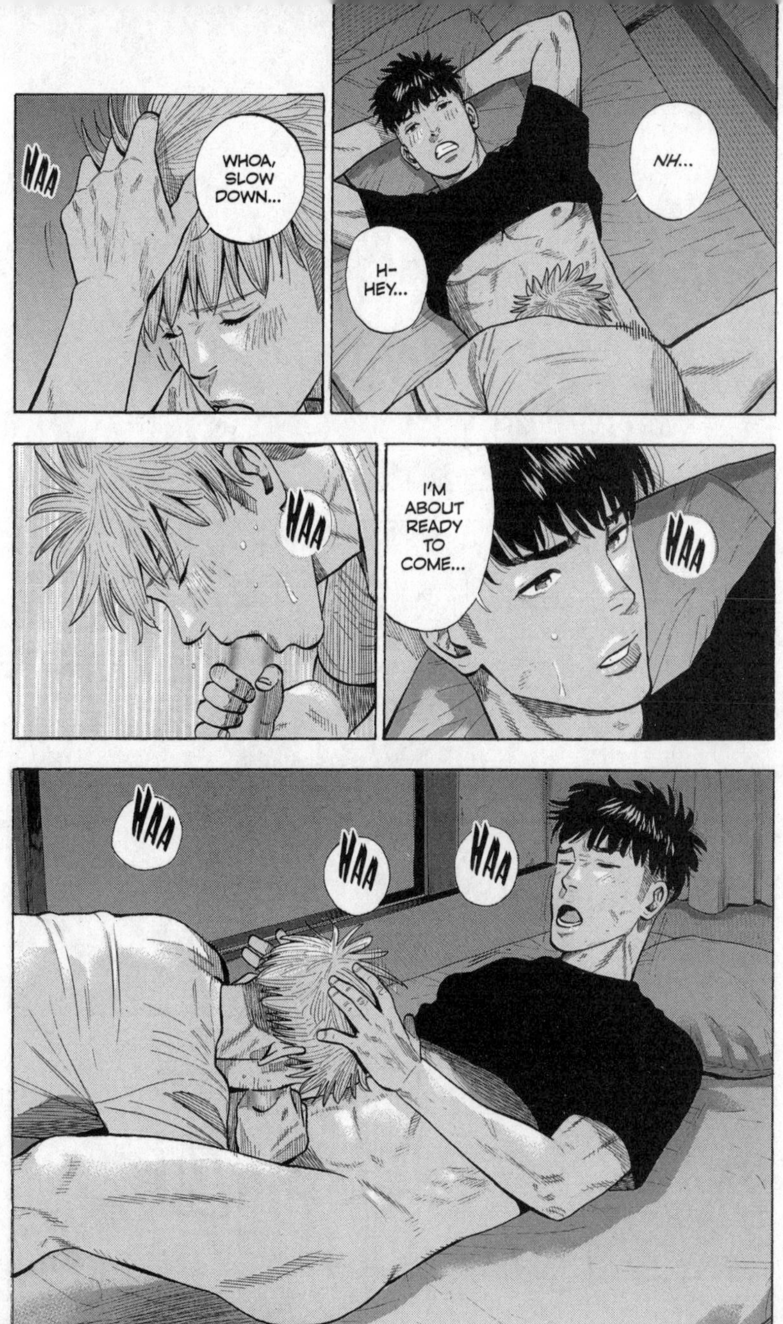
NH...
H-HEY...
WHOA, SLOW DOWN...
HAA
I'M ABOUT READY TO COME...
HAA
HAA
HAA
HAA
HAA

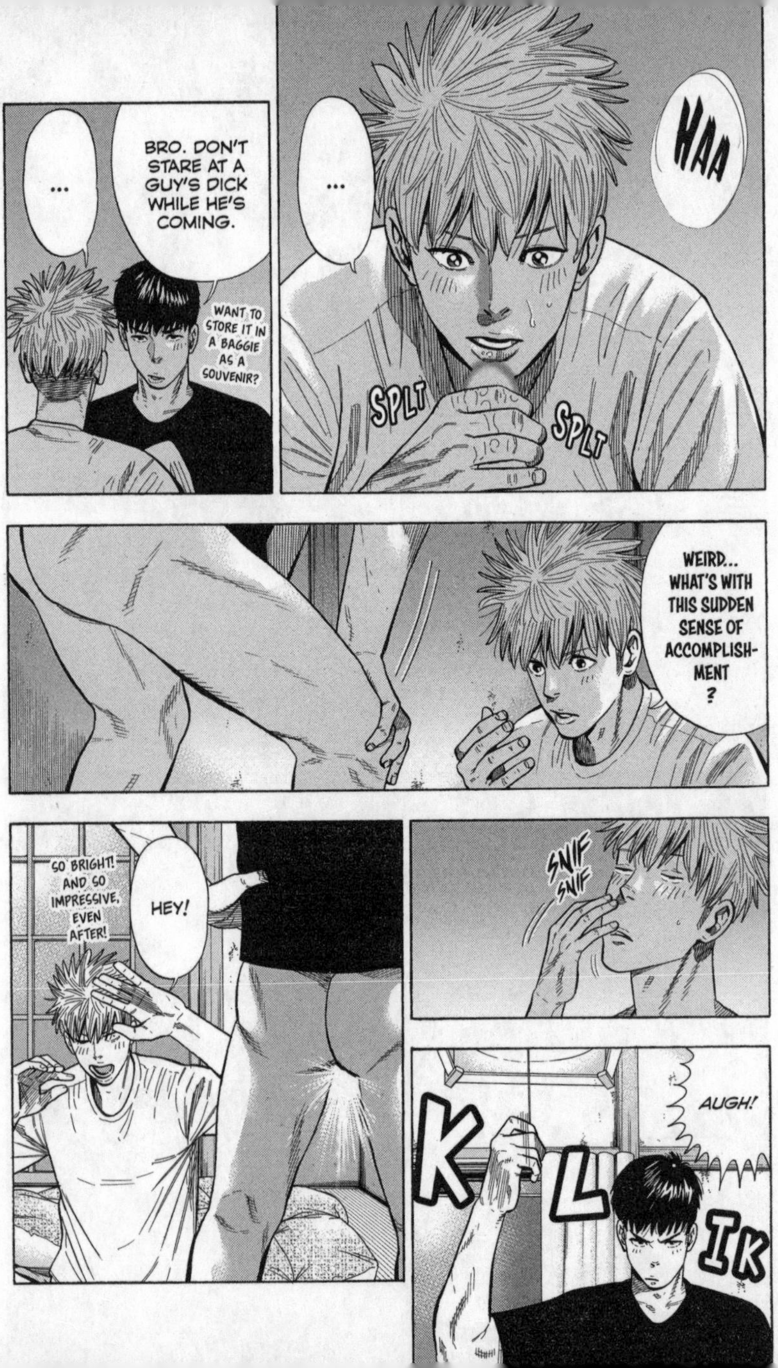
HAA
...
SPLT
SPLT
BRO. DON'T STARE AT A GUY'S DICK WHILE HE'S COMING.
...
WANT TO STORE IT IN A BAGGIE AS A SOUVENIR?
WEIRD... WHAT'S WITH THIS SUDDEN SENSE OF ACCOMPLISHMENT?
SNIF SNIF
AUGH!
KLIK
HEY!
SO BRIGHT! AND SO IMPRESSIVE, EVEN AFTER!

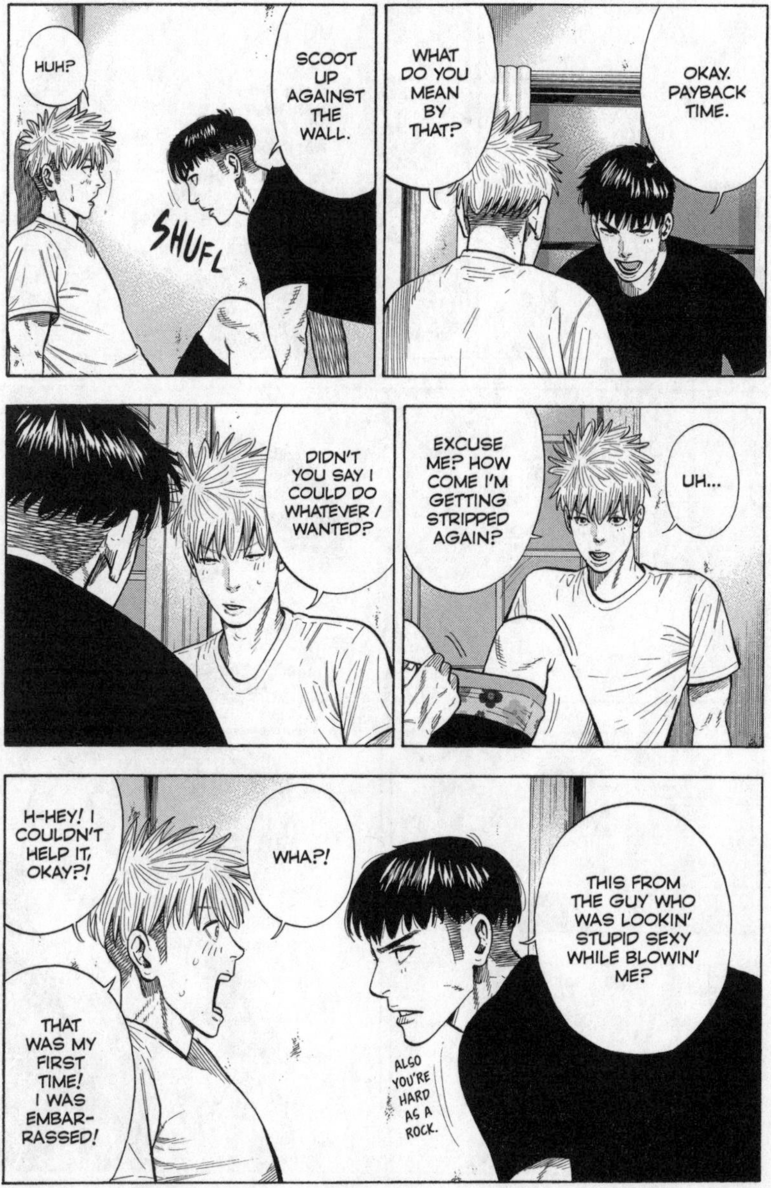
OKAY. PAYBACK TIME.
WHAT DO YOU MEAN BY THAT?
SCOOT UP AGAINST THE WALL.
HUH?
SHUFL
UH...
EXCUSE ME? HOW COME I'M GETTING STRIPPED AGAIN?
DIDN'T YOU SAY I COULD DO WHATEVER I WANTED?
THIS FROM THE GUY WHO WAS LOOKIN' STUPID SEXY WHILE BLOWIN' ME?
WHA?!
H-HEY! I COULDN'T HELP IT, OKAY?!
ALSO YOU'RE HARD AS A ROCK.
THAT WAS MY FIRST TIME! I WAS EMBARRASSED!

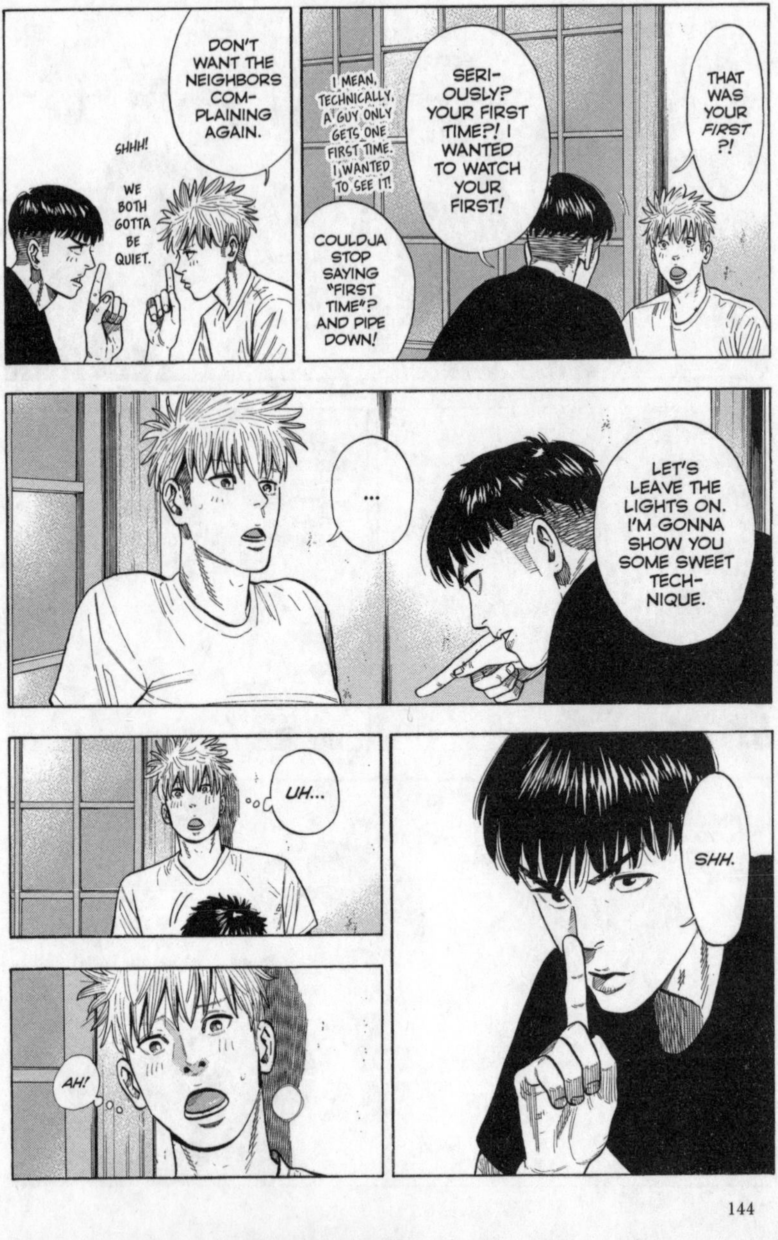
THAT WAS YOUR FIRST?!
SERIOUSLY? YOUR FIRST TIME?! I WANTED TO WATCH YOUR FIRST!
I MEAN, TECHNICALLY, A GUY ONLY GETS ONE FIRST TIME. I WANTED TO SEE IT!
COULDJA STOP SAYING "FIRST TIME"? AND PIPE DOWN!
DON'T WANT THE NEIGHBORS COMPLAINING AGAIN.
SHHH!
WE BOTH GOTTA BE QUIET.
LET'S LEAVE THE LIGHTS ON. I'M GONNA SHOW YOU SOME SWEET TECHNIQUE.
...
SHH.
UH...
AH!

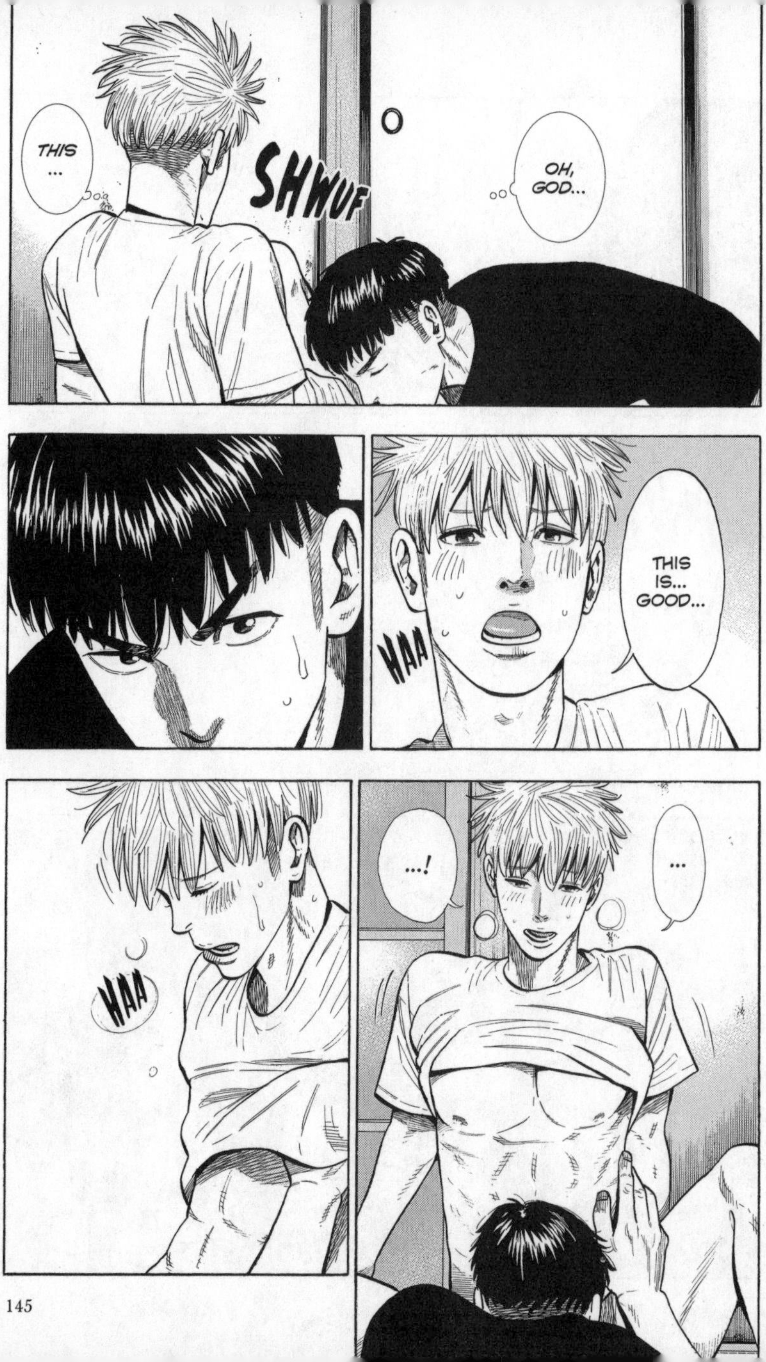
OH, GOD...
SHWUF
THIS ...
THIS IS... GOOD...
HAA
...
...!
HAA

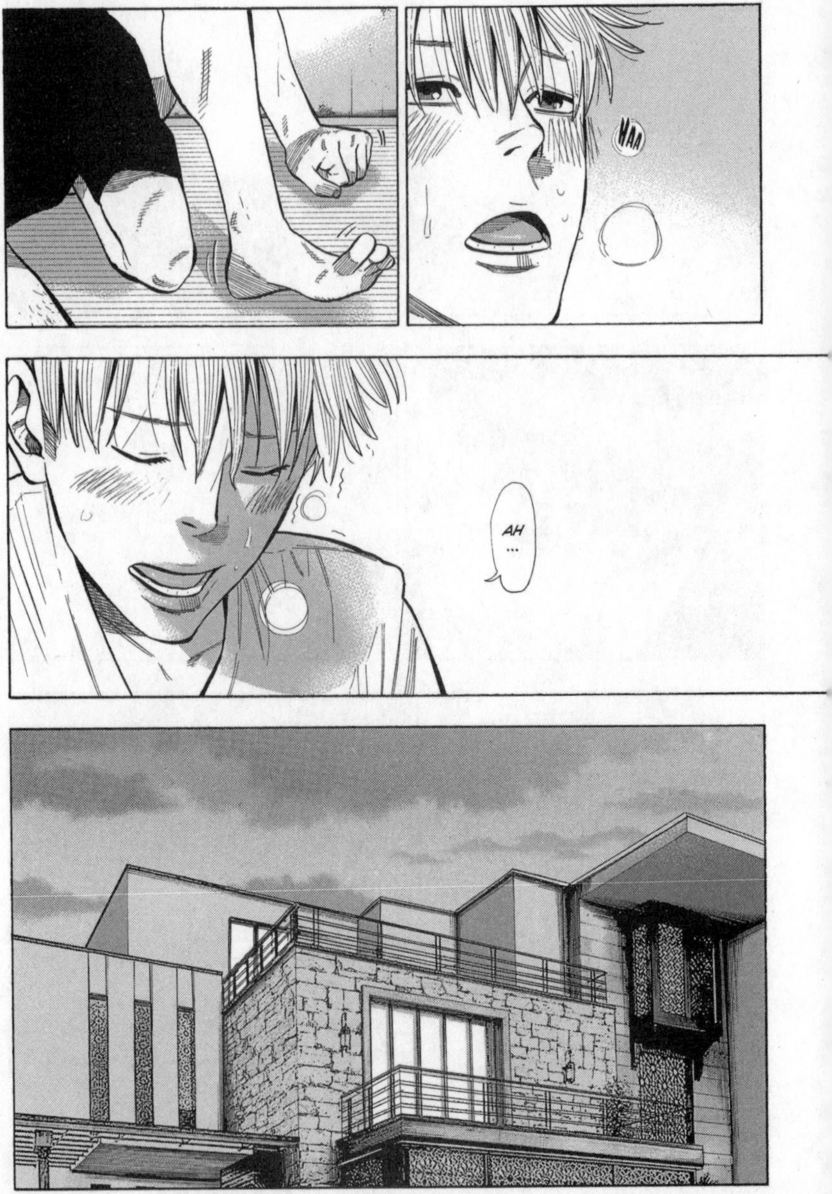
HAA
AH ...

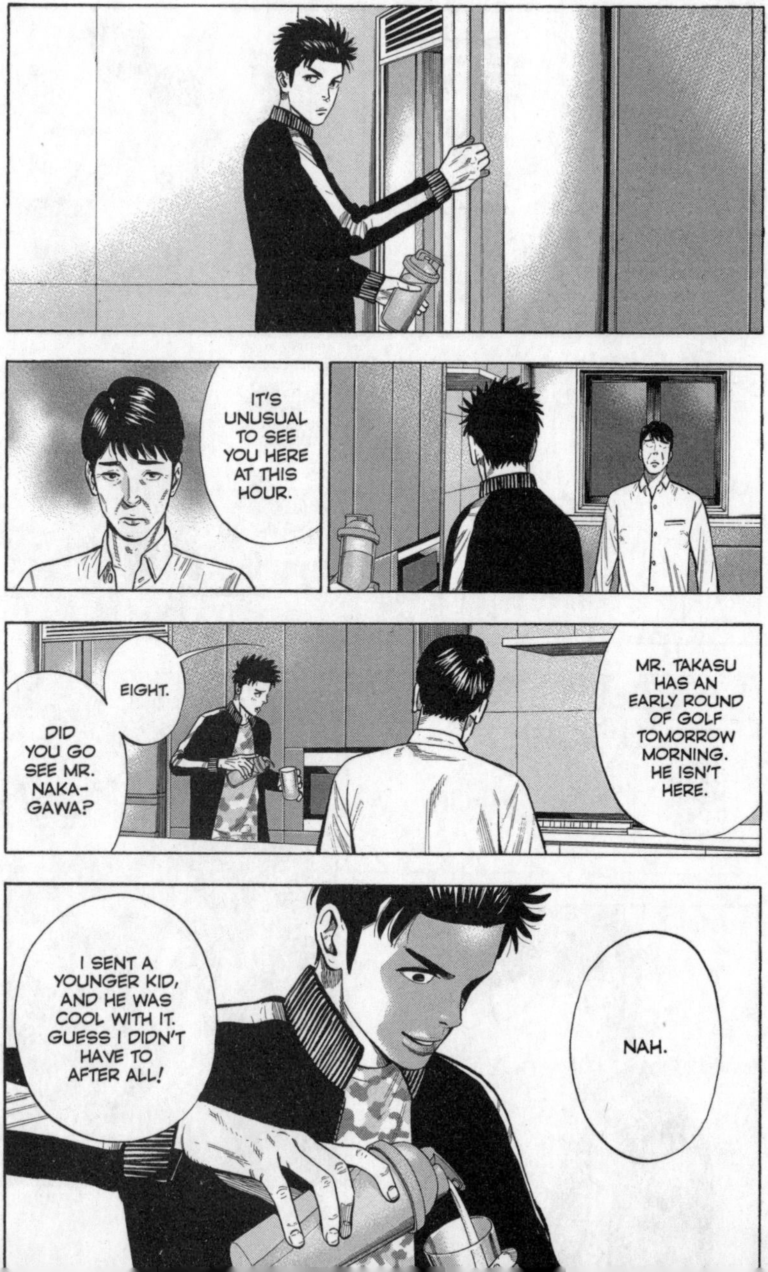
IT'S UNUSUAL TO SEE YOU HERE AT THIS HOUR.
MR. TAKASU HAS AN EARLY ROUND OF GOLF TOMORROW MORNING. HE ISN'T HERE.
EIGHT.
DID YOU GO SEE MR. NAKA-GAWA?
NAH.
I SENT A YOUNGER KID, AND HE WAS COOL WITH IT. GUESS I DIDN'T HAVE TO AFTER ALL!

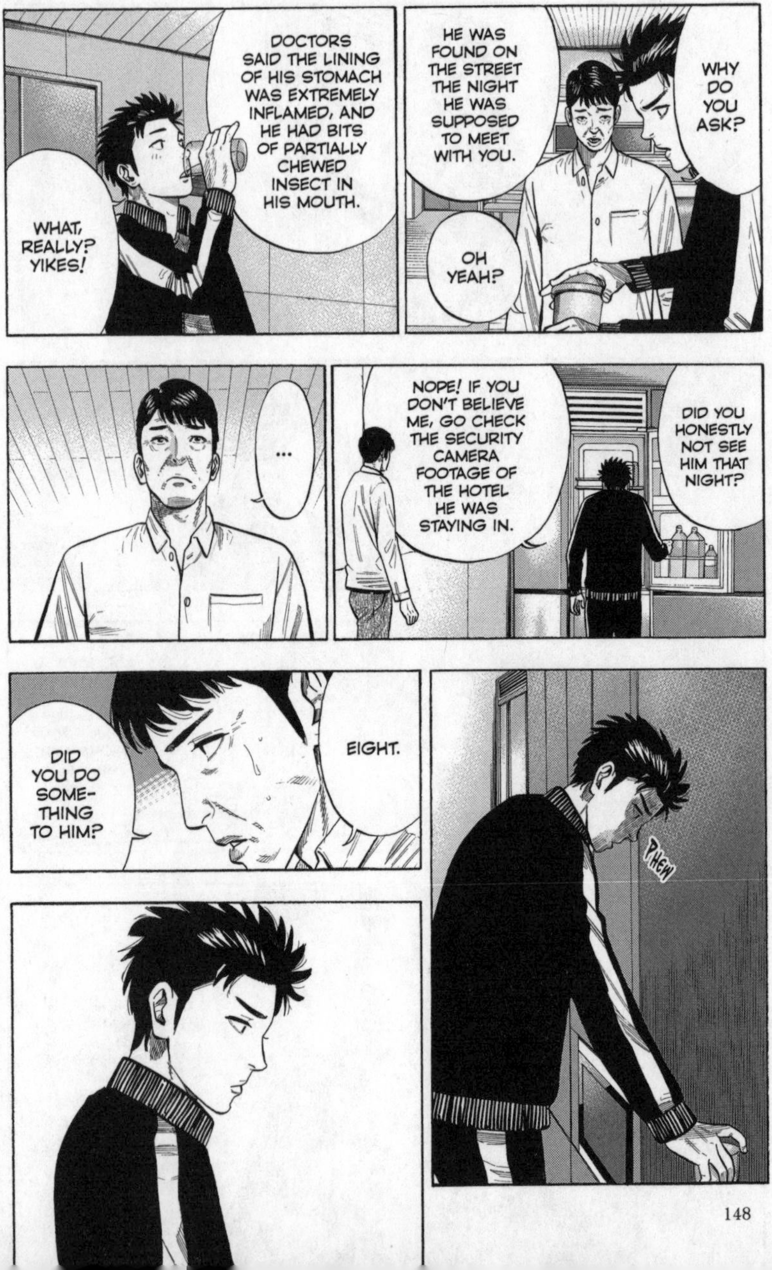
WHY DO YOU ASK?
HE WAS FOUND ON THE STREET THE NIGHT HE WAS SUPPOSED TO MEET WITH YOU.
OH YEAH?
DOCTORS SAID THE LINING OF HIS STOMACH WAS EXTREMELY INFLAMED, AND HE HAD BITS OF PARTIALLY CHEWED INSECT IN HIS MOUTH.
WHAT, REALLY? YIKES!
DID YOU HONESTLY NOT SEE HIM THAT NIGHT?
NOPE! IF YOU DON'T BELIEVE ME, GO CHECK THE SECURITY CAMERA FOOTAGE OF THE HOTEL HE WAS STAYING IN.
...
PHEW
EIGHT.
DID YOU DO SOME-THING TO HIM?

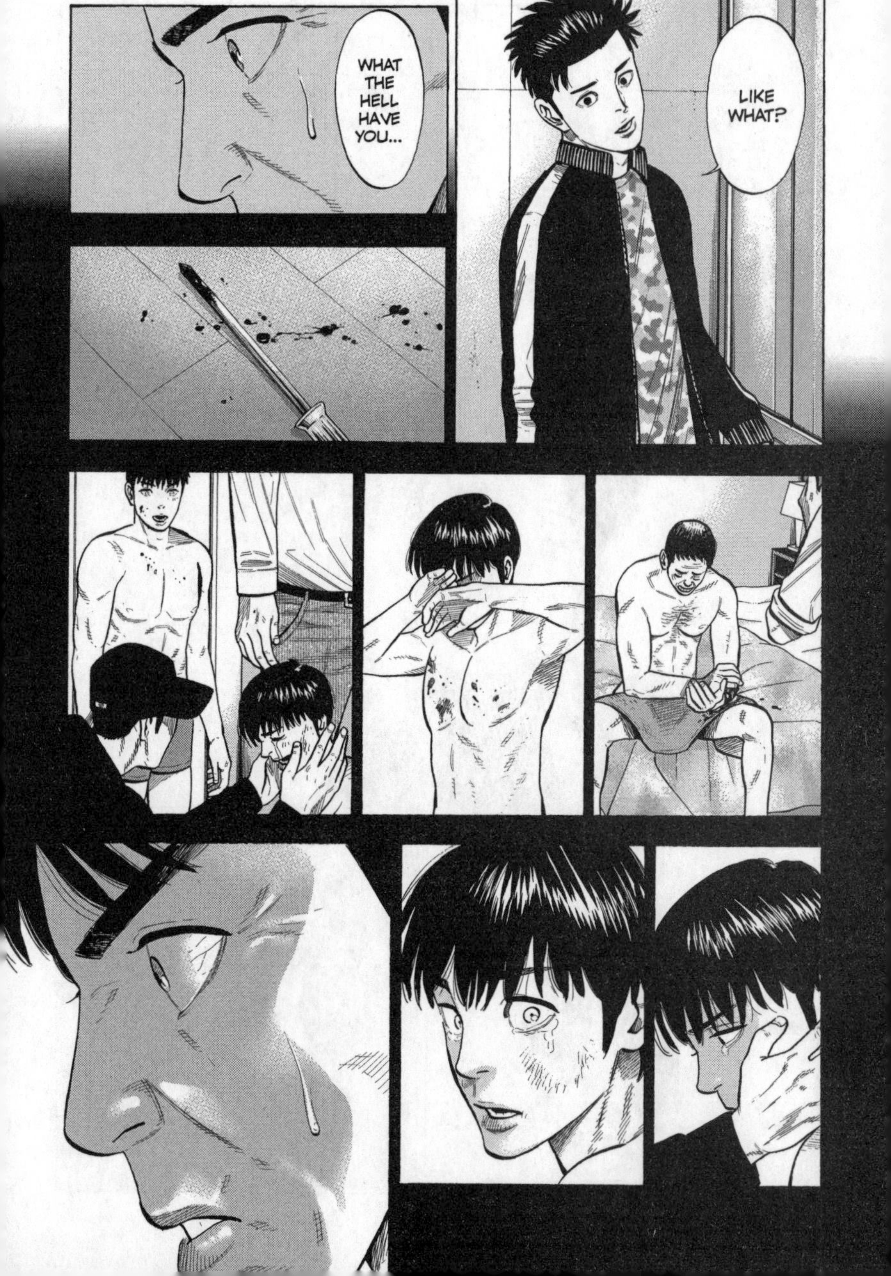
LIKE WHAT?
WHAT THE HELL HAVE YOU...

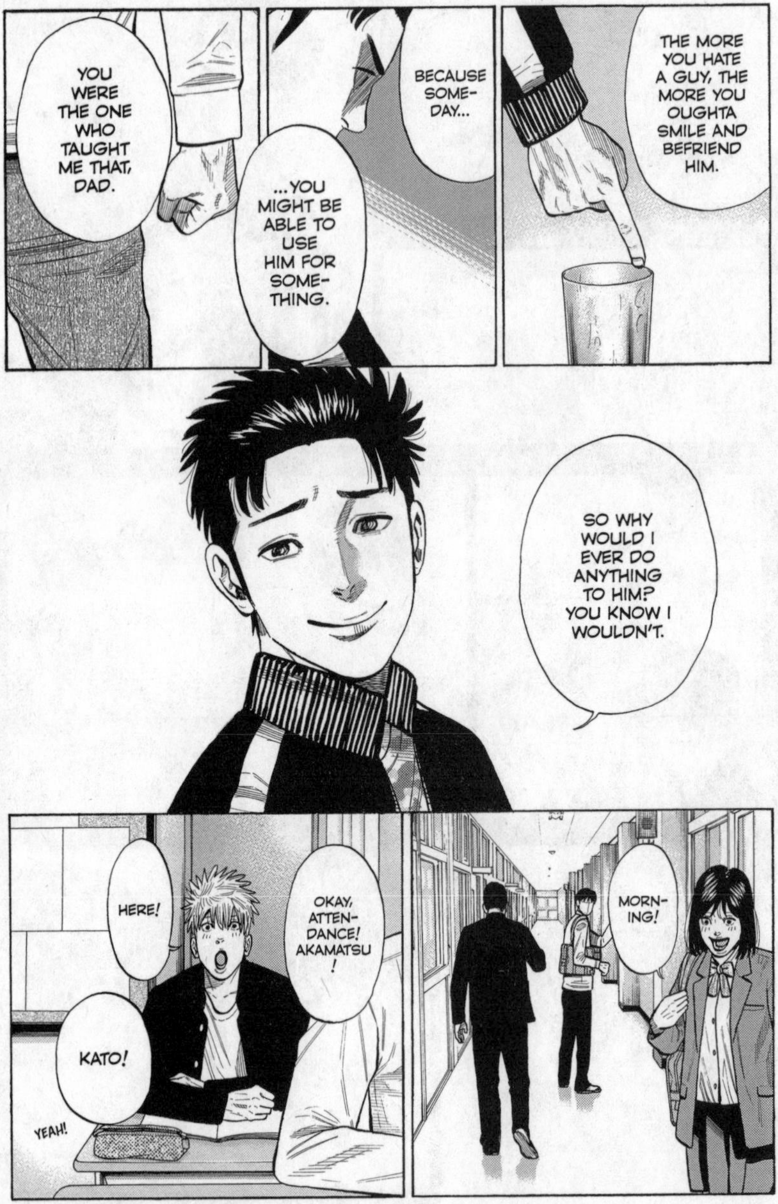

THE MORE YOU HATE A GUY, THE MORE YOU OUGHTA SMILE AND BEFRIEND HIM.
BECAUSE SOME-DAY...
...YOU MIGHT BE ABLE TO USE HIM FOR SOME-THING.
YOU WERE THE ONE WHO TAUGHT ME THAT, DAD.
SO WHY WOULD I EVER DO ANYTHING TO HIM? YOU KNOW I WOULDN'T.
MORN-ING!
OKAY, ATTEN-DANCE! AKAMATSU!
HERE!
KATO!
YEAH!

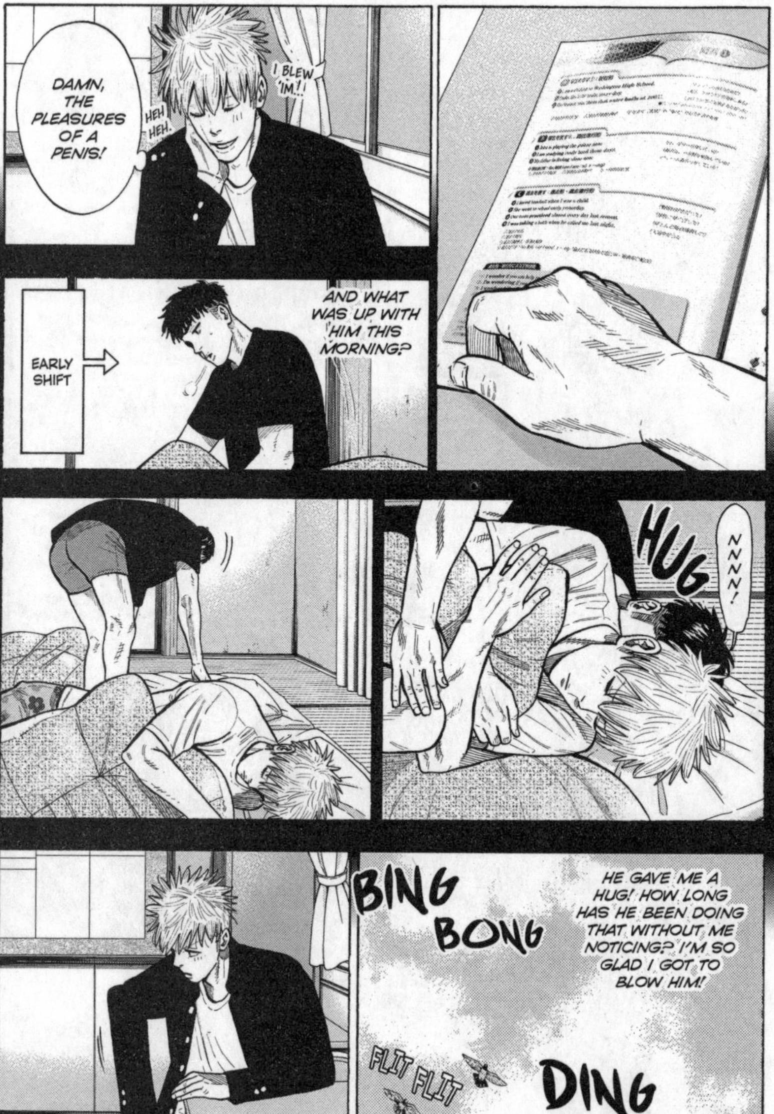
DAMN, THE PLEASURES OF A PENIS!
HEH HEH.
I BLEW 'IM!...
AND WHAT WAS UP WITH HIM THIS MORNING?
EARLY SHIFT
NNNN...!
HUG
BING BONG
HE GAVE ME A HUG! HOW LONG HAS HE BEEN DOING THAT WITHOUT ME NOTICING? I'M SO GLAD I GOT TO BLOW HIM!
DING DONG
FLIT FLIT
FLIT

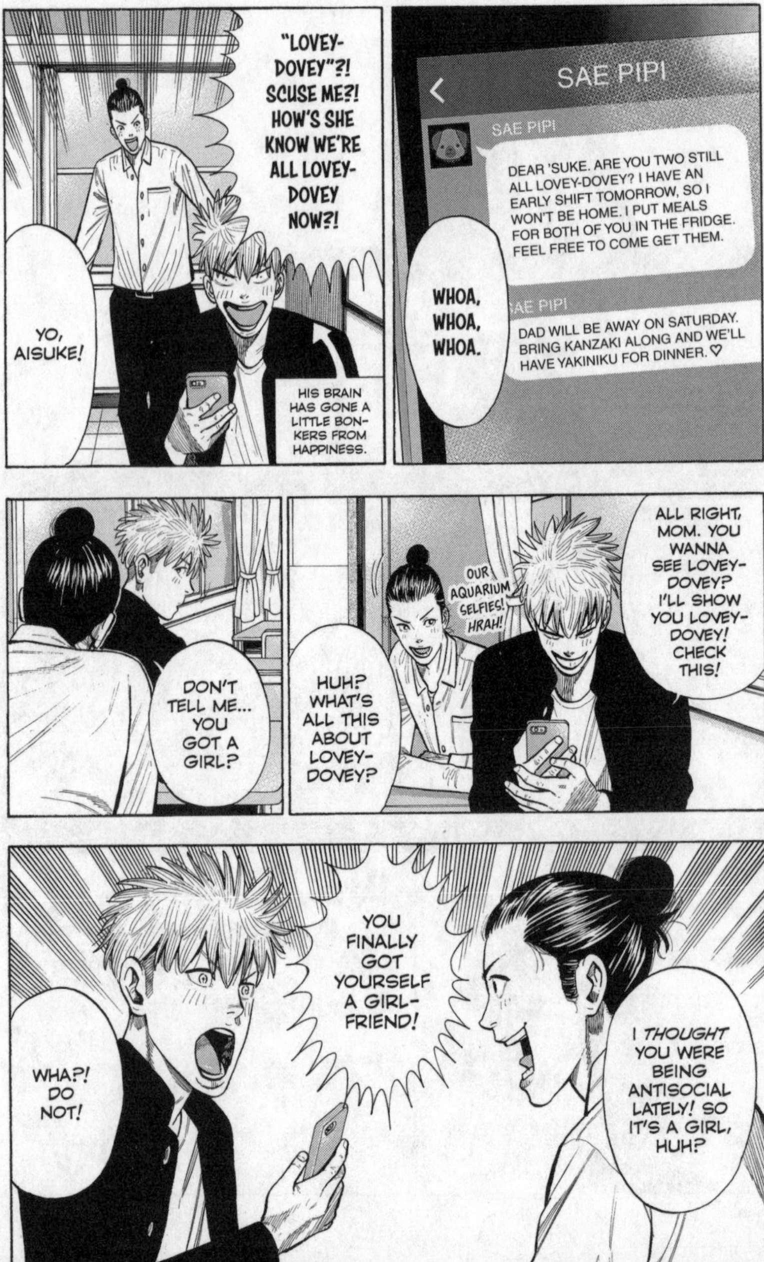
SAE PIPI
SAE PIPI
DEAR 'SUKE. ARE YOU TWO STILL ALL LOVEY-DOVEY? I HAVE AN EARLY SHIFT TOMORROW, SO I WON'T BE HOME. I PUT MEALS FOR BOTH OF YOU IN THE FRIDGE. FEEL FREE TO COME GET THEM.
SAE PIPI
DAD WILL BE AWAY ON SATURDAY. BRING KANZAKI ALONG AND WE'LL HAVE YAKINIKU FOR DINNER. ♡
WHOA, WHOA, WHOA.
"LOVEY-DOVEY"?! SCUSE ME?! HOW'S SHE KNOW WE'RE ALL LOVEY-DOVEY NOW?!
YO, AISUKE!
HIS BRAIN HAS GONE A LITTLE BONKERS FROM HAPPINESS.
ALL RIGHT, MOM. YOU WANNA SEE LOVEY-DOVEY? I'LL SHOW YOU LOVEY-DOVEY! CHECK THIS!
OUR AQUARIUM SELFIES! HRAH!
HUH? WHAT'S ALL THIS ABOUT LOVEY-DOVEY?
DON'T TELL ME... YOU GOT A GIRL?
I *THOUGHT* YOU WERE BEING ANTISOCIAL LATELY! SO IT'S A GIRL, HUH?
YOU FINALLY GOT YOURSELF A GIRL-FRIEND!
WHA?! DO NOT!

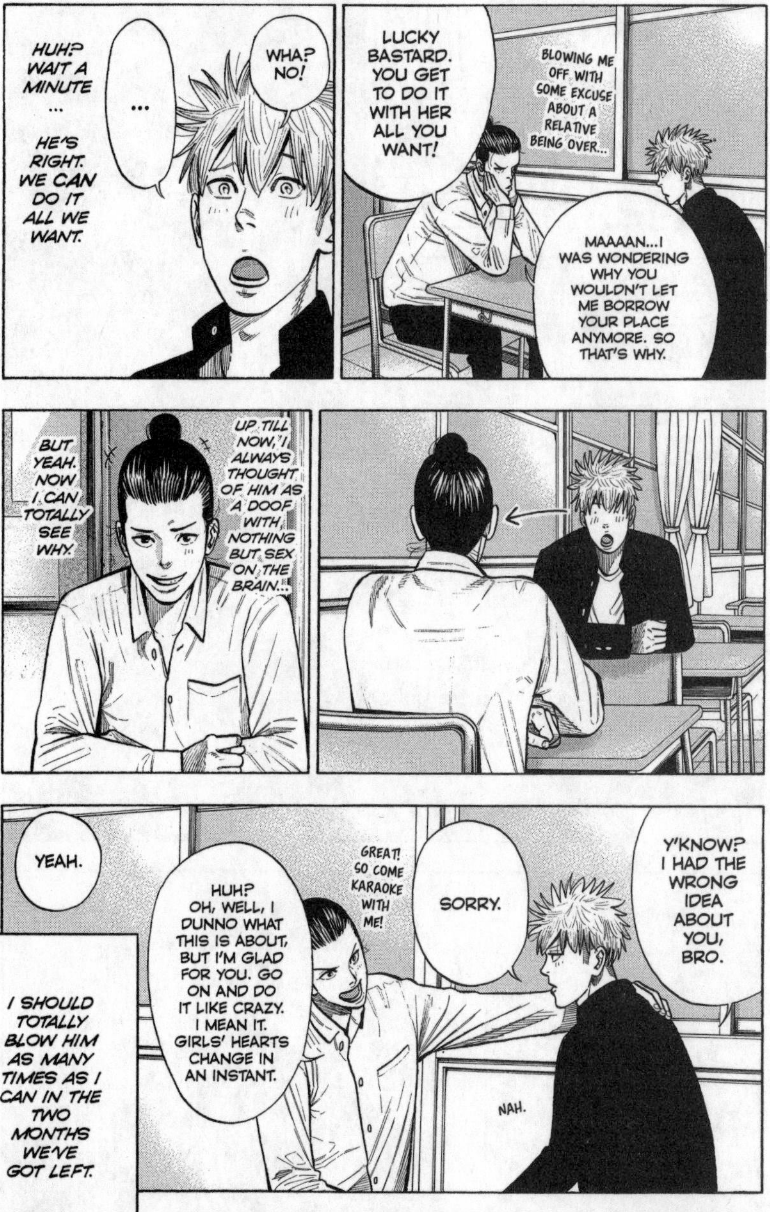
MAAAAN...I WAS WONDERING WHY YOU WOULDN'T LET ME BORROW YOUR PLACE ANYMORE. SO THAT'S WHY.
BLOWING ME OFF WITH SOME EXCUSE ABOUT A RELATIVE BEING OVER...
LUCKY BASTARD. YOU GET TO DO IT WITH HER ALL YOU WANT!
WHA? NO!
...
HUH? WAIT A MINUTE ... HE'S RIGHT. WE CAN DO IT ALL WE WANT.
UP TILL NOW, I ALWAYS THOUGHT OF HIM AS A DOOF WITH NOTHING BUT SEX ON THE BRAIN...
BUT YEAH. NOW I CAN TOTALLY SEE WHY.
Y'KNOW? I HAD THE WRONG IDEA ABOUT YOU, BRO.
SORRY.
HUH? OH, WELL, I DUNNO WHAT THIS IS ABOUT, BUT I'M GLAD FOR YOU. GO ON AND DO IT LIKE CRAZY. I MEAN IT. GIRLS' HEARTS CHANGE IN AN INSTANT.
YEAH.
GREAT! SO COME KARAOKE WITH ME!
NAH.
I SHOULD TOTALLY BLOW HIM AS MANY TIMES AS I CAN IN THE TWO MONTHS WE'VE GOT LEFT.

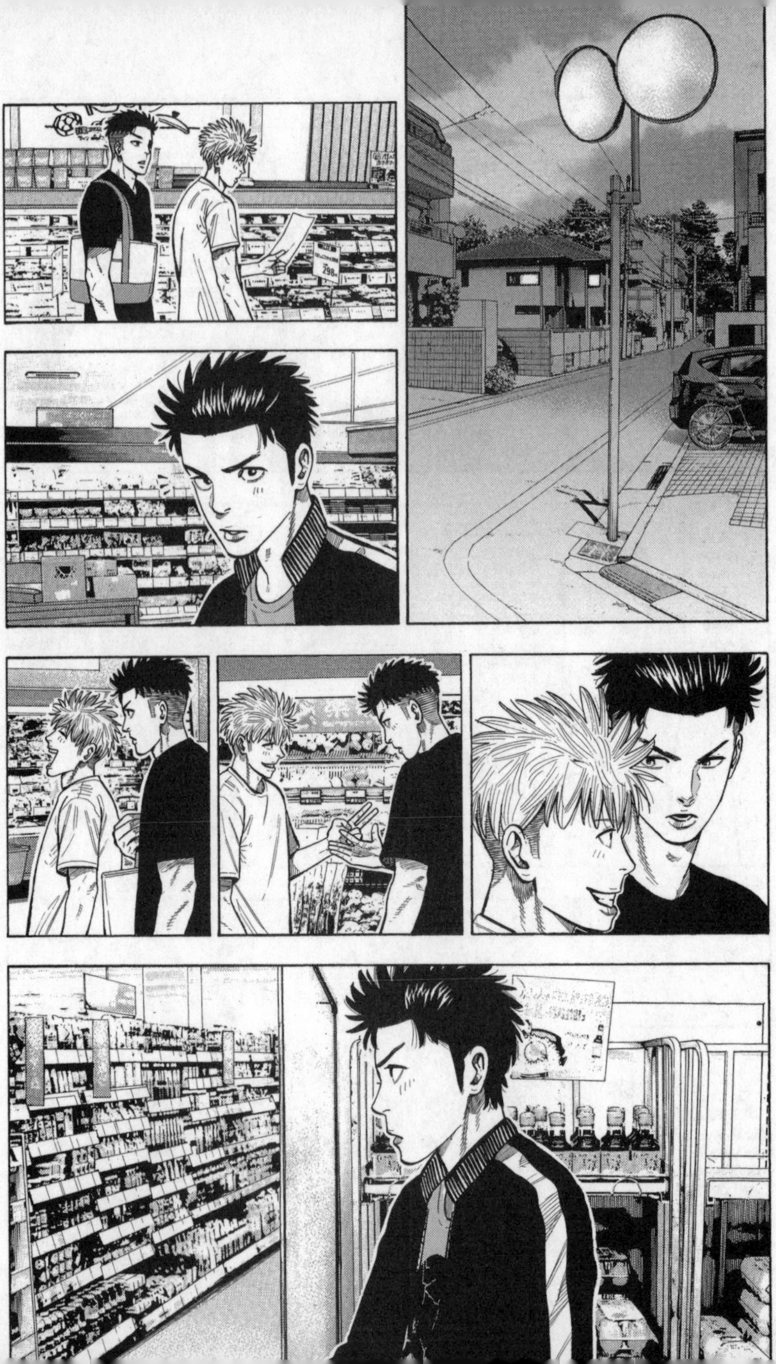

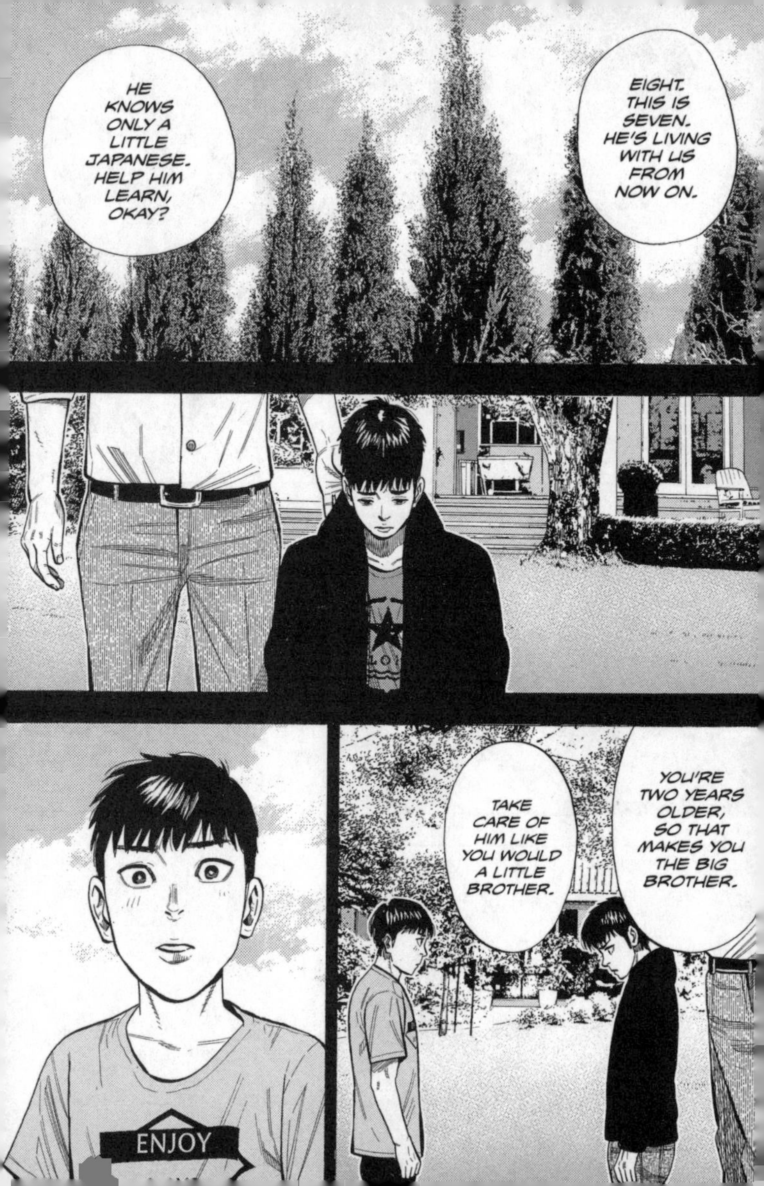
EIGHT. THIS IS SEVEN. HE'S LIVING WITH US FROM NOW ON.
HE KNOWS ONLY A LITTLE JAPANESE. HELP HIM LEARN, OKAY?
YOU'RE TWO YEARS OLDER, SO THAT MAKES YOU THE BIG BROTHER.
TAKE CARE OF HIM LIKE YOU WOULD A LITTLE BROTHER.
ENJOY

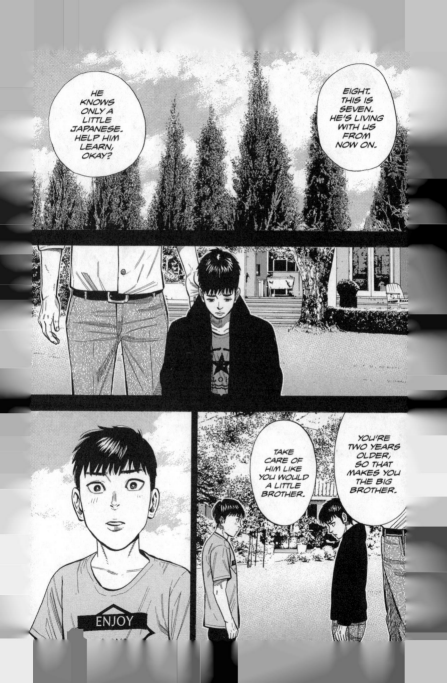

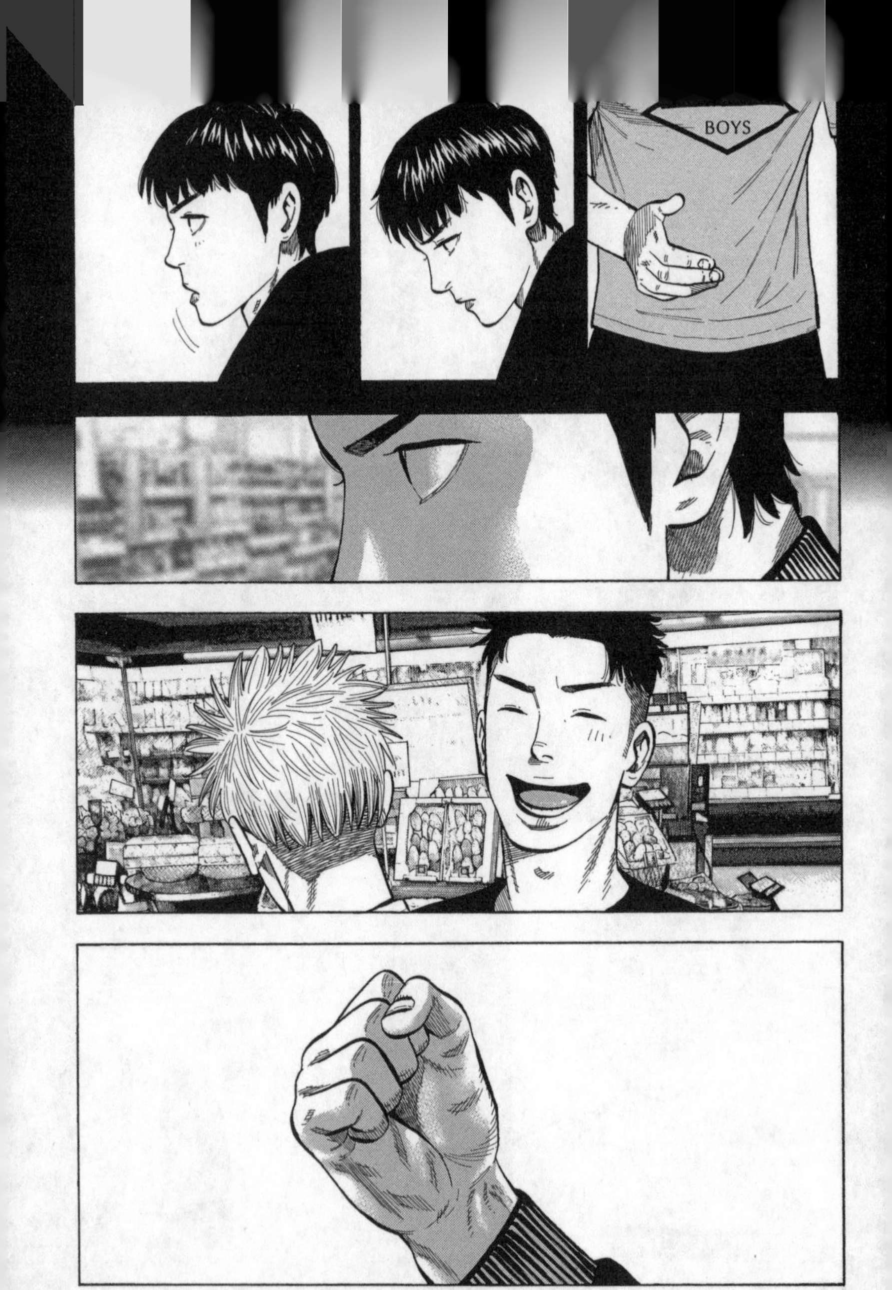
BOYS

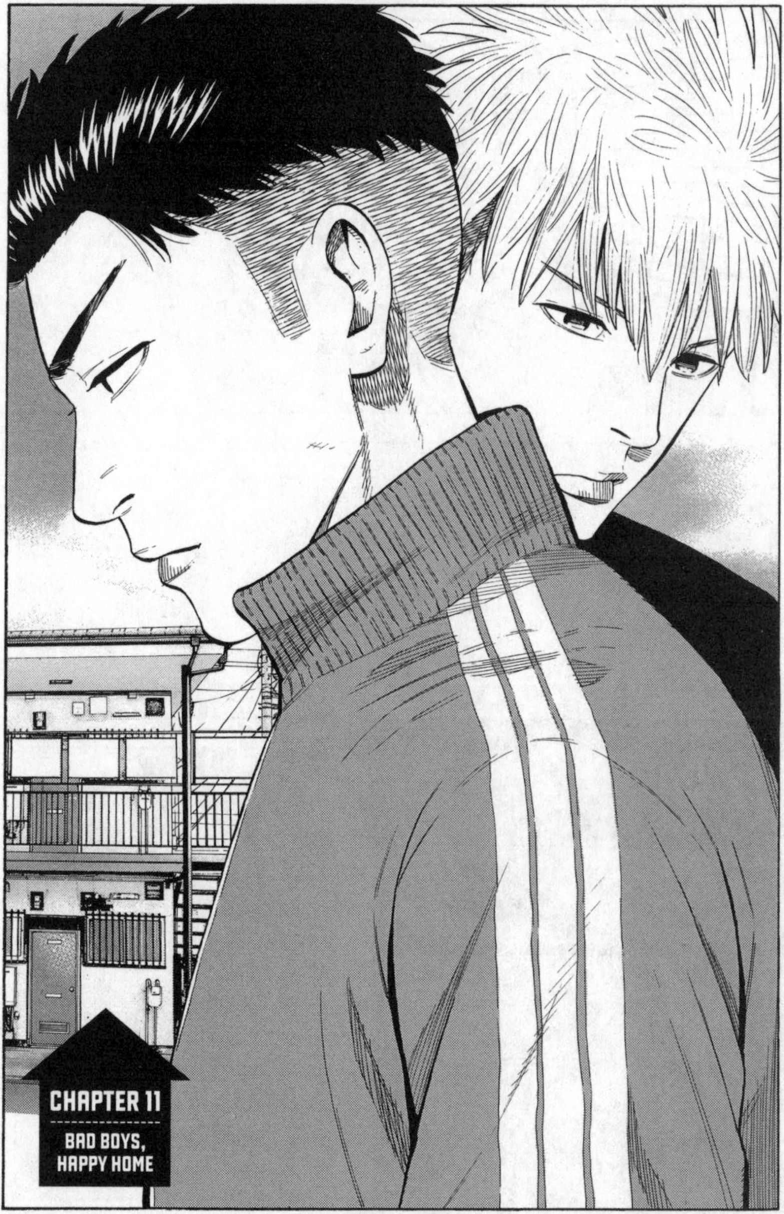
CHAPTER 11
BAD BOYS, HAPPY HOME

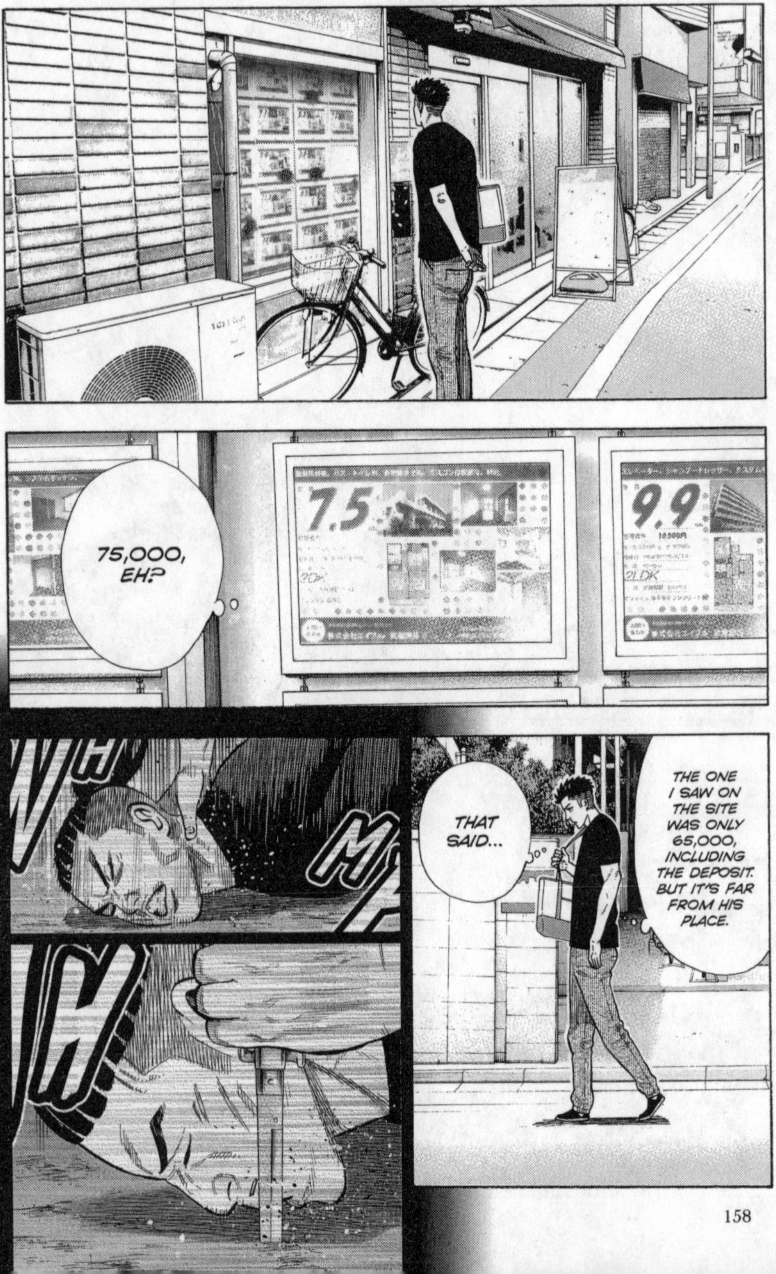
75,000, EH?
THE ONE I SAW ON THE SITE WAS ONLY 65,000, INCLUDING THE DEPOSIT. BUT IT'S FAR FROM HIS PLACE.
THAT SAID...

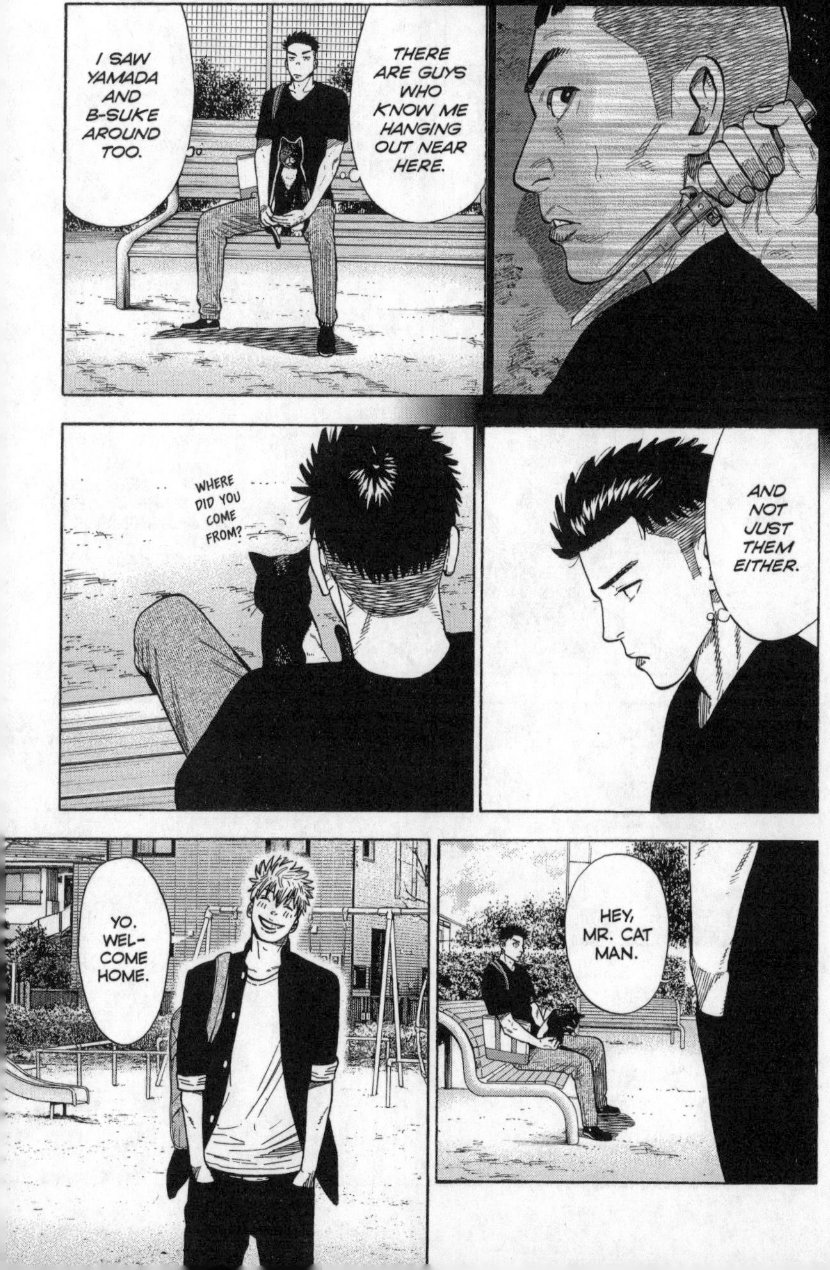
THERE ARE GUYS WHO KNOW ME HANGING OUT NEAR HERE.
I SAW YAMADA AND B-SUKE AROUND TOO.
AND NOT JUST THEM EITHER.
WHERE DID YOU COME FROM?
HEY, MR. CAT MAN.
YO. WEL-COME HOME.

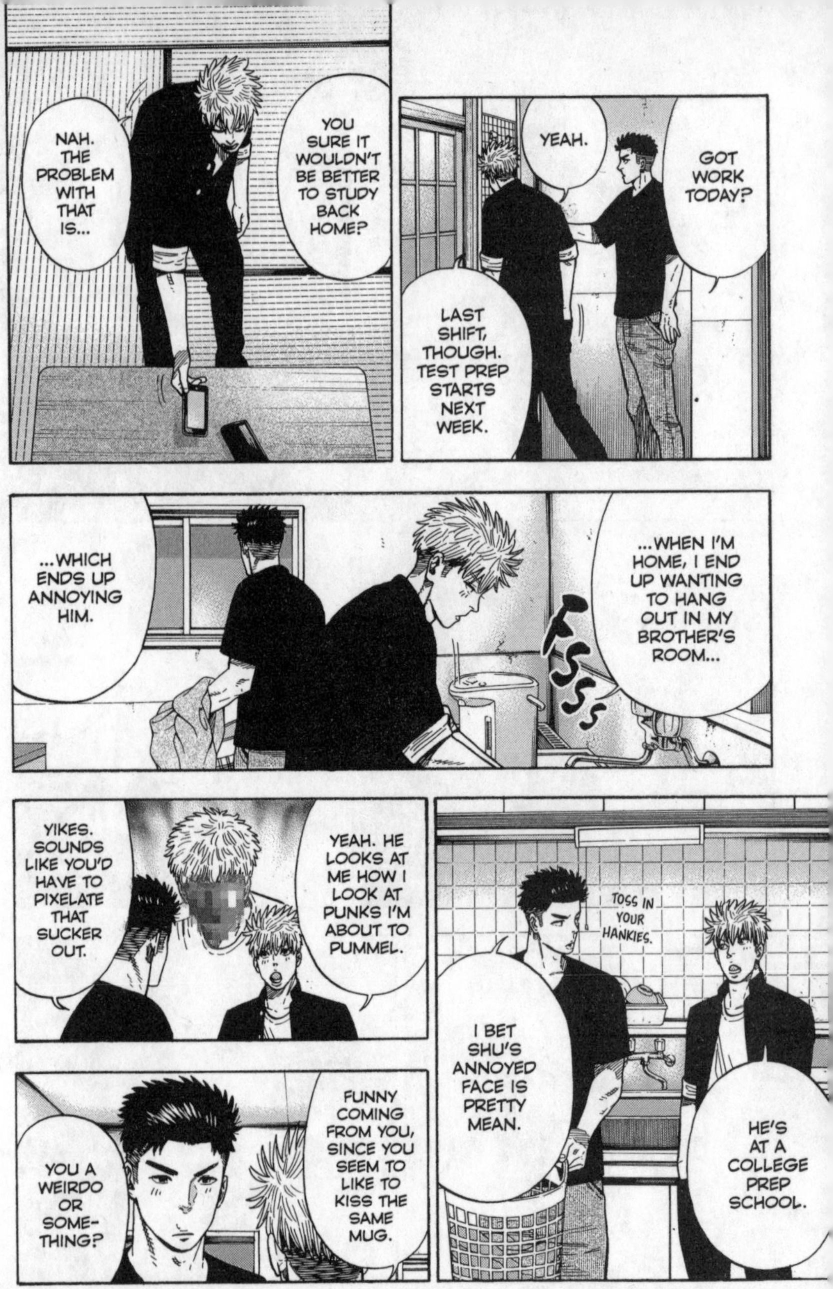
GOT WORK TODAY?
YEAH.
LAST SHIFT, THOUGH. TEST PREP STARTS NEXT WEEK.
YOU SURE IT WOULDN'T BE BETTER TO STUDY BACK HOME?
NAH. THE PROBLEM WITH THAT IS...
...WHEN I'M HOME, I END UP WANTING TO HANG OUT IN MY BROTHER'S ROOM...
TSSS
...WHICH ENDS UP ANNOYING HIM.
TOSS IN YOUR HANKIES.
I BET SHU'S ANNOYED FACE IS PRETTY MEAN.
HE'S AT A COLLEGE PREP SCHOOL.
YEAH. HE LOOKS AT ME HOW I LOOK AT PUNKS I'M ABOUT TO PUMMEL.
YIKES. SOUNDS LIKE YOU'D HAVE TO PIXELATE THAT SUCKER OUT.
FUNNY COMING FROM YOU, SINCE YOU SEEM TO LIKE TO KISS THE SAME MUG.
YOU A WEIRDO OR SOMETHING?

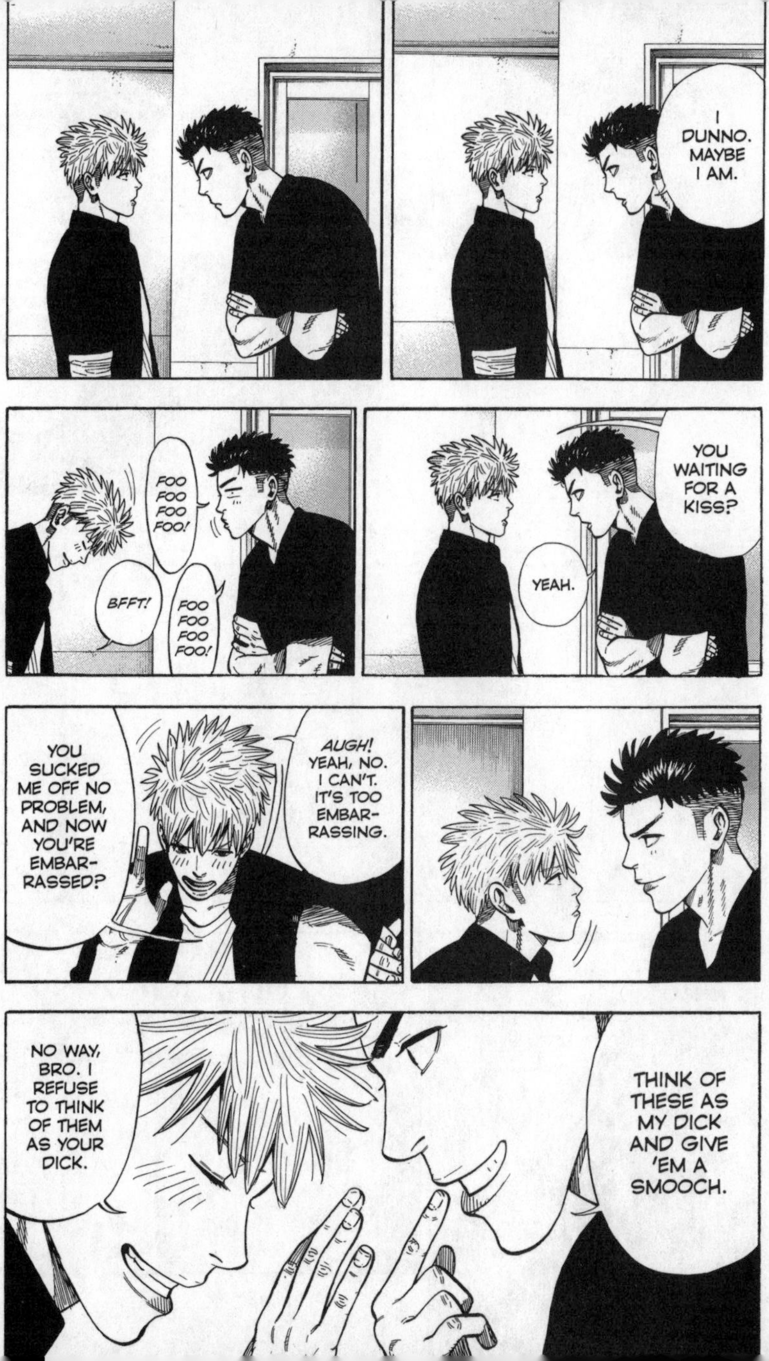

I DUNNO. MAYBE I AM.
YOU WAITING FOR A KISS?
YEAH.
FOO FOO FOO FOO!
FOO FOO FOO FOO!
BFFT!
AUGH! YEAH, NO. I CAN'T. IT'S TOO EMBARRASSING.
YOU SUCKED ME OFF NO PROBLEM, AND NOW YOU'RE EMBARRASSED?
THINK OF THESE AS MY DICK AND GIVE 'EM A SMOOCH.
NO WAY, BRO. I REFUSE TO THINK OF THEM AS YOUR DICK.

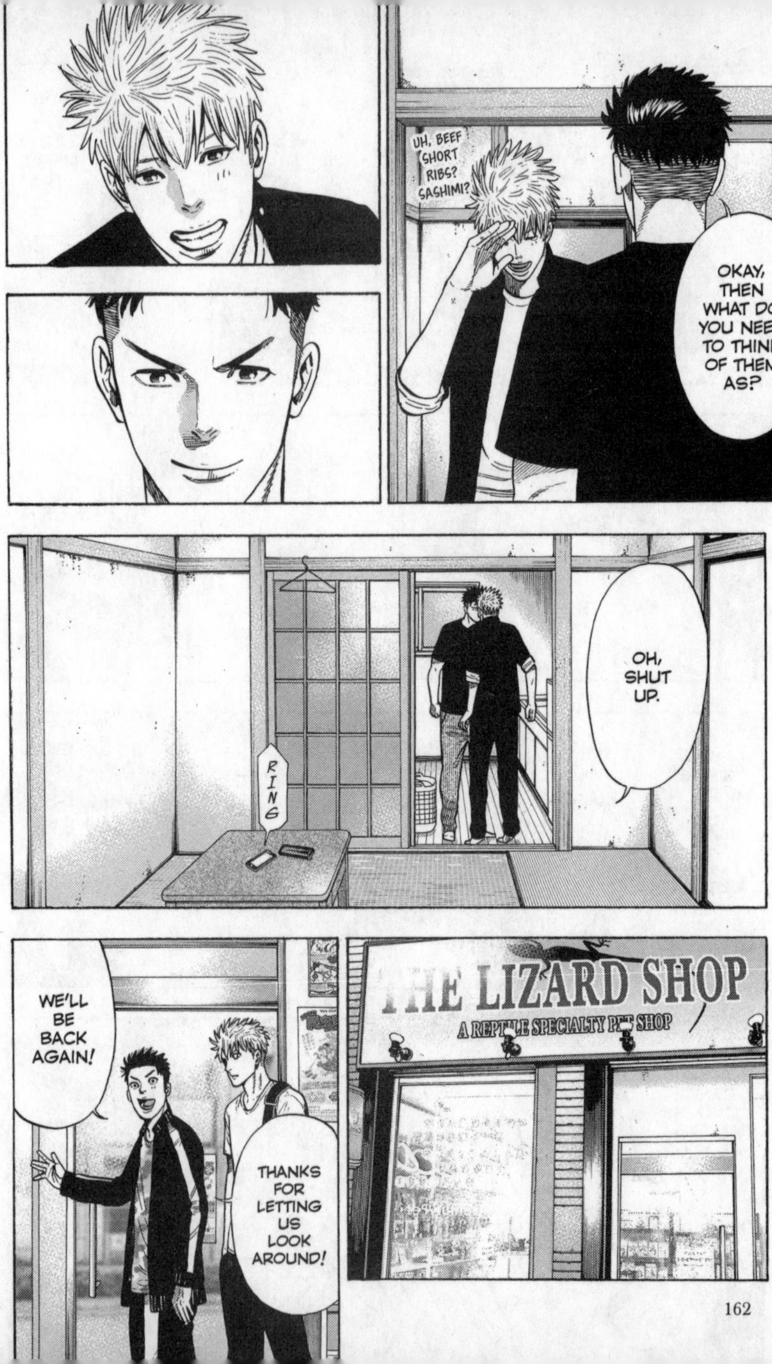
OKAY, THEN WHAT DO YOU NEED TO THINK OF THEM AS?
UH, BEEF SHORT RIBS? SASHIMI?
OH, SHUT UP.
RING
THE LIZARD SHOP
A REPTILE SPECIALTY PET SHOP
WE'LL BE BACK AGAIN!
THANKS FOR LETTING US LOOK AROUND!

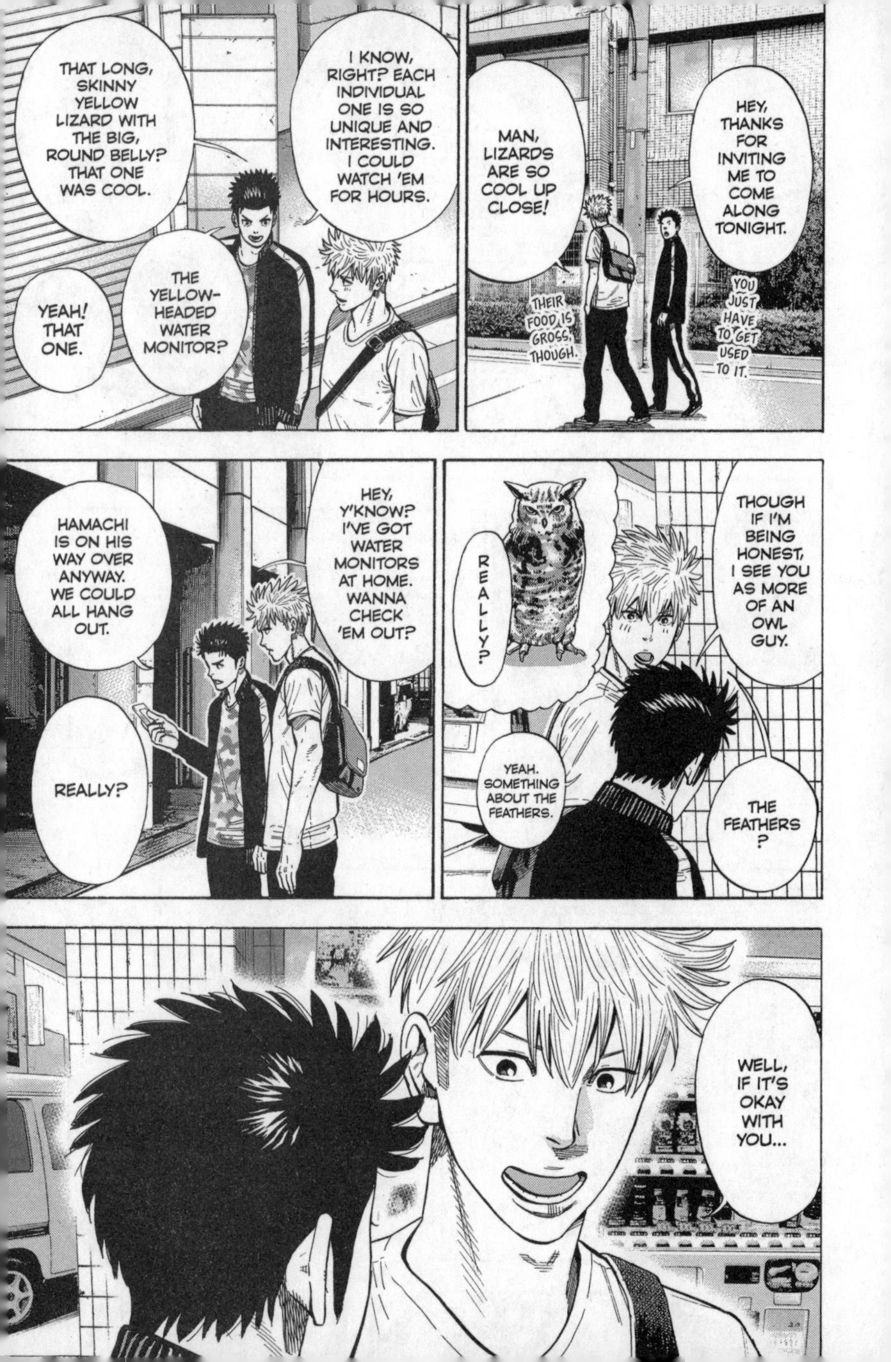
HEY, THANKS FOR INVITING ME TO COME ALONG TONIGHT.
MAN, LIZARDS ARE SO COOL UP CLOSE!
THEIR FOOD IS GROSS, THOUGH.
YOU JUST HAVE TO GET USED TO IT.
I KNOW, RIGHT? EACH INDIVIDUAL ONE IS SO UNIQUE AND INTERESTING. I COULD WATCH 'EM FOR HOURS.
THAT LONG, SKINNY YELLOW LIZARD WITH THE BIG, ROUND BELLY? THAT ONE WAS COOL.
THE YELLOW-HEADED WATER MONITOR?
YEAH! THAT ONE.
THOUGH IF I'M BEING HONEST, I SEE YOU AS MORE OF AN OWL GUY.
REALLY?
THE FEATHERS?
YEAH. SOMETHING ABOUT THE FEATHERS.
HEY, Y'KNOW? I'VE GOT WATER MONITORS AT HOME. WANNA CHECK 'EM OUT?
HAMACHI IS ON HIS WAY OVER ANYWAY. WE COULD ALL HANG OUT.
REALLY?
WELL, IF IT'S OKAY WITH YOU...

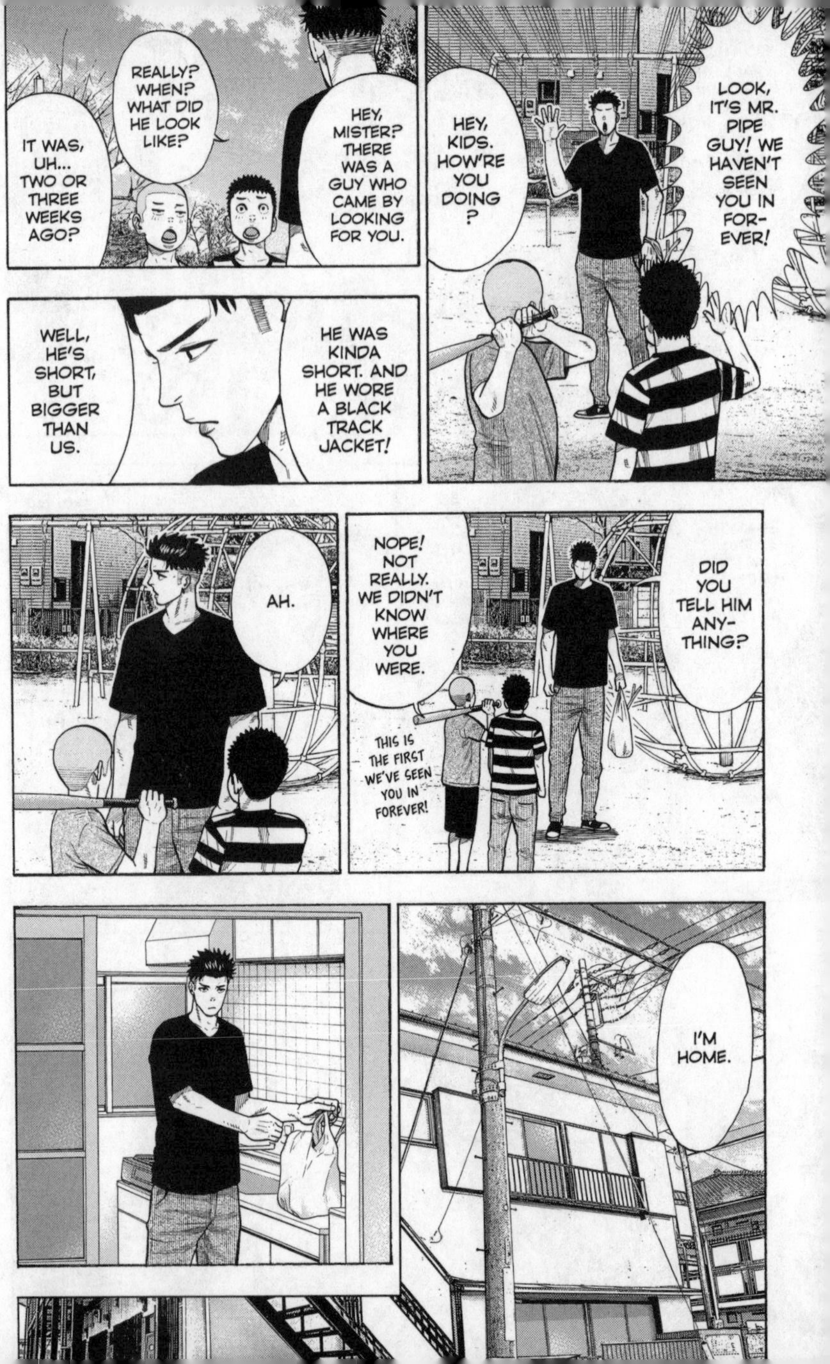
LOOK, IT'S MR. PIPE GUY! WE HAVEN'T SEEN YOU IN FOREVER!
HEY, KIDS. HOW'RE YOU DOING?
HEY, MISTER? THERE WAS A GUY WHO CAME BY LOOKING FOR YOU.
REALLY? WHEN? WHAT DID HE LOOK LIKE?
IT WAS, UH... TWO OR THREE WEEKS AGO?
HE WAS KINDA SHORT. AND HE WORE A BLACK TRACK JACKET!
WELL, HE'S SHORT, BUT BIGGER THAN US.
DID YOU TELL HIM ANYTHING?
NOPE! NOT REALLY. WE DIDN'T KNOW WHERE YOU WERE.
THIS IS THE FIRST WE'VE SEEN YOU IN FOREVER!
AH.
I'M HOME.

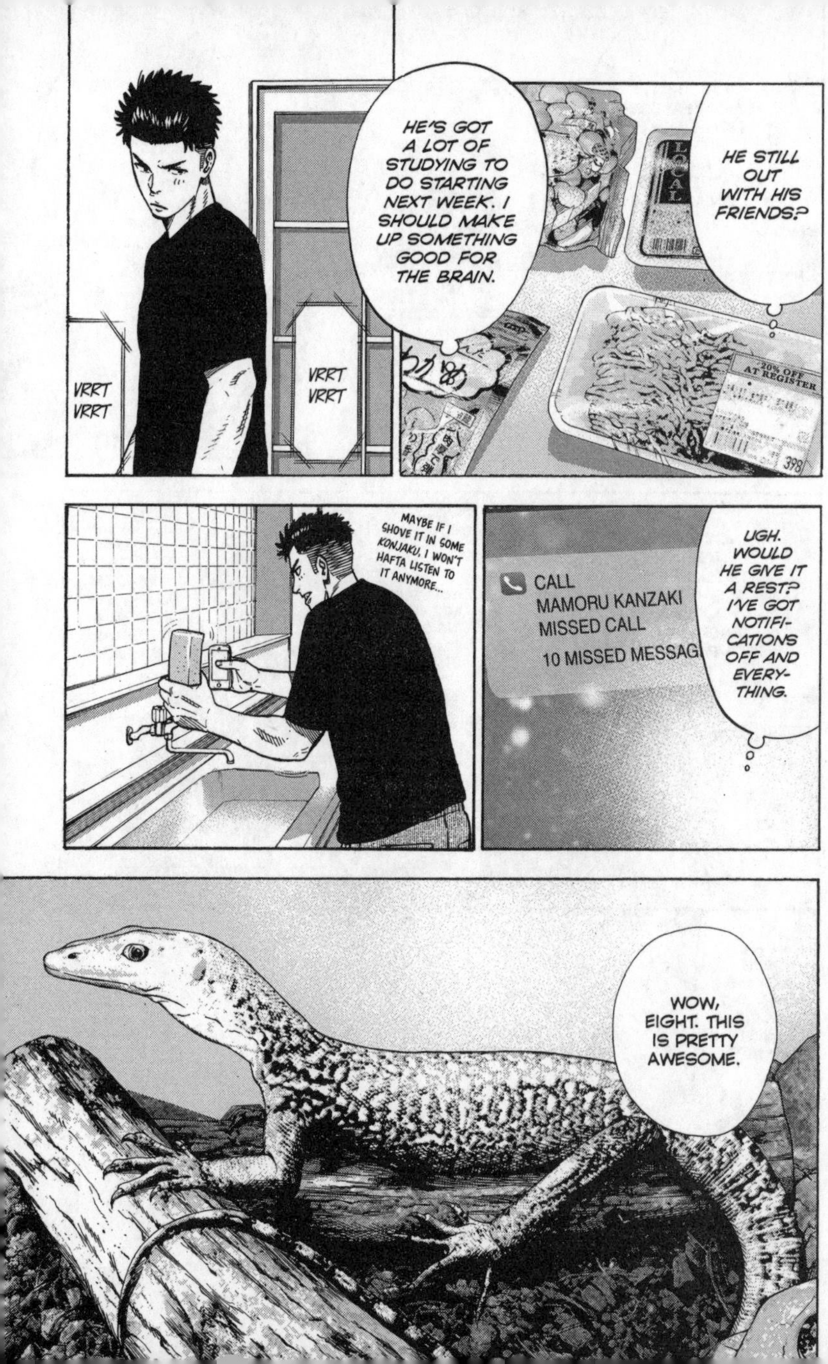
HE STILL OUT WITH HIS FRIENDS?
-20% OFF AT REGISTER
398
HE'S GOT A LOT OF STUDYING TO DO STARTING NEXT WEEK. I SHOULD MAKE UP SOMETHING GOOD FOR THE BRAIN.
VRRT VRRT
VRRT VRRT
UGH. WOULD HE GIVE IT A REST? I'VE GOT NOTIFI-CATIONS OFF AND EVERY-THING.
CALL
MAMORU KANZAKI
MISSED CALL
10 MISSED MESSAG
MAYBE IF I SHOVE IT IN SOME KONJAKU, I WON'T HAFTA LISTEN TO IT ANYMORE...
WOW, EIGHT. THIS IS PRETTY AWESOME.

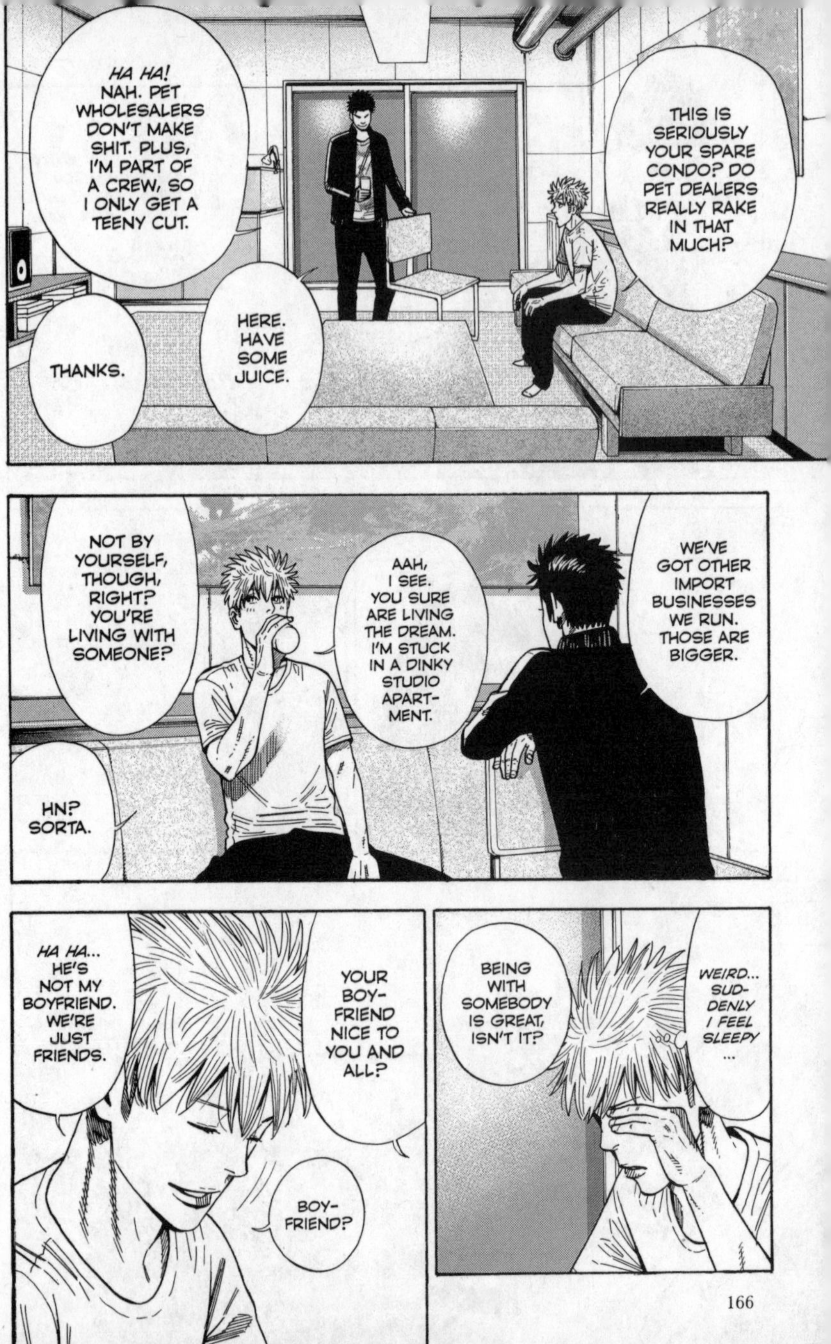
THIS IS SERIOUSLY YOUR SPARE CONDO? DO PET DEALERS REALLY RAKE IN THAT MUCH?
HA HA! NAH. PET WHOLESALERS DON'T MAKE SHIT. PLUS, I'M PART OF A CREW, SO I ONLY GET A TEENY CUT.
HERE. HAVE SOME JUICE.
THANKS.
WE'VE GOT OTHER IMPORT BUSINESSES WE RUN. THOSE ARE BIGGER.
AAH, I SEE. YOU SURE ARE LIVING THE DREAM. I'M STUCK IN A DINKY STUDIO APARTMENT.
NOT BY YOURSELF, THOUGH, RIGHT? YOU'RE LIVING WITH SOMEONE?
HN? SORTA.
WEIRD... SUDDENLY I FEEL SLEEPY ...
BEING WITH SOMEBODY IS GREAT, ISN'T IT?
YOUR BOYFRIEND NICE TO YOU AND ALL?
BOYFRIEND?
HA HA... HE'S NOT MY BOYFRIEND. WE'RE JUST FRIENDS.

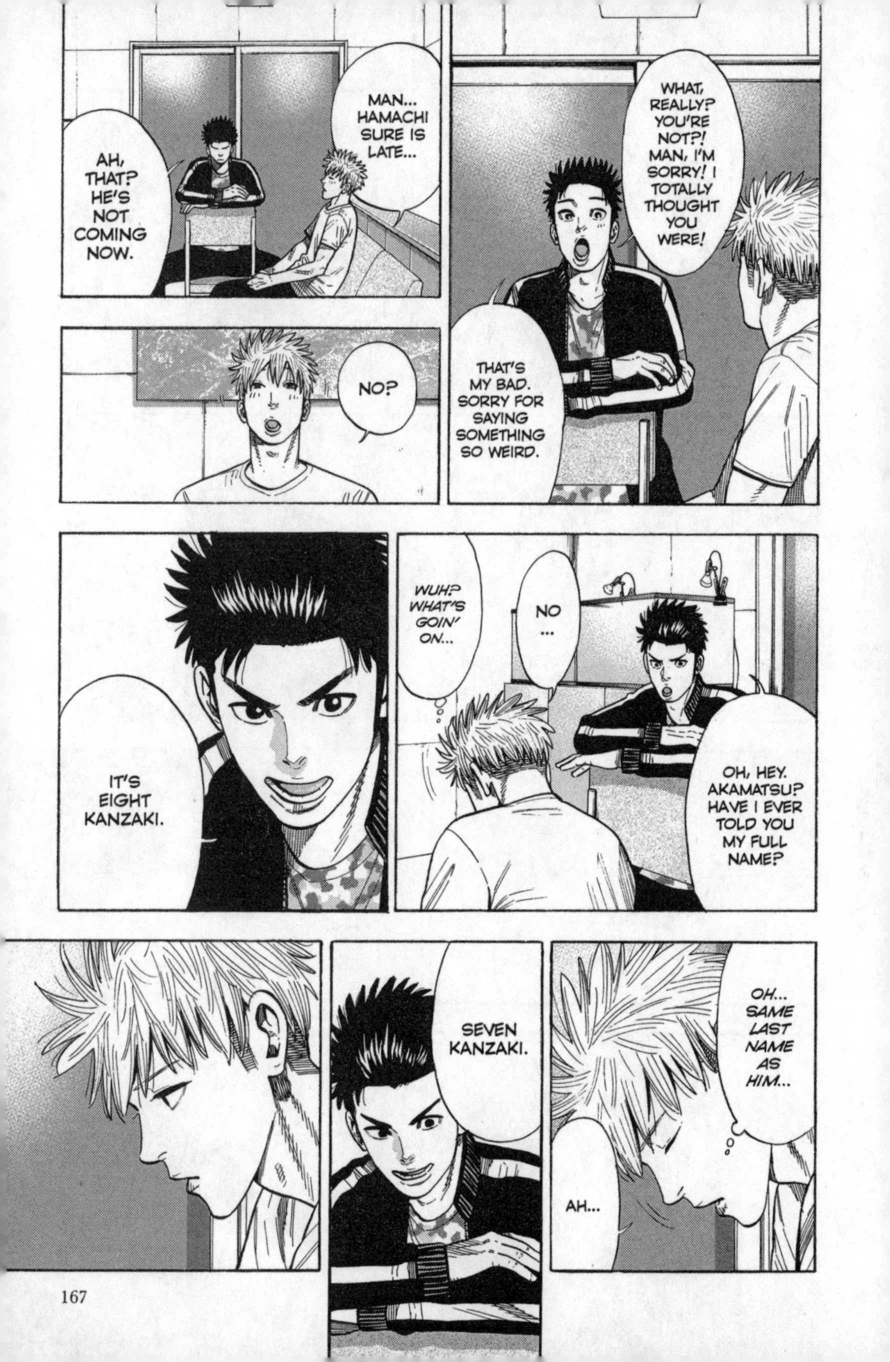
WHAT, REALLY? YOU'RE NOT?! MAN, I'M SORRY! I TOTALLY THOUGHT YOU WERE!
THAT'S MY BAD. SORRY FOR SAYING SOMETHING SO WEIRD.
MAN... HAMACHI SURE IS LATE...
AH, THAT? HE'S NOT COMING NOW.
NO?
OH, HEY. AKAMATSU? HAVE I EVER TOLD YOU MY FULL NAME?
NO ...
WUH? WHAT'S GOIN' ON...
IT'S EIGHT KANZAKI.
OH... SAME LAST NAME AS HIM...
AH...
SEVEN KANZAKI.

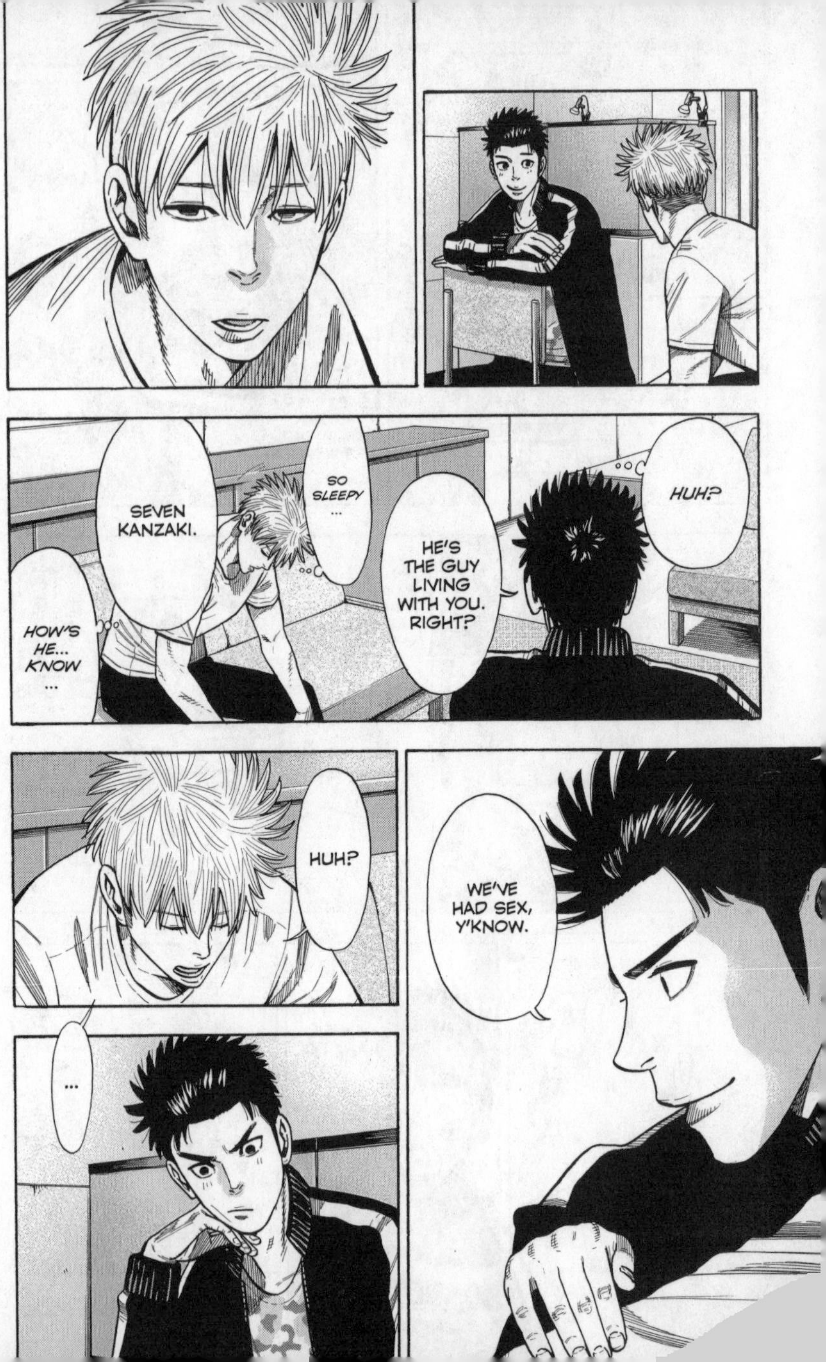
HUH?
SO SLEEPY ...
SEVEN KANZAKI.
HE'S THE GUY LIVING WITH YOU. RIGHT?
HOW'S HE... KNOW ...
WE'VE HAD SEX, Y'KNOW.
HUH?
...

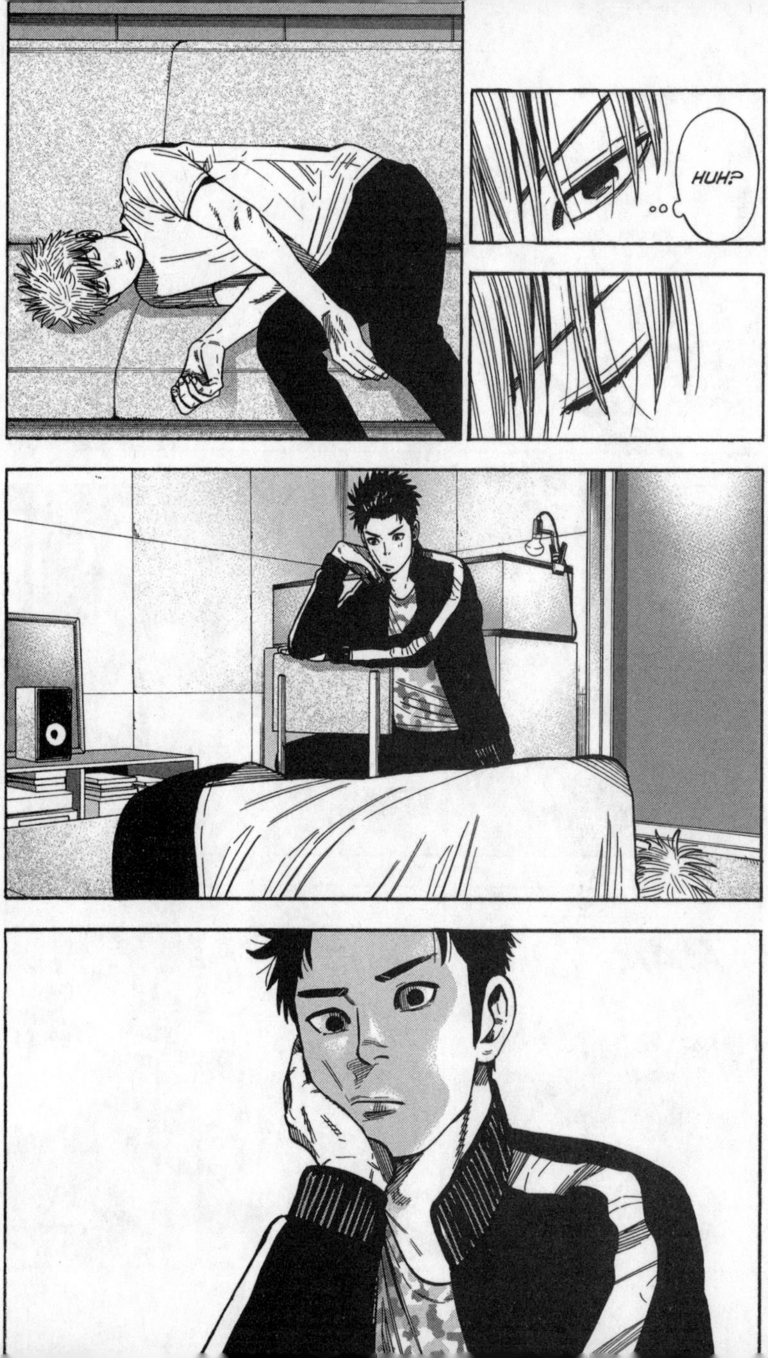
HUH?

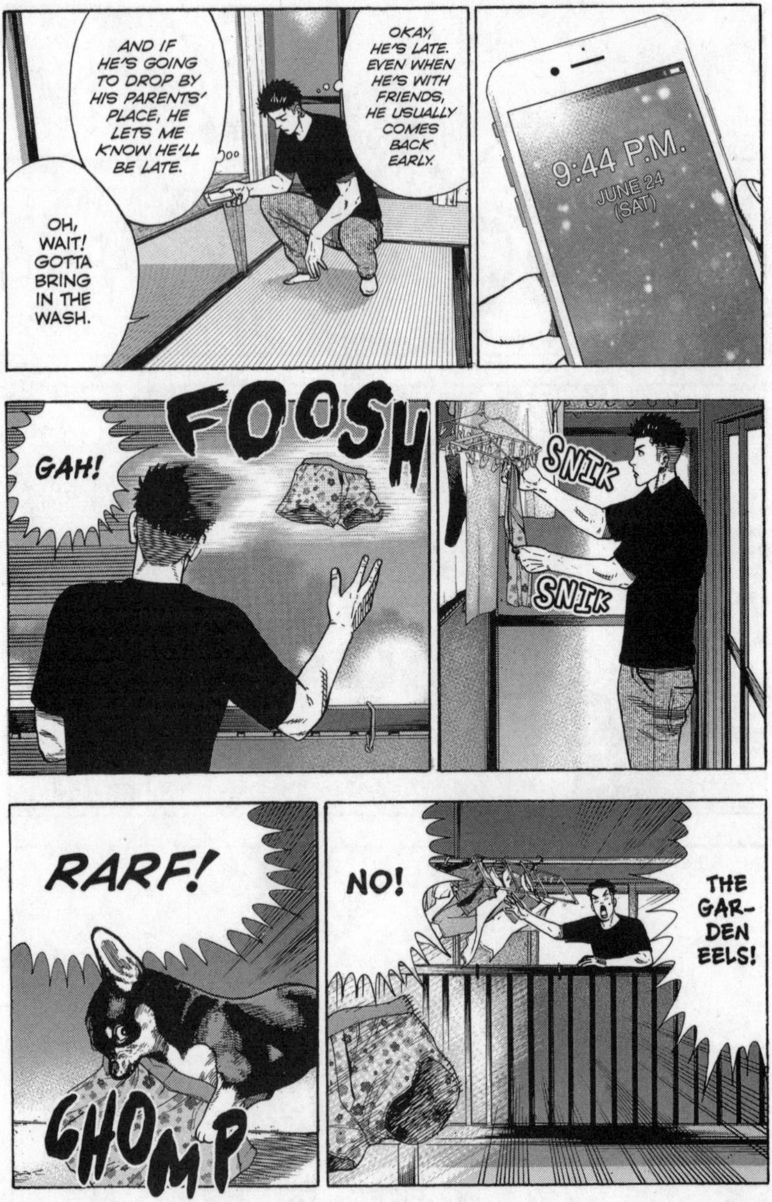
9:44 P.M.
JUNE 24 (SAT)
OKAY, HE'S LATE. EVEN WHEN HE'S WITH FRIENDS, HE USUALLY COMES BACK EARLY.
AND IF HE'S GOING TO DROP BY HIS PARENTS' PLACE, HE LETS ME KNOW HE'LL BE LATE.
OH, WAIT! GOTTA BRING IN THE WASH.
SNIK
SNIK
FOOSH
GAH!
THE GAR-DEN EELS!
NO!
RARF!
CHOMP

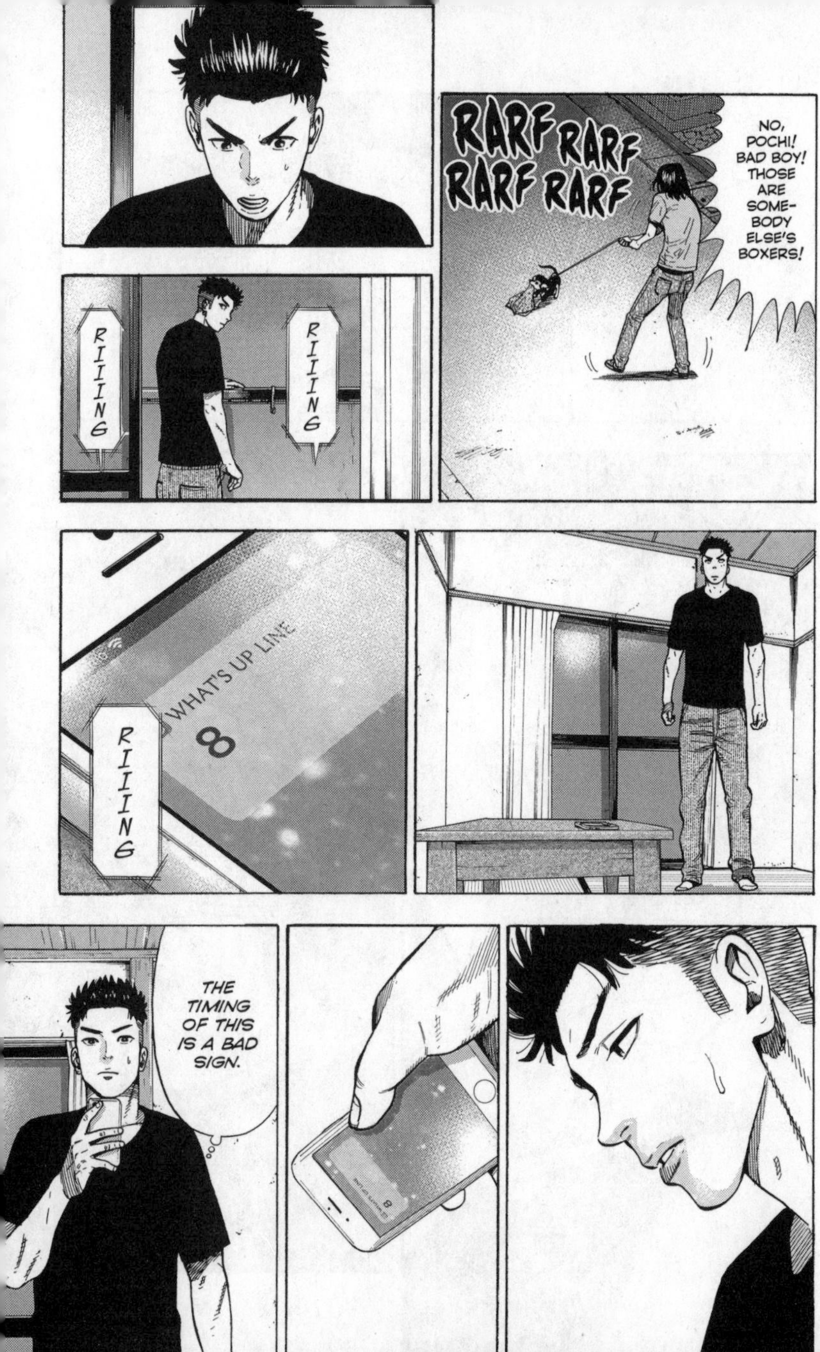
RARF RARF RARF RARF
NO, POCHI! BAD BOY! THOSE ARE SOMEBODY ELSE'S BOXERS!
RIIING
RIIING
WHAT'S UP LINE
8
RIIING
THE TIMING OF THIS IS A BAD SIGN.

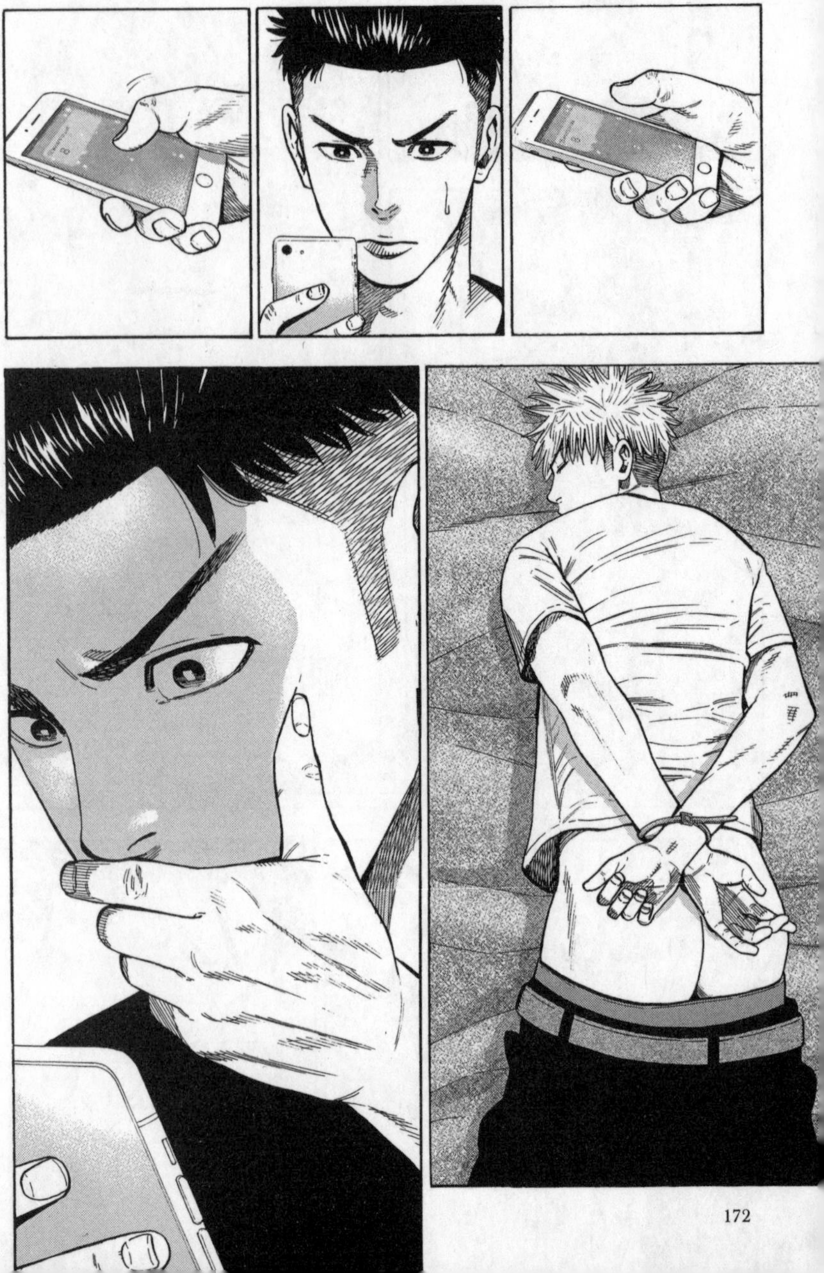

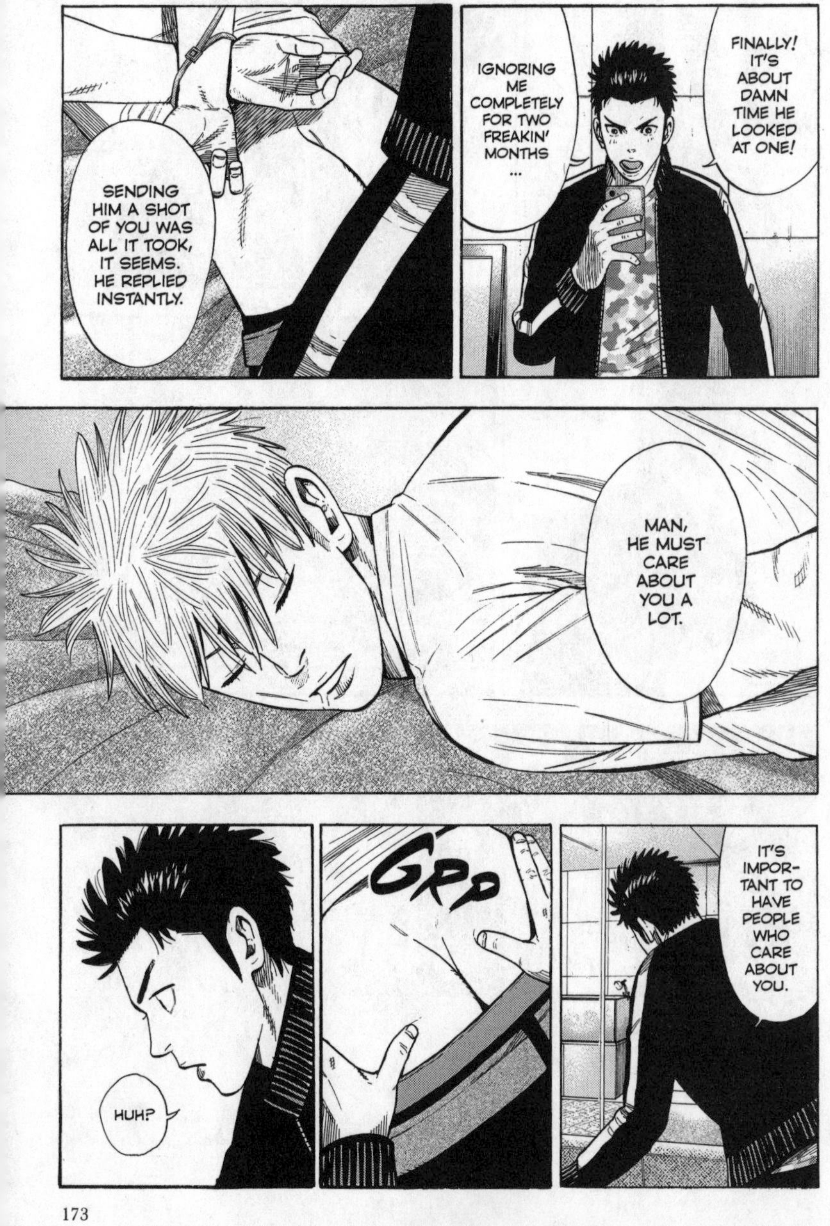
FINALLY! IT'S ABOUT DAMN TIME HE LOOKED AT ONE!
IGNORING ME COMPLETELY FOR TWO FREAKIN' MONTHS ...
SENDING HIM A SHOT OF YOU WAS ALL IT TOOK, IT SEEMS. HE REPLIED INSTANTLY.
MAN, HE MUST CARE ABOUT YOU A LOT.
IT'S IMPORTANT TO HAVE PEOPLE WHO CARE ABOUT YOU.
GRP
HUH?

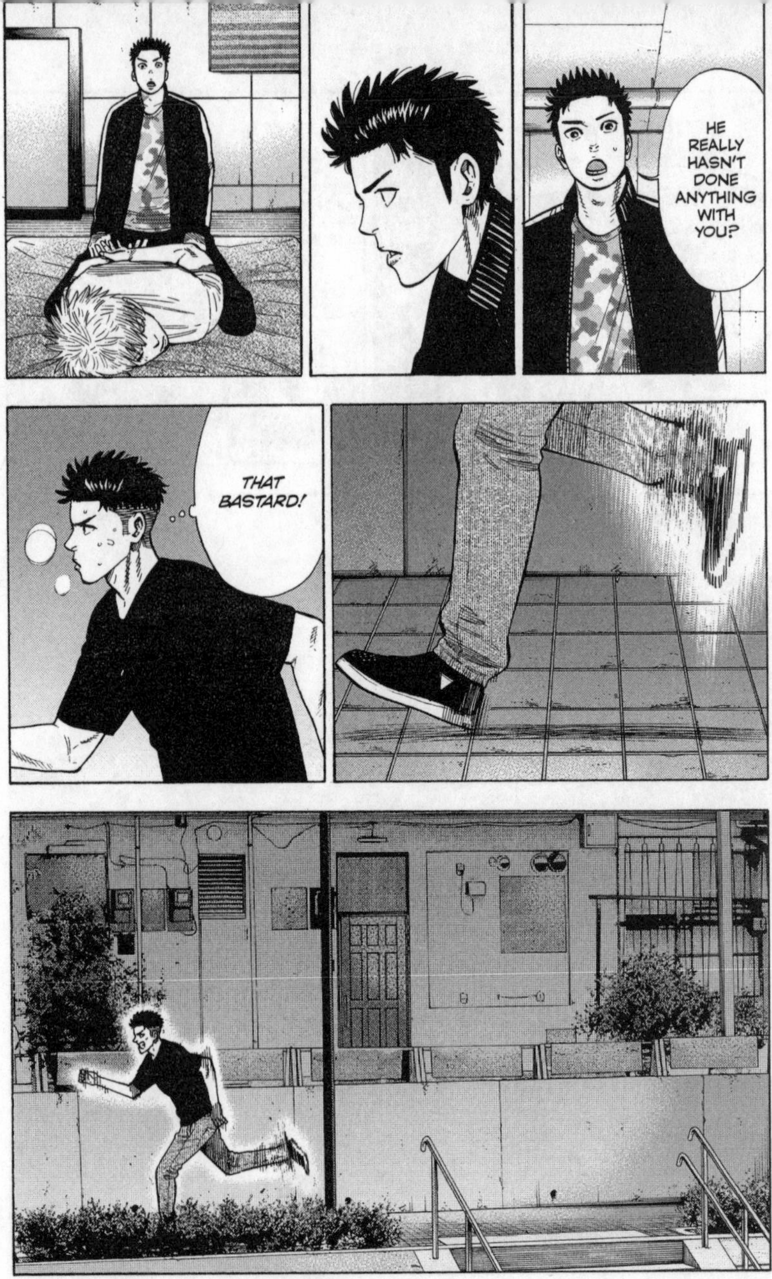
HE REALLY HASN'T DONE ANYTHING WITH YOU?
THAT BASTARD!

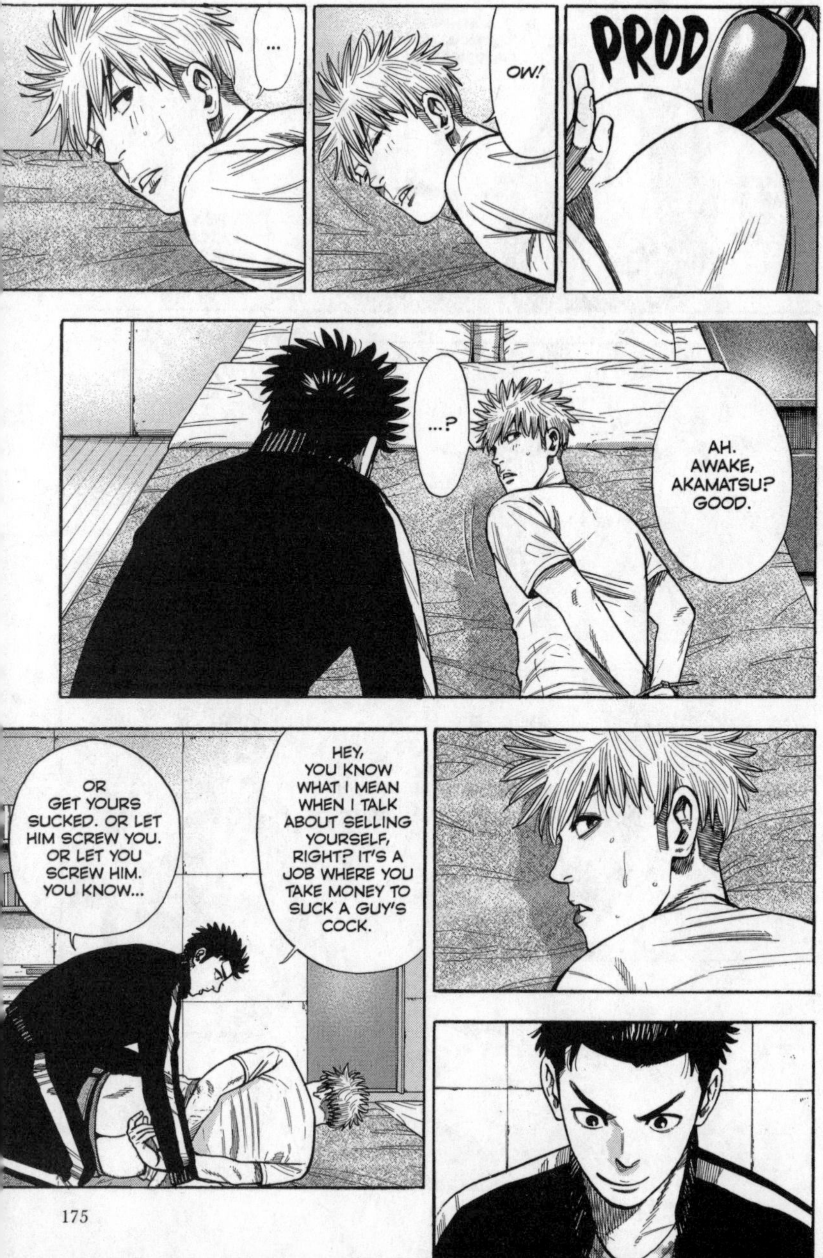
PROD
OW!
...
AH. AWAKE, AKAMATSU? GOOD.
...?
HEY, YOU KNOW WHAT I MEAN WHEN I TALK ABOUT SELLING YOURSELF, RIGHT? IT'S A JOB WHERE YOU TAKE MONEY TO SUCK A GUY'S COCK.
OR GET YOURS SUCKED. OR LET HIM SCREW YOU. OR LET YOU SCREW HIM. YOU KNOW...

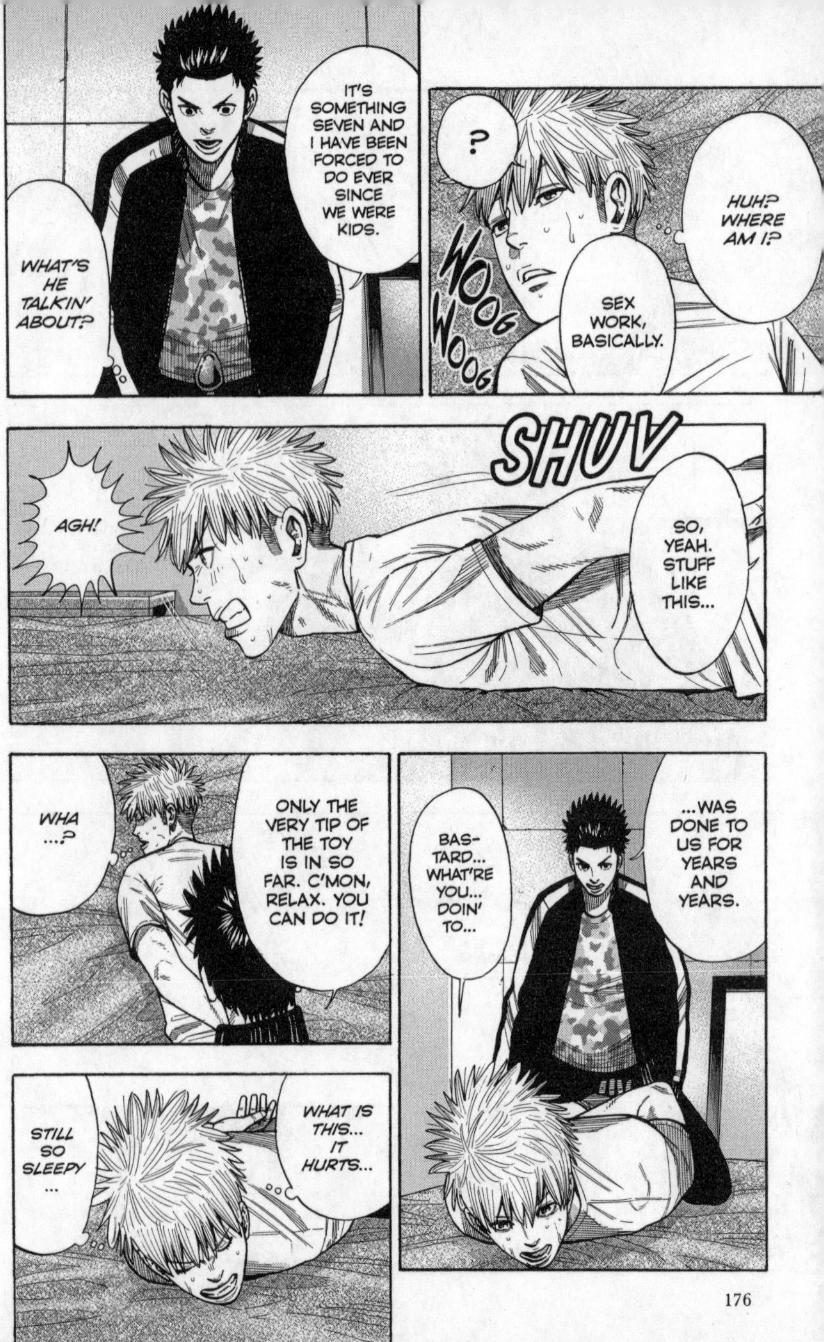
?
HUH? WHERE AM I?
WOOG WOOG
SEX WORK, BASICALLY.
IT'S SOMETHING SEVEN AND I HAVE BEEN FORCED TO DO EVER SINCE WE WERE KIDS.
WHAT'S HE TALKIN' ABOUT?
SHUV
SO, YEAH. STUFF LIKE THIS...
AGH!
...WAS DONE TO US FOR YEARS AND YEARS.
BAS-TARD... WHAT'RE YOU... DOIN' TO...
ONLY THE VERY TIP OF THE TOY IS IN SO FAR. C'MON, RELAX. YOU CAN DO IT!
WHA ...?
WHAT IS THIS... IT HURTS...
STILL SO SLEEPY ...

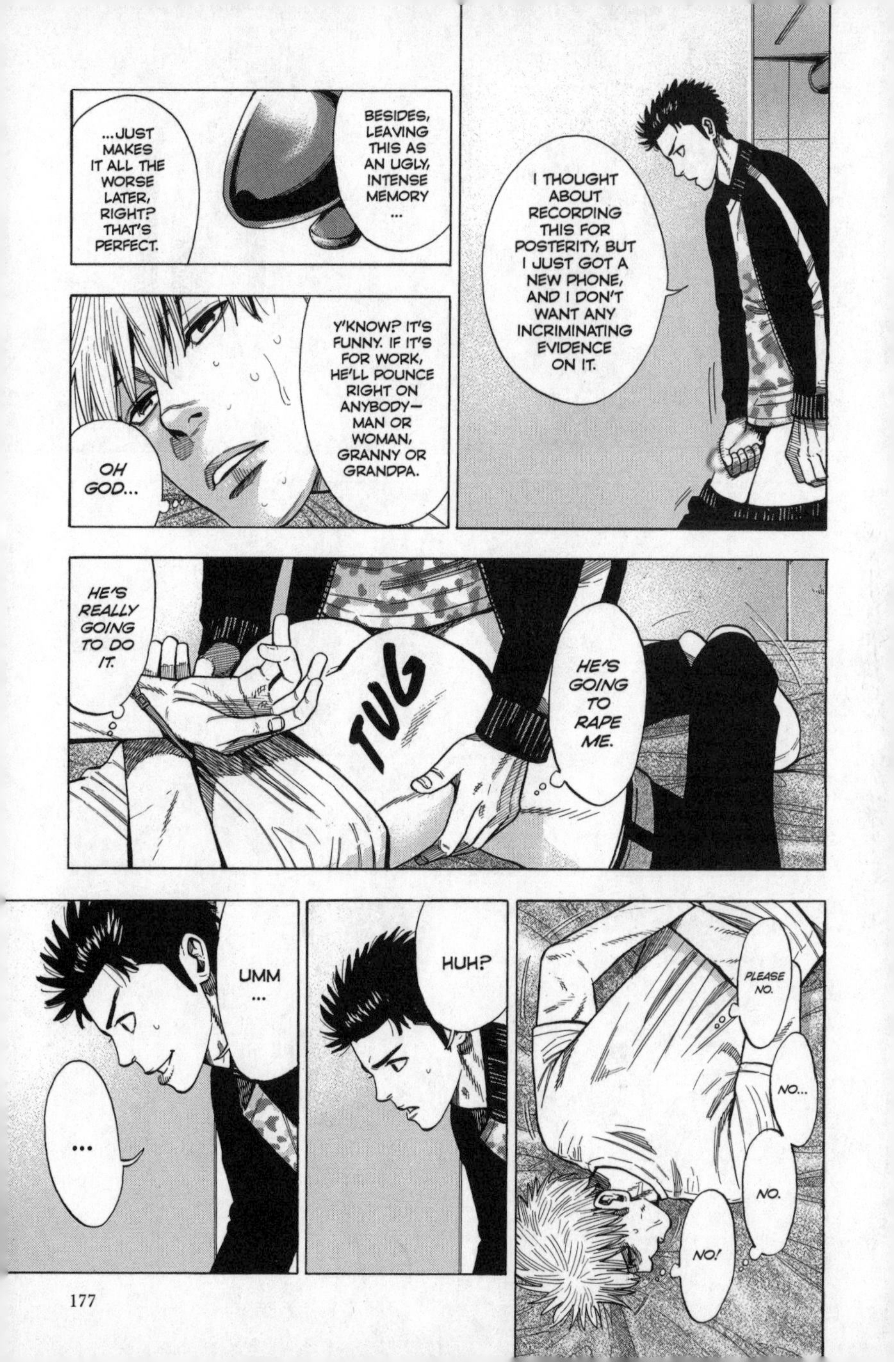
I THOUGHT ABOUT RECORDING THIS FOR POSTERITY, BUT I JUST GOT A NEW PHONE, AND I DON'T WANT ANY INCRIMINATING EVIDENCE ON IT.
BESIDES, LEAVING THIS AS AN UGLY, INTENSE MEMORY ...
...JUST MAKES IT ALL THE WORSE LATER, RIGHT? THAT'S PERFECT.
Y'KNOW? IT'S FUNNY. IF IT'S FOR WORK, HE'LL POUNCE RIGHT ON ANYBODY— MAN OR WOMAN, GRANNY OR GRANDPA.
OH GOD...
HE'S GOING TO RAPE ME.
TUG
HE'S REALLY GOING TO DO IT.
PLEASE NO.
NO...
NO.
NO!
HUH?
UMM ...
...

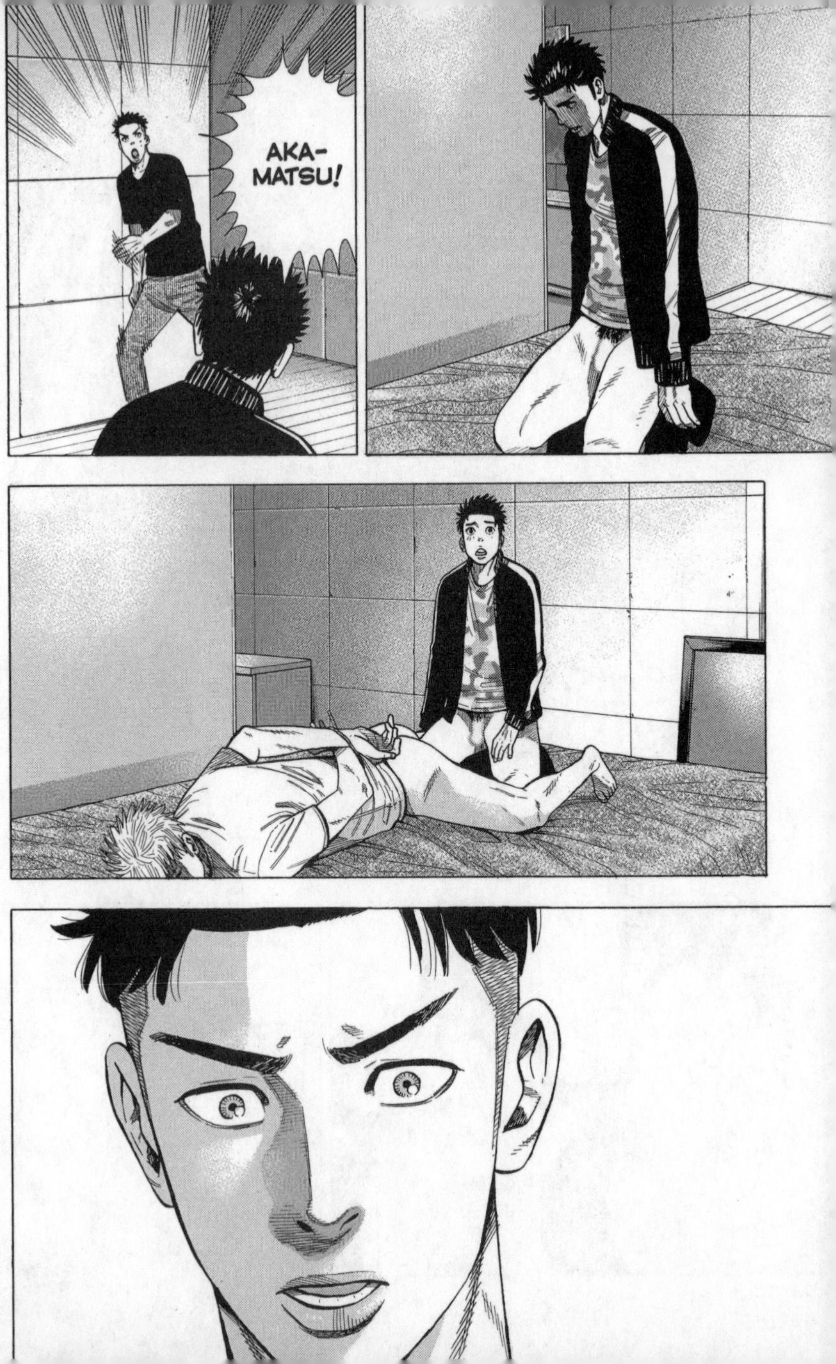
AKA-
MATSU!

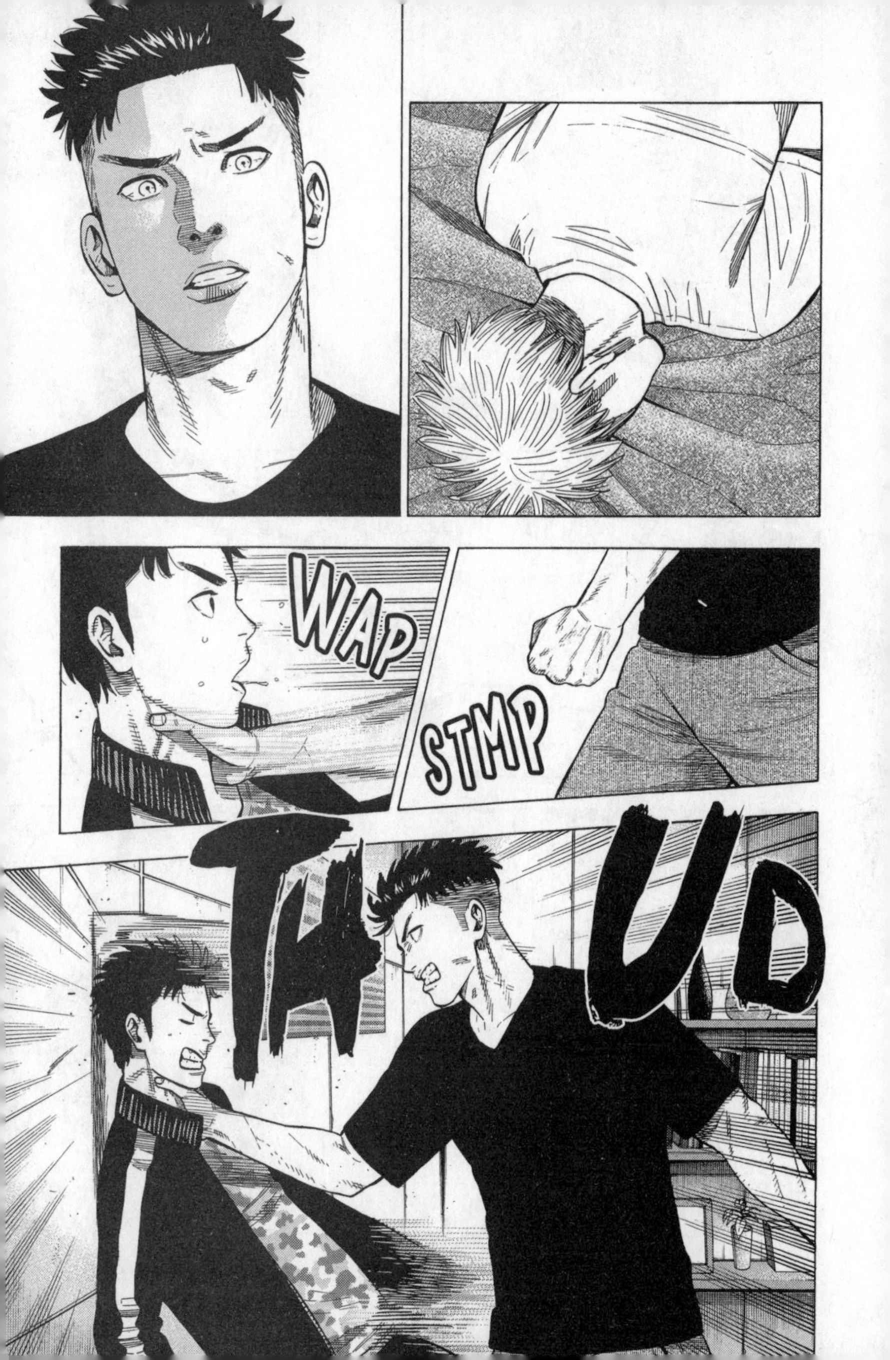
STMP
WAP
THUD

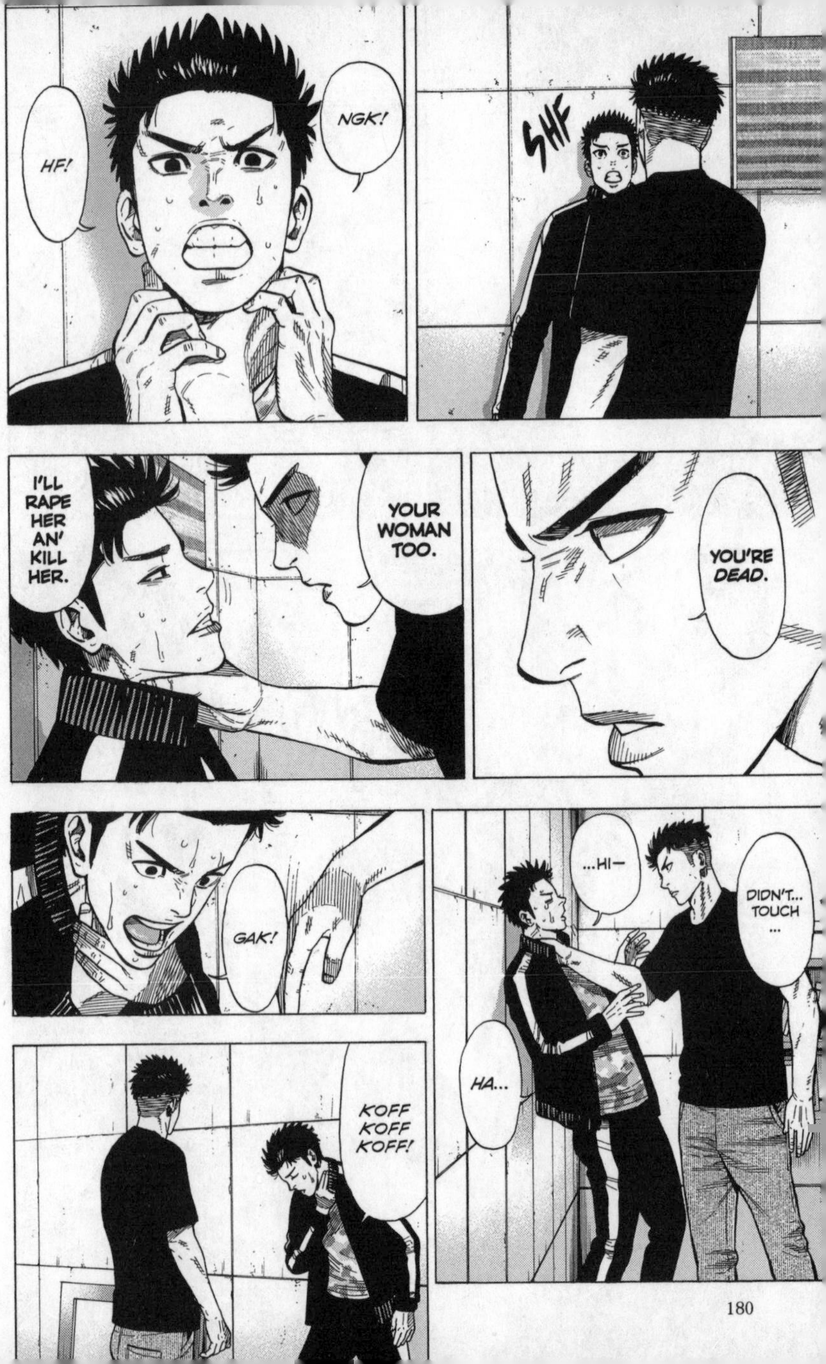
SHF
NGK!
HF!
YOU'RE DEAD.
YOUR WOMAN TOO.
I'LL RAPE HER AN' KILL HER.
DIDN'T... TOUCH ...
...HI—
HA...
GAK!
KOFF KOFF KOFF!

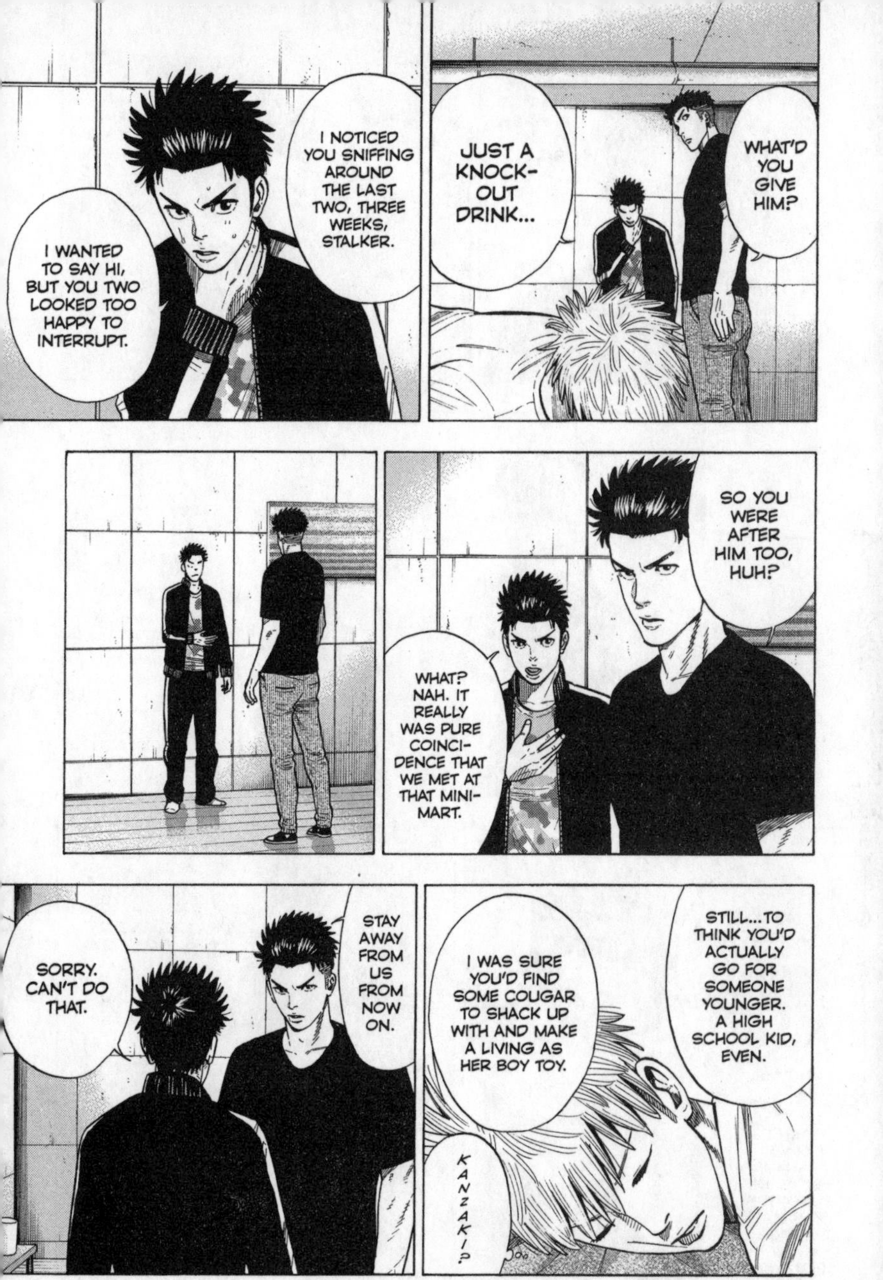
WHAT'D YOU GIVE HIM?
JUST A KNOCK-OUT DRINK...
I NOTICED YOU SNIFFING AROUND THE LAST TWO, THREE WEEKS, STALKER.
I WANTED TO SAY HI, BUT YOU TWO LOOKED TOO HAPPY TO INTERRUPT.
SO YOU WERE AFTER HIM TOO, HUH?
WHAT? NAH. IT REALLY WAS PURE COINCI-DENCE THAT WE MET AT THAT MINI-MART.
STILL...TO THINK YOU'D ACTUALLY GO FOR SOMEONE YOUNGER. A HIGH SCHOOL KID, EVEN.
I WAS SURE YOU'D FIND SOME COUGAR TO SHACK UP WITH AND MAKE A LIVING AS HER BOY TOY.
KANZAKI?
STAY AWAY FROM US FROM NOW ON.
SORRY. CAN'T DO THAT.

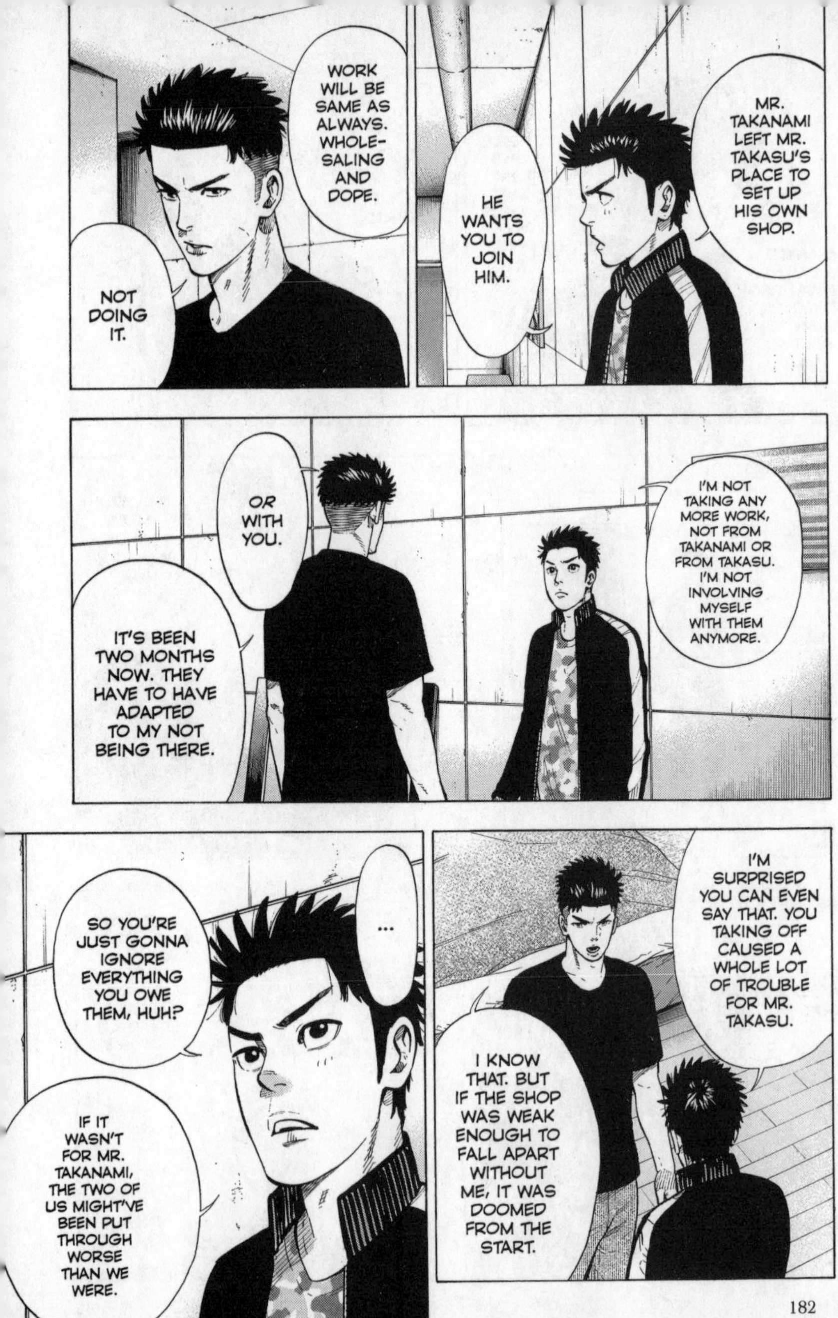
MR. TAKANAMI LEFT MR. TAKASU'S PLACE TO SET UP HIS OWN SHOP.
HE WANTS YOU TO JOIN HIM.
WORK WILL BE SAME AS ALWAYS. WHOLE-SALING AND DOPE.
NOT DOING IT.
I'M NOT TAKING ANY MORE WORK, NOT FROM TAKANAMI OR FROM TAKASU. I'M NOT INVOLVING MYSELF WITH THEM ANYMORE.
OR WITH YOU.
IT'S BEEN TWO MONTHS NOW. THEY HAVE TO HAVE ADAPTED TO MY NOT BEING THERE.
I'M SURPRISED YOU CAN EVEN SAY THAT. YOU TAKING OFF CAUSED A WHOLE LOT OF TROUBLE FOR MR. TAKASU.
I KNOW THAT. BUT IF THE SHOP WAS WEAK ENOUGH TO FALL APART WITHOUT ME, IT WAS DOOMED FROM THE START.
...
SO YOU'RE JUST GONNA IGNORE EVERYTHING YOU OWE THEM, HUH?
IF IT WASN'T FOR MR. TAKANAMI, THE TWO OF US MIGHT'VE BEEN PUT THROUGH WORSE THAN WE WERE.

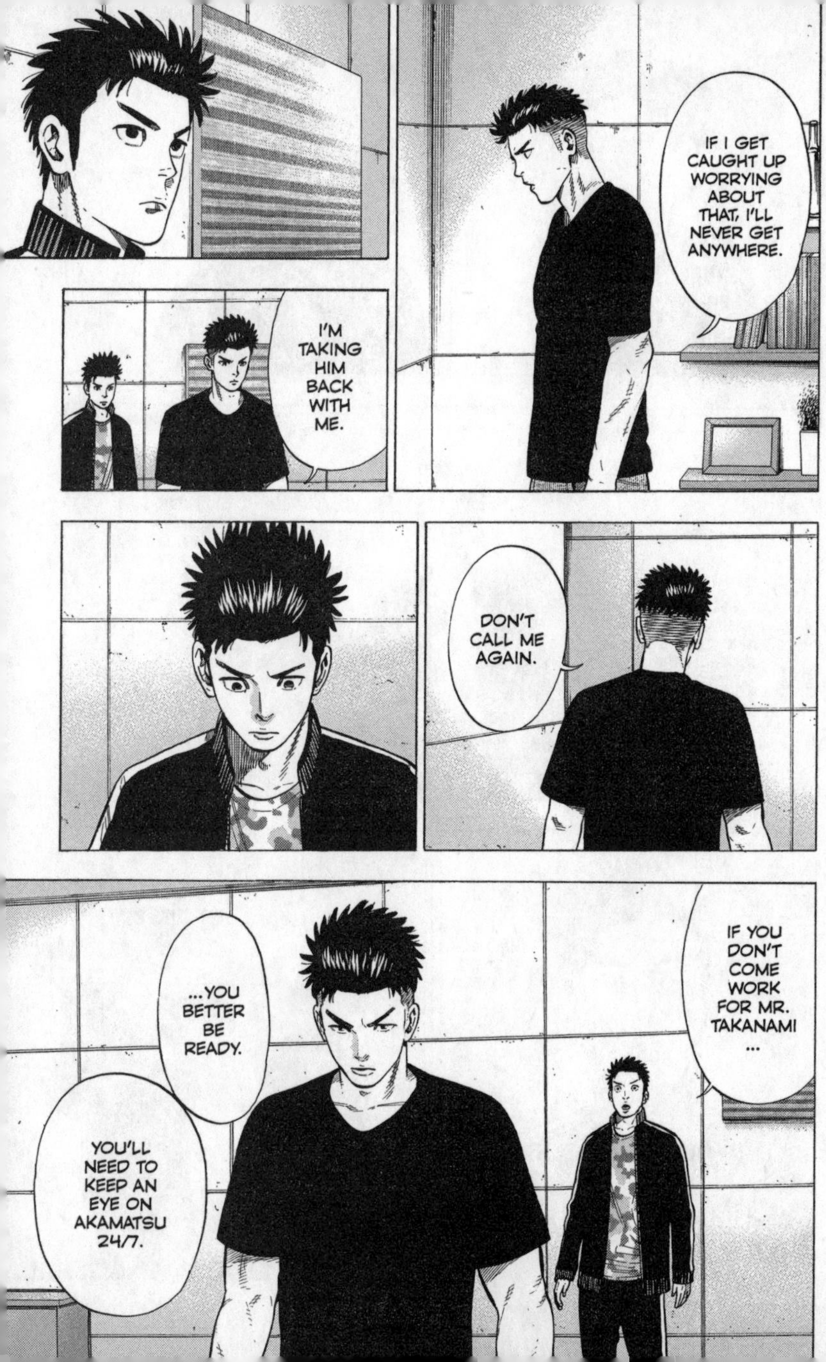
IF I GET CAUGHT UP WORRYING ABOUT THAT, I'LL NEVER GET ANYWHERE.
I'M TAKING HIM BACK WITH ME.
DON'T CALL ME AGAIN.
IF YOU DON'T COME WORK FOR MR. TAKANAMI ...
...YOU BETTER BE READY.
YOU'LL NEED TO KEEP AN EYE ON AKAMATSU 24/7.

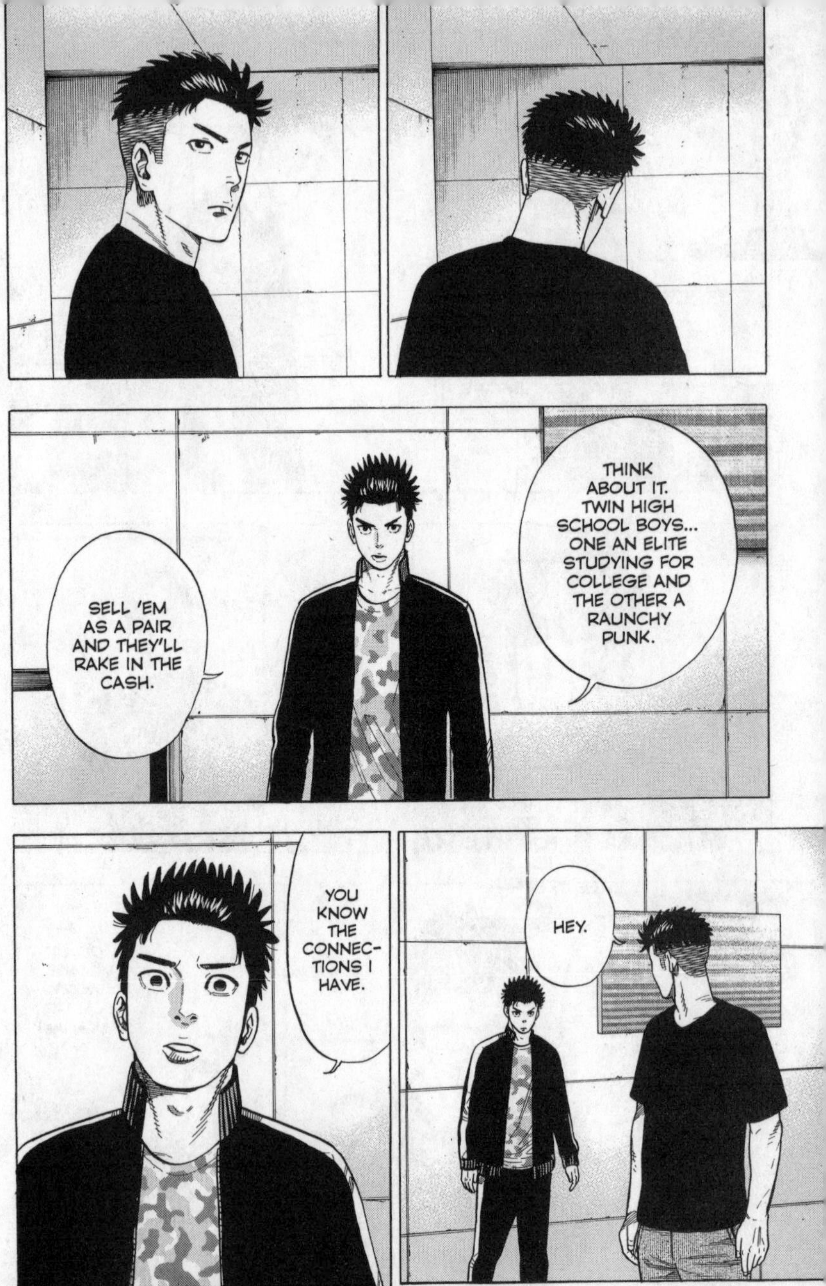
THINK ABOUT IT. TWIN HIGH SCHOOL BOYS... ONE AN ELITE STUDYING FOR COLLEGE AND THE OTHER A RAUNCHY PUNK.
SELL 'EM AS A PAIR AND THEY'LL RAKE IN THE CASH.
HEY.
YOU KNOW THE CONNEC- TIONS I HAVE.

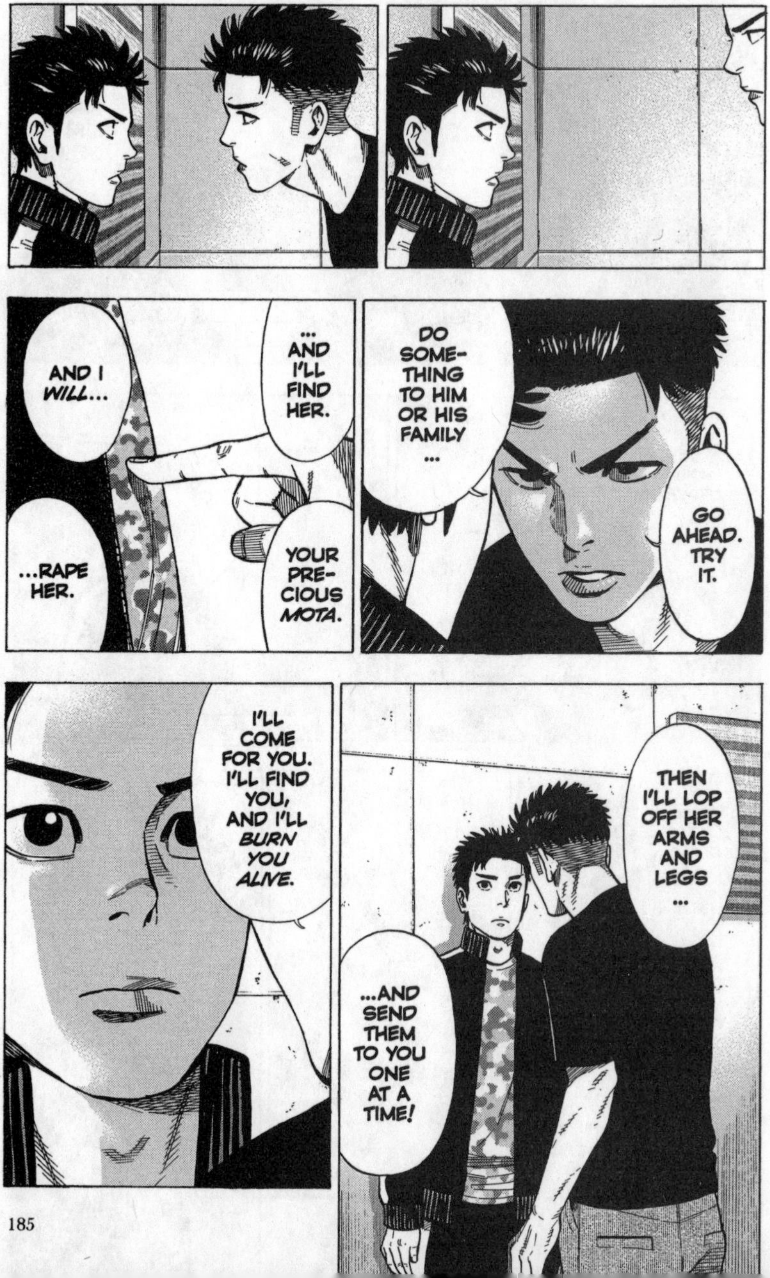
DO SOMETHING TO HIM OR HIS FAMILY ...
GO AHEAD. TRY IT.
... AND I'LL FIND HER.
YOUR PRECIOUS *MOTA*.
AND I *WILL*...
...RAPE HER.
THEN I'LL LOP OFF HER ARMS AND LEGS ...
...AND SEND THEM TO YOU ONE AT A TIME!
I'LL COME FOR YOU. I'LL FIND YOU, AND I'LL *BURN* YOU *ALIVE*.

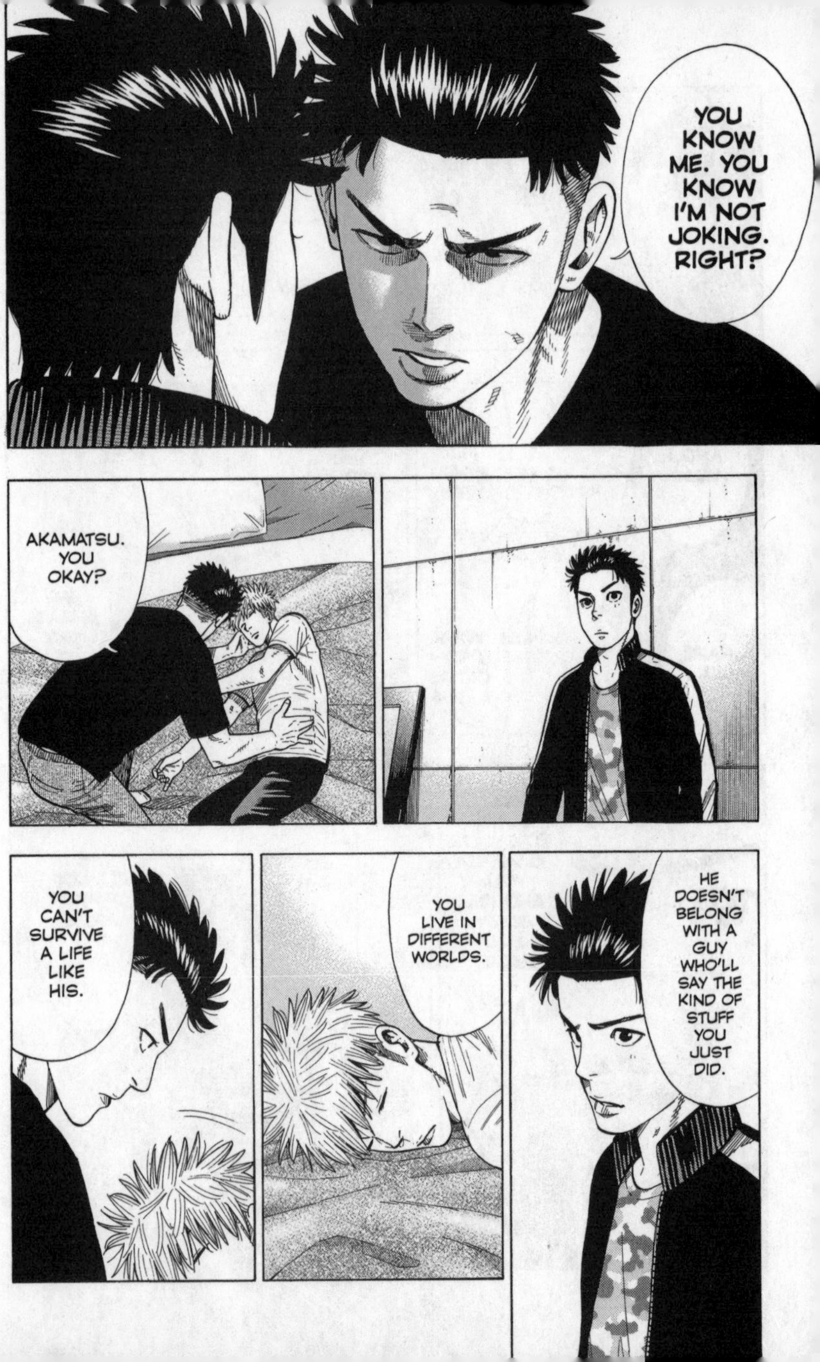
YOU KNOW ME. YOU KNOW I'M NOT JOKING. RIGHT?
AKAMATSU. YOU OKAY?
HE DOESN'T BELONG WITH A GUY WHO'LL SAY THE KIND OF STUFF YOU JUST DID.
YOU LIVE IN DIFFERENT WORLDS.
YOU CAN'T SURVIVE A LIFE LIKE HIS.

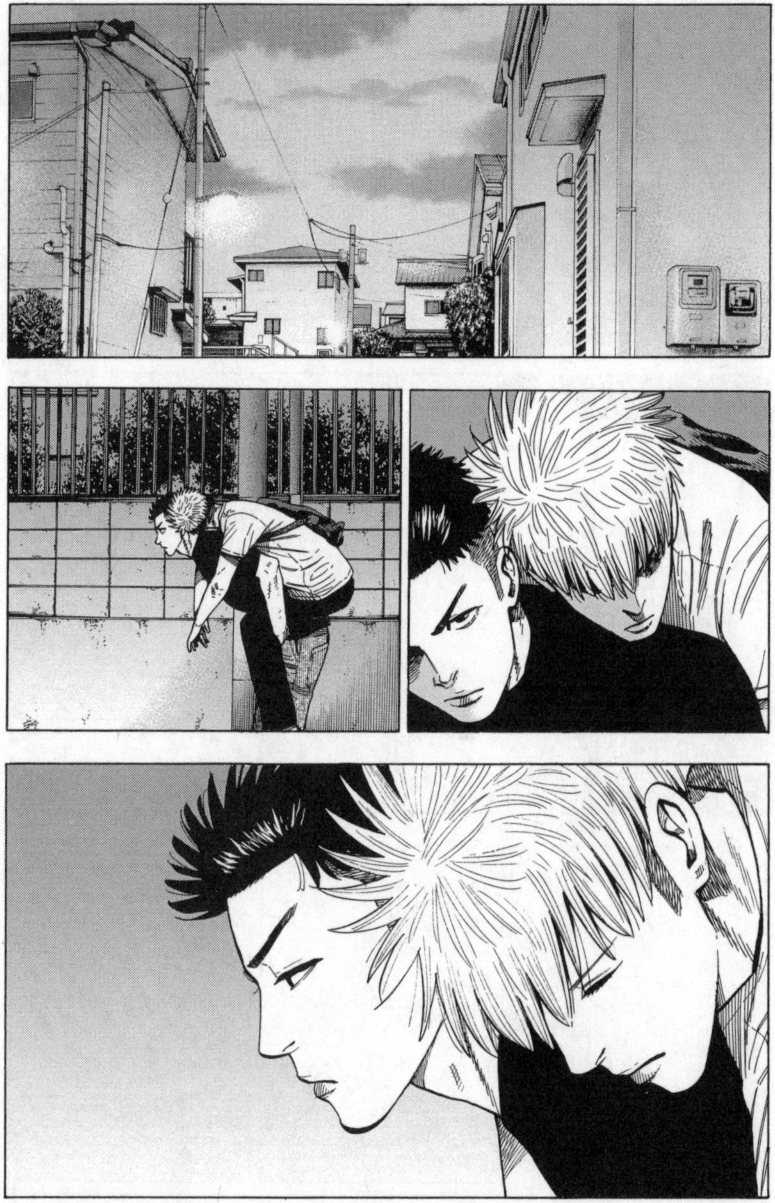

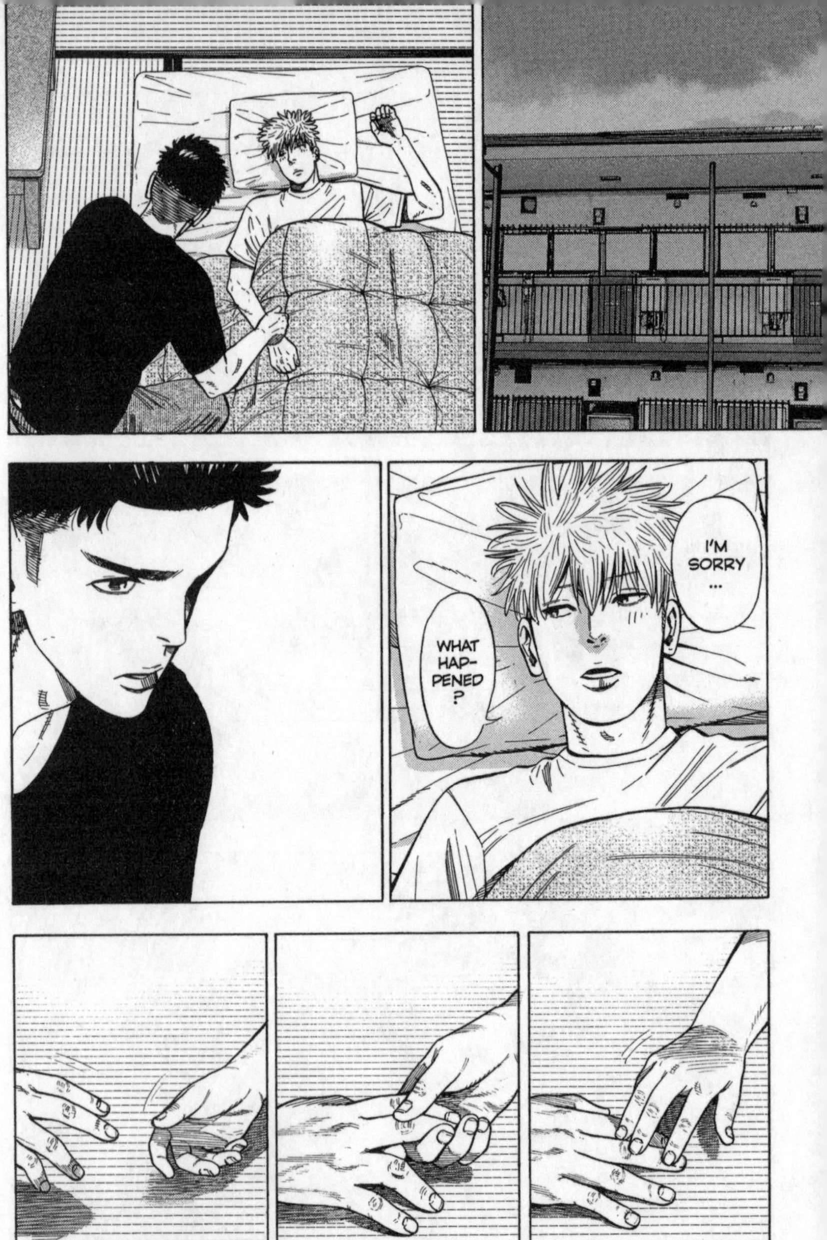
I'M SORRY ...
WHAT HAP-PENED ?

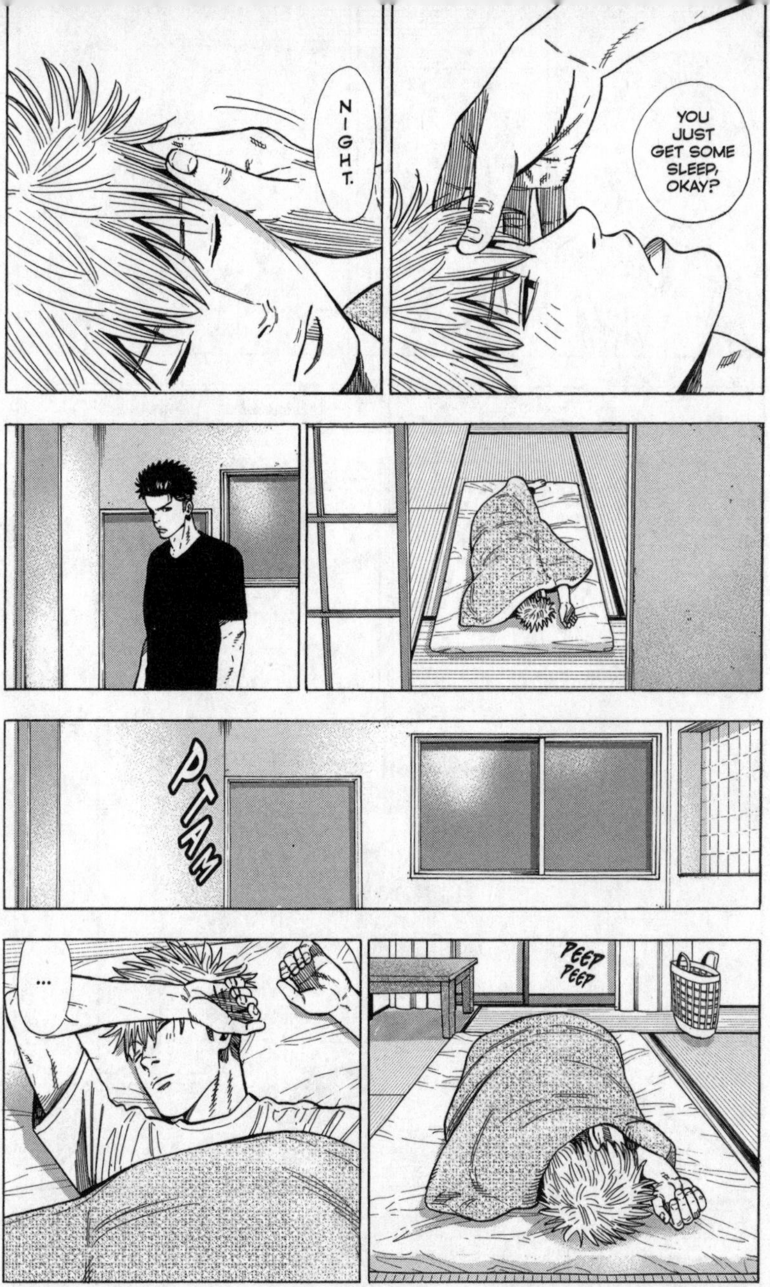
YOU JUST GET SOME SLEEP, OKAY?
NIGHT.
PTAM
PEEP PEEP
...

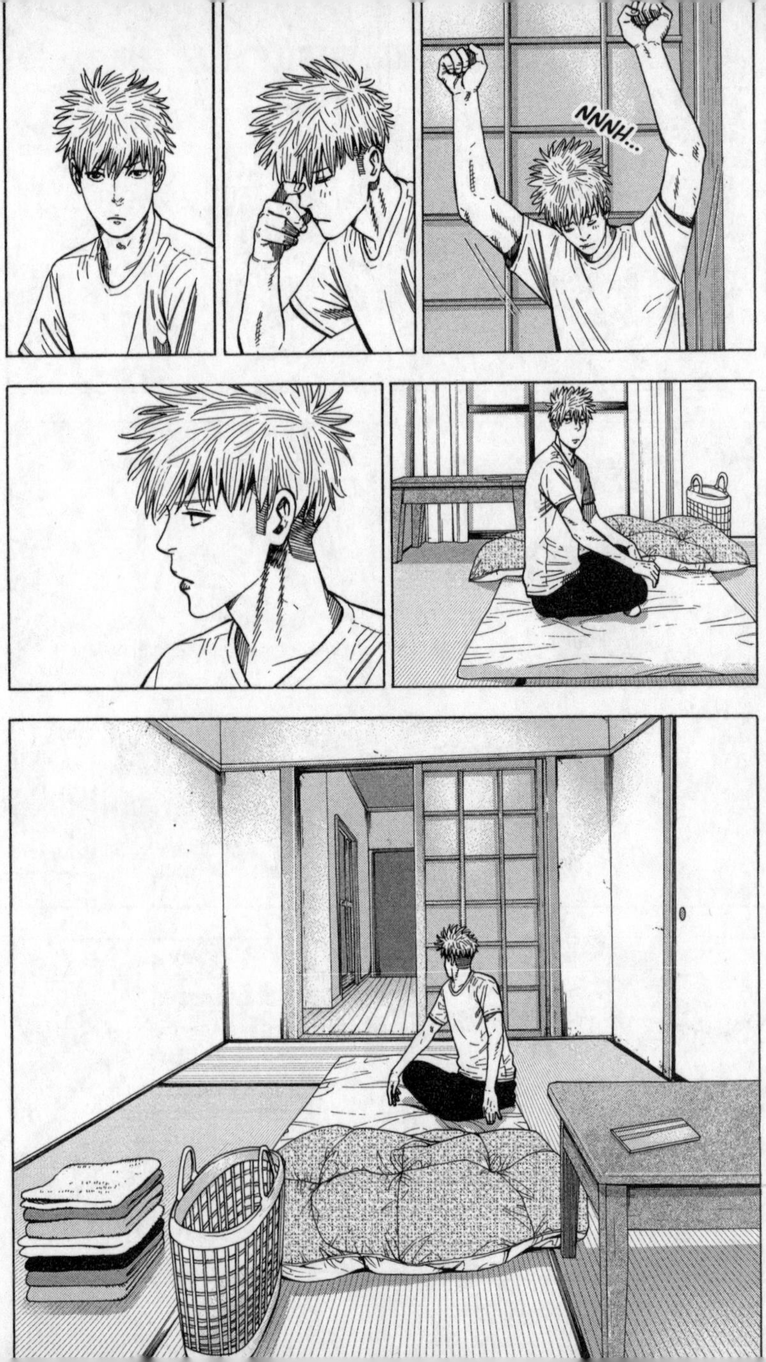
NNNH...

FISHY BAD BOYS AKAMATSU AND SEVEN

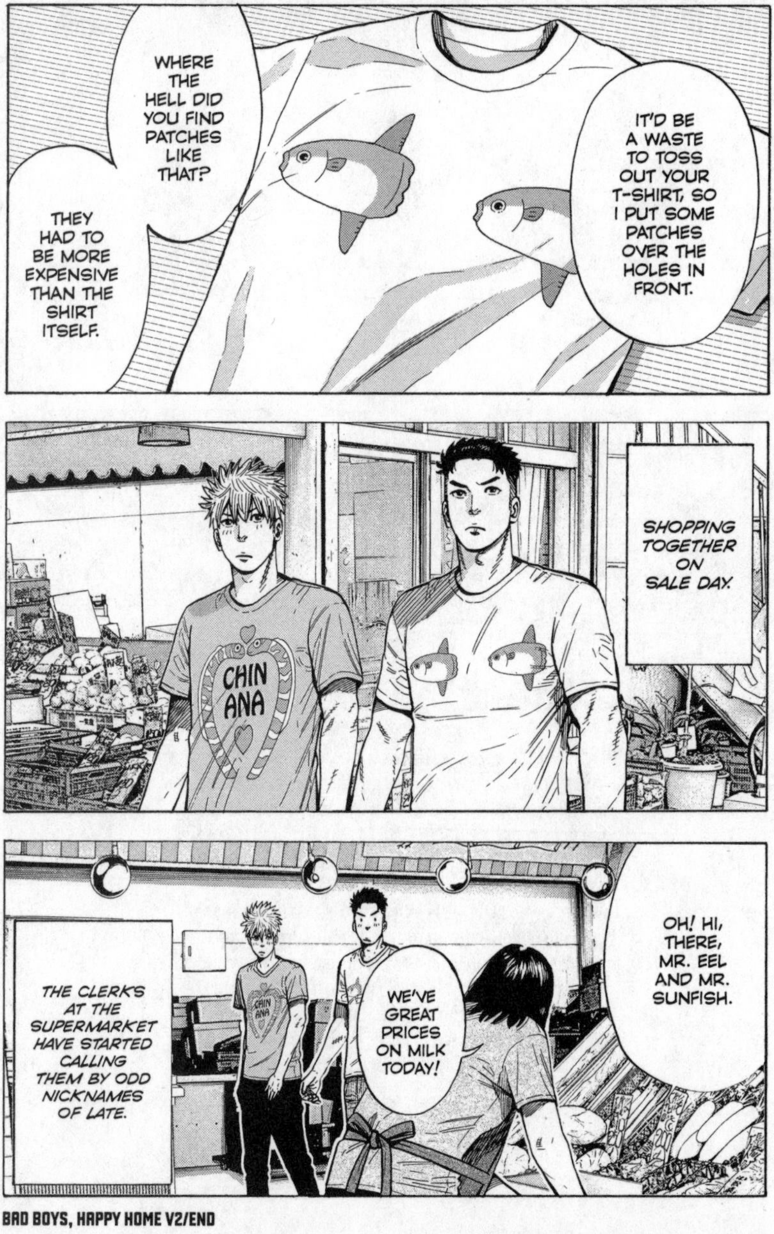
IT'D BE A WASTE TO TOSS OUT YOUR T-SHIRT, SO I PUT SOME PATCHES OVER THE HOLES IN FRONT.
WHERE THE HELL DID YOU FIND PATCHES LIKE THAT?
THEY HAD TO BE MORE EXPENSIVE THAN THE SHIRT ITSELF.
SHOPPING TOGETHER ON SALE DAY.
CHIN ANA
OH! HI, THERE, MR. EEL AND MR. SUNFISH.
WE'VE GREAT PRICES ON MILK TODAY!
THE CLERKS AT THE SUPERMARKET HAVE STARTED CALLING THEM BY ODD NICKNAMES OF LATE.

BAD BOYS, HAPPY HOME V2/END

SHOOWA
Thank you for your purchase!
This is volume 2.
I hope you enjoy it!

Hiromasa Okujima
Living with other people
is great, but I kind of
want to get a dog too.

About the Creators

Bad Boys, Happy Home may be **SHOOWA**'s
first English-language release, but she's
also been published internationally in both
French and Korean. You can find out more
about her on her Twitter page, **@shoowa**.

Although this is **Hiromasa Okujima**'s first
professional foray into boys' love, he's
created many shonen and seinen manga.
Some of his hobbies include martial arts
and collecting secondhand clothing.
You can find out more about him on his
Twitter page, **@HiromasaOkujima**.